# Researching
# Modern Evangelicalism

# Researching
# Modern Evangelicalism

## A Guide to the Holdings of the Billy Graham Center, With Information on Other Collections

Compiled by

**Robert D. Shuster,
James Stambaugh,**
and
**Ferne Weimer**

*With an Introduction by Joel Carpenter*

Bibliographies and Indexes in Religious Studies, Number 16

**GREENWOOD PRESS**
New York • Westport, Connecticut • London

**Library of Congress Cataloging-in-Publication Data**

Shuster, Robert D.
   Researching modern evangelicalism : a guide to the holdings of the
Billy Graham Center, with information on other collections /
compiled by Robert D. Shuster, James Stambaugh, and Ferne Weimer ;
with an introduction by Joel Carpenter.
      p.      cm.—(Bibliographies and indexes in religious studies,
ISSN 0742-6836 ; no. 16)
   ISBN 0-313-26478-3
   1. Billy Graham Center. Archives—Catalogs. 2. Evangelicalism—
United States—History—20th century—Sources—Bibliography—
Catalogs. 3. United States—Church history—20th century—Sources—
Bibliography—Catalogs. I. Stambaugh, James. II. Weimer, Ferne.
III. Title. IV. Series.
CD3209.W483S56    1990
016.2773'082—dc20          90-34009

British Library Cataloguing in Publication Data is available.

Library of Congress Catalog Card Number: 90-34009
ISBN: 0-313-26478-3
ISSN: 0742-6836

First published in 1990

Greenwood Press, 88 Post Road West, Westport, CT 06881
An imprint of Greenwood Publishing Group, Inc.

Printed in the United States of America

The paper used in this book complies with the
Permanent Paper Standard issued by the National
Information Standards Organization (Z39.48-1984).

10 9 8 7 6 5 4 3 2 1

# Contents

# Preface

The purpose of this guide is to describe and thus make more available an exceptional resource for Christian work and the study of American religious history: the research collections of the Billy Graham Center. The Center, a division of Wheaton College dedicated to the study of missions and evangelism, began in 1974. Since 1975, the staff of the Archives, Library and Museum have been gathering a unique collection of documents, publications and artifacts about the ways that the Christian gospel is spread, particularly by Evangelical Protestant North Americans.

The materials in our holdings were collected with the intention that they would be a continuing resource for the pastor, the missionary, the scholar, the journalist, the interested layperson and the general community. The varied interests of these different groups were kept in mind as we described our holdings and prepared the index.

The concentration in this volume is almost exclusively on the material in the Billy Graham Center building on the Wheaton College campus. A select and helpful listing of other resource centers in the country with material on the people, organizations and events of American Evangelicalism is included in the appendixes. Appendix I lists archives and manuscript repositories and Appendix II libraries.

The staff of the Archives, Library and Museum wish to gratefully acknowledge the generosity of the Billy Graham Evangelistic Association, without which the Center's collections would not exist. We also want to thank present and former directors of the Center for their support of our efforts: James Kraakevik, William Shoemaker, David Johnston and Donald Hoke.

Finally, the authors acknowledge with deep appreciation the other staff members who have contributed so much to the completion of this volume: Paul Ericksen and Magdalene Wohlschlegel of the Archives; Kenneth Gill, Daniela Bogdan, and Roberta Sommerville of the Library; and Doreen Fast and Cathy Koves of the Museum.

# Introduction:
# Studying Evangelicals

Interest in understanding Evangelical Christianity and its role in the modern world has grown considerably in recent years. The importance of learning more about Fundamentalism, Pentecostalism, and the other varieties of modern Evangelicalism has become obvious. These once-marginal religious movements and traditions have remained vigorous while other faiths have faltered, and in North America especially, Evangelicals have become much more assertive in public affairs. Their reemergence in public life has prompted renewed interest in studying Evangelicalism, and this guide is designed to help researchers locate important caches of materials for examining this complex cluster of religious movements. This book should also prove useful to researchers who are not students or professional scholars. Christian workers who need to locate materials to use for a variety of projects will find many valuable nuggets of information herein.

**A DEFINITION.**   "Evangelical" is one of those labels that is used a great deal in public discussion but is not well understood. The term means, in its simplest denotation, pertaining to the evangel, which is the Christian gospel, or good news, that God redeems sinful humanity through His son, Jesus Christ. Evangelicals have stressed that people find salvation only through personal faith in Christ's atoning death and through the life-transforming power of the Holy Spirit. They find these views to be the central theme of the Bible, which they hold to be divinely inspired and the ultimate authority for their Christian faith and practice. The label "Evangelical" also denotes these Christians' commitment to proclaim this gospel to others by word and deed.

Variations in time and place have nuanced the term's meaning and usage, and loaded it with much historic freight. The "Evangelical" label was first used by the churches of the Lutheran Reformation in the sixteenth century, but it gained wider currency during the widespread revivals of the eighteenth and nineteenth centuries, when "Evangelical" became the common label for movements of spiritual renewal and evangelistic outreach within Protestantism. This generic

understanding of "Evangelical" also makes it an appropriate label for
contemporary biblicist and charismatic movements within the Roman
Catholic Church.

In late twentieth-century usage, "Evangelical" also frequently connotes
"conservative," in that the Evangelical movements and traditions have
opposed theological liberalism and insisted on adherence to historic
Christian doctrines. The primary locations of Evangelical movements
in the first two-thirds of the twentieth century have been the nations of
the North Atlantic, and especially North America.

Evangelical Christianity also has made rapid strides outside of the
North Atlantic region, especially in the past twenty-five years. Religious statisticians claim that half of the world's Evangelicals now
reside in the so-called Third World, and they project that by the year
2000, three-fourths will be from these regions. In Africa, for example,
conversions and church-planting are projected to give that continent
more Christians than North America by the turn of the next century.
In parts of East Asia as well, notably in China and Indonesia, Evangelicals account for most of the recent dynamism Christianity has
shown. In Latin America, where conversion to Evangelical Christianity outpaces the birthrate, Pentecostalism is the fastest growing
alternative to traditional Roman Catholicism. Even in Europe, where
the Christian inheritance of the Middle Ages, the Reformation, and
the pietist/evangelical revivals of prior centuries has waned very
rapidly, fresh renewal movements have begun and are struggling
against the secular tide.


**GROWING SCHOLARLY INTEREST.**   Because of these worldwide
trends, students of religion have been scrambling to understand the
history, character, and current thrust of the varied family of movements and traditions known as Evangelicalism. In the United States,
where Evangelical revivalism was the dominant religious persuasion in
the nineteenth century, a harvest of scholarship on religion in the
Early Republic has appeared in the last twenty years, and it has
underscored an important message: to know American Evangelicals is
to know a great deal about the heart and soul of nineteenth-century
America.

Thereafter, Evangelical Christianity began to lose its cultural domi-
nance in the United States, and it seemed to be on the way out as a
significant force. Yet its surprising longevity and recent return to
prominence have suggested that understanding twentieth-century
Evangelicalism might aid our comprehension of contemporary America as well. Scholars have been working to discover why the formula
that works so well in almost every other western nation--moderni-

zation = secularization--has to be carefully qualified, if not discarded, when talking about the United States.  And in much of the Third World, the growth of Evangelicalism and modernization are concurrent, if not closely related.

Sources in North America for the study of modern Evangelicalism are bountiful, if one knows where to look.  Much of the earlier record of these movements and traditions can be found in the archives and libraries of the major denominations and their major educational and service agencies.  Studying Evangelicals over the past century becomes more difficult, because beginning with the Wesleyan holiness movement in the 1880s, Evangelicals have often broken away from the historic denominations to form their own groups, or to conduct their religious work through nondenominational, parachurch agencies.

Evangelicals' parachurch proclivity in particular has changed the shape of Christianity worldwide.  A vast and growing portion of international Christian activity has emanated from these independent, voluntarily organized and supported agencies for religious work:  foreign missionary societies, evangelistic associations, religious publishers, student fellowships, and the so-called "electronic church" of religious radio and television.

Since the typical pattern for preserving the record of the religious past has continued to follow denominational lines, much of the story of modern Christianity will be lost unless the work of parachurch agencies is documented.  Fortunately, the Archives, Library, and Museum of the Billy Graham Center have placed a major emphasis on collecting the materials of nondenominational agencies.  They have developed an unmatched array of sources to document this vigorous but still largely uncharted aspect of modern Christianity.  These collections thus provide a unique and comprehensive starting point for research and for the creation of new materials for ministry.

**THE BILLY GRAHAM CENTER.**   The Archives, Library, and Museum form the foundational components of the Billy Graham Center, a research and programs agency of Wheaton College.  The idea for a center began to take shape in 1970 when a committee was formed by the Billy Graham Evangelistic Association (BGEA) to gather materials that documented its history and the ministry of Billy Graham.  Plans began to focus on a center that would contain an archives, a library and a museum, each of which would document the BGEA's career and collect resources on the history of evangelism and missions.  This center would also develop programs to promote and support world evangelization.

After considering several sites, the committee chose Wheaton College, Billy Graham's alma mater, in 1974. Personnel were assembled soon after, and the process of developing collections and programs was begun. Construction began in 1977, and the completed structure was dedicated in 1980. It houses the Graham Center Archives, Library, and Museum, the Wheaton College Graduate School, and a cluster of programs and institutes. All of these agencies contribute to the Center's purpose: to foster research, strategy, and training for evangelism and missions.

By the late 1980s the Center's programs included an annual missionary scholar-in-residence, professional workshops and conferences on missions and evangelism, and strategic institutes in the areas of Evangelism, Prison Ministries, and Chinese Studies. Other agencies of Wheaton College that were located at the Center because of their close relationship to its purpose included the Extension Studies Program and research institutes on American Evangelicals, Christianity and Marxism, and Muslim Studies.

**THE COLLECTIONS.** The Graham Center's Archives, Library and Museum exist to serve the resource needs of the institutes at the Graham Center and two larger constituencies: people active in or training for vocational Christian service, and the scholarly community. Their collecting focus is on Protestant Christian efforts to evangelize North America and the rest of the world.

**The Archives** of the Billy Graham Center is a growing research repository with currently over 525 collections which document the role of North American Evangelicals in foreign missions and evangelism. Among its central features are sources documenting the work of Billy Graham and his evangelistic association; oral histories of missionaries, evangelists, and other Evangelical workers; the records of major evangelistic and missionary organizations such as Youth for Christ, the Overseas Missionary Fellowship (formerly China Inland Mission), and Africa Inland Mission; the editorial files of *Christianity Today* magazine; and the private papers of influential Evangelical leaders, notably Fanny Crosby, Billy Sunday, Paul Rader, Aimee Semple McPherson, Corrie Ten Boom, and Charles Colson.

**The Library** of the Billy Graham Center, which contains some 60,000 books, 125,000 microform volumes, and 800 periodicals, focuses on the history and contemporary practice of evangelism and missions. It has particularly strong collections on evangelists, revivals, and revivalism; missionary accounts of work in Asia and Africa in the nineteenth and the twentieth centuries; church growth theory and case studies; mis-

siology; the history and contemporary concerns of American Fundamentalism and Evangelicalism; and liberation theology.

**The Museum** of the Billy Graham Center has collected over 10,000
items which depict the history and character of evangelism, social
reform, and Christian spirituality in North America, and in the North
American foreign missionary enterprise. The Museum's holdings
include prints, tracts, posters, almanacs, photographs, postcards,
figurines, paintings, sculpture, road signs, ethnographic videotapes,
rare editions of the Bible, memorabilia of famous evangelists, and
other artifacts. Among its most outstanding features are the Gast
Collection of over 600 religious lithographs from the nineteenth
century, and several hundred rare tracts published by the American
Tract Society.

**RESEARCH APPLICATIONS.** Researchers usually have no trouble
thinking of ways to use collections as rich as these, but it might be
suggestive to note some of the topics that have been researched in
them already.

Investigators into the history of Fundamentalism, post-Fundamentalist
"neo-Evangelicalism," and Pentecostalism in North America have
found ample materials here; so have those studying the origins and
development of the "electronic church." The growth of indigenous
Evangelical movements in China and Africa have been researched
here; as have the roles of women, education and health care in foreign
missions; church-state relations in the recently-founded nations of the
Third World; the evolution of mission theology; and the rise of Third
World theologies.

The Graham Center Archives is a depository for the papers and
records of twentieth-century American Evangelical leaders such as
Billy Sunday and Billy Graham, and these collections have been used
repeatedly for biographical research. A major retrospective publication project, *Fundamentalism in American Religion, 1880-1950*, a
45-volume facsimile series produced in 1988 by Garland Publishing,
drew the majority of its titles from the Graham Center Library. A
number of publishers have found rich visual material at the Graham
Center Museum for illustrating their books and magazines. The
resources for many more projects are in the collections, and they are
readily accessible to researchers of numerous kinds and levels of
expertise.

**USING THIS BOOK.** This reference book is designed to introduce
researchers--whether they are scholars, writers, librarians, college

students, workers in Christian ministries, or simply inquisitive people--
to the collections of the Billy Graham Center. It also contains a
valuable chapter with annotated entries on other libraries and archives
in North America that have significant holdings on modern Evangelicalism.

The chapters on the Graham Center Library and Museum give
detailed introductions to those departments' collections, discussing
their thematic strengths and featured holdings and services. It is
impossible, of course, to give a comprehensive inventory of both of
these repositories in a single volume. The lengthy chapter on the
Archives, however, will provide both an overview and an annotated
catalog of its more than 525 processed collections with a list of the
subjects significantly treated in each collection.

By examining the book's extensive index of subjects and names (which
is drawn mainly from the archives but includes entries from the other
two resources as well), the reader can find out quickly what the three
Graham Center collections and other North American holdings offer
in his or her area of interest. This book thus allows the user to get
either a general overview of the main features of these collections or
direct information as to their holdings on a particular topic.


**ACCESS TO THE COLLECTIONS.**    The Archives, Library, and
Museum of the Billy Graham Center are constantly acquiring and pro-
cessing new materials. Their staffs welcome researchers' questions
about their holdings, which will of course supercede the coverage of
this book by the time it is published.

The Archives puts detailed descriptions of each new acquisition into its
computerized catalog, and the Archives staff will conduct subject
searches and provide computer-generated annotated subject lists of
those collections which have significant holdings. These searches can
be made prior to one's visit. Researchers should direct inquiries to
the Reference Archivist of the Archives at this address: the Billy
Graham Center, Wheaton College, Wheaton, IL 60187; or make
contact by telephone at 708/260-5910.

Likewise, the Library and Museum staffs are happy to advise researchers about their holdings. They can be reached at the above address,
or by telephone: 708/260-5194 (Library); 708/260-5909 (Museum).

All three collections are open to any and all serious users, and the
staff welcomes visits. The Museum staff, however, would appreciate
prior notification of one's intention to do research in the artifact
collections so arrangements can be made. The Archives and Library

both have open admission, and the Library has open stacks. Advance contact from researchers will enable the staff to better serve them. Information about hours of operation and the availability of guest housing in the area can also be obtained with a telephone call or a letter prior to one's visit.

In addition, the Graham Center Resources Committee, comprised of officers of the three collections plus the director of the Institute for the Study of American Evangelicals, has been offering, as funding permits, a small research travel grant program. Prospective visitors seeking some assistance with the costs of extended research in the Graham Center collections should contact the Institute for the Study of American Evangelicals for information and application materials at the above address, or by telephone: 708/260-5437.

The staffs of the Graham Center Collections and the Institute for the Study of American Evangelicals are eager to promote the use of what they consider to be a vast treasure trove of materials for researching modern Evangelicalism. They offer this book with the hope that it will well serve those who want to study Evangelicals, and that many people --including Evangelicals themselves--will be enlightened by the researchers' findings.


    --- Joel Carpenter

# The Library

Currently, the Billy Graham Center Library has over 60,000 bound volumes, 125,000 items in microform and 800 periodicals. As an integral part of the Center, the Library focuses on historical and contemporary information about world evangelization.

Within this specialization are works by and about evangelists, evangelistic work, and their effects on society. There are also materials documenting the history of religious revivals, those occasions when the work of God in the lives of people was unusually evident. Another principal segment of the collection encompasses materials relating to world missions, the transmission of the Christian message across geographic and cultural boundaries.

The central focus of the collection is on the work of North American Evangelicals and their predecessors. This includes resources describing the history of American Evangelicalism in order to provide the context from which evangelization was pursued. To undergird the study of the propagation of the gospel, the Library includes a specialized reference collection geared to such research and a basic theological collection to aid analysis and evaluation.

A primary goal of the Library is to support research in the Archives and Museum by acquiring books, periodicals and pamphlets related to their collections. Thus, the reader may anticipate that information is available in the Library for virtually any topic listed in the index to this volume.

The titles and topics included in this section are only representative of what is contained in the collection. There are hundreds of resources in each area and it will be necessary to consult the library catalog for comprehensive information. While the Library acquires materials in many languages, the English titles of particular works are used here if the translation is available in the collection.

The Library participates in the OCLC computer network and most of the materials are accessible through that system. Thus it is possible to identify specific titles in the collection through another library participating in that network. Presently the OCLC system allows access by author and title. Subject search capability is currently being tested and should be available in the near future. Since a large portion of the Library's holdings are available through interlibrary loan, the collection is available even to those who are unable to travel to Wheaton College campus.

The library opened to the public in 1980 with an online computer catalog. When the company maintaining the system went out of business a few years later, the Library was left with a microfiche catalog which had to be supplemented with a card catalog. Wheaton College is currently in the process of installing a new computer system which will eventually include all of the resources on campus. This will make it possible to produce a microfiche catalog of the Billy Graham Center Library collection for use at off campus locations.

**EVANGELISM COLLECTION.** The core collection of materials on evangelistic work was acquired in late 1975 from a private collector, Richard Owen Roberts, who served as director of the Library until 1979.

Several kinds of materials are included in the evangelism collection. First, there are primary sources represented by the published works from the pens of evangelists, among which are doctrinal essays, sermons, correspondence, memoirs, autobiographies, and devotional literature. Second, historical materials include biographies, works treating particular evangelistic movements or specific periods of revival, and select denominational histories. Another category is methodological studies that relate to Christian evangelism, including personal evangelism, mass evangelism, and media evangelism. Miscellaneous materials within this division include studies relating to the psychology of religion and conversion, hymnals associated with evangelistic activity, and training materials used as a means to evangelize or follow up personal decisions. Also, materials pertaining to Christian organizations, such as the Salvation Army, the Young Men's Christian Association, or to general movements such as the Sunday school, are collected for their impact on the advance of the Christian gospel.

Primary sources for the study of American church history before 1820 may be found in the *Early American Imprints* microcard collection produced by the American Antiquarian Society. This collection includes some 80,000 books and pamphlets published in America from the beginning of printing in 1639 to 1819. Early evangelistic work in

America included the missionary efforts of John Eliot and David
Brainerd among the Indians. The library collection includes bio-
graphies and autobiographical works of both. John Eliot published the
first Bible in America for the Massachusetts Indians. The library owns
an autographed edition of Wilberforce Eames' *Bibliographic Notes on
Eliot's Indian Bible and on His Other Translations and Works in the
Indian Language of Massachusetts* (Washington, 1890), and a limited
edition (150) copy of *John Eliot and the Indians, 1652-1657: Being
Letters Addressed to Rev. Jonathan Hanmer*, edited by Eames (New
York, 1915). The Library also has an 1865 facsimile reprint of Eliot's
Indian tract, "The Day Breaking if not the Sun Rising of the Gospel
with the Indians of New England."

The Library holds several editions of Brainerd's autobiography, including the 1765 edition published in Edinburgh entitled: *An Account of
the Life of the Late Reverend Mr. David Brainerd, Minister of the
Gospel, Missionary to the Indians, from the Honourable Society in
Scotland, for the Propagation of Christian Knowledge*.

Other unusual items related to evangelistic work with the Indians of
North America include Scripture portions in the Cherokee language,
such as *Genesis, or The First Book of Moses* (1856).

Revivalism in America is documented in a number of secondary
sources, including Frank Beardsley's *A History of American Revivals*
(1912), Gordon Hall's *The Sawdust Trail* (1964), and William Warren
Sweet's *Revivalism in America* (1944).

The Great Awakening of 1740 was the first major revival in America.
Introductory works include Edwin Scott Gaustad's *The Great Awaken-
ing in New England* (1957), Charles Hartshorn Maxson's *The Great
Awakening in the Middle Colonies* (1920), Mary Hewitt Mitchell's *The
Great Awakening and Other Revivals in the Religious Life of Connec-
ticut* (1934), Joseph Tracy's *The Great Awakening: A History of the
Revival of Religion in the Time of Edwards and Whitefield* (1841), and
J. William T. Youngs' *God's Messengers: Religious Leadership in
Colonial New England, 1700-1750* (1970).

The collection includes several scarce items by leaders in the Great
Awakening. Gilbert Tennent is represented by *The Espousals or, A
Passionate Persuasive to a Marriage with the Lamb of God, in a Sermon
upon Gen. xxiv. 49* (Boston, 1741) and *Some Account of the Principles
of the Moravians* (London, 1743). The Library holds three early works
by Jonathan Edwards: *Some Thoughts Concerning the Present Revival
of Religion in New-England and the Way in which It Ought to Be Ack-
nowledged and Promoted* (Edinburgh, 1743), *A Treatise Concerning
Religious Affections* (Boston, 1746) and *An Humble Inquiry into the*

*Rules of the Word of God, Concerning the Qualifications Requisite a Complete Standing and Full Communion in the Visible Christian Church* (Boston, 1749). The Library has the second edition of George White-field's first published sermon, "The Nature and Necessity of Our New Birth in Christ Jesus, in Order to Salvation" (London, 1737).

The first awakening in America was characterized by controversy and criticism which many times took place in public through published letters and essays. Two letters by the revivalist Whitefield are entitled: *A Letter to the Reverend Mr. John Wesley in Answer to His Sermon, Entituled, Free-grace* (London, 1741) and *An Expostulatory Letter, Addressed to Nicholas Lewis, Count Zinzendorff, and Lord Advocate of the Unitas Fratrum* (London, 1753).

The major critic of the revival, Charles Chauncy, wrote *The Outpouring of the Holy Ghost* (Boston, 1742) and *Seasonable Thoughts on the State of Religion in New-England* (Boston, 1743). Two lesser known items are William Hobby's *An Inquiry into the Itinerancy, and the Conduct of the Rev. Mr. George Whitefield, an Itinerant Preacher: Vindicating the Former against the Charge of Unlawfulness and Inexpediency, and the Latter against Some Aspersion, which Have Been Frequently Cast upon Him* (Boston, 1745), and *Some Occasional Thoughts on the Influence of the Spirit: with Seasonable Cautions against Mistakes and Abuses* (Boston, 1742).

A periodical, *The Christian History; Containing Accounts of the Revival and Propagation of Religion in Great-Britain & America*, was published by Thomas Prince during the height of revival activity.

The Second Great Awakening began at the end of the eighteenth century. Catharine Cleveland's *The Great Revival in the West, 1797-1805* (1916), John B. Bole's *The Great Revival, 1787-1805* (1972), and Charles Keller's *The Second Great Awakening in Connecticut* (1968) are among the best secondary sources for this period. Other works include: Charles A. Johnson's *The Frontier Camp Meeting* (1955) and Bernard A. Weisberger's *They Gathered at the River: The Story of the Great Revivalists and Their Impact upon Religion in America* (1948).

Primary source materials for the period include Nathan Perkins' *Two Discourses on the Grounds of the Christian's Hope: Containing a Brief Account of the Work of God's Holy Spirit in a Remarkable Revival of Religion in West-Hartford, in the Year 1799* (Hartford, 1800). *The Autobiography of Peter Cartwright, the Backwoods Preacher* (New York, 1857) and *The Pioneer Preacher: or, Rifle, Axe, and Saddle-Bags* (New York, 1860), described as the "vivid life story of a nearly blind itinerant" (William Milburn), are two examples of a number of diaries and autobiographies of itinerant preachers and circuit riders held by the Library.

Again criticism arose against certain aspects of the revival. Two examples are Orville Dewey's *Letters of an English Traveller to His Friend in England, on the "Revivals of Religion" in America* (Boston, 1828) and A. Cleveland Coxe's *Revivalism and the Church: A Letter to a Reviewer, in Reply to Several Articles in the New-Englander* (Hartford, 1843).

Periodicals also document this period. Bennet Tyler's *New England Revivals* contained extracts from the *Connecticut Evangelical Magazine*, of which the Library holds a complete run. The *Panoplist* later developed into the *Missionary Herald*, official organ of the American Board of Commissioners for Foreign Missions. A complete run on microfilm of the *New York Observer* provides a valuable source for evangelistic and revival activity throughout much of the nineteenth century, including background material on the general American religious atmosphere in which such activity took place. Another rich source of information is the *New York Evangelist*, although only a limited run is held at present.

Several secondary sources provide general overviews of nineteenth- and twentieth-century revivalism in America. William McLoughlin's *The American Evangelicals, 1800-1900* and Timothy Lawrence Smith's *Revivalism and Social Reform: American Protestantism on the Eve of the Civil War* treat the evangelistic efforts of the nineteenth century. Twentieth century revivalism is documented in McLoughlin's *Modern Revivalism: Charles Grandison Finney to Billy Graham* and James Edwin Orr's books, e.g. *The Flaming Tongue: The Impact of 20th Century Revivals*.

Orr's *The Second Evangelical Awakening in America* is a secondary source to the 1857 "prayer" revival, while Samuel Irenaeus Prime provides contemporary accounts in *Five Years of Prayer* (1864), *The Power of Prayer Illustrated in the Wonderful Displays of Divine Grace at the Fulton Street and Other Meetings in New York and Elsewhere* (1859), *Prayer and Its Answer* (1882), and *Fifteen Years of Prayer in the Fulton Street Meeting* (1872).

Works by and about evangelists of this period provide a wealth of information about their activities and revival. The collection includes Charles Finney's *Lectures on Revivals of Religion* (London, 1839) as well as Daniel Wilhelm Nelson's 1964 dissertation, "B. Fay Mills: Revivalist, Social Reformer and Advocate of Free Religion." Biographical works of Moody include his son's *The Life of Dwight L. Moody* (New York, 1900) as well as later biographies such as James F.

Findlay's *Dwight L. Moody: American Evangelist, 1837-1899* (1969) and John Charles Pollock's *Moody: A Biographical Portrait of the Pacesetter in Modern Mass Evangelism* (1963).

Much of the recent material concentrates on various approaches to evangelistic work. Examples are: James Edgar Smith, *Friendship Evangelism* (1959), George W. Peters, *Saturation Evangelism* (1970), Rebecca Manley Pippert, *Pizza Parlor Evangelism* (1978), Ross Pilkinton, *Life-Style Evangelism* (1980), Bruce A. Rowlison, *Creative Hospitality as a Means of Evangelism* (1981) and John Wimber, *Power Evangelism* (1986).

In keeping with the ministry of Billy Graham, the collection includes information about mass evangelism such as George Sweeting, *The Evangelistic Campaign*, and Sterling W. Huston, *Crusade Evangelism and the Local Church*.

Media evangelism is also an important topic of current concern. Examples are: Gleason H. Ledyard, *Sky Waves: The Incredible Far East Broadcasting Company Story*, Razelle Frankl, *Televangelism,* and William Packard, *Evangelism In America: From Tents to TV*.

**WORLD MISSIONS COLLECTION.**    The World Missions Collection is comprised of historical, sociocultural, and theological materials pertaining to evangelism across cultural boundaries at home and overseas.

Included in the historical materials are works that deal wholly or in part with the history of Christian missions, including the histories of mission societies and agencies, denominational missions, missions to a particular locale or people, autobiographies, biographies, memoirs and correspondence of missionaries and mission leaders. The collection is strongest in nineteenth- and twentieth-century works, but there is considerable source material for earlier Catholic missions such as the *Monumenta Missionum*, the critically edited records of early Jesuit missions, and *The Jesuit Relations and Allied documents*, the record of Jesuit missionaries in New France, 1610-1791.

General historical works include such titles as Adolf von Harnack, *The Mission and Expansion of Christianity in the First Three Centuries*, Kenneth Scott Latourette, *History of the Expansion of Christianity*, Stephen Neill, *A History of Christian Missions*, and J. Herbert Kane, *A Global View of Christian Missions, from Pentecost to the Present*. More in-depth coverage is available through works addressing specific geographic areas such as Charles Pelham Groves, *The Planting of Christianity in Africa*, Kenneth Scott Latourette, *History of Christian Missions in China*, and Julius Richter, *History of Missions in India*.

Nineteenth-century Protestant mission material includes Joseph Tracy's *History of the American Board of Commissioners for Foreign Missions* (1842), Gardner Spring's *Memoirs of the Rev. Samuel J. Mills* (1820), and Colin B. Goodykoontz's *Home Missions on the American Frontier, With Particular Reference to the American Home Missionary Society*. Significant microform collections include the *Papers of the American Home Missionary Society, 1816-1936*, the *Missionary Society of Connecticut Papers, 1759-1948*, and *American Indian Correspondence -- The Presbyterian Historical Society Collection of Missionaries' Letters, 1833-1893*. This material is supplemented by periodical literature such as the *Connecticut Evangelical Magazine*, the *Panoplist, Missionary Herald at Home and Abroad*, the *New York Missionary Magazine*, the *Massachusetts Missionary Magazine*, the *Massachusetts Baptist Missionary Magazine*, and the *United Brethren's Missionary Intelligencer*.

Twentieth-century mission history is well documented in books and magazines as well as conference proceedings, reports from mission societies, and other publications of Christian agencies. Samples of these materials are the proceedings of the famous World Missionary Conference at Edinburgh in 1910, the published papers of the meetings of the International Missionary Council, proceedings of the various Student Volunteer Movement conventions, and the *Addresses and Papers of John R. Mott*.

Among the major microform holdings are the *Human Relations Area Files, New Religious Movements in Primal Societies, Papers of the American Board of Commissioners for Foreign Missions, Archives of the Council for World Mission, Joint International Missionary Council, Papers of the American Sunday School Union* and *Conference of British Missionary Societies Archives* (which includes those of the London Missionary Society).

The theology and science of missions are primary collecting areas for the Library. Standard introductions to the field include: Gerald H. Anderson, *The Theology of Christian Mission*, J. H. Bavinck, *An Introduction to the Science of Mission*, and J. Verkuyl, *Contemporary Missiology: An Introduction*. Two recent additions are Alan Richard Tippett, *Introduction to Missiology*, and Karl Müller, *Mission Theology: An Introduction*.

A broad range of publications are acquired in this area in an attempt to maintain an extensive collection. Included are such classics as William Carey, *An Enquiry Into the Obligation of Christians to Use Means for the Conversion of the Heathens,* and Roland Allen, *Missionary Methods: St. Paul's or Ours*. Other significant titles are Johannes Munck, *Paul and the Salvation of Mankind*, George W. Peters, *A*

*Biblical Theology of Missions*, Hendrik Kraemer, *From Mission-Field to Independent Church*, Johannes Christiaan Hoekendijk, *The Church Inside Out*, and Daniel Thambyrajah Niles, *Upon the Earth: The Mission of God and the Missionary Enterprise of the Churches*. Numbered among the authors whose works are collected in addition to those included above are: Rufus Anderson, Gustav Warneck, Julius Richter, Josef Schmidlin, Alphons Mulders, Pierre Charles, Max Alexander Cunningham Warren, Peter Beyerhaus, and J. Herbert Kane.

Several topics within the field of missions are singled out for special attention because of their importance. The Ecumenical Movement is one such important topic. All of the publications of the World Council of Churches are collected along with selected materials from other ecumenical bodies. Also included in this concentration are the secondary publications such as R. Pierce Beaver, *Ecumenical Beginnings in Protestant World Missions*, William Richey Hogg, *Ecumenical Foundations*, Ruth Rouse and Stephen Neill, *A History of the Ecumenical Movement*, M. M. Thomas, *Towards a Theology of Contemporary Ecumenism,* and Willem Visser't Hooft, *The Genesis and Formation of the World Council of Churches*.

Another important modern topic is Liberation Theology. The Library attempts to collect all English language materials on the subject with representative samples of the important authors' original works in other languages. Included in this collection are such publications as Rubem A. Alves, *A Theology of Human Hope*, Mortimer Arias, *Salvacion es Liberacion*, Clodovis Boff, *Theology and Praxis*, Leonardo Boff, *Introducing Liberation Theology*, Gustavo Gutiérrez, *A Theology of Liberation,* and Juan Luis Segundo, *Liberation of Theology*.

Also encompassed within the division of missions are theological studies coming out of the Third World (i.e., indigenous theological literature from Africa, Asia, Latin America, Oceania). The Library has placed a special emphasis on gathering together a wide variety of theological literature from the Evangelical church in developing countries, including books, pamphlets and periodical literature in a variety of native languages. This literature forms the primary material for the study of the contextualization of the gospel. Analytical studies in this area include Kwesi A. Dickson, *Theology in Africa,* and Choan-Seng Song, *Third-Eye Theology: Theology in Formation in Asian Settings*.

Concern for contextualized expressions of Christianity around the world has become one of the most important issues in modern missions. Some of the important publications analyzing this issue are John Stott and Robert T. Coote, eds., *Gospel & Culture*, Charles H. Kraft, *Christianity in Culture, Ministry in Context*, Morris A. Inch, *Doing*

*Theology Across Cultures*, Bruce J. Nicholls, *Contextualization: A Theology of Gospel and Culture*, and William J. Larkin, *Culture and Biblical Hermeneutics*.

Adjunct materials to missions literature include ethnography, demography, comparative religion, and social psychology. Attention is given to collecting works in which Christianity (and especially missionary activity/influence) is treated within the context under consideration. Examples are Edwin W. Smith's *The Golden Stool*, Eugene Albert Nida's *Message and Mission*, Paul G. Hiebert's *Anthropological Insights for Missionaries*, and Norman B. Tindale's *Aboriginal Tribes of Australia*. Other representative titles include Kenneth Cragg's *The Christian and Other Religion*, Raimondo Panikkar's *The Unknown Christ of Hinduism*, Lynn De Silva's writings on Buddhism and Christianity, and E. Bolaji Idowu's *African Traditional Religion*.

Of special interest is the extensive collection of theses and dissertations (both foreign and American) pertaining to evangelism and missions. Included in this collection are the numerous church growth studies that are produced each year at Fuller Theological Seminary and other Evangelical schools of world mission. The Library attempts to acquire research produced at Third World institutions which is often unavailable to the Western world.

In addition to a growing backfile of retrospective periodicals pertaining to mission activity, the Library is presently receiving about 500 periodicals of missiological importance. These can be roughly divided into three categories: a) research-oriented journals, e.g., the *International Bulletin of Missionary Research*, *International Review of Missions*, *Missiology*, *Norsk Tidsskrift for Misjon*, *Neue Zeitschrift für Missionswissenschaft*, and *Zeitschrift für Mission*; b) journals focusing on subjects supplementary to missions, e.g., those dealing with culture or anthropology, such as *Anthropos*, *Third World Resources*, and *International Journal of Intercultural Relations*, or theological journals focusing on a particular region, e.g., *African Theological Journal*, *Al-mushir* (Pakistan), *Boletín Teológia* (Latin America), *Caribbean Journal of Religious Studies*, and *Revista Ecclesiástica Brasilia*; c) periodicals that include house organs of mission organizations or sending agencies and ecumenical organizations, e.g., *Afroscope* (Association of Evangelicals of Africa and Madagascar), *AIM International*, *Asian Church Today* (Evangelical Fellowship of Asia), *Breakthrough* (Slavic Gospel Association), *Christian Conference of Asia News*, *SIM Now* and *Latin America Evangelist* (Latin America Mission) or sundry titles with missiological implications such as *AF Press Clips* and *Background Notes on the Countries of the World*.

The Library acquires microform editions of periodicals which are otherwise unavailable. In some cases, collections of periodicals are filmed together and handled as a set. An example of such a collection was produced by Greenwood Press and entitled *Missionary Periodicals from the China Mainland.*

**REFERENCE COLLECTION.** The reference collection was developed to complement the Library's general holdings in missions, evangelism, revival and church history and to serve as the starting point for research in those areas. The foundation of the collection is the 685-volume *National Union Catalog, Pre-1956 Imprints,* a listing by author of books published before 1956 and held by the Library of Congress and other American libraries. The set encompasses some ten million entries and indicates the locations of books in more than 700 libraries. With its supplements from 1956 to the present, the *National Union Catalog* serves as an unparalleled tool for finding copies of American publications not held by the Library. The *British Museum General Catalogue of Printed Books* similarly lists British publications by author.

The collection includes standard works in biblical studies, church history, religion and theology, as well as more specialized sources such as subject encyclopedias. *The Encyclopedia of Religion* edited by Mircea Eliade and the *World Christian Encyclopedia* edited by David B. Barrett are two of the most important works. These are supplemented by more specific publications such as *The Encyclopedia of Unbelief, Encyclopedia of Asian Civilization, Encyclopedia of Islam* (both old and new editions), *The Encyclopedia of American Religions,* and the *Encyclopedia of American Religious Experience.*

Encyclopedias covering various traditions within the Christian Church also contribute to the understanding of world evangelization. Examples of these useful publications are *Encyclopedia of Southern Baptists, Encyclopedia of the Lutheran Church, The Mennonite Encyclopedia,* and *The Brethren Encyclopedia.*

Other useful resources are histories of the various regions of the world. The Library acquires the history series published by Cambridge University Press including such titles as *Cambridge History of China* and *Cambridge History of Iran.*

Particular emphasis has been placed on the acquiring of indexes, bibliographies and bibliographical guides such as *Missionalia, Bibliographia Missionaria, Bibliotheca Missionum,* and Livinius Vriens, *Critical Bibliography of Missiology.* To these have been added sources with a much narrower focus; for example, *The Chinese Recorder Index* and the cumulative indexes for selected South African mission publications:

*The Net Cast in Many Waters*, *The Missions Field* and *The Cape to the Zambezi*.

The core of the missions reference collection is comprised of both historical and current resources. *The Encyclopaedia of Missions*, edited by Edwin Munsell Bliss, was first published in 1891. A second edition was produced in 1904. This work contains important information which is still valuable for research today as is evidenced by the appearance of a reprint of the second edition in 1975. Other older publications include: the *Statistical Atlas of Christian Missions* produced in 1910 in conjunction with the international missionary conference held at Edinburgh that year, *World Statistics of Christian Missions*, that was published by U.S. and British agencies and intended to include all Protestant missions in Latin America which had been omitted in the 1910 compilation, and the *World Missionary Atlas* (1925).

Later resources include the *Encyclopedia of Modern Christian Missions: The Agencies* (1967), the *Dictionary Catalog of the Missionary Research Library* (1968), and the *Concise Dictionary of the Christian World Mission* (1971). These are also somewhat dated resources, but important for the study of missions.

These historical materials are supplemented by more current information sources. The most recent of these is the *Lexikon Missionstheologischer Grundbegriffe* (1987). Another important work is the *Handbuch der Ökumenik* (1985). A third German language publication is an annual entitled *Jahrbuch Mission*.

Contemporary English language resources of this nature have not been forthcoming. However, in their place three serial publications have emerged to provide current information for mission studies. These publications are produced primarily through the effort the Missions Advanced Research and Communications Center (MARC) and include the *Mission Handbook*, Unreached Peoples series and the World Christianity series.

While the collecting of reference sources in fields related to missiology has been selective, the Library is, nonetheless, attempting to establish sound support materials in the allied disciplines of communications, area studies, ethnology, and linguistics. The Library seeks out published catalogs of important ethnic and area study collections held by other libraries (e.g., the Herskovits collection of Africana at Northwestern University). Other specialized items include the bibliographical series of the Asian Mass Communications Research and Information Centre, the series of historical/cultural dictionaries published by Scarecrow Press, the World Bibliographical Series published by Clio, the *Handbook of Latin American Studies,* and Lambros Comitas' *The Complete Caribbeana,* 1900-1975, an indispensable bibliography for the history of missions to the West Indies.

The Library has increased its already extensive access to Americana and Early American Imprints with the addition of the *New Sabin* bibliographical guide to the bibliographies by Evans, Shaw-Shoemaker, Roorbach and Kelly. Other noteworthy acquisitions are the University of Cape Town School of Librarianship Bibliographical Series, including *David Livingstone: A Catalogue of Documents*, compiled by Gary W. Clendennen, and the *American Missionary Association Archives*.

Welcome additions to the reference collection are two recent publications by Richard Owen Roberts, *Revival Literature: An Annotated Bibliography with Biographical and Historical Notices* (1987) and *Whitefield: A Bibliographic Record of Works By, For, and Against George Whitefield: With Annotations, Biographical and Historical Notes* (1988).

**BILLY GRAHAM COLLECTION.**    The only materials collected comprehensively are those relating to the life and ministry of Billy Graham. These non-circulating materials are housed in the Special Collections Room and duplicates are made available for borrowing through the regular circulating collection.

The bulk of the materials consist of works by and about Billy Graham. All forms of published information in all languages are collected by the Library. The goal is to acquire every edition of each title from Dr. Graham's first publication, *Peace with God (1953),* to his most recent title, *Answers to Life's Problems (1988),* and biographical works ranging from John Charles Pollock, *Billy Graham: The Authorized Biography* (1966), to Marshall Frady, *Billy Graham: A Parable of American Righteousness* (1979).

A significant part of this collection is the numerous theses produced through the scholarly evaluation of Dr. Graham's ministry. Examples are Donald Allen Waite, "The Evangelistic Speaking of Billy Graham, 1949-1959" (Ph.D. Thesis, Purdue University, 1961), Bill Vaughn, "Billy Graham: A Rhetorical Study  in Adaption" (Ph.D. Thesis, University of Kansas, 1972), Larry Joe Davis, "Interpretation of Scripture in the Evangelistic Preaching of William Franklin 'Billy' Graham" (Ph.D. Thesis, Southern Baptist Theological Seminary, 1986) and Jerry Berl Hopkins, "Billy Graham and the Race Problem, 1949-1969" (Ph.D. Thesis, University of Kentucky, 1986).

Several of Billy Graham's family are also involved in ministries which interrelate with his own. Their publications are included in the Graham Collection. Examples include *A Time For Remembering: The Ruth Bell Graham Story* and Gigi Graham Tchividjian, *Sincerely....Gigi*.

Also included are materials by and about the ministry team of the Billy Graham Evangelistic Association such as Clifford B. Barrows, *Crusade Hymn Stories*, and George Beverly Shea, *Then Sings My Soul;* associate evangelists such as Grady Baxter Wilson, *Count It All Joy*, John Wesley White, *Arming for Armageddon,* Abdiyah Akbar Abdul-Haqq, *Sharing Your Faith With a Muslim*, Howard O. Jones, *Shall We Overcome?* and Leighton Frederick Sandys Ford, *Good News Is for Sharing*; musicians such as Ethel Waters, *His Eye Is On the Sparrow,* and Norma Zimmer, *Norma*; and other significant people related to his ministry such as Joni Eareckson Tada, *Joni,* and Corrie Ten Boom, *Corrie Ten Boom: Her Life, Her Faith*.

In addition to materials describing the various Billy Graham crusades around the world, the proceedings of and reports about other major events he has sponsored are included in this collection. Examples are International Congress on World Evangelization (Lausanne, 1974), *Let the Earth Hear His Voice*, First International Conference for Itinerant Evangelists (Amsterdam, 1983), *The Work of an Evangelist,* and Second International Conference for Itinerant Evangelists (Amsterdam 1986), *The Calling of an Evangelist*.

**THEOLOGICAL EDUCATION BY EXTENSION.**    Theological education by extension has become an important part of Christian education in the Third World. Developed in the 1960's, this method of education was promoted in response to the thousands of pastors and church leaders who were unable to take advantage of traditional education.

The development of TEE is reported in Ralph D. Winter, ed., *Theological Education by Extension* (1969). An effort was made to keep track of the proliferation of TEE programs and a directory was published in 1974 by Wayne C. Weld, *The World Directory of Theological Education by Extension*.

In recent years the field has become so large and diverse that it is impractical to attempt to document it. However, the library acquires publications about TEE including newsletters from various regions of the world, such as *CUP of T.E.E.* from the Pakistan Committee for Theological Education by Extension and *Paftee Bulletin* from the Philippine Association for Theological Education by Extension.

In addition, a curriculum collection of TEE materials from around the world is maintained. The establishment of this collection was made possible through a grant from the Committee to Assist Ministry Education Overseas (CAMEO). It was CAMEO which also played an important role in the development of the TEE movement, providing much of the support and organization during the formative years.

**MK COLLECTION.** The MK collection is a special resource which deals with different aspects of educating the children of missionaries, including their personal development and cultural adjustment to being "third-culture kids." The collection originated at the office of the Children's Education Department of Wycliffe Bible Translators.

After Wycliffe staff gathered numerous magazine articles and some unpublished theses and dissertations, an annotated bibliography was compiled for their own use. The collection was later deposited at the Billy Graham Center Library in order to make it available to others outside their organization. The Library continues to add to the collection and maintain the bibliography in an unannotated form.

Samples of the published titles from the collection include: the proceedings of the First International Conference on Missionary Kids (Manila 1984) entitled *New Directions in Missions: Implications for MKs*, C. John Buffam, *The Life & Times of an MK* (1985), William C. Viser, *It's OK to be an MK* (1986), and Ruth E. Van Reken, *Letters I Never Wrote* (1985).

**PRISON MINISTRY COLLECTION.** More than 400 agencies in the United States are dedicated to prison ministry. Many exist for only a short time and new ones spring up to carry on the work. Others, like Charles Wendell Colson's Prison Fellowship and Chaplain Ray's International Prison Ministry, are well established. They produce regular publications, *Jubilee* and *Prison Evangelism Magazine* respectively. Interest in collecting prison ministry materials at the Library was prompted by the Center's Institute for Prison Ministries. A significant literature had emerged from the work of these agencies which was illusive. Books, magazines, newsletters, tracts, brochures, and videos are now being preserved to document this effort. Publications from more than 250 agencies are now included in the collection which is partly housed in the Library's vertical file.

In addition to direct ministry to inmates, there has been a concerted effort to bring about reform in prisons. This includes making the public, especially Christians, aware of problems within the prison system. Examples are John R. W. Stott and Nick Miller, editors,

*Crime and the Responsible Community* (1980), Charles Wendell Colson, *America's Prison Crisis* (1987) and Donald Smarto, *Justice and Mercy* (1987).

# The Museum

The Museum collection complements the other resources of the
Graham Center. During the formative stages of development the
resource divisions of the Center collaborated to divide up the collecting task in a way which would eliminate unnecessary duplication and
overlapping of efforts. Materials are divided up according to content,
type, period, and their appropriateness to the resource itself. Another
result of that effort is that the Archives and Library can be viewed
more as pure information bases, while the Museum serves more as a
visual repository which illustrates the history and witness of Evangelical Christianity. The Museum collection contains images and objects
which focus on historic, symbolic, and aesthetic highlights of American
Evangelical Christianity and its antecedents. Because of its historic
and theological position, Evangelical Christianity has not left behind
much material culture of the type that is usually found in museums. It
is and has been in the past primarily a religion of spoken and written
words rather than images or artifacts. Consequently, much of the
Museum's collection consists of material normally associated with
archives and libraries. To understand the distinctions between them it
might be well to give one example. Both the Library and Museum
collect books, but they do it from entirely different perspectives. The
Library collects books for information and research and is concerned
only with the content of the books. The Museum collects books as
objects and is concerned with their symbolic and historic importance.
Therefore, the Museum's collection is filled with rare books, first editions, fine printing, and illustrated books. Likewise, the Museum and
Archives collect photographs but the Museum specializes in nineteenth
century photography while the Archives centers on twentieth century
material.

In two instances, collections were transferred to facilitate the task of
the researcher. In 1984 the entire manuscript collection of the Museum was deaccessioned and turned over to the Archives, so that all
manuscript material is now located in the Archives. Likewise, the Museum's pamphlet collection was transferred to the Library in 1989.

The Museum contains approximately 25,000 objects. Only a small portion of the collection is on permanent display in the Museum's exhibits. Temporary exhibits allow the Museum to showcase various aspects of its collections throughout the year. The temporary exhibits reflect a mixture of historic subjects, topics, contemporary Christian art and recent work of the Billy Graham Evangelistic Association. Of particular note is the Museum's highly acclaimed Sacred Arts exhibit which is held each spring. This all media national juried art show features the best of contemporary religious artwork from around the country.

The Museum's greatest strength is in nineteenth century material. The collection also contains small amounts of material from the eighteenth century and earlier and the first half of the twentieth century. More recent material is represented in the Museum's unique collection of contemporary Christian artwork. Most of the collections are flat printed material such as books, photographs, artwork, paper ephemera, and prints of all kinds. The Museum's Gast collection contains over 700 religious lithographs, including several unique copies of Currier and Ives prints. The portrait collection contains over 4,000 items. A collection of religious tracts runs to 8,000 pieces from 186 different publishers and spans three centuries. The Museum's contemporary art collection contains over 200 objects. All of Dr. Billy Graham's personal memorabilia which is not of an archival nature is housed in the Museum. But this is just a sampling of some of the special collections within the Museum's overall holdings. The narrative which follows this introduction is meant to be a chronological walk through the Museum's collections. Its purpose is to acquaint the reader with the scope of the collections and some of its highlights. It is by no means comprehensive but will give the potential user enough acquaintance with the collecting strategy so he can determine for himself what potentially might be found in the collections and what probably will not be found there.

The collection is housed in the Museum storage areas on the fourth floor of the Billy Graham Center. Those persons wishing to do research in the collections may do so from 9 a.m. to 3 p.m., Monday through Friday. If a researcher is planning a trip to the Museum, it is advisable to write or call ahead so that the staff can be better prepared to help with the project. The Museum's mailing address and phone number are: Billy Graham Center Museum, 500 E. College Ave., Wheaton, IL 60187; (708) 260-5909.

The Museum utilizes a computerized catalogue which is also available in hard copy. A handy one volume abbreviated Museum catalogue is also available for beginning searchers in the collection.

In addition to the main catalogue, there are a number of specialized tools to help the researcher. A topical index is available for the tract collection so that it can be accessed by subjects. The Museum also keeps a complete set of slides of all the artwork in the collection as well as an artist's file.

The staff of the Museum welcomes inquiries by mail and will do limited searches. Photocopies and photographic copies or slides are available. If only a small number of copies are needed, they are provided free of charge. If a large quantity is needed, they will be provided to the researcher at cost. For current costs please contact the Museum. The Museum will lend objects to other institutions on a limited basis. This is done on a case by case basis and inquiries should be sent to the Director of the Museum.

**THE EIGHTEENTH CENTURY AND BEFORE.** Appropriately, the earliest object in the Museum is a leaf from a twelfth century Bible written in a beautiful Carolingian book hand. Since the Bible is the primary source and inspiration of all Christian teaching, it is well represented throughout the collection. Most of the important editions in the transmission of Scripture can be found either in complete volumes or individual leaves. Fifteenth century examples include the *Gutenberg Bible* (1450-55), the first *Jenson Bible* (1476), *The Nurnberg Bible* (1483), and the *Koberger Latin Bible* (1497). The sixteenth century saw the introduction of many new versions of Scripture and among the Museum's holdings are *Erasmus' Bible* (1522), the *Coverdale Bible* (1535), *The Great Bible* (1544), *Matthew's Bible* (1549), the *Bishop's Bible* (1568), and *The Geneva Bible* (1588). During the seventeenth century the most famous of all English Bibles was produced - *The King James* or *Authorized Version* of 1611. During the eighteenth century the first European language Bible was printed in America by Christopher Saur in Germantown, Pennsylvania (1743). And after the American Revolution, the need for a new supply of Bibles prompted Robert Aitken of Philadelphia to print the first American Bible (1782) in the English language.

In the case of extremely rare volumes or Bibles where there are only one or two known copies, the Museum has acquired facsimiles for study. This category would include such works as the *Codex Alexandrinus* (4th century), the *Book of Kells* (9th century), the *Wycliffe New Testament* (1388), a complete *Gutenberg Bible* (1450-55), the *Tyndale New Testament* (1526), and the *Bay Psalm Book* (1640). The age of illuminated manuscripts is represented in a series of beautiful facsimiles done by Verlag Muller, and Schindlar of Stuttgart, Germany. There are examples from *The New Minster ("Grinbald") Gospels, Le Psautier De Saint Louis, Les Tres Riches Heures du Jean Due de Berry, The Bedford Hours*, and the *Psalter of Henry the Lion*.

Since the beginning of printing there has been a rich tradition of miniature books, and there have been many editions of the Bible done in a miniature scale. Most of these were done for children, but others were created for ease of transportation. The Museum's collection dates back to the seventeenth century and includes such important works as Jeremiah Rich's New Testament in Shorthand (1659), John Taylor's *Verbum Sempiternum*, and *The Bible in Miniature*, or *A Concise History of the Old and New Testaments* by E. Newberry (1780). There are also many American editions of thumb Bibles, but most of these come from the nineteenth century.

Christian symbols and art of the sixteenth and seventeenth centuries are amply illustrated in the *Index Iconologicus*. This work is a microfiche collection compiled by Dr. Karla Longedijk and consists of 60,000 alphabetically filed entries. The photographs are indexed by subject themes, content or artist. Together these parts form an index of subject matter complete with literary, theological and historical background.

Evangelical Christianity both in England and America has its roots in the Protestant Reformation, and, therefore, this historical period is covered in the collections. Most of the items in this area consist of prints and medallions of the major reformers which were done during the eighteenth, nineteenth, and twentieth centuries. Figures who are represented include: Martin Luther, John Calvin, John Knox, Philip Melanchton, John Huss, Thomas Cramner, and Ulric Zwingli.

If there is a geographic center to Christianity, it would have to be Jerusalem. The Museum has gathered a small number of important early maps and prints of the Holy City. The earliest printed depiction of Jerusalem comes from the *Nurnberg Chronicle* published by Anton Koberger in 1493. Three of the most beautiful prints of Jerusalem come from George Braun and Franciscus Hogenberg's *Civitates Orbis Terrarum*, published in Cologne between 1572 and 1617. From this work the Museum has beautiful hand colored copies of *Hierosolyma Urbs Sancta, Iudeae* (1575), and *Ierusalem, et Surburbia Eius* (1588). The collection also has a lovely 11" x 48" panoramic view of the city published by Cornelius de Bruy in Delft (1698). Another interesting map of the Middle East, *Tabula Geographica in Qua Paradisus* by Petrus Plancius (London, 1609), features fifteen medallions depicting scenes from Chapters I-IX of Genesis.

Protestant evangelism in this country began with work among the American Indians. Early evidence of the work can be seen in an act of English parliament printed in 1649. This *Act for the Promoting and Propagating the Gospel of Jesus Christ in New England* appropriated

monies to support the work of John Eliot and the Mayhew family.
John Eliot's Bible in the Algonquin language became the first Bible
printed in America (1663) and the Museum has a number of leaves
from this famous work.  A number of early Puritan tracts relating to
Indian missions were reprinted during the 1860s by Joseph Sain.
Among these works are: *New England's First Fruits With Divers Other
Special Matters Concerning That Country* (1643), *The Clear Sunshine of
the Gospel Breaking Forth Upon the Indians in New England* (1648),
*The Light Appearing More and More Towards the Perfect Day* (1651),
*Straight Out of Weakness: or a Glorious Manifestation of the Further
Progress of the Gospel Among the Indians in New England* (1652), and
*A Further Manifestation of the Progress of the Gospel, Among the
Indians in New England* (1659).

In Georgia, Governor James Oglethorpe commissioned Anglican
clergyman Thomas Wilson to write a guide book for missionaries to
use in teaching Indians and slaves, and the result was *An Essay Toward an Instruction for the Indians* (1740).  This important and popular
work went through many editions, and the Center has a fine copy of
the first edition printed in London by J. Osborn and W. Thorn.

An account of Eleazar Wheelock's Indian Mission School which later
became Dartmouth can be found in *A Brief Narrative of the Indian
Charity School, in Lebanon in Connecticut, New England* (1766).  An
account of the work of Experience Mayhew contains the testimonies of
Indians and is titled, *Indian Converts: or Some Account of the Lives
and Dying Speeches of a Considerable Number of the Christianized
Indians of Martha's Vineyard in New England* (1727).

The Mather family helped shape and chronicle Puritan life for three
generations, and some of their works are included in the Museum.
Richard Mather's *A Platform of Church Discipline* (1680) outlined the
polity that governed the church for nearly a century.  Early Puritan
church history is first recounted in Cotton Mather's monumental work,
*Magnalia Christi Americana* (1702).

John and Charles Wesley indirectly influenced colonial American religion through their association with George Whitefield and the spread
of the Methodist church during the last half of the eighteenth century.

Charles Wesley is represented in a large mezzotint engraving which
depicts him preaching to North American Indians.  There are numerous items featuring John Wesley, including ceramic busts, plates,
plaques, and cups.  Prints include, *Providential Deliverance of John
Wesley From Fire*, February 9, 1709, *Rev. John Wesley Preaching on His
Father's Tomb*, *The Rev. John Wesley Preaching in the Gwennap Am-
phitheatre*, *The Death of the Rev. John Wesley A.M.*, and portraits.

**THE FIRST GREAT AWAKENING.**   Jonathan Edwards, the fore-
most American proponent of the awakening, published several works
addressing the intellectual and emotional influences of conversion
from a theological perspective.  A first edition of *A Treatise Concerning Religious Affections* (1746), in the collection, documents his analysis
of religious experience.

In 1738 George Whitefield first arrived in America to establish an
orphanage in Georgia, as illustrated in a scaled drawing in *The Or-
phan-House Accounts* (1741) from the collection.  Returning to America in 1739 to promote the orphanage, he traveled from Georgia
through the Southern and Middle colonies to New England preaching
the message of salvation.  His dramatic and efficacious preaching
brought criticism from the opponents of the awakening, evidenced by
several publications in the collection in defense of or in opposition to
Whitefield's preaching.  Even Benjamin Franklin published a volume
of Whitefield's sermons.  Witness to his overall popularity and the
impact of his seven preaching tours in America are the many portraits
of Whitefield contained in the collection and an extra illustrated
biography with 156 tipped in prints entitled, *The Life of the Rev.
George Whitefield* (1866).

**THE SECOND GREAT AWAKENING.**   Though national in scope,
this revival had two distinct components.  In the north, it began in the
universities with the young men training to be ministers and where
Timothy Dwight (president of Yale College, 1795-1817) was instrumental through his writings and his leadership.  The collection contains published sermons and essays by Timothy Dwight and Lyman
Beecher.  As a result of revival in the universities, the Christian
community developed a greater sense of social consciousness.  Benevolent organizations were formed to accomplish a wide-ranging program
of evangelization and social reform.  Adoniram Judson helped establish the American Board of Commissioners for Foreign Missions
(ABCFM) in 1810, the first foreign mission society in America.  Along
with a portrait of Judson, the collection contains several items related
to the ABCFM and this early phase of its foreign missionary zeal,
including receipts for gifts, membership certificates, and a tin toleware
missionary collection box (ca. 1820).

The American Bible Society was founded in 1816 to promote the distribution of the Bible in America.  *The First Annual Report of Mana-
gers of the American Bible Society* (1817) and *Speeches Delivered at the
Anniversary* (1821) represent some of the holdings in the collection.

First organized in 1817, the Sunday and Adult School Union (SASU)
became known as the American Sunday School Union (ASSU) in

1825. Initial concerns were to foster Sunday schools and to publish suitable literature for them. The Museum's collection includes an undated tract published by the SASU, numerous ASSU books, pamphlets and tracts from as early as 1826, several celluloid buttons with Scripture verses, and a sample case of 50 books distributed in the mid-1800s to Sunday school libraries.

The result of a merger between the New York Religious Tract Society (NYRTS, 1812) and the New England Tract Society (NETS, 1814), the American Tract Society (ATS) was established in 1825. Modeled after the Religious Tract Society (RTS, London, 1799), they determined to publish and distribute tracts of Evangelical truth to different denominations as inexpensively as possible. The collection of early ATS publications includes some early annual reports, a number of undated tracts; several almanacs from 1824 and later; and a bound volume of early tracts, *The Publications of the American Tract Society*, Vol. I (1824), which contains the society's constitution. The collection also includes: a tract published in 1820 by the NETS; a tract published in 1824 by the NYRTS; and several undated tracts published by the RTS.

In the South, the frontier of the time, the camp meeting became the dominant means for promoting revival, as illustrated in an outstanding collection of over 40 different prints on the subject. A large hand-colored lithograph entitled, *Sing-Sing Camp Meeting, 1838* (1839), depicts a typical early camp ground complete with tents, speaker's stand and benches. Unique to the collection is the only known painting of a camp meeting (ca. 1820).

While camp meetings were first organized and promoted by Presbyterians, it was the Methodists who established them as an institution. Greatly influenced by John and Charles Wesley, and their practice of using traveling preachers to evangelize rural areas, Francis Asbury established and promoted circuit riders in America. In one of three prints depicting circuit riders in the collection, Asbury appears on horseback in a chromolithograph (ca. 1860). Other materials found in the collection that relate to Methodism in America include: more than 50 portraits of ministers taken from the *Cyclopedia of Methodism*; an undated lithograph of *The First Methodist Church and Parsonage in America--John Street, New York*; a hand-colored lantern slide of the log church where, in 1790, Asbury held the first Methodist Conference in Kentucky; two different prints celebrating the centenary of Methodism in America (1866); a bicentennial program from John Street Methodist Church, New York (the oldest Methodist Society in America, 1966); and numerous artifacts commemorating the bicentennial of American Methodism (1984).

The vision to evangelize the world, rekindled by the Second Great Awakening, renewed evangelistic and missionary activity among native Indians. A half-plate daguerreotype (ca. 1845) of Rev. Abel Bingham and his Indian converts is the earliest known photograph of missionary activity in America.

**TEMPERANCE MOVEMENT.**   Among the social reform movements inspired by the revivalism of the Second Great Awakening was the temperance movement which, in most cases, advocated total abstinence rather than the temperate use of alcohol. A law prohibiting the sale and use of alcohol was passed in Maine in 1846, and temperance advocates pushed for other states to pass the "Maine Law," as illustrated by a broadside advertising a "mass meeting of the friends of temperance and advocates of the Maine Law" (1853), and a pamphlet, *Maine Liquor Law* (1853), documenting a court case challenging such laws. Several prints illustrate the debilitating effects of alcohol, like *The Black Valley Rail Road* (1863), a chromolithograph. Other temperance items include:  almanacs from as early as 1833; materials related to the Women's Christian Temperance Union (founded in 1874); and publications of local, regional and national temperance societies.

**FULTON STREET PRAYER MEETING.**   Sometimes referred to as the Third Great Awakening, the period from 1857-1859 was marked by a revival of a different nature. Based upon the format of the noon-time prayer meeting organized by Jeremiah Lanphier in New York City (1857), the prayer meeting revival swept across the nation during a period of financial disaster. A wood engraving entitled, *The Fulton Street Prayer-Meeting*, appeared in *Harper's Weekly* (Supplement, September 30, 1871) to celebrate the opening of the new chapel for the Fulton Street noon prayer meeting on January 23, 1871.

**CIVIL WAR.**   Originating in the unresolved moral dilemma of slavery, tensions between the North and the South continued to escalate throughout the middle of the nineteenth century and culminated in the Civil War (1861-1865). The collection contains a number of ante-bellum publications defending or denouncing slavery, including one of the most significant works of Theodore Dwight Weld, *American Slavery As It Is:  The Testimony of a Thousand Witnesses* (1839), which linked newspaper accounts of slavery to biblical judgment. Harriet Beecher Stowe's influential novel also helped to fuel the cause of the abolitionists. A chromolithographed poster with the same title as the book demonstrates the popularity of *Uncle Tom's Cabin* (1851).

The United States Christian Commission, conceived in 1861 at a convention of delegates from Young Men's Christian Associations, distributed Christian literature and organized prayer meetings among

Union soldiers.  As stated in the *First Annual Report of the United States Christian Commission* (1863), "the object of the commission was to promote the spiritual and temporal welfare of the officers and men of the United States army and navy, in cooperation with chaplains and others."

Although no single organization can be solely credited, a remarkable revival took place among the Confederate troops during the war.  The Confederate States Bible Society was organized at Augusta, Georgia, in 1862, to provide Bibles for the South.  Now very rare, a copy of the *New Testament* (1862) printed in Atlanta, Georgia, is in the collection. This was the only publication ever printed by the society.

In the mid-to late-nineteenth century America, culture was dominated by Protestantism, and prevailing moral values reflected an over-whelmingly Protestant heritage.  A prime example of this is found in the prints contained in the Gast Collection.

**THE GAST COLLECTION.**   The Gast Collection consists of 785 prints from the late nineteenth century, collected over a period of fifty years by Rev. Stuart F. Gast, an Anglican minister.  The majority of the prints are lithographs or chromolithographs, although some steel engravings and woodcuts are included.  Over half of the collection are small prints (9 x 12 inches or smaller), with those remaining evenly distributed between medium (12 x 17) and large (20 x 28) prints.

Nearly half of the collection are prints published by Charles Currier, Nathaniel Currier, or Nathaniel Currier and James Merrit Ives (better known as Currier and Ives), forming the largest collection of Currier/Currier and Ives religious prints.  Most of the other promi-nent publishers of the time are also represented; they include:  L. Turgis, James Baillie, Kelloggs & Comstock, Kellogg & Thayer, D.W. Kellogg & Co., E.B. & E.C. Kellogg, T. Kelly, G.S. Peters, Sarony & Major, Haskell & Allen, and H.R. Robinson.

Illustrations of scenes directly related to the Bible are the most com-mon, including a series on the life of Christ and several versions of *The Lord's Prayer*.  *The Ten Commandments* is one print published by Nathaniel Currier which has not previously been listed in any cata-logue raisonne.  It is a medium (13 x 9, plate only) handcolored litho-graph with the Ten Commandments set in different typefaces, with commandments I-V and X in a single column, and commandments VI-IX in two columns.  Two angels with trumpets flank the title at the top of the print.

Several prints reflect the social and religious values of the time by depicting sentimental religious scenes of children in prayer, family devotion, Bible reading, sacred mottos, and Christian virtues, depicted as fruits in *The Tree of Life-The Christian* published by Nathaniel Currier. *The Tree of Life*, with a trunk of "Hope" and "Love," has 28 labeled fruits (virtues). It rises from the ground of "Faith" and "Repentance." At left, an angel repulses Satan from attacking the tree with an ax, while at right, another angel waters the tree. This print is contrasted with a companion print, *The Tree of Death*. *The Sinner* is also a small (12 1/4 x 8 1/2, plate only) hand-colored lithograph published by Nathaniel Currier. The leafless "Tree of Death," with a trunk labeled "Pride" and "Selfwill," rises from the ground of "Unbelief." Its branches are labeled "Lust of the Flesh," "Pride of Life," and "Lust of the Eye," and they bear a total of 29 labeled fruits (sins). At left, Satan, with the fires of hell raging behind him, waters the tree, while at right, a skeleton (death) prepares to attack the tree with an ax.

Significant family events, such as marriages, births and deaths, were memorialized on illustrated certificates and family registers. Some historical scenes from church history and portraits of famous religious leaders round out the collection.

**EPHEMERA COLLECTION.** Religious sentiment is prevalent in popular nineteenth century American culture and is evident in the ephemera of the period. Literally, "of the day," ephemera generally refers to something short-lived and, in the collection, more specifically refers to any printed item normally discarded after its intended use.

Among the earlier printed ephemeral items in the collection are some communion tokens or "love-feast tickets" dated as early as 1800. These tokens were distributed to church members as a pledge or guarantee of their right to receive communion and to protect the sacrament from abuse by unworthy persons. Documenting another privilege of church membership (a designated seat during church services), are notices and receipts of pew rents dated as early as 1820.

Generally used as a vehicle to convey information, and particularly effective when used for advertising, the broadside was a popular means of communicating during the eighteenth and nineteenth centuries. The breadth of subject matter of the broadsides in the collection is quite extensive. In 1798 the Commonwealth of Massachusetts passed *An Act to Prevent Profane Cursing and Swearing*. Consisting of 69 quatrains, *A Wonderful Account* (1831) relates the events surrounding the conversion and death of Mrs. Sarah Pebbles who died at the age of 24 years. Other broadsides announce meetings, advertise publications, voice opinion, or strive to persuade opinion on specific social issues (such as temperance), or relate personal experiences.

What began as a handwritten commendation from a teacher in recognition of good behavior, diligent study or punctuality, evolved into intricately designed and attractively illustrated rewards of merit. The collection contains a rather large, ornate manuscript reward presented to a pupil for "carefully studying and accurately reciting twenty Scripture lessons." Several rewards of merit from the early part of the century represent the single printing technique (usually in black) with woodcut scenes of events derived from Scripture. Although these were sometimes printed in a single color or hand-colored, chromolithographed rewards were not prevalent until sometime after the 1850s. Exquisite examples of these are contained in the collection and also feature verses from Scripture.

In a similar way, cards with Scripture verses, sacred mottos or religious poetry were richly embellished with florals, rural scenes or expressions of personal piety. Though not technically rewards of merit, they were often utilized as such. The collection boasts a wide variety of styles and sizes, and consists of over 850 individual cards, including some die-cuts, embossed cards and lace paper. The collection also contains more than 1350 Sunday school lesson picture cards published between 1881 and 1947 by various suppliers of Sunday school materials.

Other ephemeral items in the collection include: letterhead, printed envelopes, letter circulars, calendars, tickets, trade cards, pledge cards, certificates, handbills, and greeting cards.

**URBAN EVANGELISM**. The steady decline of religious influence on society as a whole progressed rapidly in the post-Civil War era as it witnessed the shift from a predominantly rural America to an urbanized society. The prevalent belief that the individual, and not the church (or a particular denomination), was the basic religious unit lead to the success of prominent preachers like Dwight L. Moody.

Returning from a successful evangelistic tour of Great Britain in 1875, Dwight L. Moody and his singing partner, Ira D. Sankey, held evangelistic services in most of America's major cities. The collection contains many prints of services conducted by this team, including a hand-colored wood engraving entitled, *The Revivalists In Brooklyn-- Opening Service of Messrs. Moody and Sankey In the Rink,* which appeared in the November 6, 1875 issue of *Harper's Weekly*. Other related materials include: *The North-Western Hymn Book* (a pre-fire Chicago imprint compiled by Moody, 1868), a pair of hand-colored lithograph portraits of Moody and Sankey published by Currier & Ives, Staffordshire figures of both Moody and Sankey, and almost 40 portraits of Moody and 20 portraits of Sankey.

While free from denominational affiliations, Moody's emphasis on the importance of the local church in spiritual growth, service and evangelism led to a strategy of centrally-located evangelistic services, widespread publicity and extensive church cooperation. The teams of R. A. Torrey/Charles M. Alexander and J. Wilbur Chapman/Charles M. Alexander organized evangelistic campaigns in similar ways. The collection contains a small amount of material on these evangelists and their activities, including a series of buttons used to identify the various groups organized for Chapman's campaign under the motto of "The King's Business."

The lessened emphasis on denominational affiliation and the population shift from rural to urban areas encouraged the formation of some of the earliest parachurch organizations in America. The Young Men's Christian Association (YMCA, 1851) and the Young Women's Christian Association (YWCA, 1866) were designed as centers of evangelism to young people moving to the cities. Their purpose is outlined in the constitution and by-laws of *The Boston Young Men's Christian Association* (1852). A collection of fifteen chromolithographed World War I posters represent the crucial ministry of the YMCA as one of the two official government relief agencies during World War I.

Officially established in the United States in 1880, the Salvation Army's effort to evangelize the masses outside of ordinary church influences focused on the slums or large cities. Published in 1890, William Booth's *In Darkest England and the Way Out* included a chromolithograph of the same title depicting the plight of "the victims of vice and poverty." A collection of photographic postcards and wood engravings illustrate the implementation of his design to meet the fundamental need of these people, both temporal and spiritual. During the war the Salvation Army assisted the YMCA and the Red Cross, establishing their reputation for openhanded generosity and for the doughnuts which they distributed to the troops in France. *A Man May Be Down But He's Never Out!* (1919), a World War I poster, advertises the Salvation Army's Home Service Fund Campaign.

Concern over the state of misery and hopelessness in skid rows and slums led to the formation of store-front rescue missions. Two books in the collection describe the founding and work of Jerry McAuley's Water Street Mission in New York: *Jerry McAuley: His Life and Work* (1885) and *Down In Water Street for Twenty-Five Years* (1897). Several photographs represent the work of Mel Trotter who was instrumental in starting over sixty rescue missions after directing a rescue mission in Grand Rapids.

A desire to educate and properly train young people for Christ's service was a by-product of the social gospel and a renewed interest in
missions.  The United Society for Christian Endeavor was founded in
1881 by Rev. Francis E. Clark with a stated purpose "to promote an
earnest Christian life among its members, to increase their mutual
acquaintance, and to make them more useful in the service of God."
An illustrated history of the society, *World Wide Endeavor: The Story
of the Young People's Society for Christian Endeavor from the Beginning
and in All Lands*, was written by Francis E. Clark and published in
1895.  Numerous stereoviews, postcards, badges, buttons and ribbons
in the collection are from annual conventions held by the society
between 1892 and 1915.  The collection also contains an autographed
cabinet photograph of the founder.

**THE TABERNACLE ERA.**    The use of tabernacles, crude temporary
wooden structures, enabled evangelists to combine the centrally-
located mass evangelistic meeting with an extensive organization and
publicity campaign.  The collection contains 80 postcards with interior
and exterior views of tabernacles.  Thirty of these are of tabernacles
built for Billy Sunday campaigns.

Billy Sunday's effective use of the tabernacle kept him in the public
view.  A unique four foot long photograph depicts Sunday and his
campaign workers outside the tabernacle built for his Chicago campaign of 1918.  Flamboyant and dynamic, Sunday captured America's
attention with his stories, impersonations and vaudeville antics, taking
on modernist theologians, saloon keepers, lukewarm church members,
and anyone else he considered to be an enemy of the church.  His
unrestrained preaching style is impressively portrayed in many of the
nearly sixty photographic postcards of Sunday and his family (ca. 1908-
1910), a small cast statue (1915), and a George Bellows lithograph
simply titled, *Billy Sunday* (ca. 1923).  Another Bellows print, *The
Sawdust Trail* (1917), shows Sunday receiving those who came forward
at the evangelist's invitation.

The Fundamentalist/Modernist controversy of the 1920's destroyed the
unity that had existed among Protestant churches involved in large-
scale urban evangelism.  Between 1910 and 1915 those defending
historic positions of Christian orthodoxy issued a series of booklets in
defense of their position.  Volume I of *The Fundamentals*, from which
the term "Fundamentalism" is derived, is in the collection.  Many of
the more than 750 lantern slides of cartoons E. J. Pace produced for
*The Sunday School Times* depict modernism as a very real and peril-
ous threat to Fundamentalist orthodoxy.

At the same time, many fundamentalist organizations considered
modernism to be a threat to the foreign mission endeavor.  Because of

their concern over what they perceived as a redefinition of the
missionary's message and task, fundamentalists formed new
interdenominational missions agencies designed to reach specialized
constituencies. Missions-related objects in the collection consist of
both personal artifacts belonging to missionaries and anthropological
artifacts indigenous to the culture in which they ministered. Some examples are: a Chinese passport (1914) issued to a British missionary
whose name translated into Chinese meant "Reveal the Way," a Chinese Bible given to Jonathan Goforth (missionary to China from 1888
to 1934), two Bibles and a Greek New Testament that belonged to Jim
Elliot (one of the five missionaries martyred in 1955 by the Auca Indians of Ecuador), and a hand-woven reed basket that was tied to a
rope dangling from an airplane which represents the first contact between the missionaries and the Auca Indians (as pictured in *Through
Gates of Splendor* and *Jungle Pilot*).

**THE POSTCARD COLLECTION.** At the turn of the twentieth century fervor for collecting postcards and displaying them in albums was
a universal phenomenon. This craze, considered the Golden Age of
the picture postcard, developed unexpectedly as a result of newly re-
fined printing techniques. Picture postcards were viewed as a means
of preserving memories and were treated more like mementos than
vehicles for communication. A large collection of more than 700 postcards depicting scenic views of church buildings represents the sou-
venir status applied to postcards.

As an example of its use as a greeting card, the collection includes
more than 150 picture postcards used to express Christmas and Easter
greetings, dating from 1905 through 1948. Also used to solicit attendance at meetings, Sunday school and church, the picture postcard was
a perfect way to announce special events. The collection contains
more than 200 Rally Day cards from 1909-1966 and over 100 Sunday
school cards from 1909-1955.

Many postcards were used to express creeds, mottos of the faith,
Scripture verses and religious poetry, or to illustrate events from
Scripture. A special series of *The Holy Scripture In Pictures* consists of
120 postcards from the original designs of Robert Leinweber, illustrating events from both the Old and New Testaments. More than 100
postcards in the collection are of religious poetry or hymn texts,
including two different complete sets of the hymn text, *Rock of Ages*.

Probably the most popular religious postcards were chromolithographed sets of "The Lord's Prayer" (a series of eight postcards) and
"The Ten Commandments" (a series of ten postcards). Four different
complete sets of "The Lord's Prayer" (ca. 1910) and two different com-

plete sets of "The Ten Commandments" (ca. 1910) are in the collection.

Exemplifying the versatility of the postcard, the collection also contains several postcards relating to the following subjects: temperance and prohibition, portraits of prominent religious leaders, scenes of foreign and home missions work, reproductions of religious art and gospel wagons.

**REGIONALISM AND AFRICAN AMERICAN RELIGION.** Following the First World War, and concurrent with the Great Depression and World War II, rising social consciousness and nationalistic trends were conveyed in the work of artists like John Stuart Curry and John McGrady. Focusing on familiar scenes of everyday life in different regions of the country, these "regionalists" essentially documented the diverse cultural identity of an emerging nation. The collection contains a number of lithographs and woodcuts portraying religion in the South and in the African American community. Among them are: *Holy Rollers* (John Stuart Curry, 1930), *Proverbs 6:9* (Wayman Adams, ca. 1930), *Baptism In Big Stranger Creek* (John Stuart Curry, 1932), *Revival* (Isac Friedlander, 1933), *Experience Meeting, Massydony* (Prentiss Taylor, 1934), *'Speriences Meeting* (Palmer Schoppe, ca. 1935), *Church Supper* (Frank Hartley Anderson, 1936), *Easter Morning* (Olin Davis, n.d.), *Assembly Church* (Prentiss Taylor, 1936), and *Swing Low Sweet Chariot* (John McGrady, 1941).

Some items in the collection document the impact of Christianity on Afrrican Americans in America and early missionary activity among slaves, as evidenced in *An Account of the Endeavors Used by the Society for Propagation of the Gospel in Foreign Parts, to Instruct Negroe Slaves in New York* (London, 1730). A letter circular distributed by the Bethel Baptist Association in 1856 recommends a "special missionary of the Gospel" be sent to the slave population in the region. Another circular sent out by the Southern Aid Society in 1858 mentions that "at least half of our fifty or sixty missionaries devote their time chiefly to the religious instruction of slaves and free blacks."

Significant to the collection are two items relating the religious experience to two individuals, one slave and one free African American. *Poems on Various Subjects, Religious and Moral* (1773) is a first edition copy of original poetry written by an educated negro slave, Phyllis Wheatley. *The Missionary Preacher, or a Brief Memoir of the Life, Labours, and Death of John Stewart, (Man of Colour), Founder, Under God of the Mission Among Wyandotts at Upper Sandusky, Ohio* (1827) relates the work of a African American missionary to the Wyandott Indians.

Other items in the collection illustrate the religious life of the African American community, including: two sepiatone photographs of baptisms in Culpepper, Virginia, with both white and African American people looking on (ca. 1910s), several postcards of baptism scenes (ca. 1905-1915), nearly forty prints of African American congregations, churches, revival meetings, weddings and funerals, and some stereotypical caricatures.

**FINE PRINTING.**   By the turn of the twentieth century, reaction to the effects of industrialization on book printing had led to the revival of the artistic ideals and fine craftsmanship of the Middle Ages.  The movement combined elements from the fine arts and the useful arts to produce a functionally and artistically unified work of art.  Ranging from designs based purely on typography to lavishly illustrated works complete with initials and borders, both commercial and private presses participated in the endeavor to produce finely printed books in limited editions.

One of the earliest examples of fine printing in the collection is *A New Biblia Pauperum Containing XXXVIII Pictures Concerning the Life, Parables, Vertues, & Seyenges of Our Lord & Sauyour Ihesu Christ,* published by Unwin Brothers (London, 1877).  It is entirely without illustration.  The typography, binding, layout and design elements work together to imitate a fifteenth-century book.

The Doves Press, a private press, was established in 1900 by Thomas James Cobden-Sanderson and Emery Walker to print books that would effectively use typography "to communicate, without loss by the way, the thought or image intended to be communicated by the author." *The English Bible* (1902-1905), a five volume set, is completely without ornament or illustration.  Calligraphic initials printed in red ink begin each book of the Bible.

The Nonesuch Press, founded in 1923, combined the efficiency of a commercial press with the design of a private press to produce a book of respectable appearance at a moderate price, and thus put fine books in the realm of the general public. *The Holy Bible*, published in five volumes between 1924 and 1927, contained illustrations at the beginning and end of each volume, and minimal ornamentation at the beginning of each book of the Bible.

*The Four Gospels* (1931), published by the Golden Cockerel Press, was designed by Eric Gill.  He used beginning words as the decorative element in an otherwise unillustrated text, intertwining the woodcut letters with human forms in a way that was reminiscent of manuscript illumination, yet strikingly different.

The Limited Editions Club was founded in 1929 by George Macy to publish books for its subscribers at a rate of one volume a month. The titles were chosen by the subscribers from the classics of literature. They were then edited by reputable scholars, illustrated by famous artists, designed by the most talented typographers, and produced by the best printers in Europe and America. The Museum's collection contains the following Limited Editions Club publications: *The Four Gospels* (Leipzig, 1932), *The Pilgrim's Progress* (New York, 1941), *The Book of Job* (New York, 1946), *The Book of Ruth* (New York, 1947), *The Book of Psalms* (New York, 1960), *The Book of Proverbs* (New York, 1963), *The Book of Ecclesiastes* (New York, 1968), *The Sermon on the Mount* (Oxford, 1977), and *The Book of the Prophet Isaiah* (New York, 1979).

The collection also contains two sets of typographical solutions addressing the problems associated with printing the Bible. *Liber Librorum* (1955) contains 43 examples of typographical solutions by leading international book designers assembled into sets at Stockholm in celebration of the 500th anniversary of the Gutenberg 42-line Bible. *Typographie Der Bibel* (Stuttgart, 1962) contains 27 pamphlets of studies and typographical designs assembled to celebrate the 150th anniversary of the Wurttembergischen Bible Institute.

**CHILDREN'S LITERATURE.**    Some of the earliest literature published in England and America exclusively for the use of children were instructional aids in the form of hornbooks, catechisms and primers. The nineteenth century hornbook in the collection consists of the alphabet and "The Lord's Prayer" printed on paper that is covered with translucent horn to prevent it from being soiled and attached to a wooden board with a narrow band of brass.

New England catechisms, forerunners of *The New England Primer*, instructed children in the first principles of piety and morality. The text, based on the essential doctrines and duties of religion, was formatted by way of questions and answers which the child memorized. *The Orthodox Christian: or, A Child Well Instructed in the Principles of the Christian Religion: Exhibited in a Discourse by Way of Catechizing*, the first edition of the Andover Catechism, was published in 1738. The first American printing of the Episcopal Catechism after the separation from the British Church, *The ABC With the Church of England Catechism* (1785), left blanks for the words "king" and "him" with instructions for the teacher to fill the blanks with words suited to a republican government. *Milk for Babes, or A Catechism in Verse: For Children* (1822) provides the answers of the catechism in quatrains. Numerous other editions of catechisms were published, including the following: *The Baptist Catechism* (Wilmington, 1809), *A Catechism Containing the First Principles of Religious and Social Duties* (Haverhill,

1809), *A Short Catechism for Young Children* (Morris-Town, 1818), *An Epitome of Scripture Doctrine, Comprised in a Catechism* (Boston, 1821), *A Catechism: Compiled and Recommended by the Worcester Association of Ministers* (Worcester, 1821), *The Shorter Catechism* (New York, 1830), *The Shorter Catechism* (Philadelphia, 1832), *Dr. Watts' First Catechism* (Philadelphia, 1832), *The Westminster Assembly's Shorter Catechism* (Boston, 1839), and *Milk for Babes* (Northampton, 1840).

*The New England Primer* was the most popular schoolbook for children in New England, as evidenced by the numerous editions that were issued. The earliest issue extant was printed in Boston in 1727. Most editions contained an alphabet lesson in couplets, the Shorter Catechism, Dr. Watts' Cradle Hymn, and the woodcut of martyr John Rogers, with only slight variances. The Museum's collection of New England primers includes copies of the following editions: Boston (1777), frequently reprinted, Albany (1818), Pittsburgh (n.d.), Philadelphia (1839), Worcester (n.d.), and Boston (n.d.). Two other primers of interest in the collection are: *The Evangelical Primer* (Boston, 1819), which was more of a catechism than a primer, and *The Bible Primer* (New York, 1873), which based all of its reading lessons on biblical passages.

The popularity of *The New England Primer* was due in part to its illustrations. Also one of the most popular children's books of the eighteenth century, *The History of the Holy Jesus* (1749), was one of the first illustrated books in America. Its sixteen woodcut illustrations juxtaposed the contemporary Puritan dress with the biblical subject matter of the text in a curious fashion.

Illustrated portions of Scripture and thumb Bibles, which were developed from abridged histories of the Bible, were popular as easy ways to learn biblical and moral instruction, and were often published on a miniature scale. The collection contains several examples: *The Holy Bible Abridged, of the History of the Old and New Testament Illustrated with Notes and Adorned with Cuts for the Use of Children* (New York, 1790), *The Bible* (Philadelphia, ca. 1796), *History of the Bible* (Boston, 1814), *Scripture History Designed Particularly for the Improvement of Youth* (New York, 1829), *History of the Bible* (New London, 1831), *The Child's Bible with Plates* (Philadelphia, 1834), *The Bible In Miniature for Children with Twenty-Five Engravings* (Worcester, 1835), and *The Child's Pictorial History of the Bible* (Buffalo, 1857 and 1862).

Hieroglyphical Bibles, popular in the late eighteenth century, were used as an easy way to teach Scripture to children. By inserting emblematic figures into the text to replace certain words, Bible lessons were made more attractive as well as profitable.  The collection contains two early examples, whose lengthy titles reflect their noble goals: *The Hieroglyphick Bible; or, Select Passages in the Old and New Testaments, Represented with Emblematical Figures, for the Amusement of Youth: Designed Chiefly to Familiarize Tender Age, in a Pleasing and Diverting Manner, with Early Ideas of the Holy Scriptures* (Hartford, 1800) and *A New Hieroglyphical Bible, for the Amusement and Instruction of Children: Being a Selection of Some of the Most Useful Lessons and Interesting Narratives from Genesis to the Revelations* (Hartford, 1820).

*The Pilgrim's Progress* by John Bunyan, a work that was not originally intended for children, nevertheless became one of the most popular and influential children's books ever written.  Published in America in 1798, *The Christian Pilgrim* was arranged especially for children.  The second American edition of *The Christian Pilgrim* (1807), in the collection, originally belonged to John W. Barber, who later published *Bunyan's Pilgrim's Progress, From This World To That Which Is To Come, Exhibited in a Metamorphosis, or a Transformation of Pictures* (ca. 1840), also in the collection.  Its five leaves fold to form fifteen woodcut illustrations.  Other items in the collection related to *The Pilgrim's Progress* include:  a Limited Editions Club publication (1941), a set of 12 chromolithographed cards published by the Religious Tract Society (London, n.d.), a facsimile of the 1679 edition published by Paradine (London, 1978), a special edition published by C. Arthur Pearson, Ltd. (London, n.d.) with illustrations by George Woolliscroft Rhead, Frederick Rhead, and Louis Rhead, over 200 prints taken from various publications, and two ceramic plates with scenes of Christian's pilgrimage.

**TRACT COLLECTION.**    Produced especially for poor people, chapbooks were popular among children as well as adults.  They were the result of the efforts of people such as Hannah More to convert and instruct the spiritually ignorant and to preserve them from radical influence.  With the publication of these Cheap Repository Tracts (1795-1798) the prolific and profitable venture of tract publishing began.  Appearing in the form of broadside ballads, some of the earliest tracts in the collection are by Hannah More (ca. 1795).  These tracts and those produced as chapbooks were extremely popular in England.  The committee formed for their distribution eventually led to the formation of the Religious Tract Society.  Three volumes of bound chapbooks in the collection contain numerous "penny tracts" written by Hannah More and her helpers.

In working with the poor and the young, evangelicals made extensive use of tracts.  From the narrative tracts of 1795-1800 there developed several categories: the historical tract designed to promote a Protestant view of history, the missionary tract, the didactic tract, and the tract of warning that called attention to pressing social evils of the day.

Many of the nineteenth century tracts in the collection were published by the Religious Tract Society, and American Tract Society, or the American Sunday School Union. At least half of these were especially designed for children. Other publishers of tracts from this time period represented in the collection include: the Hartford Evangelical Tract Society, the Tract Association of Friends, the Episcopal Female Tract Society, and the Evangelical Tract Society. Independent printers who also published tracts are represented in the collection: Sidney Babcock (New Haven), S. M. Crane (New York), Mahlon Day (New York), Kiggins & Kellogg (New York), and Rufus Merrill & Co. Concord).

Due to their convenient size, simple design, concise message and nominal price, tracts have remained a popular and effective means of distributing the gospel message. A collection of nearly 8,000 twentieth century tracts represent 186 publishers. Among the best represented publishers are: Concordia Tract Mission, Faith, Prayer & Tract League, Forward Movement Publications, Good News Publishers, InterVarsity Press, and Words of Hope.

A complete collection of tracts published by the Billy Graham Evangelistic Association consists of 283 titles (1951-1989), most of which are transcriptions of messages preached by Billy Graham on the *Hour of Decision* broadcast. Many of these titles have multiple copies due to the number of times they have been reprinted.

**THE BILLY GRAHAM MEMORABILIA.** The Museum's collection of Dr. Billy Graham's memorabilia consists of nearly 1,000 items. Most of these relate to Dr. Graham's travels on behalf of the Billy Graham Evangelistic crusades and special speaking engagements. The type of items in this collection include: crusade mementos, awards, plaques, trophies, certificates, degrees, keys to cities, gifts given to Dr. Graham in appreciation of his work, and a few personal artifacts.

**CONTEMPORARY CHRISTIAN ART.** The Museum's collection of contemporary Christian art features more than 200 works encompassing both fine art and folk art. The decline of religious imagery in fine art during the nineteenth century and its virtual disappearance in the twentieth century is markedly contrasted with the emphasis placed on the spiritual realm in much of the folk art produced in recent years.

Some folk artists document the religious life of their community while others attempt to relate their own religious experiences or personal concepts of spiritual truth through their work, reflecting not only their personal faith, but also their cultural environment. *The Revival* (1984), a hand-painted, carved wooden sculpture by Roy K. Pace, depicts a church revival scene.

The visionary works of Howard Finster, a retired minister, uniquely convey his own interpretations of Scripture passages and biblical concepts, often serving as a verbal witness of his beliefs. The collection contains more than ten pieces of his art, including two original paintings which consist of visual images combined with text.

The combination of visual artistic expression and function, prevalent in folk art, is evidenced in two pieces used as vehicles for communication. An early twentieth century quilt in the collection contains 12 panels with short exhortative and declarative phrases taken directly from Scripture. A large painted aluminum roadside sign by Brother Harrison Mayes succinctly challenges the passer-by to "Get Right With God."

In the mainstream of the fine art world, the spiritual dimension of man and especially religious belief has been largely ignored in recent times by both the church and the art community. Christians in the Visual Arts (CIVA) and the New York Arts Group have been established in an attempt to facilitate the networking of artists for mutual support and encouragement.

Many Christian artists attempting to convey meaning through their art draw upon the past but then relate the message of Christianity in a contemporary idiom. The title of Jeff Thompson's mixed media construction, *Homage to Grunewald* (1981), draws by inference upon the sixteenth century crucifixion altar piece by the German painter Matthias Grunewald.

The influence of icons used as aids to worship, meditation and prayer can be seen in the "contemporary icons" of Sheila Keefe, many of which deal with entombments and are done in a primitive and timeless style. *Fresco Study I* (1983) and *Fresco Study II* (1983) both have entombed bodies (of Christ and of Lazarus, respectively) and Scripture references carved and painted on wooden panels.

By drawing upon stylistic elements of various historical periods, Edward Knippers simultaneously imparts a timelessness to the massive figures in his paintings and a historical context for the Christian subject matter. In *Crucifixion* (1985) the muscularity of the nude body of Christ dramatically emphasizes the necessity of the Incarnation as a source of redemption for modern man.

While drawing upon the traditional subject matter contained in Scripture for inspiration, Tanja Witkowski uses the expressive quality of color to convey the "timeless spiritual, emotional and psychological truth of the biblical account." The Museum's collection of her work consists of 15 paintings, all of which are based upon narratives found in Scripture.

The difficult possibility of visually interpreting the reality of a spiritual realm through the limitations of a physical medium is represented in the work of Donald Forsythe. Two of the three works by Forsythe in the collection are mixed media collages in which he attempts to depict the "substance and mystery of God's activity in the lives of his people, and in controlling events." They are: *King of a Realm So Royal* (1986) and *Spiritual Infirmity* (1986).

The works of other contemporary Christian artists attempting to deal with this struggle of producing religious art in a secular society are represented in the collection. These include the following works: *Going Home* (1985), a hand-painted wooden assemblage by George Lorio; *Searching, I Take the Blind to See the Show* (1985), an acrylic collage by Michael Mallard; *Historical Dislocations: The Expulsion* (ca. 1987), by Chris Anderson; *Fire of Thorns* (1988), by Tim Lowly; and *No Mercy* (1988), by Fred Del Guidice.

# The Archives

The Archives has the narrowest collecting policy of the three Graham Center resources. The staff acquires documents about North American Protestant, nondenominational, Evangelical efforts to spread the gospel. This includes the records of faith missions, the papers of evangelists, the files of youth groups, materials relating to prison ministry, the tapes and films of radio and television ministries and documents from many other types of Christian work besides. The nucleus of the Archives' holdings is made up of the records of the Billy Graham Evangelistic Association. About one fifth of the processed collections are from the BGEA.

This collecting policy is unusual among American religious archives. Almost all other repositories document an institution, namely a denomination. The BGC Archives is documenting an activity. The policy was framed so as to preserve valuable materials which other archives were not acquiring, such as the files of the nondenominational evangelistic organizations and faith missions which provide so much of the leadership and direction of Evangelical Protestantism.

As of January 1990, the Archives contained 2500 linear feet of processed materials and an additional 3300 linear feet of unprocessed records. The processed materials form 525 collections and include such diverse elements as paper records, audio tapes, films, video tapes, computer tapes, photographs, slides, negatives, and microforms. On the following pages, most of the processed holdings are briefly described. For every collection described below, there is a guide available for use in the reading room of the Archives. These guides can be over a hundred pages long and describe the individual collections in much greater detail than the brief entries in this volume allow.

A few words should be said about materials that have not been described below. Unprocessed materials are not included, although researchers can have limited access to them in many cases. Among the as yet unprocessed materials in the Archives are the records of Bill Glass Evangelistic Association, Inter-Varsity Christian Fellowship of the United States, Latin American Mission, Moody Memorial Church of Chicago, National Religious Broadcasters, Voice of Calvary Ministries, World Evangelical Fellowship, films of Percy Crawford's television program: *Youth on the March* (first broadcast in 1949) and the 1986 International Congress of Itinerant Evangelists as well as papers and/or oral history interviews with people such as Charles Colson, radio station HCJB co-founder Clarence Jones, and many other Christian workers. Microfilm collections purchased by the Archives from micropublishers were in most cases not included since they are available for use at other institutions as well. If a collection includes other items besides the microfilm, such as CN# 143, or if the film was created in whole or in part by the efforts of the Center, such as CN# 61, then they are described below. Finally, for reasons of space, several small collections were not included.

The collection descriptions on the following pages are intended to give a general idea of the contents of individual collections and to give an indication of the kind of topics that can be researched through them. The first line gives the collection number: CN# XXX. In a few cases, the number includes the letters SC: CN# SCXXX. This means that the collection is a small collection which is less than half a cubic foot in size and includes no tapes, photographs or film. The second line is the name of the creator or creators and or subjects of the documents in the collection followed by birth and death dates, in the case of people, or incorporation and dissolution dates in the case of an organization. In a few cases, such as CN# 102 or CN# 356, the staff has artificially put similar types of materials together in one collection, and in those cases this line refers to the subject matter of the material.

The third line describes the type of collection. There are four kinds of collections in the Archives. The first are *records*, which are the files of an organization. These include such things as correspondence of officers of the organization, minutes of meetings, personnel files, reports, newsletters and manuals. Also under this heading would be the files of a temporary organization, such as a committee set up to run a congress or conference. An example of this is CN# 176. The second type of collection is called *papers*. These are the personal documents of an individual including letters, diaries, scrapbooks, home movies. If the Archives has both an oral history interview with an individual and some or all of his or her papers, then the whole collection is called papers. The third type of collection is called *interview* or *interviews*. This consists solely of oral history interviews taped by the BGC Archives staff with various individuals involved in Christian work. In the interviews, the interviewees discuss their family background, education, conversion, ministry, major political, military, or social events they witnessed or participated in, reflections on their work and other relevant topics. The last type of collection is called *ephemera*. These contain one or a few items by or about an individual or organization, but they were received from sources other than the subject or the subject's heirs and cannot be considered the subject's papers or records. The third line also gives the dates covered by the material in the collection. If there are major chronological gaps in the collection, this is indicated by putting the range of dates for the overwhelming majority of the documents in parentheses, like this: 1922 (1957-1968) 1974; n.d. The symbol "n.d." means that there are several documents in the collection with no date. The years given for interviews are the years in which the interviews were conducted, not the time period covered by the interviews.

Following these three lines is a brief narrative description of the collection. This usually includes some biographical or historical information and a few sentences about the subjects covered by the documents.

This brief description is followed by a line on the volume which lists the number of boxes and/or other types of materials in the collection. A box might be a document case, which is a little less than half a cubic foot or a record carton, which is a cubic foot. The purpose of this line is to give a very rough idea of the size of the collection.

The last item in each entry is the list of major topics. These include the names of people, places, events, organizations and subjects for which there is information in the collection. Often a collection will contain a great deal of information on subjects with little direct relationship to missions or evangelism. The papers of many missionaries to China, for example, contain much information about the Sino-Japanese War. In most cases, the subject headings are those of the Library of Congress. Most, but not all, of the entries entered under "MAJOR TOPICS" are also in the index of this volume.

*EXAMPLE:*

CN# 205 *[Collection number]*
Carlson, Robert Dean; 1928- *[Creator and/or subject of collection, birth-death or organization-dissolution dates]*
Interviews; 1982 *[Type of collection, dates of collection]*

*Oral history interviews with Carlson in which he discusses his boyhood in China and Tibet, the condition of the Christian church in those countries, social and religious customs, and the Chinese language.* *[Brief description]*

Vol: 2 Audio Tapes *[Volume]*

*(MAJOR TOPICS: Agricultural societies; Assemblies of God; Assemblies of God--Missions; Bible--Publication and distribution; Buddhists in China; Buddhists in Tibet; Carlson, Robert Dean; Children of missionaries; China; Christian and Missionary Alliance)*

All of the collections described are available for use in the reading room of the Archives. Approximately a third of the collections have some restriction placed on their use. In some cases, this means that documents can be used in the reading room but cannot be photocopied. In other cases, portions of a collection are closed until a specific date except to researchers with the written permission of the donor of the collection. The researcher is required to use xerox or microfilm copies in a few cases because of the fragile condition of the originals. Information on the specific restrictions, if any, attached to particular collections can be obtained from the staff.

Several of the Archives collections are available for interlibrary loan, either on microfilm or on audio tape. A complete list of collections that can be loaned is available on request. There is also a biannual checklist, entitled *From the Archives of the Billy Graham Center*, which describes recently processed collections, new acquisitions, and current research in the Archives. Persons wishing to borrow through interlibrary loan or to subscribe to the checklist should contact the Reference  at the address on page vii.

As of January 1, 1990, the Archives reading room was open from 10:00 a.m. to 6:00 p.m. Monday to Friday, 10:00 a.m. to 2:00 p.m. on Saturday, except for holidays. The collections are open to all. Past users include scholars working on dissertations or books, journalists, pastors looking for sermon topics or illustrations, students working on assignments, evangelists and other Christian workers investigating ways to improve their ministries, television and film production companies searching for illustrative materials, book and magazine editors searching for photographs, laypersons gathering information for church activities and conferences, and the casually curious. All are welcome.

CN# 282
**Adolph, Bonnie Jo; 1933-**
Interviews; 1984

Tape of an oral history interview with Mrs. Adolph which mainly covers the years of her life between 1954 and 1974 during which time she attended Wheaton College, married Harold Adolph, and served with him as a missionary of the Sudan Interior Mission in Ethiopia.

Vol: 2 Audio Tape

(MAJOR TOPICS:  Adolph, Bonnie Jo Adelsman; Adolph, Harold Paul; Animism; Children of missionaries; Children--Conversion to Christianity; Christian and Missionary Alliance (CMA); Christmas; Church and state in Ethiopia; Conversion; Coptic Church; Courtship; Ethiopia; Evangelistic work--Ethiopia; Evangelistic work--Taiwan; Family; Illinois; Intercultural communications; Johnson, Torrey Maynard; Marriage; Medical care--Ethiopia; Missionaries--Recruitment and training; Missions to Animists; Missions, Medical; Missions--Bangladesh; Missions--Ethiopia; Missions--Taiwan; Muslims in Ethiopia; Panama; Sex role; Sudan Interior Mission (SIM); Taiwan; Wheaton College, IL; Women--Religious life; Women in missionary work; Worship)

%%%%%%%%%%%%

CN# 169
**Adolph, Harold Paul; 1932-**
Interviews; 1981

Tapes of interviews with Adolph in which he talks about his boyhood in  China, his education at  Wheaton College, and his activities in Ethiopia as a medical missionary.

Vol: 2 Audio Tapes

(MAJOR TOPICS:  Adolescence; Adolph, Harold Paul; Adolph, Paul Earnest; Animism; Children of missionaries; China; Communism; Coptic Church; Edman, Victor Raymond; Ethiopia; Haile Selassie; Illinois; Language: Amharic; Language: Chinese; Medical care--Ethiopia; Missions to Animists; Missions to Muslims; Missions, Medical; Missions--China; Missions--Ethiopia; Muslims in Ethiopia; Narramore Christian Foundation; Overseas Missionary Fellowship (China Inland Mission); Panama; Shanghai, China; Sino-Japanese Conflict, 1937--1945; Sudan Interior Mission (SIM); Wheaton College, IL; World War II)

%%%%%%%%%%%%

CN# 81
**Africa Inland Mission; 1896-**
Records 1902-1985; n.d.

Correspondence, minutes, reports, personnel files, photographs,
slides, tapes, etc., relating to the mission's work in Africa from its
founding.  Documents describe the process of recruiting and
training missionaries, development of an administrative structure,
relations with other missions, development of the Africa Inland
Church, changes in Africa and African Christianity following the
independence of African nations from colonial status, and the
work in Kenya, Uganda, Zaire, Tanzania, Sudan, the Central
African Republic, and other countries.  Hundreds of tapes of
AIM's radio program, *Letter From Africa*, are also included.

Vol: 39 boxes, Audio tapes, Films, Negative, Oversize Materials,
Photographs, Slides

(MAJOR TOPICS: Africa Inland Church; Africa Inland Mission
(AIM); Agricultural societies; American Council of Christian Chur-
ches; Angola; Animism; Assemblies of God; Association of Evangelicals of Africa and Madagascar (AEAM); Australia; Barnett, William
John; Barrows, Clifford B; Belgium; Bible--Translating; Bob Jones
University, SC; Canada; Catholic Church in Malawi; Catholic church
in Sudan; Catholic Church in Tanzania; Catholic Church in Zaire;
Catholic Church--Missions; Catholic Church--Relations; Central
African Republic; Child Evangelism Fellowship; Child welfare; Children of missionaries; Christian education (theory); Christian educa-
tion--Kenya; Christian education--Tanzania; Christian educa-
tion--Uganda; Christian education--Zaire; Christian leadership; Chris-
tian literature--Publication and distribution; Church and social problems; Church and state in Central African Republic; Church and state
in Comoro Islands; Church and state in Kenya; Church and state in
Mozambique; Church and state in Namibia; Church and state in
Seychelles Islands; Church and state in Tanzania; Church and state in
Uganda; Church and state in Zaire; Church of Christ in the Congo;
Church work with students; Church work with youth; City missions;
Colonies; Communication; Communication in organizations; Com-
munism; Communism--Mozambique; Congo Protestant Council;
Conversion; Corporations, Religious--Taxation; Davis, Ralph T;
Disease: Leprosy; Disease: Venereal disease; Divination; Ecumenical
movement; Education--Curricula; Education--Kenya; Educa-
tion--Reunion Island; Education--Tanzania; Eglise Evangelique du
Congo Oriental (EVACO); Engstrom, Theodore "Ted" Wilhelm;

Ethiopia; Ethnocentrism; Evangelicalism; Evangelistic work--Belgium;
Evangelistic work--Central African republic; Evangelistic work--Kenya;
Evangelistic work--Sudan; Evangelistic work--Tanzania; Evangelistic
work--Uganda; Evangelistic work--Zaire; Famine--Kenya; Famine--Ug-
anda; Fund raising; Fundamentalism; Graham, William Franklin
"Billy"; Great Britain; Hospitals--Central African Republic; Hospi-
tals--Kenya; Hospitals--Tanzania; Hospitals--Zaire; Hurlburt, Charles
E; Indigenous church administration; Intercultural communications;
Interdenominational Foreign Mission Association (IFMA); Interna-
tional Missionary Council; Ironside, Henry Allan "Harry"; Islam
(theology); Islam--Cameroon; Islam--Comoro Islands; Islam--Ghana;
Islam--Guinea; Islam--Kenya; Islam--Morocco; Islam--Nigeria; Is-
lam--Relations--Christianity; Islam--Sierra Leone; Islam--Sudan;
Islam--Tanzania;  Islam--Uganda; Ivory Coast; Kenya; Kenyatta,
Ngina; Kikuyu people, Kenya; Language in missionary work: Lan-
guage: Swahili; Lindsell, Harold; Madagascar; Marriage; Masai people,
Kenya; Mass media in missionary work; Mau movement; Mission
Aviation Fellowship (MAF); Missionaries, Lay; Missionaries, Resign-
ation of; Missionaries--Recruitment and training; Missions to Muslims;
Missions, Medical; Missions--Central African Republic; Missions---
Comoro Islands; Missions--Educational work; Missions--Kenya; Mis-
sions--Seychelles; Missions--South Africa; Missions--Sudan; Missions---
Tanzania; Missions--Uganda; Missions--Zaire; Moody Bible Institute,
IL; Mozambique; Nairobi, Kenya; National Association of Evangeli-
cals; National Council of Churches; National Holiness Association;
Nationalism; Navigators; New Zealand; Nigeria; Organizational
change; Orphans and orphan-asylums; Congresses and conferences---
Pan African Christian Leadership Assembly, 1976; Pentecostalism---
Kenya; Presidents--United States; Pygmies; Racism; Radio in religion;
Refugees--Sudan; Refugees--Uganda; Religion and music; Rift Valley
Academy, Kenya; Roosevelt, Theodore; Scott Theological College,
Machakos, Kenya; Scott, Peter Cameron; Seume, Richard Herman;
Sex role; Seychelles; Skinner, Thomas; Social change; Social classes;
South Africa; Stam, Peter; Sudan; Sudan Interior Mission (SIM);
Tanzania; Taylor, Kenneth Nathaniel; Torrey, Reuben Archer Sr;
Transportation--Kenya; Trotman, Dawson; Uganda; Unevangelized
Fields Mission; War; World Council of Churches; World War II;
Worship; Wycliffe Bible Translators; Wyrtzen, John Von Casper
"Jack"; Zaire; Zambia)

%%%%%%%%%%%%

CN# 177
**Alford, Zoe Anne; 1912-**
Papers; 1925-1983; n.d.

Correspondence, manuscripts, lecture notes, curriculum materials,
circular  prayer letters, financial records, clippings, maps, promotional materials,  minutes, photographs, newsletters, an audio
taped interview with Alford, etc., all relating to her missionary
work in India and New Mexico among the Navajo Indians.  The
collection provides a broad overview of Alford's education, preparation and missionary career with The Evangelical Alliance
Mission (TEAM), particularly at Union Biblical Seminary, as well
as of indigenous and foreign Christian work in India.  The time
period covered is 1920 to 1977.

Vol: 11 boxes, 1 Audio Tape, Photographs

(MAJOR TOPICS:  Alford, Zoe Anne; Bible Institute of Los Angeles
(BIOLA), CA; Christian education (theory); Christian educa-
tion--India; Church growth--India; Correspondence schools and cour-
ses; Education--Curricula; Education--India; Evangelical Alliance
Mission, The (TEAM); Evangelical Fellowship of India; Graham,
William Franklin "Billy"; Hinduism (theology); Hindus in India; India;
Indians of North America; Missions from underdeveloped areas;
Missions--Educational work; Missions--India; Missions--United States;
Moody Bible Institute, IL; Muslims in India; Navajo Indians; Nonfor-
mal education; Sex role; Smith, Wilbur Moorehead; Tenney, Helen
Jaderquist; Tenney, Merrill Chapin; Vacation schools, Christian;
Wheaton College, IL; Women--Religious life; Women in missionary
work)

%%%%%%%%%%%%

CN# SC105
**American Association for Jewish Evangelism**
Ephemera; 195?

Brochure, probably from the 1950s, advertising an AAJM film
entitled *Three Minutes to Twelve*.  The movie was about the place
of the Jews in New Testament prophecy and the creation of the
nation of Israel as part of the fulfillment of that prophecy.

(MAJOR TOPICS: American Association for Jewish Evangelism;
Bible--Prophecies; Israel; Judaism; Mass media in religion; Missions to

Jews; Moving-pictures in church work; Moving-pictures--Moral and religious aspects; Religion and music)

%%%%%%%%%%%%

CN# SC99
**American Bible Society**
Ephemera; 1833-1853; n.d.

Nine letters and one annual report from members of the American Bible Society addressed to Rev. J. C. Brigham, Secretary, and Mr. Joseph Hyde, General Agent and Assistant Treasurer. Letters contain information on finances, orders and reports on sales of Bibles, notices of obituaries of members, and other data relating to the Society.

(MAJOR TOPICS: American Bible Society; Bible--Publication and distribution)

%%%%%%%%%%%%

CN# SC70
**American Board of Commissioners for Foreign Missions**
Ephemera; 1848-1917

Miscellaneous collection of items including a biography of missionary Harriet Newell, d. 1813; two engraved certificates issued for contributions of a dime to Mission School Enterprise, 1857, and Morning Star, a missionary ship, 1866; historical sketch of a mission in Micronesia, 1852-1883; a program for the Congregational Home Missionary Society's diamond jubilee and a letter from India by John and Margaret Miller, 1917.

(MAJOR TOPICS: American Board of Commissioners for Foreign Missions; Boston, MA; Massachusetts; Missions--United States)

%%%%%%%%%%%%

CN# 339
**American Board of Missions to Jews; 1894-**
Ephemera; n.d.

One 13-minute tape of Radio program #6, titled *The Promise of Tomorrow*, produced by the American Board of Missions to Jews. Narrated by Charles L. Feinberg and directed to friends of Jewish Christians, the brief talk discusses Jewish views of heaven. A brief news report about Israel and the Middle East is included, with reference to New Testament prophecies about the apocalypse.

Vol: 1 audio tape

(MAJOR TOPICS: American Board of Missions to the Jews; Evangelistic work--Israel; Feinberg, Charles Lee; Israel; Judaism; Mass media in religion; Missions to Jews; Radio in religion)

%%%%%%%%%%%%

CN# SC43
**American Tract Society**
Ephemera; 1854-1858

Several handwritten letters from the American Tract Society offices in Rochester, Niagara, and Toronto; some of the duties and responsibilities of the colporteurs.

(MAJOR TOPICS: American Tract Society; Canada; Evangelistic work--Canada; Evangelistic work--United States; Great Britain; London, England; Toronto, ON)

%%%%%%%%%%%%

CN# 231
**Anderson, Ian Rankin (1912-1982) and Helen Mount (1909 - )**
Papers; 1928-1982

Correspondence, diaries, articles, clippings, manuscripts, photographs, newsletters, songbooks, etc., related to the Andersons' mission work with Overseas Missionary Fellowship. The materials thoroughly document their careers among the Chinese in China until 1951, in Taiwan until 1956, and in the Philippines until 1971, and again in Taiwan until 1974. Documents also reflect their work as regional representatives for OMF following their retirement in 1974.

Vol: 1 box, Oversize Material, Photographs, Slides

(MAJOR TOPICS: Anderson, Helen Mount; Anderson, Ian Rankin; Bible colleges; Bible--Translating; China; China--Description and travel; China--History; China--Religion; Christian education of adults; Christian education of children; Christian education--China; Christian education--Philippines; Christian education--Taiwan; Communism--China; Conversion; Education--Philosophy; Evangelistic work--China; Evangelistic work--Taiwan; Far East Broadcasting

Company; Frame, Helen Grace Nowack; Frame, Raymond William;
India; Indigenous church administration; Kuo min tang (China);
Language in missionary work; Language: Chinese; Mass media in
missionary work; Missionaries, Withdrawal of; Missionaries--Leaves
and furloughs; Missions to Chinese; Missions--biblical teaching; Mis-
sions--China; Missions--Educational work; Missions--Philippines;
Missions--Taiwan; Mormons and Mormonism; Overseas Missionary
Fellowship (China Inland Mission); Philippines; Radio in missionary
work; Radio in religion; Reorganized Church of Jesus Christ of Latter
Day Saints; Sino-Japanese Conflict, 1937-1945; Sunday schools; Taiwan; Taylor, James Hudson; ten Boom, Cornelia Arnolda Johanna;
Women--Religious life; Women in missionary work, World War II)

%%%%%%%%%%%%%

CN# 114
**Appelman, Hyman Jedidiah; 1902-1983**
Ephemera;  1964-1978; n.d.

Brochures and pamphlets highlighting Appelman's evangelistic
ministry and an audio tape of Appelman's personal testimony.

Vol: 1 box, 1 Audio Tape

(MAJOR TOPICS: Appelman, Hyman Jedidiah; Chicago, IL; Edman,
Victor Raymond; Evangelistic work--Soviet Union; Evangelistic work-
-United States; Fundamentalism; Graham, William Franklin "Billy";
Los Angeles, CA; New York City, NY; Persecution--Soviet Union;
Sermons, American; Soviet Union)

%%%%%%%%%%%%%

CN# 407
**Arctic Missions, Inc.; 1951-**
Records;   1947-1985; n.d.

Correspondence, reports, brochures, and other material document-
ing the work of Arctic Missions, Inc. (formerly Alaska Missions
Inc.), a group of nondenominational missionaries in Alaska and
Canada (principally British Columbia) involved in rural evangelis-
tic work and Christian education among the Indian, Aleut and
Inuit people.

Vol: 1 box

(MAJOR TOPICS:  Aeronautics in missionary work; Alaska; Alcoholics; Aleut people, USA; Arctic Mission, Inc; Baptism; Bible

colleges; Bob Jones University, SC; Canada; Catholic Church; Catholic
Church in Canada; Catholic Church--Relations with Protestants;
Charismatic movement; Christian education (theory); Christian educa-
tion of adolescents; Christian education of adults; Christian education
of children; Christian education--Canada; Christian education--United
States; Cities and towns; City missions; Conversion; Correspondence
schools and courses; Divorce; Education, Higher; Education--Canada;
Education--Philosophy; Education--United States; Evangelistic work---
Canada; Evangelistic work--United States; Frizen, Edwin Leonard Jr;
Fund raising; Fundamentalism; Glossolalia; Indigenous church ad-
ministration; Interdenominational Foreign Mission Association
(IFMA); Indians of North America; Language in missionary work;
Mass media in missionary work; Mass media in religion; Mission-
aries--Recruitment and training; Missions--Canada; Missions--Edu-
cational work; Missions--Finance; Missions--Rural work; Missions---
Study and teaching; Missions--United States; Moravian Church--Mis-
sions; Moravians; Nationalism; Occult sciences; Orthodox Eastern
Church; Orthodox Eastern Church--Relations; Slavic Gospel Association; Vaus, James Arthur; Wycliffe Bible Translators)

%%%%%%%%%%%%

CN# 180
**Armerding, Carl; 1883-1987**
Interviews; 1981

Oral history interview with Armerding in which he describes his
career as a missionary preacher, teacher, and administrator. The
interview also contains information on his itinerant missionary
service in Honduras, 1912-14; preaching for Brethren Assemblies
in the British West Indies, United States, and Canada; and years
spent on the faculties of Dallas Theological Seminary, Moody
Bible Institute, and Wheaton College between 1936-1962. Discussion of the church in Latin America, 1912-1981; the work of
Central American Mission and Latin America Mission; and reminiscences of Billy Sunday, "Gipsy" Smith, Dr. H. A. Ironside,
James Hudson Taylor, and Dr. Will H. Houghton.

Vol: 1 Audio Tape

(MAJOR TOPICS: Armerding, Carl E; Armerding, Hudson Taylor;
Brethren; Brethren Church--Missions; CAM International; Catholic
Church; Catholic Church in Honduras; Catholic Church--Missions;
Dallas Theological Seminary; Evangelistic work--Honduras; Evangelis-
tic work--United States; Houghton, William Henry; Ironside, Henry
Allan "Harry"; Latin America Mission; Missions--Central America;
Missions--Honduras; Moody Bible Institute, IL; New Mexico; Overseas

Missionary Fellowship (China Inland Mission); Plymouth Brethren;
Plymouth Brethren--Missions; Smith, Rodney "Gipsy"; Sunday, William
Ashley "Billy"; Taylor, James Hudson; Townsend, William Cameron;
Wheaton College, IL)

%%%%%%%%%%%%

CN# 197
**Asher, Virginia Healey; 1869-1937**
Papers; 1903-1941 n.d.

Correspondence, diaries, autograph book, booklets, clippings,
tracts, photographs, and a negative relating to the evangelistic
activities of Asher and her husband William, and their work in
association with Billy Sunday, Homer Rodeheaver, Charles Fuller,
William Biederwolf, Melvin Trotter, J. Wilbur Chapman, and
others.

Vol: 1 box, Photographs, Negatives

(MAJOR TOPICS: Asher, Virginia Healey; Asher, William; Bieder-
wolf, William Edward; Chapman, John Wilbur; Cities and towns; City
missions; Evangelistic work--United States; Fuller, Charles Edward Sr;
Rodeheaver, Homer Alvan; Sex role; Sunday, William Ashley "Billy";
Trotter, Melvin Ernest; Winona Lake Bible Conference, IN; Women-
-Religious life)

%%%%%%%%%%%%

CN# 225
**Baptista Film Mission 1942-1965**
Records; 1908 (1939-1963) 1963; n.d.

Correspondence, diaries, newsletters, scripts, catalogs, films, and
other material related to the work of the company founded by
Charles O. Baptista to produce motion picture projection equip-
ment and evangelistic films. This collection contains much information on the beginnings of the Christian film industry.

Vol: 1 box, Audio Tapes, Films, Photographs, Video Tapes

(MAJOR TOPICS: American Bible Society; Animism; Baptista Film
Mission; Baptista, Charles Octavia; Belief and doubt; Bible--Criticism,
interpretation, etc.; Broadcasting station: HCJB, Ecuador; Cambodia;
Catholic Church in Philippines; Chicago Gospel Tabernacle; Chicago,
IL; China; Christian drama; Church and state in Vietnam; Church
work with military personnel; Communism; Conversion; Ecuador;

Edman, Victor Raymond; Evangelical Alliance Mission, The (TEAM);
Evangelistic work--Japan; Evangelistic work--Korea; Evangelistic
work--Mexico; Evangelistic work--United States; Evangelistic work---
Vietnam; Film: *Pilgrim's Progress*; Graham, William Franklin "Billy";
Ironside, Henry Allan "Harry"; Israel; Japan; Jerusalem, Israel; John-
son, Torrey Maynard; Jones, Clarence Wesley; Jones, Robert R Jr
"Bob"; Kerr, Maxwell A; Korea; Mexico; Missions--Mexico; Missions---
Vietnam; Moving-picture industry--United States; Moving-pictures in
church work; Moving-pictures--Moral and religious aspects; Nigeria;
Organizational change; Orphans and orphan-asylums; Rader, Daniel
Paul; Radio audiences; Radio in missionary work; Radio in religion;
Revivals; Riley, William Bell; Shea, George Beverly; Sweeting, George;
Venezuela; Vietnam; Wang, Leland; Wheaton College, IL; Wheaton
Revival, 1950; Wilson, Walter L; Youth for Christ International)

%%%%%%%%%%%%

CN# 248
**Barnett, William John; 1909-**
Interviews; 1983-1983

Three interviews with Barnett in which he describes his childhood
in Kenya with his pioneer Africa Inland Mission parents, experiences with Masai people and attendance at Rift Valley Academy;
high school in the U.S. in Columbia, SC, and at Columbia Bible
College and Wheaton College; receiving an M.D. degree from
Albany Medical College, Albany, NY, 1945; return to Africa with
his wife as a missionary for Africa Inland Mission in a hospital
ministry in Kenya between 1951 and 1983.

Vol: 3 Audio Tapes

(MAJOR TOPICS: Adolescence; Africa Inland Mission (AIM);
African Americans; Agricultural societies; Animism; Baptism; Barnett,
William John; Bible colleges; Boarding schools--Kenya; Capital punishment; Children of missionaries; Christian education--Kenya; Church
development, New; Church growth--Kenya; College students--Religious
life; Columbia Bible College, Columbia, SC; Conversion; Family;
Hurlburt, Charles E; Intercultural communications; Kenya; Language
in missionary work; Language: Swahili; Masai people, Kenya; Mis-
sionaries--Recruitment and training; Missions, Medical; Missions---
Kenya; Missions--Rural work; Nursing; Orphans and orphan-asylums;
Poverty; Prayer; Rift Valley Academy, Kenya; Sex role; Student
Foreign Mission Fellowship; Village communities; Women--Religious
life; Women in missionary work; Worship)

%%%%%%%%%%%%%

CN# 57
**Bartel, Susan Schultz; 1900-**
Interviews; 1978-1979

Four tapes of interviews of Mrs. Loyal Bartel; these interviews
describe her education and preparation for missions work, her
work and that of her husband in China, her impressions of Chinese events and culture, and other topics.  The collection also
contains photographs.

Vol: 4 Audio Tapes, Photographs

(MAJOR TOPICS: Anglicans; Bartel, Loyal; Bartel, Susan; Catholic
Church--Missions; Chicago Hebrew Mission; China; Christian and
Missionary Alliance (CMA); Church and state in China; Church of
England--Missions; Cities and towns; City missions; Evangelistic
work--China; Goforth, Jonathan; Hawaii; Kuo min tang (China);
Lutheran Church--Missions; Lutherans; Missions--China; Moody Bible
Institute, IL; Muslims in China; Nee, Watchman; Pacific Garden
Mission, IL; Sex role; Shanghai, China; Sino-Japanese Conflict, 1937--
1945; Teng, Hsiao-ping; Wang Ming Tao; Women--Religious life;
Women in missionary work; World War II)

%%%%%%%%%%%%%

CN# 128
**Beecher, Henry Ward  1813-1887**
Ephemera; 1875-1893  n.d.

An autograph, photograph, and newspaper clippings.  The clippings include reminiscences by his widow and posthumously published articles by Beecher.  Also includes a 176-page booklet of
first eight days of the lawsuit brought against Beecher for adultery
in 1874-1875.

Vol: 1 box

(MAJOR TOPICS: Beecher, Henry Ward; Evangelistic work--United
States)

%%%%%%%%%%%%

CN# 213
**Bell, Sarah Margaret "Sally"; 1939-**
Interview; 1982

Oral history interview of about 100 minutes, in which Sally Bell
describes her mission work with radio station HCJB in Quito,
Ecuador, 1965 to 1976.

Vol: 1 Audio Tape

(MAJOR TOPICS: Anglicans; Bigamy; Broadcasting station: HCJB,
Ecuador; Canada; Catholic Church in Ecuador; Catholic Church--Re-
lations; Christian Service Brigade; Church of England; Costa Rica;
Ecuador; Family; Graham, William Franklin Jr "Billy"; Jones, Clarence
Wesley; Language in missionary work; Larson, Reuben Emmanuel;
Mass media in religion; Missions--Ecuador; Pioneer Ministries; Rac-
ism; Radio in missionary work; Radio in religion; Sex role; Toronto,
ON; Van Der Puy, Abraham Cornelius; Wheaton College, IL; Witch-
craft)

%%%%%%%%%%%%

CN# 209
**Bertermann, Eugene Rudolph; 1914-1983**
Records; 1955-1981; n.d.

Correspondence, reports, minutes, manuscripts, photographs,
phonograph records, and other materials relating to Bertermann's
involvement in religious broadcasting, particularly in regard to his
responsibilities as president and one of the board of directors of
National Religious Broadcasters; executive director and board
member of Far East Broadcasting Company; and one of the
planners of the ecumenical evangelistic effort known as Key '73.
Bertermann was also a leader in the television efforts of the
Lutheran Church-Missouri Synod and was for many years associated with the program *The Lutheran Hour*, although there is
little about this in the BGC collection.

Vol: 19 boxes, 1 Audio Tape, Oversize Materials, Phonograph
Records, Photographs

(MAJOR TOPICS: African Americans; American Lutheran Church;
Argentina; Armstrong, Benjamin Leighton; Assemblies of God; Auto-
mation; Baptists; Belief and doubt; Bell, Lemuel Nelson; Bertermann,
Eugene R; Bible--Publication and distribution; Bowman, Robert H;

Brazil; Broadcasting station: ELWA, Liberia; Broadcasting station:
HCJB, Ecuador; Burma; Cambodia; Campus Crusade for Christ;
Carlson, Frank; Carter, James Earl "Jimmy"; Catholic Church in
United States; Censorship; Chile; China; Christian leadership; Chris-
tian literature--Publication and distribution; Church and social prob-
lems; Church and state in Korea; Church and state in United States;
Communication; Communism--China; Communism--Soviet Union;
Conlan, John Bertrand; Conversion; District of Columbia; Ecuador;
Ecumenical movement; Eisenhower, Dwight David; Epp, Theodore H;
Ethics; Ethiopia; Evangelical Alliance Mission, The (TEAM); Evan-
gelicalism; Evangelistic work--Brazil; Evangelistic work--Great Britain;
Evangelistic work--Guatemala; Evangelistic work--Japan; Evangelistic
work--Mexico; Evangelistic work--Soviet Union; Evangelistic work---
United States; Family; Federal Communications Commission; Ford,
Gerald Rudolph; Fund raising; Fundamentalism; Graham, William
Franklin "Billy"; Great Britain; Guatemala; Hatfield, Mark Odom;
Henry, Carl Ferdinand Howard; Hong Kong; Hudson, Arthur William
Goodwin; India; Indonesia; Intercultural communications; Interna-
tional Christian Broadcasters; Japan; Jesus to the Communist World;
Jones, Clarence Wesley; Jones, Robert R Sr "Bob"; Key '73; Kim, Billy
(Jang Hwan); Korea; Language in missionary work; Language: Por-
tuguese; Laos; Legislators--United States; Lutherans; Marquardt,
Horst; Mass media in religion; McLuhan, Herbert Marshall; Method-
ists; Mexico; Missions Advanced Research and Communications
Center (MARC); Missions--Interdenominational cooperation; Mov-
ing-pictures in church work; Mundt, Karl Earl; National Association of
Broadcasters (NAB); National Association of Evangelicals; National
Council of Churches; National Religious Broadcasters; Nixon, Richard
Milhous; Organizational change; Panama; Pentecostals; Periodical:
*Christianity Today*; Personnel management; Philippines; Pornography;
Prayer; Presbyterians; Presidents--United States; PTL Network; Radio
audiences; Radio in missionary work; Radio in religion; Radio Pro-
gram: *Heaven and Home Hour*; Radio program: *Hour of Decision*;
Radio Program: *Old Fashioned Revival Hour*; Seventh Day Adventists;
Seychelles; Singapore; Soviet Union; Space flight; Supreme Court;
Sweeting, George; Taiwan; Talmage, Thomas Dewitt; Television in
religion; Television program: *PTL Club*; Thailand; Tokyo, Japan;
Trans World Radio; Underground Evangelism; United States; Uruguay; Van Der Puy, Abraham Cornelius; Vietnam; Vietnamese Con-
flict; Washington, DC; Wilson, George McConnell; World Evangelical
Fellowship (WEF); World Literature Crusade; World Vision Interna-
tional; Wurmbrand, Richard; Wyrtzen, John Von Casper "Jack";
Zimmerman, Thomas Fletcher)

%%%%%%%%%%%%

CN# 18
**BGEA: Administrative Assistant, Crusade Services; 1950-**
Records; 1966-1971

Files of the administrative assistant (Stan Cover) to the executive
assistant/office manager. Some correspondence, schedules, and
position description, but most of the files either deal with the
shipping of supplies to particular associate evangelist crusades or
contain samples or sample books of the kind of supplies the
BGEA had in stock.

Vol: 3 boxes

(MAJOR TOPICS: Adams, Lane G; Alaska; Barrows, Clifford B; Bell,
Ralph Shadell; Billy Graham Evangelistic Association (BGEA);
Canada; Colorado; Evangelistic work--Canada; Evangelistic work--Uni-
ted States; Graham, William Franklin "Billy"; Gustafson, Roy W;
Haqq, Akbar Abdul; Jones, Howard O; Mississippi; North Carolina;
Pennsylvania; Virginia; White, John Wesley; Wilson, Grady Baxter;
Wisconsin)

%%%%%%%%%%%%

CN# 198
**BGEA: Albuquerque Evangelistic Crusade, Greater; 1952**
Records; 1951-1953

Correspondence, legal documents, financial records, and executive
committee minutes of the corporation formed to organize and
administer a series of Billy Graham evangelistic meetings in
Albuquerque, New Mexico. Minutes outline all procedures involved, including construction of a tabernacle for the meetings.

Vol: 1 box

(MAJOR TOPICS: Albuquerque, NM; Barrows, Clifford B; Beavan,
Gerald "Jerry"; Billy Graham Evangelistic Association (BGEA);
Evangelistic work--United States; Graham, William Franklin "Billy";
Haymaker, Willis Graham; New Mexico; Wilson, Grady Baxter)

%%%%%%%%%%%%

CN# 26
**BGEA: Audio Tapes; 1950-**
Records; 1962-1976; n.d.

This collection contains 74 audio tapes which include sermons, talks, question and answer sessions, and addresses delivered by Billy Graham between 1962 and 1976; two Christian Life and Witness courses led by Donald Tabb; interviews for the "Hour of Decision" by Tabb; and two tapes by Cliff Barrows discussing music and evangelism.

Vol: 74 Audio Tapes

(MAJOR TOPICS: Adams, Lane G; Alabama; American Revolution Bicentennial, 1776-1976; Annenberg, Walter H; Askew, Reubin O'-Donovan; Assassination; Athletes in Action; Athletes--Religious life; Atlanta, GA; Barrows, Clifford B; Bible--Prophecies; Billy Graham Evangelistic Association (BGEA); Black, Cyril Wilson (Sir); Boone, Charles Eugene "Pat"; Bright, William Rohl "Bill"; Briscoe, Jill; Campus Crusade for Christ; Canada; Catholic Church in Ireland; Catholic Church--Relations; Christian education--United States; Christian leadership; Christian life; Christianity and economics; Clergy; Communication; Communism; Congresses and conferences--Explo '72; Conversion; Corts, John Ronald; Counseling; Death; Deyneka, Peter Sr; District of Columbia; Edwards, Jonathan Sr; Evangelicalism; Evangelistic invitations; Evangelistic sermons; Evangelistic work (Christian theology); Evangelistic work--Australia; Evangelistic work--Brazil; Evangelistic work--Canada; Evangelistic work--Germany; Evangelistic work--Great Britain; Evangelistic work--India; Evangelistic work--Ireland; Evangelistic work--Mexico; Evangelistic work--New Zealand; Evangelistic work--South Africa; Evangelistic work--United States; Evans, Dale; Faith; Fife, Eric; Film: *Hiding Place, The*; Forgiveness; Free will and determinism; Freedom (Theology); Freedom of will; Fuller, Charles Edward Sr; Georgia; Graham, Ruth Bell; Graham, William Franklin "Billy"; Great Britain; Gustafson, Roy W; Hall, Myrtle; Hamblen, Stuart; Hawaii; Hell; Hill, Edwin V; Holy Spirit; Hudson, Arthur William Goodwin; Humility; Illinois; Ireland; Jews; Jews in United States; Jones, Howard O; Jones, Robert R Jr "Bob"; Kennedy, John Fitzgerald; Kentucky; Kim, Billy (Jang Hwan); Korea; Law; Lindsay, Harold; London, England; Melvin, Billy Alfred; Mexico; Mexico City, Mexico; Mooneyham, W Stanley; Moving-pictures in church work; Moving-pictures--Moral and religious aspects; National Association of Evangelicals; New York (state); Nixon, Richard Milhous; Nonformal education; North Carolina; Obedience; Ohio; Orr, James Edwin; Peace; Prayer; Prayer groups; Presidents--United States;

Radio in religion; Radio program: *Hour of Decision*; Radio Program: *Old Fashioned Revival Hour*; Reconciliation; Religion and music; Religion and science; Religion and sports; Religious liberty; Repentance; Resurrection; Riggs, Charles A; Rogers, Roy; Salvation; Schuller, Robert Harold; Sermons, American; Sexual ethics; Shea, George Beverly; Sin; Smith, Edward R "Tedd"; Smith, Kathryn Elizabeth "Kate"; Smith, Rodney "Gipsy"; Sports; Stott, John Robert Walmsley; ten Boom, Cornelia Arnolda Johanna; Texas; Trinity Bible College (Florida Bible Institute), FL; United States--Church History--Colonial period, ca 1600-1775; United States--History--Colonial period, ca 1600-1775; Vietnamese Conflict; Washington (state); Washington, DC; Watergate Affair, 1972-1974; Waters, Ethel; Wheaton College, IL; Wilson, Grady Baxter; Wilson, Thomas Walter Jr; Worship; Youth---Religious life; Youth--Societies and clubs)

%%%%%%%%%%%%%

CN# 245
**BGEA: Billy Graham Evangelistic Association, Ltd [Australia]; 1959-**
Records; 1958-1980

Correspondence, promotional materials, procedure books, posters, telegrams, clippings, minutes of meetings, financial reports, photographs, slides, films, video cassettes, audio tapes, phonograph records, etc., relating to the operations (both in Australia and the South Pacific) of the Billy Graham Evangelistic Association, Ltd., and its predecessor, Hour of Decision, Ltd.; coordination of showings of films of the BGEA subsidiary World Wide Pictures movie; and the production of the Australian edition of *Decision* magazine.  The collection also documents many evangelistic activities, such as the 1968, 1969, and 1979 Billy Graham Crusades and the television broadcast of these meetings.

Vol: 31 boxes, 4 Audio Tapes, 2 Films, Negatives, Oversize Materials, Phonograph Records, Photographs, Slides, Video Tapes

(MAJOR TOPICS: Hatori, Akira; Australia; Barrows, Clifford B; Beavan, Gerald "Jerry"; Billy Graham Evangelistic Association (BGEA); Billy Graham Evangelistic Association, Ltd [Australia]; Billy Graham Evangelistic Association, Ltd [Great Britain]; Cities and towns; Congresses and conferences--Asia-South Pacific Congress on Evangelism, 1968; Congresses and conferences--World Congress on Evangelism, 1966; Dain, Arthur John; Emery, Alan C Jr; Evangelical Literature Overseas; Evangelistic invitations; Evangelistic sermons; Evangelistic work--Australia; Evangelistic work--New Zealand; Evangelistic work--Papua New Guinea; Evangelistic work--Singapore; Far

East Broadcasting Company; Ferm, Lois Roughan; Ferm, Robert O; Ford, Leighton Frederick Sandys; Graham, Ruth Bell; Graham, William Franklin "Billy"; Great Britain; Gustafson, Roy W; Hall, Myrtle; Haqq, Akbar Abdul; India; Indonesia; Italy; Malaysia; Mass media in religion; Mooneyham, W Stanley; Moving-picture audiences; Moving-pictures in church work; Moving-pictures--Moral and religious aspects; Nelson, Victor B; Netherlands; New Zealand; Organizational change; Palms, Roger Curtis; Papua New Guinea; Periodical: *Decision*; Philippines; Pollock, John Charles; Radio in religion; Richards, Cliff; Riggs, Charles A; Salvation Army; Shea, George Beverly; Singapore; Smyth, Walter Herbert; Sydney, Australia; Television in religion; Walter F Bennett and Co; Waters, Ethel; Wilson, George McConnell; Wilson, Grady Baxter; Wilson, Thomas Walter Jr; Wirt, Sherwood Eliot; World Wide Pictures)

%%%%%%%%%%%%%

CN# 9
**BGEA: Billy Graham Evangelistic Association, Ltd [Great Britain]; 1955-**
Records; 1954-1976; n.d.

Records of the director of the British office of the BGEA. This collection also contains a selection of replies written by Rev. Alan C. Stephens to people writing to Billy Graham for counseling.

Vol: 4 boxes

(MAJOR TOPICS: Barrows, Clifford B; Beavan, Gerald "Jerry"; Billy Graham Evangelistic Association (BGEA); Billy Graham Evangelistic Association, Ltd [Great Britain]; Brown, William Frederick "Bill" Sr; Congresses and conferences--International Congress on World Evangelization, 1974; Congresses and conferences--World Congress on Evangelism, 1966; Cook, Robert Andrew; Counseling; Dain, Arthur John; Evangelistic work--Great Britain; Ferm, Lois Roughan; Ford, Gerald Rudolph; Ford, Leighton Frederick Sandys; Graham, Ruth Bell; Graham, William Franklin "Billy"; Great Britain; Halverson, Richard C; Lindsell, Harold; London, England; Missions--Educational work; Muntz, John Palmer; Nelson, Victor B; Olford, Stephen Frederick; Palms, Roger Curtis; Periodical: *Decision*; Presidents--United States; Pollock, John Charles; Richards, Cliff; Shea, George Beverly; Smyth, Walter Herbert; Wilson, George McConnell; Wilson, Grady Baxter; Wilson, Thomas Walter Jr; Wirt, Sherwood Eliot)

%%%%%%%%%%%%

CN# 245
**BGEA: Billy Graham Evangelistic Association Ltd [Hong Kong];**
**1973-**
Records; 1973-1982

Correspondence, promotional materials, editorial guidelines, tracts, guest books, incorporation articles, stationery, official seals, audio tapes, a scrapbook, and other materials relating to the operations of the office. Documents outline the ongoing activities of the office, the principal task of which was the publication of a Chinese edition of *Decision* magazine. Other BGEA programs in Hong Kong and southeast Asia were coordinated there as well.

Vol: 2 boxes, 16 Audio Tapes, Photograph

(MAJOR TOPICS: Bell, Ralph Shadell; Billy Graham Evangelistic Association (BGEA); Billy Graham Evangelistic Association [Hong Kong]; China; Church work with refugees; Evangelistic work--Hong Kong; Film: *Hiding Place, The*; Graham, William Franklin "Billy"; Gustafson, Roy W; Hong Kong; Jones, V Samuel; Malaysia; Missions to Chinese; Periodical: *Decision*; Philippines; Thailand; World Wide Pictures)

%%%%%%%%%%%%

CN# 34
**BGEA: Billy Graham Evangelistic Association [Japan]; 1967-**
Records; 1966-1976; n.d.

Correspondence, posters, reports, etc. of the Tokyo branch, started in 1967. Records relate mostly to the office's publishing of *Ketsudan No Toki* (the Japanese edition of the BGEA's tabloid *Decision*); involvement in the showing of the films of World Wide Pictures, a BGEA subsidiary; the production and distribution of the film *Shiokari Toki*; and arranging for BGEA television programs to be broadcast. The collection also contains some correspondence from the 1967 Tokyo International Crusade.

Vol: 1 box, Photographs

(MAJOR TOPICS: Billy Graham Evangelistic Association (BGEA); Billy Graham Evangelistic Association [Japan]; Cities and towns; Communication; Evangelical Alliance Mission, The (TEAM); Evangelistic work--Japan; Graham, William Franklin "Billy"; Japan; Missions--Japan; Palms, Roger Curtis; Periodical: *Decision*; Pollock, John

Charles; Tokyo, Japan; Wilson, George McConnell; Wirt, Sherwood
Eliot; World Wide Pictures)

%%%%%%%%%%%%%%

CN# SC34
**BGEA: Billy Graham World's Fair Pavilion; 1950-**
Press Packet; 1964-1965

A packet apparently given to the press on the occasion of the
ground breaking and the dedication of the Billy Graham pavilion.
The packet contains information on Graham's life and ministry;
biographies of the architect (Edward Durell Stone) and contrac-
tors for the pavilion; and photographs of Graham, Stone, the
pavilion, and press reports.

(MAJOR TOPICS: Billy Graham Evangelistic Association (BGEA);
Evangelistic work--United States; Graham, William Franklin "Billy";
New York. World's Fair, 1964-1965; Stone, Edward Durell)

%%%%%%%%%%%%%%

CN# 24
**BGEA: Billy Graham's News Conferences; 1950-**
Records;  1963-1976

Tapes of press conferences held by Billy Graham, usually in
conjunction with a crusade.  Topics discussed cover a wide spec-
trum of theological, social, political, and economic matters, both
foreign and domestic.

Vol: 13 Audio Tapes

(MAJOR TOPICS: Australia; Becker Amendment; Billy Graham
Evangelistic Association (BGEA); Church and state in United States;
Civil rights movement; Communication; Communism; Dixon, Jeanne
L; Dulles, John Foster; Ecumenical movement; Evangelicalism; Evan-
gelistic work--Australia; Evangelistic work--New Zealand; Evangelistic
work--United States; Graham, William Franklin "Billy"; Hargis, Billy
James; Humphrey, Hubert Horatio; John XXIII (Pope); Kennedy,
John Fitzgerald; Kennedy, Robert Francis; King, Martin Luther;
Legislators--United States; Los Angeles, CA; McIntire, Carl Curtis;
National Council of Churches; New York City, NY; New Zealand;
Nixon, Richard Milhous; Paisley, Ian Richard Kyle; Pentecostals; Pike,
James; Poor People's March on Washington, 1968; Presidents--United
States; Profanity; Religion in the public schools--United States; Rob-
erts, Granville Oral; Rockefeller, Nelson Aldrich; Schools--Prayers;

Vietnamese Conflict; Witchcraft; World Council of Churches; World
Wide Pictures; Youth--Religious life)

%%%%%%%%%%%%%

CN# 45
**BGEA: Blue Ridge Broadcasting Corp., The 1962-**
Records; 1959-1975

Correspondence, memos, reports, pamphlets, newsletters, photographs, tapes from the North Carolina radio station controlled by
the BGEA.  The collection mainly deals with the details of the day
to day operation of the station and its participation in the work of
the BGEA.

Vol: 7 boxes, 51 Audio Tapes, Photographs

(MAJOR TOPICS: Adams, Lane G; Baptists; Barrows, Clifford B;
Bell, Lemuel Nelson; Billy Graham Evangelistic Association (BGEA);
Blinco, Joseph D; Charlotte, NC; China; Church and state in United
States; Communication; Congresses and conferences--Explo '72;
Congresses and conferences--US Congress on Evangelism, 1969;
Congresses and conferences--World Congress on Evangelism, 1966;
Evangelistic work--Israel; Evangelistic work--United States; Federal
Communications Commission; Ford, Leighton Frederick Sandys;
Glenn, John Herschel Jr; Gordon-Conwell Divinity School; Graham,
Ruth Bell; Graham, William Franklin "Billy"; Hall, Myrtle; Harvey,
Paul; Ireland; Israel; Johnson, Lyndon Baines; Kennedy, John Fitz-
gerald; Moving-pictures in church work; National Association of
Broadcasters (NAB); Nixon, Richard Milhous; North Carolina; Prayer
groups; Presidents--United States; Radio in religion; Radio program:
*Hour of Decision*; Radio Program: *Old Fashioned Revival Hour*; Riggs,
Charles A; Sermons, American; Shea, George Beverly; Southern
Baptist Convention; Taiwan; Taylor, Clyde Willis; Tennessee; Viet-
namese Conflict; Walter F Bennett and Co; Wilson, Thomas Walter
Jr)

%%%%%%%%%%%%%

CN# 10
**BGEA: Board of Trustees Books; 1950-**
Records; 1951-1978; n.d.

Books of photographs prepared for members of the BGEA board
of trustees depicting important events in the history of the As

sociation, yearly activities, and property owned by the Association.

Vol: 1 box

(MAJOR TOPICS: Billy Graham Evangelistic Association (BGEA);
Evangelistic work--United States; Graham, William Franklin "Billy";
Nebraska; Organizational change)

%%%%%%%%%%%%

CN# 360
**BGEA; 1950-**
Clipping File; 1932 (1949-1986) 1986; n.d.

This collection consists entirely of newspaper clippings, magazine
clippings, and some news releases about the work of Billy Graham
and the Billy Graham Evangelistic Association.  There are over
350 scrapbooks of newspaper clippings.  One hundred and
sixty-five books contain newspaper clippings from a single crusade.
These are followed by over 200 scrapbooks of clippings referring
to BGEA activities within a country.  Over 40 countries are represented, although over half of the 200 books deal with the United
States.  Then there are a few miscellaneous scrapbooks about
BGEA films and special events.  In the next section are over 450
scrapbooks of magazine articles about Graham and/or the BGEA.
The articles in these books are mostly from United States periodicals and there are three indexes to their contents. All of the
scrapbooks are on microfilm.  The collection also includes several
boxes of loose clippings which are arranged solely by date.

(MAJOR TOPICS:  Bakker, James Orsen "Jim"; Bakker, Tammy
Faye; Billy Graham Center, IL; Billy Graham Evangelistic Association
(BGEA); Carter, James Earl "Jimmy"; Church and state in Poland;
Church and state in the Soviet Union; Church work with military
personnel; Colson, Charles Wendell; Congresses and conferences---
Explo '72; Congresses and conferences--International Conference for
Itinerant Evangelists, 1983; Congresses and conferences--International
Congress on World Evangelization, 1974; Congresses and confer-
ences--Urbana Missionary Conventions; Congresses and conferences---
World Congress on Evangelism, 1966; Corporations, Religious--Taxa-
tion; Eisenhower, Dwight David; Ford, Leighton Frederick Sandys;
Graham, Ruth Bell; Graham, William Franklin "Billy"; Johnson,
Lyndon Baines; Kennedy, John Fitzgerald; Nixon, Richard Milhous;
Presidents--United States; Radio program: *Hour of Decision*; Reagan,
Ronald Wilson; Riggs, Charles A; Roberts, Granville Oral; Shea,
George Beverly; Television in religion; ten Boom, Cornelia Arnolda

Johanna; Truman, Harry S; Watergate Affair, 1972-1974; Waters, Ethel; Wheaton College, IL)

%%%%%%%%%%%%%

CN# SC90
**BGEA: Columbia Crusade Executive Committee; 1949-1950**
Records; 1949-1950

Minutes of the executive committee of the 1950 Columbia, SC Billy Graham crusade. Topics discussed include finance, building a tabernacle, and publicity. The book also contains lists of committee members and some of the participating pastors.

(MAJOR TOPICS: Billy Graham Evangelistic Association (BGEA); Columbia, SC; Evangelistic work--United States; Graham, William Franklin "Billy"; Haymaker, Willis Graham; Hoke, Donald Edwin; South Carolina)

%%%%%%%%%%%%%

CN# 16
**BGEA: Crusade Procedure Books; 1950-**
Records; 1957-1975

Procedure books compiled during different Billy Graham Crusades which contain materials of the various committees planning the crusade, such as the executive committee, and committees for publicity, choir, ushers, special events, councils, and others. Materials include such things as minutes, form letters, publicity, instruction sheets, audit statements, etc.

Vol: 126 boxes

(MAJOR TOPICS: Adams, Lane G; Alabama; Albuquerque, NM; Arizona; Atlanta, GA; Australia; Belgium; Bell, Ralph Shadell; Boston, MA; California; Charlotte, NC; Chicago, IL; Christian education of adults; Christian education of children; Christian education--Australia; Christian education--Belgium; Christian education--Canada; Christian education--Germany; Christian education--Great Britain; Christian education--Japan; Christian education--Mexico; Christian education--Norway; Christian education--Philippines; Christian education--Singapore; Christian education--United States; Church work with students; Cities and towns; Colorado; Communication in organizations; Connecticut; Corporations--Finance; Correspondence schools and courses; Counseling; Evangelicalism; Evangelistic work--Australia; Evangelistic work--Belgium; Evangelistic work--Germany; Evangelistic

work--Great Britain; Evangelistic work--Japan; Evangelistic work---
Mexico; Evangelistic work--New Zealand; Evangelistic work--Singa-
pore; Evangelistic work--United States; Georgia; Germany; Graham,
William Franklin "Billy"; Great Britain; Hawaii; Illinois; Indiana; Iowa;
Japan; Kentucky; London, England; Los Angeles, CA; Louisiana;
Maryland; Mass media in religion; Massachusetts; Mexico; Mexico
City, Mexico; Michigan; Minneapolis, MN; Minnesota; Mississippi;
Missouri; Moving-pictures in church work; Nebraska; Nevada; New
Mexico; New York (state); New York City, NY; New Zealand; North
Carolina; North Dakota; Norway; Ockenga, Harold John; Ohio;
Oklahoma; Oregon; Organizational change; Pennsylvania; Prayer
groups; Singapore; South Carolina; South Dakota; Sydney, Australia;
Tennessee; Texas; Tokyo, Japan; Toronto, ON; Virginia; Voluntarism;
Washington (state); Wisconsin)

%%%%%%%%%%%%

CN# 12
**BGEA: Executive Assistant for Team Activities; 1950-**
Records; 1961-1970; n.d.

Materials relating to the various duties of the holder of the joint
offices of the BGEA's office manager and executive assistant to
the vice president in charge of Team activities. Some of the duties
included supervision of the stenographic pool, handling of personnel matters, preparation of supplies for evangelistic crusades, etc.
Because some of the holders of the post had previously been
deeply involved in some of Graham's crusades, files for those
particular crusades are included in this collection even when the
crusade occurred before the individual's term as office manager.

Vol: 16 boxes

(MAJOR TOPICS: Adams, Lane G; Alabama; Alaska; Arizona;
Arkansas; Australia; Barrows, Clifford B; Bell, Ralph Shadell; Billy
Graham Evangelistic Association (BGEA); Blinco, Joseph D; Boston,
MA; Brown, William Frederick "Bill" Sr; California; Canada; Chicago,
IL; Colorado; Congresses and conferences--Asia-South Pacific Con-
gress on Evangelism, 1968; Congresses and conferences--West African
Congress on Evangelism, 1968; Congresses and conferences--World
Congress on Evangelism, 1966; Connecticut; Denmark; District of
Columbia; Evangelistic work--Australia; Evangelistic work--Canada;
Evangelistic work--Caribbean; Evangelistic work--Denmark; Evangelis-
tic work--Great Britain; Evangelistic work--New Zealand; Evangelistic
work--Puerto Rico; Evangelistic work--Singapore; Evangelistic work---
United States; Evangelistic work--Vietnam; Ferm, Robert O; Georgia;

Graham, William Franklin "Billy"; Great Britain; Haqq, Akbar Abdul;
Hawaii; Haymaker, Willis Graham; Huston, Sterling W; Idaho; Illinois;
Indiana; Iowa; Johnson, Torrey Maynard; Jones, Howard O; Kansas;
Kentucky; London, England; Los Angeles, CA; Louisiana; Maine;
Malaysia; Maryland; Massachusetts; Miami, FL; Michigan; Mississippi;
Missouri; Montana; Mooneyham, W Stanley; Navigators; Nebraska;
Nelson, Victor B; Nevada; New Hampshire; New Jersey; New Mexico;
New York (state); New York City, NY; New Zealand; Nigeria; North
Carolina; North Dakota; Ockenga, Harold John; Ohio; Oklahoma;
Oregon; Pennsylvania; Puerto Rico; Rhode Island; Riggs, Charles A;
Shea, George Beverly; Singapore; Smyth, Walter Herbert; South
Carolina; South Korea; Tennessee; Texas; Vangioni, Fernando V;
Vietnam; Virginia; Walter F Bennett and Co; Washington (state);
Waters, Ethel; West Virginia; White, John Wesley; Wilson, George
McConnell; Wilson, Grady Baxter; Wilson, Thomas Walter Jr; Wirt,
Sherwood Eliot; World Wide Pictures)

%%%%%%%%%%%%

CN# 19
**BGEA: Ferm, Robert O.; 1911-**
Papers; 1949-1980; n.d.

Correspondence, manuscripts, questionnaires, photographs, minutes of meetings, schedules, statistics, and more relating to Ferm's
many and varied posts within the Billy Graham Evangelistic
Association. Some of these posts were research assistant to
Graham, coordinator of various crusades, co-editor of *Decision*
and dean of the schools of evangelism held for each evangelistic
crusade. The collection also contains letters written by people
reacting to the work of Graham and the BGEA, many descriptions
of conversion experiences of individuals attending BGEA crusades
or who watched a crusade on television, and information on the
internal functioning of the BGEA.

Vol: 15 boxes

(MAJOR TOPICS: Adams, Lane G; Alabama; Alaska; Albania; Albu-
querque, NM; Anglicans; Argentina; Arizona; Arkansas; Atlanta, GA;
Australia; Baptists; Barrows, Clifford B; Beavan, Gerald "Jerry";
Belize; Bell, Lemuel Nelson; Berry, Lowell W; Bible--Publication and
distribution; Billy Graham Evangelistic Association (BGEA); Blinco,
Joseph D; Boston, MA; Brazil; Bright, William Rohl "Bill"; Brown,
John Elward; Buddhism (theology); Buddhists in Taiwan; Butt, How-
ard E Jr; California; Canada; Catholic Church; Catholic Church in
United States; Catholic Church--Relations; Chicago, IL; Christian
education--Great Britain; Christian education--United States; Church

and social problems; Church of England; Clergy; Colorado; Communication; Connecticut; Conversion; Counseling; Cults; Delaware; District of Columbia; Ecumenical movement; Egypt; Emery, Alan C Jr; Episcopalians; Ethiopia; Evangelistic work--Argentina; Evangelistic work--Australia; Evangelistic work--Brazil; Evangelistic work--Canada; Evangelistic work--Great Britain; Evangelistic work--Hong Kong; Evangelistic work--Ireland; Evangelistic work--Israel; Evangelistic work--Japan; Evangelistic work--Mexico; Evangelistic work--New Zealand; Evangelistic work--Nigeria; Evangelistic work--Paraguay; Evangelistic work--Soviet Union; Evangelistic work--Sweden; Evangelistic work--Switzerland; Evangelistic work--Taiwan; Evangelistic work--United States; Evangelistic work--Uruguay; Evans, Robert Philip; Far East Broadcasting Company; Federal Republic of Germany; Ferm, Lois Roughan; Ferm, Robert O; Florida; Ford, Leighton Frederick Sandys; France; Fuller, Charles Edward Sr; Georgia; Graham, William Franklin "Billy"; Great Britain; Greece; Gustafson, Roy W; Haiti; Haqq, Akbar Abdul; Harper, Redd; Haymaker, Willis Graham; Henry, Carl Ferdinand Howard; Hillis, Charles Richard "Dick"; Hispanic Americans; Hoke, Donald Edwin; Hong Kong; Hudson, Arthur William Goodwin; Huston, Sterling W; Iceland; Idaho; Illinois; India; Indiana; Iowa; Ireland; Israel; Italy; Japan; Jones, Howard O; Jordan; Judaism; Judd, Walter Henry; Kansas; Kentucky; Kenya; Lebanon; Legislators--United States; Liberia; London, England; Los Angeles, CA; Louisiana; Luce, Henry R; Maine; Malaysia; Maryland; Massachusetts; Methodists; Mexico; Mexico City, Mexico; Miami, FL; Michigan; Missions to Buddhists; Missions, Medical; Missions--Educational work; Mississippi; Missouri; Montana; Mooneyham, W Stanley; Nebraska; New Hampshire; New Jersey; New Mexico; New York (state); New York City, NY; New Zealand; Nigeria; Nonformal education; North Carolina; O C Ministries; Ockenga, Harold John; Ohio; Oklahoma; Olford, Stephen Frederick; Oral Roberts Evangelistic Association; Oral Roberts University, Tulsa, OK; Oregon; Pakistan; Palermo, Louis; Palermo, Phil; Paraguay; Pennsylvania; Pentecostals; Periodical: *Christian Century, The*; Periodical: *Decision*; Peru; Philadelphia, PA; Philippines; Pollock, John Charles; Poverty; Radio in religion; Radio program: *Hour of Decision*; Rhode Island; Rice, John Richard; Riggs, Charles A; Roberts, Granville Oral; Shea, George Beverly; Shufelt, John Stratton; Sierra Leone; Smith, Oswald Jeffrey; Smyth, Walter Herbert; South Carolina; Southern Baptist Convention; Soviet Union; Sweden; Sydney, Australia; Taiwan; Taylor, Herbert John; Television in religion; Tennessee; Texas; Tokyo, Japan; Uruguay; Utah; Vangioni, Fernando; Vaus, James Arthur; Vermont; Vietnam; Vietnamese Conflict; Virginia; Walter F Bennett and Co; Washington (state); Waters, Ethel; West Virginia; White, John Wesley; Wilson, Grady Baxter; Wilson, Thomas Walter Jr; Wirt, Sherwood Eliot; Wisconsin; World Council of Churches; World Wide

Pictures; Wyoming; Youth for Christ International; Zimbabwe; Zondervan Publishing House)

%%%%%%%%%%%%

CN# 13
**BGEA: Field Director of Associate Crusades; 1950-**
Records; 1962-1976

Materials relating to the responsibilities of the field director, a BGEA executive based first in Atlanta, then in Minneapolis. Associate crusades were those of BGEA evangelists other than Billy Graham. Some of these responsibilities included investigating the possibility of a crusade in a community, appointing an associate (director) for setting up the crusade and training local counselors, scheduling crusade music teams, communicating with the associate evangelists, etc. John Dillon was the field director for the entire period of time covered by this body of records.

Vol: 70 boxes, 39 Audio Tapes, Oversize Materials, Photographs

(MAJOR TOPICS: Adams, Lane G; Alabama; Alaska; Arizona; Atlanta, GA; Bahamas; Barrows, Clifford B; Bell, Ralph Shadell; Bermuda; Billy Graham Evangelistic Association (BGEA); Blinco, Joseph D; Boston, MA; Bryant, Anita; California; Canada; Chicago, IL; Colorado; Congresses and conferences--World Congress on Evangelism, 1966; Counseling; Delaware; Evangelicalism; Evangelistic work--Bahamas; Evangelistic work--Barbados; Evangelistic work--Bermuda; Evangelistic work--Caribbean; Evangelistic work--Great Britain; Evangelistic work--Indonesia; Evangelistic work--Ireland; Evangelistic work--Jamaica; Evangelistic work--Liberia; Evangelistic work--New Zealand; Evangelistic work--Singapore; Evangelistic work--Switzerland; Evangelistic work--United States; Evangelistic work--Vietnam; Evangelistic work--Zimbabwe; Evans, Robert Philip; Fellowship of Christian Athletes; Ferm, Robert O; Florida; Ford, Leighton Frederick Sandys; Georgia; Graham, William Franklin "Billy"; Great Britain; Gustafson, Roy W; Haqq, Akbar Abdul; Haymaker, Willis Graham; Huston, Sterling W; Idaho; Illinois; India; Indiana; Inter-Varsity Christian Fellowship; Iowa; Ireland; Jamaica; Jones, Howard O; Kansas; Kentucky; Kenya; Liberia; Louisiana; Maine; Malaysia; Maryland; Massachusetts; Michigan; Minneapolis, MN; Minnesota; Mississippi; Missouri; Montana; Nairobi, Kenya; National Association of Evangelicals; National Negro Evangelical Association; Nelson, Victor B; New Jersey; New York (state); New York City, NY; New Zealand; Nonformal education; North Carolina; North Dakota; Ohio; Oregon; Organizational change; Pennsylvania; Philadelphia, PA; Philippines; Riggs, Charles A; Sermons, American; Shea, George Beverly; Shufelt,

John Stratton; Singapore; Smyth, Walter Herbert; South Carolina; South Dakota; Switzerland; Tennessee; Vangioni, Fernando V; Vaus, James Arthur; Vietnam; Virginia; Walter F Bennett and Co; Washington (state); Waters, Ethel; West Virginia; White, John Wesley; Wilson, George McConnell; Wilson, Grady Baxter; Wilson, Thomas Walter Jr; Winona Lake Bible Conference, IN; Wirt, Sherwood Eliot; Wisconsin; Wyoming; Zimbabwe)

%%%%%%%%%%%%

CN# 113
**BGEA: Films and Video Tapes; 1950-**
Records; 1955-1987; n.d.

Films and video tapes of the BGEA's subsidiary, World Wide Pictures. Most of these programs are the broadcast versions of BGEA crusades in various cities around the world.

Vol: 363 Films, 112 Video Tapes

(MAJOR TOPICS: Alabama; American Revolution Bicentennial, 1776-1976; Arizona; Athletes--Religious life; Atlanta, GA; Australia; Barrows, Clifford B; Beavan, Gerald "Jerry"; Bell, Lemuel Nelson; Bell, Ralph Shadell; Berlin, Germany; Billy Graham Center, IL; Billy Graham Evangelistic Association (BGEA); Blinco, Joseph D; Brazil; California; Campus Crusade for Christ; Canada; Caribbean; Carter, James Earl "Jimmy"; Cash, Johnny; Catholic Church in United States; Catholic Church--Relations; Charlotte, NC; Chicago, IL; Christian life; Christianity and economics; Church and state in Hungary; Church and state in Poland; Church and state in the Soviet Union; Church and state in United States; Church work with families; Church work with military personnel; Church work with students; Church work with the deaf; Church--biblical teaching; Cities and towns; Colorado; Colson, Charles Wendell; Columbia, SC; Communication; Communism; Congresses and conferences--Asia-South Pacific Congress on Evangelism, 1968; Congresses and conferences--Explo '72; Conlan, John Bertrand; Connally, John Bowden; Denmark; Denver, John; Dole, Robert J; Ecumenical movement; Evangelicalism; Evangelistic work---Australia; Evangelistic work--Brazil; Evangelistic work--Canada; Evangelistic work--Caribbean; Evangelistic work--Denmark; Evangelistic work--Hungary; Evangelistic work--New Zealand; Evangelistic work--Soviet Union; Evangelistic work--Sweden; Evangelistic work---United States; Evangelistic work--Yugoslavia; Evans, Dale; Fellowship of Christian Athletes; Film: *Hiding Place, The*; Film: MR TEXAS; Florida; Ford, Leighton Frederick Sandys; Frost, David Paradine; Garroway, Dave; George, Jeannette Clift; Georgia; Glass, William; Graham, Ruth Bell; Graham, William Franklin "Billy"; Great Britain;

Gustafson, Roy W; Hall, Myrtle; Hamblen, Stuart; Haqq, Akbar
Abdul; Harper, Redd; Harvey, Paul; Hatfield, Mark Odom; Hawaii;
Hines, Jerome; Hull, James Roger; Hungary; Hustad, Donald Paul;
Illinois; Indiana; Indians of North America; Irwin, James Benson;
Jones, Howard O; Karlsson, Evie Tornquist; Kennedy, John Fitzgerald;
Kentucky; Kivengere, Festo; Kristofferson, Kris; Landry, Thomas
Wade; Legislators--United States; London, England; Los Angeles, CA;
Mass media in religion; McDonald, James "Jimmie"; Michigan; Min-
nesota; Mississippi; Missouri; Montana; Moving-pictures in church
work; Moving-pictures--Moral and religious aspects; National
Religious Broadcasters; New York (state); New York City, NY; New
Zealand; Nixon, Richard Milhous; North Carolina; North Dakota;
Ohio; Oregon; Organizational change; Osei-Mensah, Gottfried B;
Parenthood; Pennsylvania; Periodical: *Decision*; Philadelphia, PA;
Philippines; Pierce, Robert Willard "Bob"; Presidents--United States;
Race relations; Religion and sports; Richards, Cliff; Richardson,
Robert Clinton "Bobby"; Rio de Janeiro, Brazil; Rogers, Roy; Salva-
tion Army; Sermons, American; Sex role; Shea, George Beverly;
Skinner, Thomas; Slavery; Smathers, George A; Smith, Edward R
"Tedd"; Smyth, Walter Herbert; South Carolina; South Dakota; Space
flight; Sweden; Sydney, Australia; Television in religion; ten Boom,
Cornelia Arnolda Johanna; Tennessee; Texas; Vietnamese Conflict;
Virginia; Warner, John William; Washington (state); Watergate Affair,
1972-1974; Waters, Ethel; Wheaton College, IL; White, John Wesley;
Wilson, Grady Baxter; Wisconsin; World Wide Pictures; Wyoming;
Youth for Christ International; Yugoslavia)

%%%%%%%%%%%%

CN# 1
**BGEA: Haymaker, Willis Graham; 1895-1980**
Papers; 1917-1970; n.d.

Correspondence, reports, photographs, and other material relating
mainly to Haymaker's work over twenty years as advance man and
crusade director for Billy Graham crusades, although some of the
material is also from his work for other evangelists, such as Bob
Jones Sr. and Gipsy Smith. The collection contains information on
both the internal workings of the Billy Graham Evangelistic
Association and on arrangements for particular crusades.

Vol: 8 boxes, Oversize Materials, Photographs

(MAJOR TOPICS: Adams, Lane G; Alabama; Albuquerque, NM;
Appelman, Hyman Jedidiah; Arizona; Arkansas; Atlanta, GA; Bar-
rows, Clifford B; Beavan, Gerald "Jerry"; Berlin, Germany; Boston,
MA; Brown, William Frederick "Bill" Sr; Butt, Howard E Jr; Califor-

nia; Canada; Colorado; Columbia, SC; Congresses and conferences---
World Congress on Evangelism, 1966; District of Columbia; Eisen-
hower, Dwight David; Evangelicalism; Evangelistic work--Canada;
Evangelistic work--France; Evangelistic work--Great Britain; Evan-
gelistic work--United States; Ferm, Robert O; Florida; Ford, Leighton
Frederick Sandys; France; Fundamentalism; Georgia; Graham, Ruth
Bell; Graham, William Franklin "Billy"; Great Britain; Haymaker,
Willis Graham; Illinois; Indiana; Jones, Howard O; Jones, Robert R Sr
"Bob"; Kennedy, Robert Francis; Kentucky; London, England; Los
Angeles, CA; Louisiana; Massachusetts; Miami, FL; Michigan; Missis-
sippi; Missouri; Mooneyham, W Stanley; New Jersey; New Mexico;
New York (state); New York City, NY; North Carolina; Ockenga,
Harold John; Ohio; Organizational change; Paris, France; Pennsyl-
vania; Philadelphia, PA; Pollock, John Charles; Presidents--United
States; Riggs, Charles A; Shea, George Beverly; Smith, Rodney "Gi-
psy"; Smyth, Walter Herbert; South Carolina; Tennessee; Texas;
Toronto, ON; Virginia; Washington (state); Washington, DC; West
Virginia; Wilson, Grady Baxter; Wilson, Thomas Walter Jr; Wirt,
Sherwood Eliot; Wisconsin)


%%%%%%%%%%%%

CN# 141
**BGEA: History Project; 1950-**
Records; 1970-1986; n.d.

Tapes and transcripts of oral history interviews conducted by Dr.
Lois Ferm with hundreds of persons who had some involvement
with the Billy Graham Evangelistic Association, Billy Graham, or
an international or regional congress on evangelism. Transcripts
include information on a wide variety of other evangelistic
endeavors as well. Collection also contains office files relating to
the search by the BGEA among Crusade workers, etc. for materials documenting Graham's career.

Vol: 45 boxes, 43 Audio Tapes, 361 Audio Tape Cassettes, 1 Film,
Negatives, 1 Phonograph Record, Photographs, Slides

(MAJOR TOPICS: Adams, Lane G; African Americans; Alaska;
Albuquerque, NM; Alexander, Charles McCallon; Amsterdam, Neth-
erlands; Anglicans; Animism; Argentina; Arizona; Armerding, Hudson
Taylor; Assemblies of God; Athletes--Religious life; Atlanta, GA;
Australia; Austria; Bangladesh; Baptists; Barrows, Clifford B; Belgium;
Belief and doubt; Bell, Lemuel Nelson; Bell, Ralph Shadell; Berry,
Lowell W; Biederwolf, William Edward; Billy Graham Center, IL;
Billy Graham Evangelistic Association (BGEA); Billy Graham Evan-
gelistic Association, Ltd [Australia]; Bolten, John; Boston, MA; Broad-

casting station: ELWA, Liberia; California; Canada; Catholic Church
in France; Catholic Church in Ghana; Catholic Church in Hungary;
Catholic Church in Italy; Catholic Church in Philippines; Catholic
Church in Poland; Catholic Church in United States; Charismatic
movement; Charlotte, NC; Chicago, IL; Chile; China; Chinese in
foreign countries; Christian and Missionary Alliance (CMA); Christian
education (theory); Christian education--Argentina; Christian educa-
tion--Canada; Christian education--Great Britain; Christian educa-
tion--India; Christian education--United States; Christian leadership;
Christian Worker's Foundation; Christianity Today, Inc; Church and
social problems; Church and state in Hungary; Church and state in
Poland; Church and state in the Soviet Union; Church of England;
Church of the Nazarene; Church work with families; Church work with
military personnel; Church work with single people; Church work with
students; Church work with the aged; Church work with youth; Cities
and towns; City missions; Colorado; Columbia, SC; Com-
munism--China; Communism--Hungary; Congresses and conferences---
International Conference for Itinerant Evangelists, 1983; Congresses
and conferences--International Conference for Itinerant Evangelists,
1986; Congresses and conferences--International Congress on World
Evangelization, 1974; Congresses and conferences--World Congress on
Evangelism, 1966; Connecticut; Conversion; Costa Rica; Cunville,
Rieweh Robert; Czechoslovakia; Dain, Arthur John; Divorce; Dodds,
Gilbert L; Dunlop, Merrill; Ecumenical movement; Egypt; Eskimos;
Evangelicalism; Evangelistic invitations; Evangelistic work--Argentina;
Evangelistic work--Australia; Evangelistic work--Austria; Evangelistic
work--Bangladesh; Evangelistic work--Belgium; Evangelistic
work--Brazil; Evangelistic work--Canada; Evangelistic work--Chile;
Evangelistic work--China; Evangelistic work--Denmark; Evangelistic
work--Egypt; Evangelistic work--France; Evangelistic work--Germany;
Evangelistic work--Ghana; Evangelistic work--Great Britain; Evangelis-
tic work--Guatemala; Evangelistic work--Hungary; Evangelistic work---
India; Evangelistic work--Indonesia; Evangelistic work--Italy; Evan-
gelistic work--Japan; Evangelistic work--Kenya; Evangelistic
work--Korea; Evangelistic work--Lebanon; Evangelistic work--Liberia;
Evangelistic work--Malawi; Evangelistic work--Mexico; Evangelistic
work--Morocco; Evangelistic work--Mozambique; Evangelistic work---
Netherlands; Evangelistic work--New Zealand; Evangelistic
work--Nigeria; Evangelistic work--Papua New Guinea; Evangelistic
work--Paraguay; Evangelistic work--Peru; Evangelistic
work--Philippines; Evangelistic work--Poland; Evangelistic work--Sierra
Leone; Evangelistic work--South Africa; Evangelistic work--Soviet
Union; Evangelistic work--Sweden; Evangelistic work--Switzerland;
Evangelistic work--Taiwan; Evangelistic work--Tanzania; Evangelistic
work--Uganda; Evangelistic work--United States; Evangelistic work---
Uruguay; Evangelistic work--Venezuela; Evangelistic
work--Yugoslavia; Evangelistic work--Zaire; Evangelistic work--Zimba-

bwe; Evans, Robert Philip; Ferm, Lois Roughan; Ferm, Robert O;
Film: *Mr. Texas*; Florida; Ford, Leighton Frederick Sandys; France;
Fund raising; Georgia; Germany; Ghana; Graham, Ruth Bell; Graham,
William Franklin "Billy"; Great Britain; Greater Europe Mission
(GEM); Guatemala; Gustafson, Roy W; Halverson, Richard C; Ham,
Mordecai Fowler; Ham-Ramsey Revival, Charlotte, NC, 1934; Hansen,
Kenneth Norman; Haqq, Akbar Abdul; Haymaker, Willis Graham;
Hoke, Donald Edwin; Hong Kong; Hull, James Roger; Hungary;
Idaho; Illinois; Independent churches; India; Indians of North Ameri-
ca; Indonesia; Integration; Inter-Varsity Christian Fellowship--United
States; Interdenominational cooperation; International Church of the
Four Square gospel; Ireland; Italy; Japan; Jarman, Walton Maxey;
Jesus people; Johnson, Torrey Maynard; Jones, Howard O; Kennedy,
John Fitzgerald; Kentucky; Kenya; Kim, Billy (Jang Hwan); King,
Martin Luther; Korea; Kresge, Stanley Sebastian; Landry, Thomas
Wade; Lausanne Committee for World Evangelization; Lausanne,
Switzerland; Lebanon; Liberia; London, England; Los Angeles, CA;
Louisiana; Lutherans; Malawi; Marquardt, Horst; Mass media in
religion; Massachusetts; McCall, Duke Kimbrough; Methodists; Mexico; Michigan; Minneapolis, MN; Minnesota; Missions from underdeveloped areas; Missions, Medical; Missions--Bangladesh; Mis-
sions--Belgium; Missions--China; Missions--Denmark; Mis-
sions--Ghana; Missions--Great Britain; Missions--India; Mis-
sions--Interdenominational cooperation; Missions--Liberia; Mis-
sions--Mozambique; Missions--Nigeria; Missions--Portugal; Mis-
sions--Theory; Missions--United States; Missouri; Moody Bible Institute, IL; Moody Church, IL; Mormons and Mormonism; Morocco;
Moscow, Soviet Union; Moving-pictures in church work; Mozambique;
Muslims in Egypt; Navigators; Nelson, Victor B; Netherlands; Nevada;
New Hampshire; New Mexico; New York (state); New York City, NY;
New Zealand; Nigeria; Nixon, Richard Milhous; North Carolina;
Norway; Ockenga, Harold John; Ohio; Olford, Stephen Frederick;
Oregon; Orthodox Eastern Church--Soviet Union; Pakistan; Palau,
Luis; Papua New Guinea; Paraguay; Patterson, Vernon William;
Pennsylvania; Pentecostals; Periodical: *Christianity Today*; Periodical:
*Decision*; Peru; Philippines; Poland; Pollock, John Charles; Prayer;
Prayer groups; Presbyterians; Presidents--United States; Prisoners--So-
viet Union; Prisoners--United States; Prisons--Missions and charities;
Race relations; Racism; Radio in religion; Radio program: *Hour of
Decision*; Religion and music; Religion and sports; Riggs, Charles A;
Riley, William Bell; Rio de Janeiro, Brazil; Rodeheaver, Homer
Alvan; Romania; Rookmaaker, Hendrik; Salvation Army; Sanny,
Lorne Charles; Seattle. Century 21 World's Fair, 1962; Seventh Day
Adventists; Shea, George Beverly; Smith, Oswald Jeffrey; Society of
Friends; South Africa; South Carolina; Southern Baptist Convention;
Soviet Union; Stott, John Robert Walmsley; Sudan Interior Mission
(SIM); Sunday, Helen Amelia Thompson; Sunday, William Ashley

"Billy"; Sweden; Switzerland; Sydney, Australia; Taiwan; Tanzania; Taylor, Herbert John; Television in religion; Television program: *Hour of Decision*; ten Boom, Cornelia Arnolda Johanna; Tennessee; Texas; Tokyo, Japan; Toronto, ON; Torrey, Reuben Archer Sr; Trans World Radio; Trotman, Dawson; Uganda; United Bible Societies; United Church of Canada; United States; Uruguay; Van Kampen, Robert Cornelius; Vaus, James Arthur; Venezuela; Voluntarism

%%%%%%%%%%%%

CN# 191
**BGEA: Hour of Decision Radio Program; 1950-**
Records; 1950-1980

Recordings of the Billy Graham Evangelistic Association's weekly radio program, which included music, announcements about evangelistic meetings, and a sermon by Graham or an associate. Many programs make references to then-current political or social events.

Vol: 2300 Audio Tapes

(MAJOR TOPICS: Atlanta, GA; Barrows, Clifford B; Beavan, Gerald "Jerry"; Belief and doubt; Billy Graham Evangelistic Association (BGEA); Church work with families; Church--Biblical teaching; Communication; Conversion; Death; Evangelicalism; Evangelistic work--United States; Family; Ford, Leighton Frederick Sandys; Georgia; Graham, William Franklin "Billy"; Indiana; Korean War; Love (Theology); Mass media in religion; Prayer; Radio in religion; Radio program: *Hour of Decision*; Religion and music; Sermons, American; Sex role; Shea, George Beverly; Sin; Values; Wilson, George McConnell; Wilson, Grady Baxter; Winona Lake Bible Conference, IN)

%%%%%%%%%%%%

CN# 23
**BGEA: Leighton Ford Crusade Office; 1950-**
Records; 1964-1973

Correspondence, minutes, invoices, newspaper clippings, films, audio tapes, photographs, etc., relating to crusades preached by Leighton Ford and a few other associate evangelists and directed by Norman Pell and Irv Chambers. There are usually several files for each crusade containing detailed financial, personnel, and organizational information. Particularly interesting are the films and tapes of crusades.

Vol: 20 boxes, 25 Audio Tapes, 21 Films, Negatives, Photographs, 2 Videotapes

(MAJOR TOPICS: Australia; Belief and doubt; Billy Graham Evangelistic Association (BGEA); California; Canada; Colorado; Connecticut; Conversion; Counseling; Crowds; Evangelistic work--Australia; Evangelistic work--Canada; Evangelistic work--Great Britain; Evangelistic work--New Zealand; Evangelistic work--United States; Family; Florida; Ford, Leighton Frederick Sandys; Georgia; Great Britain; Illinois; Indiana; Iowa; Manning, Ernest G; Marriage; Michigan; Minnesota; Mississippi; Missouri; New Zealand; Nonformal education; Oklahoma; Pennsylvania; Philadelphia, PA; Prayer; Presidents--United States; Reconciliation; Sermons, American; Sex role; Skinner, Thomas; South Dakota; Tennessee; West Virginia; Wisconsin; Youth--Religious life)

%%%%%%%%%%%%

CN# 102
**BGEA: Phonograph Records; 1950-**
Records; 1952-1978

This collection consists of phonograph records produced by the BGEA to be distributed as gifts to supporters of the organization. Each recording usually includes sermons and/or musical selections. Musical selections are by BGEA staff members, such as George Beverly Shea, Tedd Smith, and Cliff Barrows. NonBGEA phonograph records received by the Archives from the BGEA are also included in the collection such as material from Key '73 and Barry Moore crusades.

Vol: 30 Phonograph Records

(MAJOR TOPICS: American Bible Society; Australia; Barrows, Clifford B; Billy Graham Evangelistic Association (BGEA); Canada; Cash, Johnny; Evangelistic work--Australia; Evangelistic work--Canada; Evangelistic work--Great Britain; Evangelistic work--United States; Ford, Leighton Frederick Sandys; Graham, William Franklin "Billy"; Great Britain; Hall, Myrtle; Hustad, Donald Paul; Key '73; London, England; Mickelson, Paul; Missions--Great Britain; New York (state); New York City, NY; North Carolina; Radio program: *Hour of Decision*; Religion and music; Sankey, Ira D; Shea, George Beverly; Smith, Edward R "Tedd"; Switzerland; Sydney, Australia; Texas; Toronto, ON; Waters, Ethel; Wilson, Grady Baxter)

%%%%%%%%%%%%

CN# SC13
**BGEA: Portland Gospel Crusade Executive Committee; 1949-1950**
Records; 1949-1950

Minutes of Executive Committee of the Billy Graham evangelistic
meetings held in Portland, Oregon.

(MAJOR TOPICS: Billy Graham Evangelistic Association (BGEA);
Evangelistic work--United States; Graham, William Franklin "Billy";
Oregon)

%%%%%%%%%%%%

CN# 30
**BGEA: Southern California Crusade Breakfast; 1950-**
Ephemera; 1963

Recording of a breakfast meeting held for prominent church
leaders and laymen participating in the 1963 Southern California
Crusade. Almost all of the tape is taken up by Billy Graham's talk
on the need of America for revival and on how a crusade is
planned and executed. Also on the tape are a few comments by
crusade director Walter Smyth and a song by George Beverly
Shea. The meeting was held in Los Angeles at the Biltmore Bowl.

Vol: 1 Audio Tape

(MAJOR TOPICS: California; Evangelistic work--United States;
Graham, William Franklin "Billy"; Los Angeles, CA)

%%%%%%%%%%%%

CN# 22
**BGEA: Southern California Crusade Seminary Program; 1950-**
Records; 1962-1963

Two notebooks containing correspondence, schedules, budgets, and
staff and student evaluations relating to programs held in conjunction with the 1963 Los Angeles Crusade to train seminary students
in evangelism methods. This was one of a series of trial programs
which eventually resulted in the start of the school of evangelism
component of major crusades. There are also two audio tapes of

addresses given at the 1963 Southern California Crusade Seminary
Program.

Vol: 1 box, 2 Audio Tapes

(MAJOR TOPICS: Adams, Lane G; Berry, Lowell W; Billy Graham
Evangelistic Association (BGEA); Brown, William Frederick "Bill" Sr;
Christian education--United States; Counseling; Evangelistic work---
United States; Ferm, Robert O; Ford, Leighton Frederick Sandys;
Graham, William Franklin "Billy"; Nonformal education; Sermons,
American; Smyth, Walter Herbert)

%%%%%%%%%%%%%%

CN# 25
**BGEA: Sydney School of Evangelism; 1950-**
Records; 1968

This collection is comprised solely of tapes made of the lectures
on all aspects of mass evangelism given in April, 1968, at the
Sydney School of Evangelism which was a seminar for pastors and
others run by the Billy Graham Evangelistic Association in conjunction with the 1968 Sydney Crusade.

Vol: 7 Audio Tapes

(MAJOR TOPICS: Barrows, Clifford B; Billy Graham Evangelistic
Association (BGEA); Christian education--Australia; Evangelistic
work--Australia; Evangelistic work--United States; Graham, William
Franklin "Billy"; Gustafson, Roy W; Haqq, Akbar Abdul; Nelson,
Victor B; Nonformal education; Sermons, American; Smyth, Walter
Herbert; Sydney, Australia; White, John Wesley; Wirt, Sherwood
Eliot)

%%%%%%%%%%%%%%

CN# 27
**BGEA: Team Meeting; 1950-**
Records; 1969

Tape recording of the November, 1969, team (staff) meeting held
by the Billy Graham Evangelistic Association on Marcus Island,
Florida. The BGEA annually held a combination retreat, year end
review and planning session for its upper echelons. Speakers at
this meeting included Billy Graham and Leighton Ford.

Vol: 1 Audio Tape

(MAJOR TOPICS: Evangelistic work--United States; Graham, William Franklin "Billy"; Organizational change)

%%%%%%%%%%%%

CN# 17
**BGEA: Vice-President of Crusade Organization and Team Activities; 1950-**
Records; 1949-1979, n.d.

Correspondence, forms, tapes, newspaper clippings, audits, oversize materials, photographs, crusade files, etc., which relate to the BGEA Vice-President's responsibility for supervising the mechanics of organizing a Billy Graham crusade. Crusade files contain information about planning, arrangements, scheduling special events, executive committees, follow-up, the School of Evangelism, etc. Files are from crusades in many cities in the United States as well as Canada, Hong Kong, Manila, and Taipei. The collection contains numerous petitions from cities asking Graham to preach in their communities. There is more information in many of these files on Graham's crusades than on those of associate evangelists.

Vol: 49 boxes, 101 Audio Tapes, Oversize materials, Photographs

(MAJOR TOPICS: Abortion; Adams, Lane G; African Americans; Agnew, Spiro Theodore; Albert, Carl; Albuquerque, NM; Argentina; Auca people, Ecuador; Australia; Bahamas; Barrows, Clifford B.; Beavan, Gerald "Jerry"; Belfast, Ireland; Belgium; Bell, Ralph Shadell; Benny, Jack; Berlin, Germany; Billy Graham Evangelistic Association (BGEA); Boston, MA; Brazil; Campus Crusade for Christ; Canada; Carlson, Frank; Chaplains, Military; Chile; Christian literature--Publication and distribution; Church and social problems; Church architecture; Church of the Open Door, Los Angeles, CA; Church work with military personnel; Church work with students; Church work with youth; City missions; Clergy; College students--Religious life; Colombia; Columbia, SC; Congresses and conferences--Asia-South Pacific Congress on Evangelism, 1968; Congresses and conferences--World Congress on Evangelism 1966; Connally, John Bowden; Conversion; Counseling; Dain, Arthur John; Denmark; Dodds, Gilbert L; Ecuador; Eisenhower, Dwight David; Eisenhower, Julie Nixon; Europe Evangelistic invitations;Evangelistic sermons; Evangelistic work--Argentina; Evangelistic work--Australia; Evangelistic work--Belgium; Evangelistic work--Brazil; Evangelistic work--Canada; Evangelistic work--Denmark; Evangelistic work--Germany; Evangelistic work--Great Britain; Evangelistic work--Japan; Evangelistic work--Korea; Evangelistic work---New Zealand; Evangelistic work--Paraguay; Evangelistic work--Poland;

Evangelistic work--South Africa; Evangelistic work--Taiwan; Evangelistic work--United States; Evangelistic work--Uruguay; Evangelistic work--Venezuela; Evangelistic work--Vietnam; Falwell, Jerry; Finland; Ford, Leighton Frederick Sandys; Fuller, Charles Edward Sr; Germany; Graham, Ruth Bell; Graham, William Franklin "Billy"; Great Britain; Haile Selassie; Ham, Mordecai Fowler; Ham-Ramsey Revival, Charlotte, NC, 1934; Haymaker, Willis Graham; Henry, Carl Ferdinand Howard; Hong Kong; Huston, Sterling W; India; Ireland; Japan; Javits, Jacob Koppel; Johnson, Lyndon Baines; Johnson, Torrey Maynard; Jones, Howard O; Jones, Robert R Jr "Bob"; Juvenile delinquency; Kennedy, D James; Kennedy, John Fitzgerald; Kennedy, Robert Francis; Korea; Legislators--United States; Malaysia; Maoris; Marcos, Ferdinand E; McCormick, John W; McNamara, Robert Strange; Moomaw, Donald; Mooneyham, W Stanley; Moving-picture industry--United States; National Association of Broadcasters (NAB); National Broadcasting Corporation; New Zealand; Nixon, Richard Milhous; O'Brien, Pat; Ockenga, Harold John; Olympic games, Montreal, 1976; Organizational change; Paraguay; Peace; Peru; Philippines; Politics, Practical; Presidents--United States; Prisoners--United States; Race relations; Radio in religion; Religion and music; Riggs, Charles A; Rogers, Roy; Ross, James Robert; Rusk, Dean; Schirra, Walter Marty, Jr; Sermons, American; Shea, George Beverly; Smith, Edward R "Tedd"; Smyth, Walter Herbert; Social change; South Africa; Space flight; Stennis, John Cornelius; Switzerland; Taiwan; Television in religion; Templeton, Charles B; Uruguay; Vaus, James Arthur; Venezuela; Vereide, Abraham; Vietnam; Walters, Barbara; War; Wheaton College, IL; White, John Wesley; Wilson, George McConnell; Wilson, Grady Baxter; Wilson, Thomas Walter Jr; Youth for Christ International; Youth--Religious life)

%%%%%%%%%%%%

CN# 54
**BGEA: Walter F. Bennett and Co; 1943-**
Records; 1950-1977; n.d.

Films, videotapes, advertisements and artwork produced under the direction of the advertising firm Bennett and Company for the Billy Graham Evangelistic Association. This collection includes copies of the early 1950s television program *Hour of Decision* as well as later Graham broadcasts.

Vol: 23 boxes, 140 Films, 42 Video Tapes

(MAJOR TOPICS: Alabama; Albuquerque, NM; Arizona; Athletes--Religious life; Atlanta, GA; Australia; Barrows, Clifford B; Beavan, Gerald "Jerry"; Belgium; Bell, Ralph Shadell; Bible--Prophe-

cies; Billy Graham Evangelistic Association (BGEA); Blinco, Joseph
D; Bob Jones University, SC; Brazil; Bright, William Rohl "Bill";
Calcutta, India; California; Canada; Carlson, Frank; Cash, Johnny;
Charlotte, NC; Chicago, IL; Children of missionaries; Church and
state in United States; Church work with families; Church work with
students; Church work with the aged; Church work with the mentally
handicapped; Churchill, Winston Spencer; Cities and towns; Colorado;
Communication; Coptic Church; Disaster relief--India; District of
Columbia; Ethiopia; Evangelicalism; Evangelistic work--Australia;
Evangelistic work--Belgium; Evangelistic work--Brazil; Evangelistic
work--Canada; Evangelistic work--Ghana; Evangelistic work--Great
Britain; Evangelistic work--Hungary; Evangelistic work--Liberia;
Evangelistic work--New Zealand; Evangelistic work--Nigeria; Evan-
gelistic work--United States; Evangelistic work--Zimbabwe; Family;
Florida; Ford, Leighton Frederick Sandys; Georgia; Ghana; Graham,
Ruth Bell; Graham, William Franklin "Billy"; Grant, Amy; Great
Britain; Haile Selassie; Hall, Myrtle; Ham, Mordecai Fowler; Hamb-
len, Stuart; Haqq, Akbar Abdul; Harper, Redd; Harvey, Paul; Hawaii;
Hoover, Herbert Clark; Illinois; India; Indians of North America;
Jones, Robert R Sr "Bob"; Judd, Walter Henry; Karlsson, Evie Torn-
quist; Kennedy, John Fitzgerald; Kentucky; Kenya; Kivengere, Festo;
Legislators--United States; Liberia; Livingstone, David; London,
England; Los Angeles, CA; Louisiana; Marriage; Mass media in
religion; Michigan; Minneapolis, MN; Mississippi; Missouri; Moving--
pictures in church work; Moving-pictures--Moral and religious aspects;
Nairobi, Kenya; Nevada; New Mexico; New York (state); New York
City, NY; New Zealand; Nigeria; Nkruma, Kwame; Ohio; Oregon;
Osei-Mensah, Gottfried B; Pennsylvania; Philadelphia, PA; Pierce,
Robert Willard "Bob"; Presidents--United States; Prisoners--Korea;
Radio in religion; Radio program: *Hour of Decision*; Religion and
sports; Richards, Cliff; Rio de Janeiro, Brazil; Sermons, American; Sex
role; Shea, George Beverly; Smith, Oswald Jeffrey; South Carolina;
Soviet Union--Foreign relations--United States; Sports; Stennis, John
Cornelius; Tanzania; Television in religion; Television program: *Hour
of Decision*; Tennessee; Texas; Toronto, ON; Truman, Harry S;
United States--Politics and government; Vaus, James Arthur; Voelkel,
Harold; Washington (state); Washington, DC; Waters, Ethel; White,
John Wesley; Wilson, Grady Baxter; Wilson, Thomas Walter Jr; World
Wide Pictures; Zamperini, Louis Silvie; Zimbabwe)

%%%%%%%%%%%%

CN# 28
**BGEA: Wheaton Crusade Follow-Up Cards; 1950-**
Records; 1959

This collection consists of several hundred of the follow-up cards
used by the BGEA to check the progress being made by inquirers
who had come forward during Graham's Wheaton, Illinois, meetings (September 27-October 4, 1959). Each form, with the inquirer's name typed in, was given to the local minister for whose
church the inquirer had expressed a preference. The minister
returned the form, indicating whether the inquirer was attending
the church regularly and planned to become a member, and
adding any general comments the minister wished to make.

Vol: 6 boxes

(MAJOR TOPICS: Chicago, IL; Conversion; Evangelistic work--Uni-
ted States; Graham, William Franklin "Billy"; Illinois; Wheaton
College, IL)

%%%%%%%%%%%%

CN# 4
**BGEA: Williams, Harry Boyd; 1933-**
Records; 1963-1969

Correspondence, memoranda, newsletters, financial records, forms,
meeting minutes, and posters relating to Williams' activities as
director of five different crusades for the BGEA.

Vol: 3 boxes

(MAJOR TOPICS: Billy Graham Evangelistic Association (BGEA);
California; Canada; Counseling; Evangelistic work--Canada; Evangelistic work--Soviet Union; Evangelistic work--United States; Graham,
William Franklin "Billy"; Hawaii; Oregon; Texas; World Wide Pictures)

%%%%%%%%%%%%%

CN# 214
**BGEA: World Wide Pictures, Inc; 1951-**
Records;   1954(1960-1980)1980; n.d.

Films and files relating to the production and distribution of evangelistic movies and television programs, and to publicity for Billy
Graham's crusades.  Several of the publicity and crusade clippings
scrapbooks in the collection are on microfilm.

Vol: 7 Boxes, 41 Films, Microfilm, Oversize Materials, Phonograph
Records, Photographs, 2 Video Tapes

(MAJOR TOPICS: African Americans; Alabama; Apartheid; Argen-
tina; Australia; Barrows, Clifford B; Beavan, Gerald "Jerry"; Billy
Graham Evangelistic Association (BGEA); Blinco, Joseph D; Brown,
William Frederick "Bill" Sr; Calcutta, India; California; Campus
Crusade for Christ; Canada; Carmichael, Ralph; Chicago, IL; Civil
rights movement; Colorado; Congresses and conferences--World
Congress on Evangelism, 1966; Conversion; Denmark; Evangelicalism;
Evangelistic work--Australia; Evangelistic work--Canada; Evangelistic
work--Denmark; Evangelistic work--Great Britain; Evangelistic
work--Japan; Evangelistic work--New Zealand; Evangelistic
work--United States; Film: *Hiding Place, The*; Film: *Joni*; Film: *Mr
Texas*; France; Germany; Graham, Ruth Bell; Graham, William Frank-
lin "Billy"; Great Britain; Haqq, Akbar Abdul; Holocaust, Jewish;
Illinois; India; Japan; Jerusalem, Israel; Jones, Howard O; Korea;
Language: German; Language: Spanish; London, England; Los
Angeles, CA; Mass media in religion; Mission Aviation Fellowship
(MAF); Missouri; Moving-pictures in church work; Moving-pictures---
Moral and religious aspects; Netherlands; New York (state); New
York City, NY; New York. World's Fair, 1964-1965; New Zealand;
Norway; Ohio; Oregon; Organizational change; Orphans and orphan--
asylums; Papua New Guinea; Racism; Religion and music; Richards,
Cliff; Richardson, Robert Clinton "Bobby"; Salvation; Seoul, Korea;
Sermons, American; Shea, George Beverly; Smith, Edward R "Tedd";
Smith, Rodney "Gipsy"; South Africa; Sweden; Switzerland; Sydney,
Australia; Tada, Joni Eareckson; Television in religion; ten Boom,
Cornelia Arnolda Johanna; Tennessee; Texas; Tokyo, Japan; Trotman,
Dawson; United States--Race relations; Vaus, James Arthur; Waters,
Ethel; Wilson, Grady Baxter; World Vision International; World Wide
Pictures)

%%%%%%%%%%%%

CN# 195
**Biederwolf, William Edward; 1867-1939**
Papers; 1884-1922; n.d.

Sermons, speeches, scrapbooks, articles, correspondence, and other materials which document the education and evangelistic activities of Biederwolf, a turn-of-the-century preacher and educator.

Vol: 3 boxes

(MAJOR TOPICS: African Americans; Alexander, Charles McCallon; Atlanta, GA; Australia; Biederwolf, William Edward; Chapman, John Wilbur; Chicago, IL; Christian education, Outdoor; Church and social problems; Church and state in United States; Cities and towns; City missions; Colorado; Connecticut; Counseling; Edison, Thomas Alva; Evangelistic work--Australia; Evangelistic work--United States; Fundamentalism; Georgia; Indiana; Iran; Islam (theology); Kansas; Kentucky; Mills, B Fay; Moving-pictures--Moral and religious aspects; New Jersey; Ohio; Sermons, American; Smith, Rodney "Gipsy"; Stough, Henry Wellington; Sunday, William Ashley "Billy"; Talmage, Thomas Dewitt; Tennessee; Trotter, Melvin Ernest; Spanish American War, 1898; Winona Lake Bible Conference, IN)

%%%%%%%%%%%%

CN# 11
**Billy Graham Appreciation Day; 1968**
Records; 1968

Guestbook, notebook describing appreciation scroll, and notebooks of correspondence relating to the events held by Charlotte, NC, on September 10, 1968, to honor its native son, Billy Graham. The correspondence consists of invitations to sent to prominent politicians, educators, clergy, athletes, generals, and friends with their replies.

Vol: 1 box

(MAJOR TOPICS: Billy Graham Evangelistic Association (BGEA); Evangelistic work--United States; Graham, William Franklin "Billy")

%%%%%%%%%%%%

CN# 3
**Billy Graham Center; 1974-**
Records; 1967-1981

Documentation about three phases of the Billy Graham Center's existence: initial concept and planning, ca. 1970-73; construction and dedication of the building at Wheaton College, 1977-80; and records from a 1981 meeting seeking to foster local evangelism around the world.

Vol: 3 boxes, 10 Audio Tapes, Oversize Materials, Photographs, 25 Video Tapes

(MAJOR TOPICS: Alabama; Barrows, Clifford B; Billy Graham Center, IL; Billy Graham Evangelistic Association (BGEA); Christian education--United States; Communication; Education, Higher; Evangelistic work--United States; Ferm, Lois Roughan; Ford, Leighton Frederick Sandys; Gallup, George Horace III; George, Jeannette Clift; Gieser, Paul Kenneth; Graham, Morrow Coffey; Graham, William Franklin "Billy"; Hoke, Donald Edwin; Kennedy, D James; Malik, Charles; Palms, Roger Curtis; Robertson, Marion Gordon "Pat"; Sermons, American; Van Alstyne, Frances Jane "Fanny" Crosby; Wheaton College, IL; Wilson, Thomas Walter Jr)

%%%%%%%%%%%%

CN# 6
**Billy Graham: The Authorized Biography; 1966**
Manuscript; n.d.

Manuscripts and letter. The original handwritten and typed drafts of the biography by John Pollock.

Vol: 2 boxes

(MAJOR TOPICS: Evangelistic work--United States; Graham, William Franklin "Billy"; Pollock, John Charles; Singapore)

%%%%%%%%%%%%%

CN# 41
**Billy Sunday Campaign Music...**
Ephemera; 1917; n.d.

One audio tape, mostly of gospel music. Side 1 includes songs
sung by Billy Sunday co-workers, Mrs. William Asher and Homer
Rodeheaver with the choir from the 1917 Billy Sunday revival campaign in New York City. Side 2 includes Dr. Russell Conwell
telling his famous "Acres of Diamonds" story and a song by evangelist Gipsy Smith.

Vol: 1 Audio Tape

(MAJOR TOPICS: Asher, Virginia Healey (Mrs William); Conwell,
Russell Herman; Religion and music; Rodeheaver, Homer Alvan;
Smith, Rodney "Gipsy"; Sunday, William Ashley "Billy")

%%%%%%%%%%%%

CN# SC103
**Birney, James Gillespie; 1792-1859**
Ephemera; 1839

Autograph letter from abolitionist leader Birney to S. Silsbee [?] in
answer to a question about "Whether a missionary would be coun-
tenancing or conniving at slavery, by accepting a commission from
a Foreign Missionary Board, whilst that board solicited and received aid from slaveholders?"

(MAJOR TOPICS: Birney, James Gillespie; Hawaii; Missionaries--Re-
cruitment and training; Missions--United States; Slavery)

%%%%%%%%%%%%

CN# SC16
**Black, Cyril Wilson; 1902-**
Papers; 1955-1971

Crusade bulletins, newspaper articles, pamphlets, relating to
various crusades in England (mainly from the 1966 London Crusade). Black was honorary treasurer of the 1966 Crusade.

(MAJOR TOPICS: Billy Graham Evangelistic Association (BGEA);
Black, Cyril Wilson; Evangelistic work--United States; Graham, William Franklin "Billy")

%%%%%%%%%%%%%

CN# SC61
**Blanchett, Charles Isaac; 1875-1933**
Ephemera; 1908

Manuscript booklet, containing a three-verse English poem in a
pseudo-Chinese script, illustrated with nine water colors. The
poem is a satire on the perils of missionary life, apparently made
as a gift for Blanchett (a Church of England missionary to Hong
Kong) by another missionary.

(MAJOR TOPICS: Blanchett, Charles Isaac; China; Church Missionary Society, England; Missions--China; Missions--Hong Kong)

%%%%%%%%%%%%%

CN# 171
**Bobby, Mary Lee (1928- ) and Albert Edward (1925- )**
Papers; 1953-1978; n.d.

Published articles, correspondence, prayer letters, manuscript
notes, and oral histories which all concern the mission work in
Portugal of the Bobbys and others under the Evangelical Alliance
Mission. Among their activities was radio broadcasting.

Vol: 1 box, 3 Audio Tapes

(MAJOR TOPICS: Adolescence; Bobby, Albert Edward; Bobby, Mary
Lee; Boughter, C Luke; Catholic Church in Portugal; Children of
missionaries; Christian literature--Publication and distribution; Edman,
Victor Raymond; Evangelical Alliance Mission, The (TEAM); Evan-
gelistic work--United States; Family; Full Gospel Business Men's
Fellowship; Graham, William Franklin "Billy"; Humbard, Rex;
Marriage; Mass media in religion; McIntire, Carl Curtis; Mis-
sions--Portugal; Mozambique; Pentecostals; Portugal; Radio in mis-
sionary work; Radio in religion; Sabbath; Sex role; Social classes;
Spain; Television in religion; Washington, DC; Wheaton College, IL;
Witchcraft)

%%%%%%%%%%%%

CN# 98
**Booth, William; 1829-1912**
Ephemera; 1921

An audio tape with excerpts from two of Booth's sermons, one of which contains a reference to Salvation Army; two autographs of Booth, one dated 1921, one undated; one video tape of black and white photographs and filmed segments of Salvation Army activities, including Booth's funeral. Included on the video tape is a 5 minute sermon by Harry Ironside, filmed at Moody Memorial Church.

Vol: 1 box, 1 Audio Tape, 1 Video Tape

(MAJOR TOPICS: Booth, William Bramwell; Cities and towns; City missions; Evangelistic work--Great Britain; Evangelistic work--United States; Ironside, Henry Allan "Harry"; Moody Memorial Church, IL; Salvation Army; Sermons, American; Social service)

%%%%%%%%%%%%

CN# 131
**Bovyer, J Wesley and Anna Ellmers; ?-?**
Ephemera; 1937-1940

Prayer letters, photographs, and artifacts relating to two missionaries to China who directed work in an orphanage in Chinkiang, China, from 1908 until at least 1940.

Vol: 1 box, Photographs

(MAJOR TOPICS: Bovyer, Anna Ellmers; Bovyer, J Wesley; Children; China; China Nazarene Orphanage, Chinkiang, China; Missions--China; Missions--Educational work; Orphans and orphan-asylums; Overseas Missionary Fellowship (China Inland Mission); Sino-Japanese Conflict, 1937-1945; Washington (state); World War II)

%%%%%%%%%%%%

CN# 96
**Bragg, Wayne G; 1931-**
Interview; 1980

Two audio tapes of an interview with Bragg. Highlights include his mission experiences in Brazil and the Caribbean working with university students, his student days at Wheaton, and his experience at Wheaton as a faculty member.

Vol: 2 Audio Tapes

(MAJOR TOPICS: Armerding, Carl E; Bragg, Wayne G; Brazil; Castro, Fidel; Charlotte, NC; Communism--Germany; Costa Rica; Cuba; Deyneka, Peter Jr; Dominican Republic; Ecuador; Edman, Victor Raymond; Escobar, Samuel; Evangelistic work--Brazil; Ford, Leighton Frederick Sandys; Fuller Theological Seminary, CA; Fuller, Charles Edward Sr; Graham, William Franklin "Billy"; Haiti; International Fellowship of Evangelical Students; Johnson, Jimmie; Little, Paul Eagleson; North Carolina; Pennsylvania; Puerto Rico; Radio Program: *Old Fashioned Revival Hour*; Taylor, Kenneth Nathaniel; Unevangelized Fields Mission; Van Der Puy, Abraham Cornelius; Wheaton College, IL; White, John Wesley; Wilson, Grady Baxter; Woods, C Stacey; World Student Christian Federation; Youth for Christ International)

%%%%%%%%%%%%

CN# 252
**Brain, Joan Gordon (1934- ) and Brain, Robert Wesley (1928- )**
Interviews; 1983

Four taped interviews; two with Robert Brain in which he discusses his life on the mission field in Angola as a child and as an adult serving Africa Evangelical Fellowship at Catota Bible Institute until 1975, and at Manna Bible Institute in Zambia. Two interviews with Joan Brain in which she describes her decision to become a medical missionary, marriage to Robert and mission work as a nurse, teacher, and mother in Angola and Zambia.

Vol: 4 Audio Tapes

(MAJOR TOPICS: Africa Evangelical Fellowship; Angola; Bible colleges; Bible--Translating; Bobby, Albert Edward; Bobby, Mary Lee; Brain, Joan Gordon; Brain, Robert Wesley; Carnell, Edward John; Children of missionaries; Christian and Missionary Alliance (CMA);

Christian leadership; Communism--Angola; Conversion; Educa-
tion--Angola; Education--Zambia; Evangelistic work--Australia; Gordon-Conwell Divinity School; Medical care--Angola; Medical care---
Zambia; Missionaries, Withdrawal of; Missionaries--Recruitment and
training; Missions, Medical; Missions--Angola; Missions--Zambia;
Navigators; Nonformal education; Nursing; Ockenga, Harold John;
Prisoners--Zambia; Religion and music; Religion and underdeveloped
areas; Sex role; Story-telling; Sunday schools; Witchcraft; Women--Re-
ligious life; Women in missionary work; Zambia)

%%%%%%%%%%%%%

CN# 123
**Branham, William Marrion; 1905-1965**
Ephemera; 1947-1967

Photographs, films, videotapes, and over 1,200 audio tapes containing sermons preached by charismatic-healing evangelist William
Branham, including the healing portion of services. Among the
cities in which sermons were taped were Chicago, Dallas, Hous-
ton, Los Angeles, New York, and Tulsa.

Vol: 1270 Audio Tapes, 2 Films, Photographs

(MAJOR TOPICS: Alabama; Albuquerque, NM; Arizona; Arkansas;
Branham, William Marrion; California; Canada; Charismatic move-
ment; Charlotte, NC; Chicago, IL; Church--biblical teaching; Colum-
bia, SC; Connecticut; Evangelistic work--Canada; Evangelistic work---
Germany; Evangelistic work--United States; Faith--Cure; Florida;
Germany; Healers; Illinois; Indiana; Iowa; Kansas; Kentucky; Lau-
sanne, Switzerland; Los Angeles, CA; Louisiana; Maine; Mass-
achusetts; Minneapolis, MN; Minnesota; Mississippi; New Hampshire;
New Jersey; New Mexico; New York (state); New York City, NY;
North Carolina; Ohio; Oregon; Pennsylvania; Pentecostals; Puerto
Rico; Sermons, American; South Africa General Mission; South
Carolina; South Dakota; Switzerland; Tennessee; Texas; Vermont;
Washington (state); West Virginia; Wisconsin)

%%%%%%%%%%%%%

CN# 127
**Bridegroom, Kathleen Joan; 1950-**
Ephemera; 1972-1974; n.d.

Photographs, audio tapes, and prayer letters from Bridegroom's
two years as a Sudan Interior Mission worker at radio station

ELWA in Liberia. Letters discuss her teaching experiences, cultural impressions, and mission activities.

Vol: 1 Audio Tape, Photographs

(MAJOR TOPICS: Broadcasting station: ELWA, Liberia; Children of missionaries; Liberia; Mass media in religion; Missionaries, Lay; Radio in religion; Sudan Interior Mission)

%%%%%%%%%%%%

CN# 120
**Brown, John Elward, Sr.; 1879-1957**
Ephemera; 1955

Collection includes series of 35 sermons delivered by evangelist and educator Brown in 1955 on the subject "Whose Son Is He".

Vol: 12 Audio Tapes, Photograph

(MAJOR TOPICS: Brown, John Elward; Evangelistic work--United States; John Brown University, AR; Sermons, American)

%%%%%%%%%%%%

CN# 97
**Bryan, William Jennings; 1860-1925**
Ephemera; 1896-1924

Audio tape of portions of two of Bryan's speeches and a recitation. The two speeches are the "Cross of Gold" speech to the 1896 Presidential Convention and an election talk from 1908. The recitation is of the 23rd Psalm, made in 1924.

Vol: 1 Audio Tape

(MAJOR TOPICS: Bryan, William Jennings)

%%%%%%%%%%%%

CN# 262
**Buker, Raymond Bates Jr; 1925-**
Interviews; 1983

Two interviews of Buker conducted by Joel Woodruff, November 1 and 8, 1983. Buker describes his childhood growing up in Burma, his schooling, his decision to become a missionary under Conservative Baptist Foreign Mission Society, language study; evangelization, church planting, translation, and education activities in Pakistan working with Muslims and Marwari tribal people, 1954 to 1969. Also describes Buker's job as Midwestern and Western campus representative for CBFMS, 1970-1972; relocation from Denver to Wheaton as Personnel Secretary for CBFMS, 1972-.

Vol: 2 Audio Tapes, 2 Cassette Tapes

(MAJOR TOPICS: Agricultural societies; Armerding, Hudson Taylor; Athletes--Religious life; Baptists; Baptists--Missions; Bible colleges; Bible--Translating; Buker, Raymond Bates, Jr; Burma; Campus Ambassadors; Campus Crusade for Christ; Catholic Church--Missions; Catholic Church--Relations; Children of missionaries; Christian education--Pakistan; Christian leadership; Christian literature; Christianity and politics; Church and social problems; Church and state in Pakistan; Church development, New; Church growth; Church work with youth; College students--Religious life; Communication; Conservative Baptist Foreign Mission Society; Conversion; Counseling; Dodds, Gilbert L; Drug abuse; Edman, Victor Raymond; Education--Philosophy; Elliot, Philip James; Evangelistic work--Pakistan; Gaebelein, Frank; Gordon-Conwell Divinity School; Hinduism (theology); Hindus in India; Hindus in Pakistan; India; Indigenous church administration; Intercultural communications; Islam (theology); Islam--Relations--Christianity; Language in missionary work; MAP International; Medical care--Pakistan; Missionaries--Leaves and furloughs; Missionaries--Recruitment and training; Missions to Muslims; Missions, Medical; Missions--Pakistan; Muslims in Pakistan; Navigators; Pakistan; Refugees--Pakistan; Religion and music; Religion and sports; Saint, Nathanael "Nate"; Sex role; Wheaton College, IL; World War II; Worship; Youth--Religious life)

%%%%%%%%%%%%%

CN# 221
**Campus Crusade for Christ; 1951-**
Ephemera; 1960

Ten phonograph records with messages by William R. Bright, Billy Graham, Richard C. Halverson, F.J. Huegel, J. Edwin Orr, Eugenia Price, Bernard Ramm, Wilbur Smith, and others.

Vol: 1 Audio Tape, 10 Phonograph Records

(MAJOR TOPICS: Bright, William Rohl "Bill"; Campus Crusade for Christ; Evangelicalism; Evangelistic work--United States; Fundamentalism; Graham, William Franklin "Billy"; Halverson, Richard C; Orr,

James Edwin; Pierce, Robert Willard "Bob"; Price, Eugenia; Ramm, Bernard L; Sermons, American; Smith, Wilbur Moorehead; Thieme, Robert; Thomas, W Ian; Youth--Societies and clubs)

%%%%%%%%%%%

CN# 184
**Campus-in-the-Woods    1951-**
Records; 1961-1981

Personal correspondence, cards, resumes, and mission newsletters from a group of Canadian and American students who attended an Inter-Varsity summer camp, 1951, near Toronto, Canada. This collection documents an 18-year period of the lives of those who communicated with Lois Ottaway with information which was compiled by her for an informal, annual Campus-in-the-Woods Newsletter. The newsletters describes the different kinds of Christian work in which they were involved.

Vol: 2 boxes, Photographs

(MAJOR TOPICS: Baptists; Canadian Baptist Mission; Colombia; Ethiopia; Evangelical Alliance Mission, The (TEAM); Evangelistic work--United States; Evangelistic work--Zaire; India; Indonesia; Inter-Varsity Christian Fellowship; Kenya; Latin America Mission; Methodist Church--Missions; Methodists; Missions, Medical; Missions--Colombia; Missions--Educational work; Missions--India; Missions--Indonesia; Missions--Iran; Missions--Kenya; Missions--Peru; Missions--Philippines; Missions--Zaire; North Africa Mission; Peru; South Africa; Sudan Interior Mission (SIM); Wycliffe Bible Translators; Zaire; Zimbabwe)

%%%%%%%%%%%

CN# 58
**Carlson, Carol Hammond; 1895-1980**
Interview; 1978

Tape of an interview with Mrs. Carlson about her experiences on the Tibetan mission field. Subjects discussed include first entry into Tibet, reaction of the people to non-Tibetans, and the Islamic rebellion of 1929.

Vol: 1 Audio Tape

(MAJOR TOPICS: Carlson, C Edwin; Carlson, Carol Hammond; Carlson, Robert Dean; China; Christian and Missionary Alliance

(CMA); Christian and Missionary Alliance--Missions; Evangelistic
work--Tibet; Missions--China; Missions--Tibet; New York (state);
Nigeria; Tibet; Women--Religious life; Women in missionary work)

%%%%%%%%%%%%

CN# 263
**Carlson, Margaret Johanna Larson; 1927-**
Interviews; 1983

Oral history interviews with Mrs. Carlson in which she describes
her childhood as a missionary kid in Ecuador, her education at
Westmont and Wheaton Colleges, her nursing experiences, and the
missionary work she and her husband Robert did in Hong Kong at
the Christian and Missionary Alliance Seminary there.

Vol: 2 Audio Tapes

(MAJOR TOPICS: Alcoholics; Broadcasting station: HCJB, Ecuador;
California; Carlson, Margaret Johanna Larson; Carlson, Robert Dean;
Catholic Church in China; Catholic Church in Hong Kong; Children of
missionaries; China; Christian and Missionary Alliance (CMA); Chris-
tian and Missionary Alliance--Missions; Church and social problems;
Church and state in Ecuador; Colombia; Communication; Ecuador;
Edman, Victor Raymond; Family; Funeral rites and ceremonies;
Guatemala; HNGR program, Wheaton College; Hong Kong; Illinois;
Indians of South America; Indigenous church administration; Inter-
cultural communications; International relief; Jones, Clarence Wesley;
Jones, Howard; Kantzer, Kenneth Sealer; Larson, Reuben Emmanuel;
Marriage; Mass media in religion; Missionaries--Leaves and furloughs;
Missionaries--Recruitment and training; Missions--Ecuador; Mis-
sions--Finance; Missions--Hong Kong; Missions--Interdenominational
cooperation; Nursing; Panama; Parenthood; Poverty; Racism; Radio in
missionary work; Radio in religion; Sweden; Taoism; Wheaton College, IL)

%%%%%%%%%%%%

CN# 205
**Carlson, Robert Dean; 1928-**
Interviews; 1982

Oral history interviews with Carlson in which he discusses his
boyhood in China and Tibet, the condition of the Christian church

in those countries, social and religious customs, and the Chinese language.

Vol: 2 Audio Tapes

(MAJOR TOPICS: Agricultural societies; Assemblies of God; Assemblies of God--Missions; Bible--Publication and distribution; Buddhists in China; Buddhists in Tibet; Carlson, Robert Dean; Children of missionaries; China; Christian and Missionary Alliance (CMA); Christian education--China; Church and state in Tibet; Communication; Crime and criminals; Dancing--Moral and religious aspects; Evangelical Alliance Mission, The (TEAM); Evangelistic work--Tibet; Indigenous church administration; Intercultural communications; Islam--Relations--Christianity; Lamaism; Missions to Buddhists; Missions--China; Missions--Tibet; Music--United States; Muslims in China; Overseas Missionary Fellowship (China Inland Mission); Pentecostals; Persecution--Tibet; Prayer; Religion and music; Scandinavian Alliance Mission; Seventh Day Adventists; Sex role; Sin; Soviet Union; Tibet; United Church of Canada)

%%%%%%%%%%%%

CN# 196
**Case, Edna Louise Asher; 1905-**
Interviews; 1981

Oral history tape in which Case talks about her aunt, Virginia Asher, who was a co-worker of Billy Sunday and was also involved in many other evangelistic efforts. Case also discusses her impressions of Mel Trotter, Billy Sunday, Helen Sunday, her student days at Wheaton College, and her involvement in city mission work.

Vol: 1 Audio Tape

(MAJOR TOPICS: Asher, Virginia Healey; Asher, William; Case, Edna Archer; Evangelistic work--United States; Sex role)

%%%%%%%%%%%%

CN# 241
**Chapel of the Air, United States Air Force**
Ephemera; 1962

Thirty-minute black-and-white film of a telecast service held January 14, 1962, conducted by Chaplain Carl W. McGeehon; it includes a sermon by Chaplain Major Ralph R. Pace on the subject "The Living Word of God."

Vol: 1 Film

(MAJOR TOPICS: Bible--Criticism, interpretation, etc; Chaplains, Military; Church work with military personnel; Mass media in religion; Radio Program: *Chapel of the Air*; Television in religion; Television program: *Chapel of the Air*)

%%%%%%%%%%%%

CN# 77
**Chapman, John Wilbur; 1859-1918**
Papers; 1880-1918; n.d.

Purchased microfilm from the Presbyterian Historical Society of correspondence, sermons, sermon notes, photographs, newspaper clippings, scrapbooks, and memorabilia documenting the life and ministry of J. Wilbur Chapman. Materials detail Chapman's life from early education through his pastoral ministry and full-time evangelistic work. Documents also relate to Chapman's interests in Bible Conference Centers in Winona Lake, Indiana; Montreat, North Carolina; and Stony Brook, New York.

Vol: 8 Reels of Microfilm

(MAJOR TOPICS: Alexander, Charles McCallon; Asher, Virginia Healey; Asher, William; Biederwolf, William Edward; Boston, MA; Chapman, John Wilbur; Chicago, IL; Clergy; Evangelistic invitations; Evangelistic sermons; Evangelistic work--Australia; Evangelistic work---New Zealand; Evangelistic work--United States; Fundamentalism; India; Minneapolis, MN; New Zealand; Pocket Testament League; Presbyterians; Rodeheaver, Homer Alvan; Sermons, American; Stough, Henry Wellington; Sunday, William Ashley "Billy"; Sydney, Australia; Winona Lake Bible Conference, IN)

%%%%%%%%%%%%

CN# 134
**Chapman, Marian Gold; 1922-**
Ephemera; 1957-1979

Prayer letters written by Marian Chapman, a missionary with Latin American Mission in Cartagena, Colombia (1957-1975); Bogota, New Jersey (1975-1977), and in Coral Gables, Florida (1977-1979). The letters describe her educational, financial, and administrative work with the Cartagena Secondary School and LAM Cartagena offices, in addition to personal concerns about the cultural difference and political unrest.

Vol: 1 box

(MAJOR TOPICS: Caribbean; Catholic Church in Colombia; Catholic Church--Missions; Chapman, Marian Gold; Communism; Community of Latin American Evangelical Ministries; Evangelism in Depth; Graham, William Franklin "Billy"; Howard, David Morris; Latin America Mission; Missions--Colombia; Missions--Educational work; Panama; Periodical: *Decision*; South Dakota; Strachan, R Kenneth; Wheaton College, IL)

%%%%%%%%%%%%%

CN# 295
**Charlotte Evangelistic Campaigns Research Project; 1982-1983**
Records; 1915-1983

Newspaper clippings, questionnaires, audio tapes, sermon transcripts, and other documents gathered during a research project into twentieth century evangelistic meetings held in Charlotte, North Carolina, by J. Wilbur Chapman, Billy Sunday, Mordecai Ham, Billy Graham, and Leighton Ford.

Vol: 2 boxes, 8 Audio Tapes, Microfilm, Oversize Materials, Photograph

(MAJOR TOPICS: Alexander, Charles McCallon; Chapman, John Wilbur; Charlotte, NC; Evangelicalism; Evangelistic invitations; Evangelistic sermons; Evangelistic work--United States; Ford, Leighton Frederick Sandys; Fundamentalism; Graham, William Franklin "Billy"; Ham, Mordecai Fowler; Ham-Ramsey Revival, Charlotte, NC, 1934; North Carolina; Ramsey, Walter J; Sermons, American; Sunday, William Ashley "Billy")

%%%%%%%%%%%%%

CN# 33
**Chicago Call, The; 1977**
Records; 1974-1978  n.d.

Materials related to the conference which drafted the Chicago Call, a statement of young Evangelical scholars on the need for a stronger sense of tradition and greater social activism.  Files

include minutes of the planning committee and printed post
conference report.

Vol: 2 boxes

(MAJOR TOPICS: Bible--Criticism, interpretation, etc; Chicago, IL;
Church and social problems; Church--biblical teaching; Congresses
and conferences--Chicago Call Conference, 1977; Evangelicalism;
Lovelace, Richard; Sermons, American; Theology; Webber, Robert
Eugene; Wheaton College, IL)

%%%%%%%%%%%%%

CN# 133
**Chicago Gospel Tabernacle   1922-1979**
Records; 1952-1979

Church bulletins, correspondence, financial records, newspaper
clippings, form letters, reports, minutes, photographs which document the history of the Chicago Gospel Tabernacle from the
1950s until the 1970s.

Vol: 5 boxes, Photographs

(MAJOR TOPICS: Chicago Gospel Tabernacle; Chicago, IL; Cities
and towns; Dunlop, Merrill; Evangelistic work--United States; Illinois;
Independent churches; Organizational change; Rader, Daniel Paul;
Sunday schools; Taylor, Herbert John; Vacation schools, Christian;
Youth for Christ International)

%%%%%%%%%%%%%

CN# 240
**Christian Broadcasting Network (CBN); 1961-**
Ephemera; 1979

Two video tapes of the dedication ceremonies of an International
Communication Center for CBN, October 6, 1979, Virginia Beach,
Virginia.  Dedicatory address was given by Billy Graham, with
guest appearances by Ephraim Zimbalist, Jr., Andre Crouch,
William Harness, and musical groups.

Vol: 2 Video Tapes

(MAJOR TOPICS: Charismatic movement; Christian Broadcasting
Network; Communication; Evangelistic work--United States; Graham,
William Franklin "Billy"; Mass media in religion; Prayer; Religion and

music; Robertson, Marion Gordon "Pat"; Television in religion;
Zimbalist, Ephraim Jr)

%%%%%%%%%%%%

CN# 307
**Christian Films and Videos**
Records; 1980-1985; n.d.

This collection consists of productions by Evangelical filmmakers,
donated to the Archives, on topics related to missions and evangelism.

Vol: 23 Video Tapes

(MAJOR TOPICS:  African Americans; Alcoholics; Atlanta, GA;
Bibles for the World; Bunyan, John; Church and social problems;
Church growth; Church work with the aged; Colson, Charles Wendell;
Communication; Conversion; Daystar Communications; Drug abuse;
Ecumenical movement; Evangelistic work--United States; Evans,
Christmas; Georgia; Intercultural communications; Kesler, Jay Lewis;
Mass media in religion; Missions--Caribbean; Mississippi; Moravians;
Moving-pictures in church work; Multnomah School of the Bible, WA;
Perkins, John M; Preaching; Prison Fellowship; Prisoners--United
States; Prisons--Missions and charities; Sermon on the Mount; Ser-
mons, American; Voice of Calvary Ministries; Watergate Affair,
1972-1974; Wesley, John; Youth for Christ International)

%%%%%%%%%%%%

CN# 8
**Christianity Today, Inc; 1956-**
Records; 1930 (1954-1976) 1977; n.d.

Correspondence, memoranda, forms, financial reports, study
papers, and clippings from the early period of the Evangelical
Protestant journal, *Christianity Today*.  Materials relate to the
founding of the magazine; to a wide range of religious, social, and
political events; and to theological debates.  Correspondence
includes letters to and from a wide range of leaders in various
fields.  Also in the collection are press credentials; correspondence; reports of the 1966 World Congress on Evangelism held in
Berlin; records of Key '73; records of the International Congress
on World Evangelization held in Lausanne, Switzerland, in 1974;

and the extensive correspondence files of editors Carl Henry and
Harold Lindsell.

Vol: 30 boxes, 32 Audio Tapes, Photographs

(MAJOR TOPICS: Barth, Karl; Beavan, Gerald "Jerry"; Bell, Lemuel
Nelson; Berlin, Germany; Billy Graham Evangelistic Association
(BGEA); Bright, William Rohl "Bill"; Bruce, Frederick Fyvie; Brunner,
Emil; Campus Crusade for Christ; Charismatic movement; Christianity
and economics; Christianity Today, Inc; Church and social problems;
Church and state in United States; Church and state in Vietnam;
Church--biblical teaching; Communication; Communism--Vietnam;
Congresses and conferences--CELA III; Congresses and conferences---
Congress on the Church's Worldwide Mission, 1966; Congresses and
conferences--International Congress on World Evangelization, 1974;
Congresses and conferences--World Congress on Evangelism, 1966;
Congregationalists; Conlan, John Bertrand; Corporations, Religious---
Taxation; Cushing, Richard (Cardinal); Douglas, James; Evangelical-
ism; Evangelistic work--United States; Falwell, Jerry; Ford, Leighton
Frederick Sandys; Fuller Theological Seminary, CA; Gordon-Conwell
Divinity School; Graham, William Franklin "Billy"; Halverson, Richard
C; Hargis, Billy James; Hatfield, Mark Odom; Haymaker, Willis
Graham; Henry, Carl Ferdinand Howard; Hitt, Russell Trovillo; Hoke,
Donald Edwin; India; Jarman, Walton Maxey; Jones, Robert R Sr
"Bob"; Key '73; Kilby, Clyde Samuel; King, Martin Luther; Latourette,
Kenneth Scott; Lausanne Covenant; Legislators--United States;
Lindsell, Harold; Little, Paul Eagleson; Lutheran Church-Missouri
Synod; Lutherans; Marty, Martin; McIntire, Carl Curtis; Missions from
underdeveloped areas; Missions--Interdenominational cooperation;
Mooneyham, W Stanley; Moyers, Bill; National Council of Churches;
National Religious Broadcasters; Niebuhr, Reinhold; Nixon, Richard
Milhous; Ockenga, Harold John; Organizational change; Pakistan;
Peale, Norman Vincent; Periodical: *Christian Century, The*; Periodical:
*Christianity Today*; Periodical: *Sojourners*; Peru; Pew, John Howard;
Pollock, John Charles; Presidents--United States; Roberts, Granville
Oral; Schaeffer, Edith; Sex role; Smith, Oswald Jeffrey; Smith, Wilbur
Moorehead; Social change; Sullivan, Ed; Taylor, Clyde Willis; Taylor,
Kenneth Nathaniel; ten Boom, Cornelia Arnolda Johanna; Tenney,
Merrill Chapin; Tillich, Paul J; Tournier, Paul; United Church of
Christ; Vietnam; Vietnamese Conflict; Wheaton College, IL; Wilson,
George McConnell; Winter, Ralph D; Wirt, Sherwood Eliot; Women
clergy; World Evangelical Fellowship (WEF); World Home Bible
League; Wyrtzen, John Von Casper "Jack")

%%%%%%%%%%%%

CN# 91
**Committee to Assist Ministry Education Overseas (CAMEO);
1952-**
Records; 1956 (1963-1975) 1979; n.d.

Correspondence, minutes, reports, questionnaires, monographs,
and other materials dealing with the efforts of CAMEO to assist
and improve the educational institutions of American Protestant
missions. The collection also contains a great deal of information
on programmed learning techniques and on the work of various
Evangelical organizations.

Vol: 13 boxes, Photographs

(MAJOR TOPICS: Africa Evangelical Fellowship; Africa Inland
Mission (AIM); Alaska; Angola; Argentina; Armstrong, Philip E;
Assemblies of God; Baptists; Belgium; Berean Mission; Bible Institute
of Los Angeles (BIOLA), CA; Bolivia; Brazil; Brethren; Buker,
Raymond Bates Jr; CAM International; Cambodia; Cameroon; Cen-
tral African Republic; Children of missionaries; Chile; Christian and
Missionary Alliance (CMA); Christian education (theory); Christian
education--Afghanistan; Christian education--Angola; Christian educa-
tion--Argentina; Christian education--Australia; Christian education---
Bolivia; Christian education--Brazil; Christian education--Burma;
Christian education--Cameroon; Christian education--Central African
Empire; Christian education--Chile; Christian education--Colombia;
Christian education--Costa Rica; Christian education--Cuba; Christian
education--Ecuador; Christian education--El Salvador; Christian
education--Ethiopia; Christian education--Gabon; Christian educa-
tion--Ghana; Christian education--Grenada; Christian educa-
tion--Guatemala; Christian education--Guinea; Christian educa-
tion--Guyana; Christian education--Haiti; Christian educa-
tion--Honduras; Christian education--Hong Kong; Christian educa-
tion--India; Christian education--Indonesia; Christian education--Iran;
Christian education--Israel; Christian education--Jamaica; Christian
education--Japan; Christian education--Jordan; Christian educa-
tion--Kenya; Christian education--Korea; Christian education--Laos;
Christian education--Lebanon; Christian education--Liberia; Christian
education--Madagascar; Christian education--Malawi; Christian educa-
tion--Malaysia; Christian education--Mexico; Christian educa-
tion--Mozambique; Christian education--Namibia; Christian educa-
tion--Nicaragua; Christian education--Nigeria; Christian education---
Pakistan; Christian education--Panama; Christian education--Papua
New Guinea; Christian education--Paraguay; Christian education---
Peru; Christian education--Philippines; Christian education--Puerto

Rico; Christian education--Senegal; Christian education--Sierra Leone;
Christian education--Singapore; Christian education--Somali Democratic Republic; Christian education--South Africa; Christian education---
Sri Lanka; Christian education--Surinam; Christian education--Swazi-
land; Christian education--Taiwan; Christian education--Tanzania;
Christian education--Thailand; Christian education--Uganda; Christian
education--Uruguay; Christian education--Venezuela; Christian educa-
tion--Vietnam; Christian education--Zaire; Christian educa-
tion--Zambia; Christian education--Zimbabwe; Christian Reformed
Church; Church and state in Central African Republic; Colombia;
Committee to Assist Ministry Education Overseas (CAMEO); Com-
munication; Conservative Baptist Foreign Mission Society; Costa Rica;
Cuba; Dayton, Edward Risedorph; Dominican Republic; Ecuador;
Education--Angola; Education--Curricula; Education--Honduras;
Education--Kenya; Education--Laos; Education--Nigeria; Education---
Zambia; Egypt; El Salvador; Ethiopia; Evangelical Alliance Mission,
The (TEAM); Evangelical Foreign Missions Association; Evangelical
Missions Information Service; Evangelistic work--Belgium; Evangelize
China Fellowship, Inc; France; Gabon; Germany; Ghana; Gospel
Missionary Union; Greater Europe Mission (GEM); Grenada; Guate-
mala; Guinea; Guyana; Haiti; Honduras; Hong Kong; India; Indonesia;
Intercultural communications; Interdenominational Foreign Mission
Association (IFMA); Iran; Israel; Italy; Ivory Coast; Japan; Jordan;
Kenya; Korea; Laos; Latin America Mission; Lebanon; Liberia;
Madagascar; MAP International; Mennonite Brethren; Mexico; Mis-
sions--Educational work; Missions--India; Missions--Theory; Mis-
sions--Zaire; Mozambique; Muslims in Sudan; Namibia; Nicaragua;
Nigeria; Nonformal education; Norton, Hugo Wilbert; OMS Interna-
tional, Inc; Overseas Missionary Fellowship (China Inland Mission);
Panama; Papua New Guinea; Paraguay; Peru; Philippines; Portugal;
Poverty; SEND International; Senegal; Sierra Leone; Singapore;
Somali; South Africa; Southern Baptist Convention; Sri Lanka; Sudan;
Sudan Interior Mission (SIM); Taiwan; Tanzania; Teachers, training
of; Thailand; Uganda; Unevangelized Fields Mission; United Brethren
in Christ; United States; United World Mission; Uruguay; Venezuela;
Wagner, Charles Peter; Winter, Ralph D; World Evangelical Fellow-
ship (WEF); World Gospel Mission; Youth for Christ International;
Zaire; Zambia)

%%%%%%%%%%%%

CN# SC88
**Comstock, Anthony; 1844-1915**
Ephemera; 1912-1915

Letter from Comstock to Rev. H. C. Hovey, March 2, 1912,
included with annual report to "The N.Y. Society for the Suppres-

sion of Vice"; biographical questionnaire for *The Cyclopedia of American Biography* filled in by Comstock, 1915.

(MAJOR TOPICS: Comstock, Anthony; New York Society for the Suppression of Vice; Pornography)

%%%%%%%%%%%%

CN# 76
**Conant, Judson Eber; 1867-1955**
Papers; 1875-1955

Correspondence, newspaper clippings, photographs, sermon notes and personal notes relating to the ministry of Judson Eber Conant. The collection also contains ordination materials and his examination for a preaching license. Of particular interest in the oversize collection is Conant's license to preach.

Vol: 1 box, Photographs, Oversize Materials

(MAJOR TOPICS: Chicago, IL; Clergy; Conant, Judson Eber; Evangelistic work--United States; Illinois; Iowa; Michigan; Wisconsin)

%%%%%%%%%%%%

CN# 82
**Conference on Faith and History; 1967-**
Records; 1966-1978; n.d.

Correspondence, newsletters, minutes of meetings, transcripts of sessions, brochures, clippings, etc., of the Conference formed for Evangelical Christian historians.

Vol: 2 boxes

(MAJOR TOPICS: American Revolution Bicentennial, 1776-1976; Conference on Faith and History; Evans, Robert Philip; Haile Selassie; Henry, Carl Ferdinand Howard; Latourette, Kenneth Scott; Montgomery, John Warwick; Nixon, Richard Milhous; Pierard, Richard V; Presidents--United States; Reid, W Stanford; Wheaton College, IL)

%%%%%%%%%%%%%

CN# SC108
**Conference on the Return of the Lord; 1918**
Ephemera; 1918

Brochure advertising a volume of the addresses given at the Conference on the Return of the Lord. The conference was held in Philadelphia from May 28 to 30, 1918. The brochure gives some background information on the meeting as well as listing the speakers and their topics.

(MAJOR TOPICS: Bible--Prophecies; Gray, James Martin; Millennialism; Philadelphia, PA; Riley, William Bell)

%%%%%%%%%%%%%

CN# 21
**Congress on the Church's Worldwide Mission; 1966**
Records; 1964-1976

Materials relating to the mission congress which was held on Wheaton College campus in 1966 and was jointly sponsored by the Evangelical Foreign Mission Association and the Interdenominational Foreign Mission Association. Included in this collection are tapes of the major addresses and public meetings, copies of study papers, and evaluations of the Congress by magazines, organizations, and individuals.

Vol: 1 box, 26 Audio Tapes

(MAJOR TOPICS: Armerding, Hudson Taylor; Climenhaga, Arthur M; Congresses and conferences--Congress on the Church's Worldwide Mission, 1966; Evangelical Foreign Missions Association; Evans, Robert Philip; Gieser, Paul Kenneth; Interdenominational Foreign Mission Association (IFMA); Missionaries--Recruitment and training; Missions--Theory; Norton, Hugo Wilbert; Sermons, American; Taylor, Clyde Willis; Vangioni, Fernando V; Wheaton College, IL)

%%%%%%%%%%%%

CN# SC30
**Conservative Baptist Foreign Mission Society**
Policy Book    n.d.

Handbook given to missionaries and candidates which describes
the Society's background, constitution, doctrinal statement, expectations of the missionary, and personnel policies.

(MAJOR TOPICS: Baptists; Baptists--Missions; Conservative Baptist
Foreign Mission Society)

%%%%%%%%%%%%

CN# 99
**Country Church of Hollywood, The; radio program; 1933-?**
Ephemera; 1933-1937

Twenty-four recordings of broadcasts of he Country Church of
Hollywood, a religious radio program begun by Dr. William B.
Hogg in January, 1933.

Vol: 4 Audio Tapes

(MAJOR TOPICS: California; Communication; Evangelistic work---
United States; International Church of the Four Square Gospel; Mass
media in religion; Radio in religion; Radio Program: *Country Church
of Hollywood, The*; Religion and music; Sermons, American)

%%%%%%%%%%%%

CN# 259
**Cook, Donald Arthur; 1923-**
Interviews; 1983

Two interviews with Cook in which he describes service with
Overseas Missionary Fellowship in Japan between 1956-1972
includes description of administrative duties in OMF headquarters,
Japanese attitudes toward missionaries, Christianity, cultural and
religious conflicts, church growth, cooperation with other missions,
and adaptation to Japanese needs.

Vol: 2 Audio Tapes

(MAJOR TOPICS: Children of missionaries; China; Church growth; Church work with youth; Cook, Donald Arthur; Evangelical Alliance Mission, The (TEAM); Evangelistic work--Japan; Graham, William Franklin "Billy"; Hirohito, Emperor of Japan; Idols and images; Illinois; Intercultural communications; Japan; Language in missionary work; Missionaries--Recruitment and training; Missions--Japan; Overseas Missionary Fellowship (China Inland Mission); Singapore; Tokyo, Japan; Wheaton College, IL; Youth--Religious life)

%%%%%%%%%%%%

CN# 35
**Crosby, Frances Jane "Fanny" [Van Alstyne]; 1820-1915**
Papers; 1862-1915; n.d.

Thousands of manuscripts of lyrics dictated by Crosby, poetess and hymn writer. Most of the manuscripts are numbered and dated. This collection is also on microfilm.

Vol: 2 boxes

(MAJOR TOPICS: Evangelistic work--United States; Hymn writers; Religion and music; Van Alstyne, Frances Jane "Fanny" Crosby; Women--Religious life)

%%%%%%%%%%%%

CN# SC8
**Dain, Arthur John (Jack); 1912-**
Papers; 1955-1965

Correspondence, minutes, forms relating to the Billy Graham India Crusade in January/February, 1956, which Dain helped plan.

(MAJOR TOPICS: Billy Graham Evangelistic Association (BGEA); Dain, Arthur John; Evangelistic work--United States; Graham, William Franklin "Billy")

%%%%%%%%%%%%

CN# 291
**Davis, Ralph T; ?-1963**
Papers; 1935-1962; n.d.

A group of notebooks used by Davis with summaries of biblical books to be used for sermons; sermon notes and outlines; church history, data on Africa Inland Mission, geography and worldwide cultures, hymns, and other information. There is also a photo and a few clippings concerning Davis' career as a missionary and leader of Africa Inland Mission.

Vol: 2 boxes, Photographs

(MAJOR TOPICS: Africa Inland Mission (AIM); Bible--Criticism, interpretation, etc; Davis, Ralph T; Evangelistic work--United States; Moody Memorial Church, IL; Religion and music; Sermons, American; Theology)

%%%%%%%%%%%%%

CN# 273
**Day, Harold Louis; 1913-**
Interview; 1984

Tape of an oral history session in which Day tells about his experiences while working at Chicago Gospel Tabernacle during the pastorate of Paul Rader and his successor, Clarence Erickson.

Vol: 1 Audio Tape

(MAJOR TOPICS: Bible--Criticism, interpretation, etc; Chicago Gospel Tabernacle; Chicago, IL; Christian leadership; Cities and towns; City missions; Conversion; Day, Harold Louis; Dunlop, Merrill; Erickson, Clarence H; Evangelistic sermons; Evangelistic work--United States; Fund raising; Hogg, William B; Illinois; Laity; Poverty; Preaching; Rader, Daniel Paul; Religion and music; Revivals; World Wide Christian Couriers; Worship)

%%%%%%%%%%%%%

CN# 194
**Doane, William Howard; 1832-1915**
Papers; 1872-1915; n.d.

Letters, notebooks and other materials of Doane, songbook publisher, philanthropist, and hymn writer. The letters are about hymn publishing and writing and include correspondence from Ira Sankey, Fanny Crosby, Philip P. Bliss, Philip Phillips, and Dwight L. Moody's daughter-in-law.

Vol: 1 box, Photographs

(MAJOR TOPICS: Doane, William Howard; Evangelistic work---
United States; Moody, Dwight Lyman; Religion and music; Sankey, Ira
D; Van Alstyne, Frances Jane "Fanny" Crosby)

%%%%%%%%%%%%%

CN# 50
**Dunlop, Merrill; 1905-**
Interviews; 1978-1979

Oral history interviews with Dunlop in which he talks about his association with evangelist Paul Rader, early religious radio pro-
gramming in Chicago, the Chicago Gospel Tabernacle, Youth for
Christ, evangelism, and other topics.

Vol: 2 Audio Tapes, Photographs

(MAJOR TOPICS: Argentina; Bolivia; Brazil; Broadcasting station:
WMBI; Caribbean; Chicago Gospel Tabernacle; Chile; China; Church
and social problems; Cities and towns; City missions; Colombia;
Communication; Communism; Cook, Robert Andrew; Counseling;
Dunlop, Merrill; Ecuador; Evangelistic work--Argentina; Evangelistic
work--Brazil; Evangelistic work--Chile; Evangelistic work--United
States; Evangelistic work--Uruguay; Gih, Andrew; Haggai, John;
Hammontree, Homer; Hogg, William B; India; International Church
of the Four Square Gospel; Japan; Johnson, Albert Mussey; Johnson,
Bessilyn Morris; Johnson, Jimmie; Johnson, Torrey Maynard; Jones,
Clarence Wesley; Latham, Lance; McPherson, Aimee Semple; Moody
Bible Institute, IL; Moody Memorial Church, Chicago, IL; Philippines;
Philpot, Ford; Rader, Daniel Paul; Rader, Luke; Radio Program:
*Country Church of Hollywood, The*; Rodeheaver, Homer Alvan; Shea,
George Beverly; Smith, Oswald Jeffrey; Sunday, Helen Amelia Thom-
pson; Sunday, William Ashley "Billy"; Taylor, Clyde Willis; Uruguay;
Wilson, Thomas Walter Jr; Winona Lake Bible Conference, IN; Youth
for Christ International)

%%%%%%%%%%%%%

CN# 80
**Dunn, Miriam J Toop; 1913**
Papers; 1978

Manuscript of the autobiography written by Dunn relating her
missionary experiences in China and Southeast Asia with the
China Inland Mission (CIM).

Vol: 1 box

(MAJOR TOPICS: Adolescence; Beijing, China; Borden Memorial Hospital, China; Boxers (Chinese political movement); Brethren; Brethren Church--Missions; Calcutta, India; Chambers, Oswald; Chiang Kai-Shek; China; Christian literature--Publication and distribution; Church and state in China; Communism; Communism--China; Dunn, Miriam J; Evangelistic work--China; Frame, Helen Grace Nowack; Frame, Raymond William; Great Britain; Houghton, Frank; India; Japan; Kane, J Herbert; Kuo min tang (China); Liddell, Eric Henry; Malaysia; Mao Tse-tung; Medical care--China; Missions, Medical; Missions--Educational work; Moscow, Soviet Union; Nowack, Ruth Louise; Overseas Missionary Fellowship (China Inland Mission); Plymouth Brethren; Plymouth Brethren--Missions; Salvation Army; Sex role; Shanghai, China; Singapore; Stam, Elizabeth Alden Scott; Stam, John Cornelius; Taylor, James Hudson; Women--Religious life; Women in missionary work)

%%%%%%%%%%%%

CN# SC72
**Edwards, Jonathan Sr.; 1703-1758**
Ephemera; 1748-1750

One page listing receipts, unsigned, presumed to be in Edwards' handwriting; three handwritten pages of minutes of the Congregational Church, Northampton, MA, 1748-1750, making settlement of his salary, inquiring into his controversial book on communicants, and seeking to dissuade him from preaching on the opinions in this book. Transcripts of each documents are included. There is one photograph and a negative of a print of Edwards.

(MAJOR TOPICS: Congregationalists; Edwards, Jonathan Sr; Evangelistic work--United States; Great Awakening)

%%%%%%%%%%%%

CN# 92
**Ekvall, Robert Brainerd; 1898-1983**
Interviews; 1979-1980

Tapes of two interviews on Ekvall's education at Wheaton, work as a missionary in China and Tibet, activities during World War II, and return to China in 1980.

Vol: 2 Tapes

(MAJOR TOPICS: Beijing, China; Blanchard, Charles Albert; Boxers
(Chinese political movement); Buck, Pearl Sydenstricker (Mrs Richard
J Walsh); Buddhism (theology); Buddhists in China; Buddhists in
Tibet; Catholic Church--Missions; Chiang Kai-Shek; Children of
missionaries; China; China--History--1949-; Christian and Missionary
Alliance (CMA); Christian and Missionary Alliance--Missions; Church
and state in Tibet; Communism; Communism--China; Dalai Lama;
Edman, Victor Raymond; Ekvall, Robert Brainerd; Evangelistic
work--Tibet; House churches; Intercultural communications; Is-
lam--Relations--Christianity; Korean War; Kuo min tang (China);
Lamaism; Language: Chinese; Missions to Buddhists; Missions--China;
Missions--Educational work; Missions--Tibet; Muslims in China;
Mysticism; Persecution--Tibet; Presbyterians; Shanghai, China; Three--
Self Patriotic Movement; Vietnam; Wheaton College, IL; World War
I; World War II)

%%%%%%%%%%%%%

CN# 278
**Elliot, Elisabeth Howard; 1926-**
Papers; 1926-1983; n.d.

Correspondence, clippings, publicity releases, reviews, manuscripts
and tapes relating to Elliot's careers as a missionary in Ecuador
and author; includes the manuscript of *The Savage My Kinsman*
and others. One of the tapes is the audio of the television program *This is Your Life* describing Rachel Saint's work with Day-
uma; the second is an interview with Elliot which discusses her
childhood and years at Wheaton College.

Vol: 2 boxes, 2 Audio Tapes, Photographs

(MAJOR TOPICS: Aeronautics in missionary work; Auca people,
Ecuador; Belgian Gospel Mission; Belgium; Brethren; Brethren
Church--Missions; Carmichael, Amy Wilson; Children of missionaries;
College students--Religious life; Ecuador; Elliot, Elisabeth Howard;
Elliot, Philip James; Evangelistic work--Belgium; Howard, Philip E Jr;
Intercultural communications; Ironside, Henry Allan "Harry"; Kilby,
Clyde Samuel; Language in missionary work; Marriage; McIntire, Carl
Curtis; Mission Aviation Fellowship; Missions--Ecuador; Missions---
Peru; Ockenga, Harold John; Oklahoma; Olford, Stephen Frederick;
Periodical: *Sunday School Times, The*; Peru; Philadelphia, PA; Ply-
mouth Brethren; Plymouth Brethren--Missions; Prayer; Saint, Nathan-
ael "Nate"; Saint, Rachel; Sex role; Stam, Elizabeth Alden Scott;
Torrey, Reuben Archer Jr; Wheaton College, IL; Women authors;
Women in missionary work; Women--Religious life; World War II;
Wycliffe Bible Translators; Youth--Religious life)

%%%%%%%%%%%%%

CN# 277
**Elliot, Philip James; 1927-1956**
Papers; 1941-1956

Correspondence, journals, notebooks, school records, poems, clippings, drawings, and other materials describing the career of Elliot and his spiritual preparation for the mission field and death at the hands of Auca Indians.

Vol: 2 boxes

(MAJOR TOPICS: Aeronautics in missionary work; Auca people, Ecuador; Brethren; Brethren Church--Missions; College students--Religious life; Ecuador; Elliot, Elisabeth Howard; Elliot, Philip James; Evangelistic work--United States; Illinois; Indiana; Intercultural communications; Language in missionary work; Marriage; Mexico; Mission Aviation Fellowship (MAF); Missionaries--Recruitment and training; Oregon; Plymouth Brethren; Plymouth Brethren--Missions; Prayer; Saint, Nathanael "Nate"; Wheaton College, IL; Wycliffe Bible Translators)

%%%%%%%%%%%%%

CN# 187
**Elliott, Eleanor Ruth; 1908-**
Papers; 1910 (1931-1982) 1982; n.d.

Family correspondence, prayer letters, brochures, newspaper clippings, and eight taped interviews concerning Elliott's childhood in China, mission work under China Inland Mission (now Overseas Missionary Fellowship) in China and the Philippines, her experiences as an evangelist and teacher, and her life in China during the Sino-Japanese War, 1937-1945, and the civil war which followed.

Vol: 1 box, 9 Audio Tapes

(MAJOR TOPICS: American Bible Society; Bible Institute of Los Angeles (BIOLA), CA; Bible--Publication and distribution; Buddhists in China; Buswell, James Oliver Jr; Calcutta, India; California; Caste; Catholic Church in Philippines; Catholic Church--Missions; Chiang Kai-Shek; Children of missionaries; China; Christian education--China; Christian education--Philippines; Christmas; Church and social problems; Church growth--China; Church work with families; Church work with refugees; Columbia Bible College, Columbia, SC; Communism;

Conversion; Crossett, Margaret Rice Elliott; Demonology; Educa-
tion--China; Elliott, Eleanor Ruth; Evangelistic work--China; Footbinding; Frame, Helen Grace Nowack; Gandhi, Mahatma; Glover,
Robert Hall; Goforth, Jonathan; Gospel Recordings, Inc; Hong Kong;
Illinois; Independent churches; India; Indigenous church administration; Japan; Kuo min tang (China); Language in missionary work;
Medical care--China; Missionaries--Recruitment and training; Missions
to Buddhists; Missions, Medical; Missions--China; Mis-
sions--Educational work; Missions--Philippines; Moody Bible Institute,
IL; Overseas Missionary Fellowship (China Inland Mission); Pennsyl-
vania; Pentecostals; Philippines; Presbyterian Church--Missions;
Presbyterians; Rader, Daniel Paul; Rural churches--China; Scandinavian Alliance Mission; Schoerner, Katharine Hasting Dodd; SEND
International; Sex role; Shanghai, China; Silkworm culture; Sino-Japanese Conflict, 1937-1945; Social change; Social classes; South Carolina;
Stam, Elizabeth Alden Scott; Stam, John Cornelius; Taylor, James
Hudson; Tenney, Merrill Chapin; Three-Self Patriotic Movement;
Wheaton College, IL; World War II; Young Men's Christian Associa-
tion United States)

%%%%%%%%%%%%

CN# 116
**Elliott, Helen Ruth Belcher; 1927-**
Interviews; 1980

Tapes of oral history interviews conducted with Elliott, Wycliffe
missionary to the Ixil Indian tribe in Guatemala. Topics discussed
include Wheaton College during the 1950s, field experiences,
Guatemalan culture and religion, and family activities.

Vol: 3 Audio Tapes

(MAJOR TOPICS: Bible--Translating; Children of missionaries;
Crossett, Margaret Rice Elliot; Crossett, Vincent Leroy; Elliot, Philip
James; Elliot, Raymond Leroy; Elliott, Helen Ruth Belcher; Evangelis-
tic work--Guatemala; Fuller Theological Seminary, CA; Guatemala;
Hatcher, Elias Wesley; Illinois; Japan; Kansas; Language in missionary
work; Mexico; Missions--Guatemala; Missouri; Mozambique; Nida,
Eugene Albert; Oklahoma; Overseas Missionary Fellowship (China
Inland Mission); Saint, Nathanael "Nate"; Tenney, Merrill Chapin;
Wheaton College, IL; Women--Religious life; Women in missionary
work; Wycliffe Bible Translators)

%%%%%%%%%%%%

CN# 115
**Elliott, Raymond Leroy; 1924-**
Interview; 1980

Tape of oral interview with Ray Elliott, Wycliffe Bible translator
working among the Ixil Indian tribe in Guatemala. Topics covered
include educational work and life in Wheaton; translation activities; missionary training; mission responsibilities; and political,
social, and cultural events in Central America.

Vol: 2 Audio Tapes

(MAJOR TOPICS: Baptists; Bible--Translating; CAM International;
Catholic Church--Missions; Church of the Nazarene; Church of the
Nazarene--Missions; Crossett, Margaret Rice Elliot; Crossett, Vincent
Leroy; Elliot, Philip James; Elliot, Raymond Leroy; Evangelistic
work--Guatemala; Evangelistic work--Mexico; Guatemala; Illinois;
Japan; Kansas; Ladd, George Elton; Language in missionary work;
Methodists; Mexico; Missions--Guatemala; Presbyterian Church--Mis-
sions; Presbyterians; Primitive Methodist Church; Religion and music;
Saint, Nathanael "Nate"; Society of Friends; Society of Friends--Mis-
sions; Tenney, Merrill Chapin; Tozer, A W; Wheaton College, IL;
Wycliffe Bible Translators)

%%%%%%%%%%%%

CN# 208
**Embery, Doris; 1913-**
Interview; 1982

Interview with Embery in which she discusses the activities of her
parents (who were China Inland Mission workers), her education
at the CIM school in Chefoo, her reflections on the lack of uni-
queness of missionary children, and her experiences after she left
China.

Vol: 1 Audio Tape

(MAJOR TOPICS: Bell, Lemuel Nelson; Chefoo Schools; Children of
missionaries; China; Door of Hope Mission; Embery, Doris; Fraser,
James Outram; Missionaries--Recruitment and training; Mis-
sions--China; Missions--Educational work; Overseas Missionary Fellowship (China Inland Mission); Scripture Union; Shanghai, China)

%%%%%%%%%%%%%%

CN# SC31
**Evangelical Alliance Mission, The (TEAM)    1890-**
Handbook    1962

Handbook for missionaries and candidates designed to orient them
to the mission's goals, methods, and expectations. This manual
describes in great detail the various regulations and forms of
TEAM. The last section of the manual deals with specifics of visas,
baggage preparation, financial plans, and outfits for the fields
which TEAM was serving at the time such as Tibet, India, France,
Japan, Korea, the Near East, the Netherlands, Portugal, South
Africa, Swaziland, Southern Rhodesia, Taiwan, Venezuela, Colombia, New Guinea. Also in this folder is a brochure on the Mission's
Medical Aid Fund and a letter from TEAM's executive assistant
director to the executive director of the Interdenominational
Foreign Mission Association describing TEAM procedures for
reviewing candidates for mission fields.

(MAJOR TOPICS: Evangelical Alliance Mission, The (TEAM);
Missionaries--Recruitment and training)

%%%%%%%%%%%%%%

CN# 165
**Evangelical Foreign Mission Association    1945-**
Records; 1944-1978; n.d.

Files of the executive secretary of the EFMA, an association of
denominational and non-denominational foreign mission boards
created to serve common interests of members in government
relations (domestic and foreign), use of communication channels
including radio and film, cooperative purchasing/travel, and
relations between missions. Files are divided into five parts: correspondence and general files; the Five Missionary Martyrs Fund(a
trust fund set up for the families of missionaries murdered in
Ecuador in 1956); Latin American survey; miscellaneous; and
publications. The EFMA was affiliated with the National Association of Evangelicals.

Vol: 19 boxes, 14 Audio Tapes, Oversize Material, Photographs

(MAJOR TOPICS: Africa Inland Mission (AIM); American Council
of Christian Churches (ACCC); American Sunday School Union;
Angola; Argentina; Armerding, Hudson Taylor; Armstrong, Benjamin
Leighton; Armstrong, Herbert W; Armstrong, Philip E; Assemblies of

God; Assemblies of God--Missions; Association of Evangelicals of
Africa and Madagascar (AEAM); Auca Missionary Foundation; Auca
people, Ecuador; Bangladesh; Baptists; Bertermann, Eugene R;
Bolivia; Bolten, John; Bowman, Robert H; Brazil; Brethren; Breth-
ren--Missions; Broadcasting station: HCJB, Ecuador; Buker, Raymond
Bates Jr; Bulgaria; Burma; Cameroon; Caribbean; Catholic Church;
Catholic Church in Honduras; Catholic Church in Italy; Catholic
Church in United States; Catholic Church--Missions; Catholic
Church--Relations; Central African Republic; Chad; Charismatic
movement; Child Evangelism Fellowship; Chile; Christian educa-
tion--Honduras; Christian leadership; Christian literature--Publication
and distribution; Christian Reformed Church--Missions; Church and
state in Central African Republic; Church and state in Kenya; Church
and state in United States; Church and state in Zaire; Church growth;
Church of Christ in the Congo; Climenhaga, Arthur M; Coggins,
Wade Thomas; Colombia; Committee to Assist Ministry Education
Overseas (CAMEO); Communism; Congresses and conferences--Con-
gress on the Church's Worldwide Mission, 1966; Congresses and
conferences--Explo '72; Congresses and conferences--Urbana
Missionary Conventions; Congregational churches--Missions; Conser-
vative Baptist Foreign Mission Society; Cuba; Dain, Arthur John;
Dayton, Edward Risedorph; Dominican Republic; Ecuador; Ecumen-
ical movement; Edman, Victor Raymond; Education--Angola; Educa-
tion--Kenya; Eisenhower, Dwight David; El Salvador; Elliot, Elisabeth
Howard; Elliot, Philip James; Engstrom, Theodore "Ted" Wilhelm;
Ethiopia; Evangelical Alliance Mission, The (TEAM); Evangelical
Literature Overseas; Evangelicalism; Evangelistic work--Brazil; Evan-
gelistic work--Central African Republic; Evangelistic work--Korea;
Evangelistic work--Paraguay; Evangelistic work--South Africa; Evan-
gelistic work--Taiwan; Evangelistic work--Uganda; Evangelistic work---
Zaire; Far East Broadcasting Company; Federal Communications
Commission; Ford, Gerald Rudolph; Ford, Leighton Frederick Sandys;
France; Frizen, Edwin Leonard Jr; Fuller Theological Seminary, CA;
Gerber, Vergil Glenn; Gospel Recordings, Inc; Graham, William
Franklin "Billy"; Great Commission (Bible); Greece; Guatemala;
Guyana; Haiti; Hatfield, Mark Odom; Hay, Ian M; Henry, Carl
Ferdinand Howard; Hoke, Donald Edwin; Honduras; Hong Kong;
Humbard, Rex; India; Indians of North America; Indonesia; Inter-
cultural communications; Interdenominational Foreign Mission As-
sociation (IFMA); International Christian Broadcasters; International
Council of Christian Churches; International Missionary Council; Iran
(Persia); Islam (theology); Islam--Relations--Christianity; Israel; Italy;
Ivory Coast; Japan; Jews in United States; Jones, Clarence Wesley;
Jones, Robert R Jr "Bob"; Jones, Robert R Sr "Bob"; Kenya; Kim,
Billy (Jang Hwan); Korea; Korean War; Langford, Sidney; Lebanon;
Legislators--United States; Liberia; Malaysia; McArthur, Douglas;
McCully, Theodore Edward, Jr; McGavran, Donald Anderson; McIn-

tire, Carl Curtis; Medical care--Kenya; Methodists; Mexico; Mission
Aviation Fellowship (MAF); Missionaries--Recruitment and training;
Missions Advanced Research and Communications Center (MARC);
Missions to Jews; Missions to Muslims; Missions, Medical; Mis-
sions--Argentina; Missions--Bangladesh; Missions--Bolivia; Mis-
sions--Brazil; Missions--Bulgaria; Missions--Chile; Missions--China;
Missions--Colombia; Missions--Costa Rica; Missions--Cuba; Mis-
sions--Dominican Republic; Missions--Ecuador; Missions--Educational
work; Missions--El Salvador; Missions--Ethiopia; Missions--France;
Missions--French Guiana; Missions--Greece; Missions--Guatemala;
Missions--Haiti; Missions--Honduras; Missions--India; Mis-
sions--Indonesia; Missions--Interdenominational cooperation; Mis-
sions--Iran; Missions--Italy; Missions--Ivory Coast; Missions--Japan;
Missions--Kenya; Missions--Korea; Missions--Mexico; Mis-
sions--Nigeria; Missions--Pakistan; Missions--Panama; Mis-
sions--Paraguay; Missions--Peru; Missions--Philippines; Mis-
sions--Puerto Rico; Missions--Singapore; Missions--Sri Lanka; Mis-
sions--Taiwan; Missions--Uganda; Missions--Uruguay; Mis-
sions--Venezuela; Missions--Zaire; Mormons and Mormonism; Muslims in Bangladesh; Muslims in Nigeria; Muslims in Senegal; Muslims
in Sierra Leone; Muslims in Turkey; Muslims in United States; Nairobi, Kenya; National Association of Evangelicals; National Council of
Churches; National Religious Broadcasters; Navigators; Nicaragua;
Nigeria; Nixon, Richard Milhous; O C Ministries; Occult sciences;
OMS International, Inc; Organizational change; Pakistan; Panama;
Paraguay; Paris, France; Paul VI (Pope); Pentecostal Church--Mis-
sions; Peru; Philippines; Pierce, Robert Willard "Bob"; Presbyterian
Church--Missions; Presbyterians; Presidents--United States; Puerto
Rico; Radio in missionary work; Radio in religion; Ridderhof, Joy
Fanny; Saint, Nathanael "Nate"; Sanny, Lorne Charles; SEND Interna-
tional; Senegal; Sex role; Shinto; Short Terms Abroad; Sierra Leone;
Singapore; Smith, Oswald Jeffrey; South Africa; Sri Lanka (Ceylon);
Sudan Interior Mission (SIM); Sunday schools; Taiwan; Taylor, Clyde
Willis; Taylor, Kenneth Nathaniel; ten Boom, Cornelia Arnolda
Johanna; Thailand; Truman, Harry S; Turkey; Uganda; United Breth-
ren in Christ; United Brethren in Christ--Missions; Uruguay; Van Der
Puy, Abraham Cornelius; Van Kampen, Robert Cornelius; Vangioni,
Fernando V; Vatican City; Vaus, James Arthur; Venezuela; Vietnam;
Wesleyan Methodist Church--Missions; Wheaton College, IL; Wilson,
George McConnell; Wilson, Grady Baxter; Winter, Ralph D; Woods,
C Stacey; World Council of Churches; World Evangelical Fellowship
(WEF); World Radio Missionary Fellowship; World Vision Inter-
national; Youderain, Roger; Youth for Christ International; Zaire;
Zimbabwe)

%%%%%%%%%%%%

CN# 218
**Evangelical Missions Information Service    1964-**
Records; 1964-1981

Office files covering the activities of EMIS, the publications arm of
both the Evangelical Foreign Missions Association and the Interdenominational Foreign Missions Association. EMIS responsibilities included publication of several mission periodicals, organization of missionary conferences and workshops, and, for a very
brief period, arrangement of charter flights for overseas Christian
workers.

Vol: 8 boxes, Photographs

(MAJOR TOPICS: Africa Inland Mission (AIM); African Americans;
Agape Movement; Ambassadors for Christ; Andes Evangelical Mis-
sion; Assemblies of God--Missions; Association of Evangelicals of
Africa and Madagascar (AEAM); Baptists; Belgium; Bolivia; Brazil;
Brethren; Brethren Church--Missions; Buddhism (theology); Burma;
Canada; Catholic Church; CAM International; Catholic Church in
United States; Charismatic movement; Christian Anti-Communism
Crusade; Christian education (theory); Christian educa-
tion--Philippines; Church and social problems; Church and state in
Kenya; Church development, New; Church growth; Colombia; Com-
munication; Communism; Congresses and conferences--Congress on
the Church's Worldwide Mission, 1966; Congresses and conferences---
World Congress on Evangelism, 1966; Conservative Baptist Foreign
Mission Society; Conservative Baptist Home Mission Society; Cuba;
Dain, Arthur John; Egypt General Mission; Evangelical Alliance
Mission, The (TEAM); Evangelical Foreign Missions Association;
Evangelical Literature Overseas; Evangelistic work--Belgium; Evan-
gelistic work--Brazil; Evangelistic work--Chile; Evangelistic work---
Great Britain; Evangelistic work--Korea; Evangelistic work--Mexico;
Evangelistic work--Nigeria; Evangelistic work--Poland; Evangelistic
work--Taiwan; Evangeliums Rundfunk; Gerber, Vergil Glenn; Ger-
many; Graham, William Franklin "Billy"; Great Britain; Greater
Europe Mission (GEM); Honduras; Independent churches; India;
Indigenous church administration; Indonesia; Inter-Varsity Christian
Fellowship; Intercultural communications; Interdenominational For-
eign Mission Association (IFMA); International Fellowship of Evan-
gelical Students; International relief; Islam (theology); Islam--Rela-
tions--Christianity; Italy; Japan; Kenya; Korea; Language: Spanish;
Latin America Mission; Liberation Theology; Malaysia; McGavran,
Donald Anderson; McIntire, Carl Curtis; Mass Media in Religion;
Medical care--Kenya; Mennonite Church--Missions; Mexico; Mission

Aviation Fellowship (MAF); Missionary Church--Missions; Missions to Muslims; Missions, Medical; Missions--Belgium; Missions--Bolivia; Missions--Brazil; Missions--Canada; Missions--Caribbean; Missions---Chile; Missions--Finance; Missions--France; Missions--Germany; Missions--Honduras; Missions--India; Missions--Indonesia; Missions--Interdenominational cooperation; Missions--Kenya; Missions--Malaysia; Missions--Mexico; Missions--Nicaragua; Missions--Peru; Missions---Philippines; Missions--Taiwan; Nairobi, Kenya; New Jersey; Nicaragua; Nigeria; O C Ministries; OMS International, Inc; Orthodox Presbyterian Church; Padilla, Carlos Rene; Pentecostals; Philippines; Poland; Presbyterian Church--Missions; Presbyterians; Radio in missionary work; Roberts, Granville Oral; SEND International; Short Terms Abroad; Singapore; Sudan Interior Mission (SIM); Taiwan; Trans World Radio; Troutman, Charles H Jr; Unevangelized Fields Mission; Uruguay; Wagner, Charles Peter; Westminster Seminary, Philadelphia, PA; World Evangelical Fellowship (WEF); World Radio Missionary Fellowship; World Vision International; Youth for Christ International)

%%%%%%%%%%%%

CN# 243
**Evangelical Theological Society; 1949-**
Records; 1949-1982; n.d.

Correspondence, minutes of meetings, reports, financial records, annual and regional meeting brochures, membership records, directories, selected copies of publications, files on associated groups such as the American Scientific Affiliation, abstracts, reprints of papers delivered at meetings, audio tapes, photographs. Documents relate to the formation, purpose and development of the Society.

Vol: 10 boxes, 32 Audio Tapes, Oversize Materials, Photographs

(MAJOR TOPICS: American Scientific Affiliation; Baptists; Belief and doubt; Bible as literature; Bible--Criticism, interpretation, etc; Bible--Inspiration; Catholic Church; Catholic Church in United States; Congresses and conferences--World Congress on Evangelism, 1966; Evangelical Theological Society; Evangelicalism; Evangelistic work---United States; Fundamentalism; Grounds, Vernon Carl; Henry, Carl Ferdinand Howard; Homosexuality; Japan; Judaism; Kantzer, Kenneth Sealer; Lindsell, Harold; Montgomery, John Warwick; Religion and science; Smith, Wilbur Moorehead; Tenney, Merrill Chapin; Walvoord, John Flipse; Wesley, John)

%%%%%%%%%%%%

CN# 37
**Evangelicals for Social Action; 1973-**
Records; 1965-1976

Correspondence, memoranda, budgets, notes, minutes, clippings, press releases, and other records relating to the antecedents of ESA such as the Consultation on Christian Unity (1965) and Evangelicals for McGovern (1972) and to the four workshops held by ESA between 1973 and 1976. There are an especially large number of files for the initial workshop held in 1973 which issued a document known as the Chicago Declaration.

Vol: 4 boxes

(MAJOR TOPICS: Chicago Declaration; Chicago, IL; Christianity and economics; Church and social problems; Church and state in United States; Church--biblical teaching; Civil rights movement; Congresses and conferences--US Congress on Evangelism, 1969; Congresses and conferences--World Congress on Evangelism, 1966; Evangelical Women's Caucus; Evangelicalism; Evangelicals for McGovern; Evangelicals for Social Action; Jones, Rufus; National Council of Churches; Organizational change; Pierard, Richard V; Sermons, American; Sider, Ronald; Social change; Theology; Women clergy; Women--Religious life)

%%%%%%%%%%%%

CN# 279
**Evans, Elizabeth; 1899-1989**
Interviews; 1984-1985

Series of oral history interviews with Evans in which she discusses her childhood; education at Wheaton College; work with J. Elwin Wright; her Christian education activities; the origins and development of the New England Fellowship, the National Association of Evangelicals, and the World Evangelical Fellowship; and her work as a missionary in Taiwan.

Vol: 6 Audio Tapes

(MAJOR TOPICS: American Council of Christian Churches (ACCC); Baptism; Belief and doubt; Blanchard, Charles Albert; Bob Jones University, SC; Bolten, John; Boston, MA; Buddhists in Taiwan; Buswell, James Oliver Jr; Catholic Church in United States; Catholic Church--Relations; Chaplains, Military; Children--Conversion to

Christianity; Children--Religious life; Christian education (theory); Christian education of adolescents; Christian education of adults; Christian education of boys; Christian education of children; Christian education of girls; Christian education--Taiwan; Christian education--United States; Church and social problems; Church and state in India; Church work with military personnel; Cities and towns; City missions; Congregationalists; Conversion; Courtship; Dain, Arthur John; Davis, Ralph T; Edman, Victor Raymond; Emery, Allan C Sr; Evangelical Fellowship of India; Evangelicalism; Evangelistic work---Great Britain; Evangelistic work--Taiwan; Evangelistic work--United States; Evans, Elizabeth Hicks Morrell; Evans, Kathryn Morrell; Evolution; Florida; Fuller, Charles Edward Sr; Fund raising; Fundamentalism; Funeral rites and ceremonies; Glover, Robert Hall; Graham, William Franklin "Billy"; Great Britain; Hillis, Charles Richard "Dick"; India; Indigenous church administration; Intercultural communications; International relief; Ironside, Henry Allan "Harry"; Jones, Robert R Jr "Bob"; Jones, Robert R Sr "Bob"; Language: Chinese; Letourneau, Robert Gilmore; Mass media in religion; Massachusetts; McIntire, Carl Curtis; Missionaries--Recruitment and training; Missions to Buddhists; Missions--India; Missions--Taiwan; Modernist-Fundamentalist controversy; Moving-pictures in church work; National Association of Evangelicals; National Council of Churches; New England Fellowship (NEF); New Hampshire; Nyack Missionary Institute, NY; Ockenga, Harold John; Orphans and orphan-asylums; Park Street Church, Boston MA; Pentecostals; Pierce, Robert Willard "Bob"; Preaching; Presbyterian Church--Missions; Presbyterians; Rader, Daniel Paul; Radio in religion; Rice, John Richard; Riley, William Bell; Rimmer, Harry; Romania; Schaeffer, Edith; Schaeffer, Francis August; Sex role; Simpson, Albert Benjamin; Smyth, Walter Herbert; Sunday, William Ashley "Billy"; Taiwan; Taoism; Taylor, Clyde Willis; Taylor, Herbert John; Tenney, Helen Jaderquist; Vereide, Abraham; Wheaton College, IL; Women--Religious life; Women in missionary work; World Evangelical Fellowship (WEF); World War II; Wright, James Elwin; Wyrtzen, John Von Casper "Jack") %%%%%%%%%%%%

CN# 59
**Far East Broadcasting Company, Inc.    1945-**
Records; 1947-1979    n.d.

Files of FEBC, a nondenominational agency specializing in radio broadcasting and correspondence courses.  Documents include reports of the Director's Conference, president's correspondence and feasibility studies, literature and publications, broadcast policies, promotional brochures, program schedules, program sponsorship information, a Russian Micro New Testament, plus miscellaneous items.

Vol: 1 box, Photographs

(MAJOR TOPICS: Communication; Evangelistic work--Soviet Union; Far East Broadcasting Company; Missions--Europe)

%%%%%%%%%%%%%%

CN# 302
**Farah, David Livingstone; 1930-**
Interview; 1985

Two interviews with Farah, in which he discusses his upbringing, education at Wheaton College, work as an administrator with Wycliffe Bible Translators in Peru and Bolivia, and relationships with other religious bodies, national groups and governments.

Vol: 3 Audio Tapes

(MAJOR TOPICS:  Animism; Bible--Publication and distribution; Bible--Translating; Billy Graham Evangelistic Association (BGEA); Bolivia; Catholic Church; Catholic Church in Bolivia; Catholic Church in South America; Catholic Church--Relations; Chicago, IL; Christian and Missionary Alliance (CMA); Christian education--United States; Christian martyrs; Church and state in Bolivia; Church and state in United States; Church work with children; Church work with students; Cities and towns;  City missions; College students in missionary work; College students--Religious life; Communism; Conversion; Cults; Dodds, Gilbert I; Edman, Victor Raymond; Education, higher; Education--United States; Egypt; Evangelistic work--Bolivia; Evangelistic work--United States; Family; Farah, David Livingstone; Fund raising; Graham, William Franklin "Billy"; Illinois; Indians of South America; Inter-Varsity Christian Fellowship; Intercultural communications; Kantzer, Kenneth Sealer; Korean War; Language in missionary work; Lutherans; Marriage; Mass media in missionary work; Mass media in religion; Massachusetts; Mexico; Missionaries--Leaves and furloughs; Missionaries--Recruitment and training; Missions--Bolivia; Missions---Finance; Missions--Peru; Mormons and Mormonism; Nyack Missionary Institute, NY; Palau, Luis (Rev); Pentecostalism--Bolivia; Pentecostals; Peru; Prayer breakfasts; Revivals; Simpson, Albert Benjamin; Soviet Union--Foreign relations--United States; Sudan Interior Mission (SIM); Sunday schools; Syria; Television in religion; Townsend, William Cameron; Unification Church; Vangioni, Fernando V; Wheaton College, IL; Wheaton Revival, 1950; World Home Bible League; World War II; World Wide Pictures; Wycliffe Bible Translators)

%%%%%%%%%%%%%

CN# 202
**Feiner, Berea St John; 1909-**
Papers; 1834-1979; n.d.

Varied collection of mission-related items documenting work in
China, India, and Nigeria ca. 1890-1940; prison evangelism.

Vol: 1 box, Photographs

(MAJOR TOPICS: American Baptist Foreign Mission Society; Bap-
tists; Baptists--Missions; Bingham, Rowland Victor; California; China;
Church and social problems; Colorado; Courtship; Evangelistic work---
Nigeria; Evangelistic work--United States; Feiner, Berea St John;
Gideons International; India; Kane, J Herbert; Los Angeles, CA;
Missions--China; Missions--India; Missions--Nigeria; Navajo Indians;
New York (state); Nigeria; Overseas Missionary Fellowship (China
Inland Mission); Prisoners--United States; Prisons--Missions and
charities; Sudan Interior Mission (SIM); Taylor, James Hudson;
Trotman, Dawson; Wang, Josephine Aurora Kimball)

%%%%%%%%%%%%%

CN# SC109
**Feinberg, Charles Lee; 1909-**
Ephemera; n.d.

Transcripts of thirty-one messages on the book of Revelation given
over the radio by Charles L. Feinberg.

(MAJOR TOPICS: Feinberg, Charles Lee; Mass media in religion;
Radio in religion; Sermons, American)

%%%%%%%%%%%%%

CN# 143
**Finney, Charles Grandison; 1792-1875**
Papers; 1824-1887; n.d.

Purchased microfilm edition of originals in Oberlin College Library plus two letters relating to Finney, perhaps the most influential evangelist in the ante-bellum United States.  The microfilm
includes Finney's incoming correspondence, sermon outlines
1853-75, lecture outlines, and articles.  Calendar and index to the

documents is on reel one. The collection also contains a file of contemporary letters about Finney.

Vol: 9 Reels of Microfilm, 1 folder

(MAJOR TOPICS: Church and social problems; Evangelistic work--- United States; Finney, Charles Grandison)

%%%%%%%%%%%%

CN# 272
**Fitzwilliam, Jennie Kingston; 1903-**
Papers; 1926-1985; n.d.

Letters with some translation, photographs, a Lisu translation of the New Testament, combined catechism and hymnbook in the Atsi Kachin language, and four oral history interviews recorded in 1984, all related to Fitzwilliam's mission work with Overseas Missionary Fellowship (formerly China Inland Mission) among the Lisu and Kachin peoples in southern China along the Burmese border. Included are recollections of Fitzwilliam's husband, Francis, J. O. Fraser and the early history of missionary work among the Lisu, the life of the Lisu church and its indigenous administrative practices, the development of mission work among the Kachin, and internment by the Japanese.

Vol: 1 box, 5 audio tapes, photographs, slides

(MAJOR TOPICS: Advent Christian Church; Animism; Bible colleges; Bible--Translating; Burma; Chefoo Schools; Chicago, IL; Children of missionaries; China; Christian education of adults; Christian education--China; Christmas; Conversion; Death; Evangelistic work--- China; Fitzwilliam, Jennie Eliza Kingston; Footbinding; Fraser, James Outram; Gray, James Martin; Houghton, Frank (Bishop); Indigenous church administration; Intercultural communications; Kachins (Asian people); Kuhn, Isobel Miller; Language in missionary work; Language: Chinese; Liddell, Eric Henry; Lisu people, Tibet; Massachusetts; Missionaries, Lay; Missionaries, Withdrawal of; Missionaries--Recruitment and training; Missions--China; Missions--Rural work; Moody Bible Institute, IL; Overseas Missionary Fellowship (China Inland Mission); Philadelphia School of the Bible, PA; Religion and music; Rural churches--China; Sex role; Shanghai, China; Wheaton College, IL; Women in missionary work; Women--Religious life; World War II)

%%%%%%%%%%%%

CN# 122
**Fleckles, Gladys Marie; 1946-**
Interview; 1980

Interview with Fleckles in which she talks about her short term
mission experience with Overseas Missionary Fellowship in Japan.
Other topics include her graduate work at Wheaton, undergrad-
uate study at John Brown University, and work in the admissions
department of Wheaton Graduate School.

Vol: 2 Audio Tapes

(MAJOR TOPICS: Arkansas; Chicago, IL; Education--Japan; Evangelistic work--Japan; Fleckles, Gladys Marie; Illinois; Japan; John
Brown University, AR; Korea; Medical care--Japan; Missionaries, Lay;
Missionaries--Recruitment and training; Missions, Medical; Mis-
sions--Educational work; Missions--Japan; Overseas Missionary Fellowship (China Inland Mission); Soviet Union; Tokyo, Japan; Wheaton
College, IL; Women--Religious life; Women in missionary work)

%%%%%%%%%%%%

CN# 374
**Fletcher, Artis Edward; 1944-**
Interview; 1987

Oral history interview in which Fletcher talks about his childhood,
education, and work as pastor of the Mendenhall Bible Church.
Also discussed are John Perkins, Voice of Calvary Ministries, the
black church in the United States, and racial conditions in Mississippi.

Volume: 2 Audio Tapes

(MAJOR TOPICS:  African Americans; Children--Conversion to
Christianity; Church and social problems; Clergy, Training of; Conver-
sion; Crime and criminals; Evangelistic work (Christian theology);
Evangelistic work--United States; Fletcher, Artis Edward; Ku Klux
Klan; Mendenhall Ministries, The (TMM); Mississippi; Perkins, John
M; Prayer; Race relations; Racism; Sunday schools; Voice of Calvary
Ministries; Weary, Dolphus)

%%%%%%%%%%%%

CN# SC19
**Florida Bible Institute**
Lecture Notes; 1935-1938; n.d.

Notebook belonging to Billy Graham containing mimeographed notes on theological lectures.

(MAJOR TOPICS: Graham, William Franklin "Billy"; Trinity Bible College (Florida Bible Institute), FL; Preaching)

%%%%%%%%%%%%

CN# 292
**Fox, Silas Fowler; 1893-?**
Papers; 1949-1973; n.d.

Diaries, correspondence, photographs, films, and other documents that relate to Fox's career in the Telugu-speaking area of India as an independent missionary. The collection also has information on indigenous Indian evangelists.

Vol: 2 boxes, 5 Films, Photographs

(MAJOR TOPICS: Baptism; Bombay, India; Buddhists in India; Charismatic movement; Evangelistic work--India; Fox, Silas Fowler; Idols and images; India; Marriage; Mass media in religion; Medical care--India; Missions to Buddhists; Missions, Medical; Missions--India; Radio in religion; Worship)

%%%%%%%%%%%%

CN# 255
**Frame, Helen Nowack; 1908-**
Interviews; 1983

Two interviews with Frame, in which she discusses her childhood in China, decision to become a missionary for Overseas Missionary Fellowship, years in China, departure in 1951 with her husband and children, resettlement in the Philippines, work as a teacher at Faith Academy and return to the United States.

Vol: 3 Audio Tapes

(MAJOR TOPICS: Adolph, Paul Earnest; Anderson, Helen Mount; Anderson, Ian Rankin; Bible colleges; Bible--Translating; Boxers

(Chinese political movement); Buddhists in China; Buswell, James Oliver Jr; Catholic Church in China; Charismatic movement; Chiang Kai-Shek; Children of missionaries; China; Christian education--China; College students--Religious life; Demonology; Education--Philippines; Education--Zambia; Elliott, Eleanor Ruth; Evangelistic work--China; Faith Academy, Philippines; Faith--Cure; Frame, Helen Grace Nowack; Frame, Raymond William; Glossolalia; Graham, William Franklin "Billy"; Hong Kong; Houghton, Frank; Intercultural communications; Interdenominational cooperation; Japan; Language in missionary work; Language: Chinese; Manila, Philippines; Mao Tse-tung; Missionaries, Withdrawal of; Missionaries--Leaves and furloughs; Missions to Buddhists; Missions, British; Missions--China; Missions--Philippines; Moody Bible Institute, IL; Overseas Missionary Fellowship (China Inland Mission); Philippines; Shanghai, China; Stam, Elizabeth Alden Scott; Stam, John Cornelius; War; Wheaton College, IL; Wycliffe Bible Translators)

%%%%%%%%%%%%

CN# 87
**Franson, Fredrik C; 1852-1908**
Papers; 1872-1909

Microfilm of xeroxed material collected by Rev. Edward P. Torjesen on the life and ministry of nineteenth century missionary and evangelist Fredrik Franson. Materials include articles written by or about Franson in several languages. Documents are arranged chronologically by date in folders as received.

Vol: 2 Reels of Microfilm

(MAJOR TOPICS: Australia; Beijing, China; Brazil; Bulgaria; Chicago, IL; China; Colorado; Egypt; Evangelical Alliance Mission, The (TEAM); Evangelistic work--Australia; Evangelistic work--France; Evangelistic work--Germany; Evangelistic work--Great Britain; Evangelistic work--Japan; Evangelistic work--New Zealand; Evangelistic work--South Africa; Evangelistic work--Sweden; Evangelistic work---United States; Finland; France; Franson, Fredrik; Germany; Great Britain; Greece; Illinois; India; Iowa; Iran; Ireland; Japan; Korea; London, England; Minneapolis, MN; Mormons and Mormonism; Nebraska; New York (state); New Zealand; Norway; Overseas Missionary Fellowship (China Inland Mission); Panama; Shanghai, China; Simpson, Albert Benjamin; South Africa; Soviet Union; Spain; Sweden; Switzerland; Sydney, Australia; Syria; Taylor, James Hudson; Utah)

%%%%%%%%%%%%

CN# 327
**Frederick, James K; ?-?**
Interview; 1947

Interview of Frederick, made at Green Lake, WI, during the fourth
International Workshop in Audio-Visual Education, 1947, conducted by a Mr. Kearney in which Frederick discusses his career
as a pastor specializing in production of Christian films to be used
in churches, particularly for children. Included is a discussion of
his reasons for choice of actors, use of Walt Disney Studios, and
measuring the effectiveness of a film ministry.

Vol: 1 Audio Tape

(MAJOR TOPICS:  California; Cathedral Films; Children--Religious
life; Christian education of children; Christian education--United
States; Church work with children; Communication; Disney, Walter;
Frederick, James K; Interdenominational cooperation; Lutherans;
Mass media in religion; Moving-pictures in church work; Sunday
schools)

%%%%%%%%%%%%

CN# 382
**Freed, Paul Ernest; 1918-**
Interview; 1981

Interview with Paul Freed about how he founded Trans World
Radio in 1952, the history of the development of its administrative
policies and work from that time to 1981, and about the use of
radio in missionary work. Freed also discusses his childhood as
the son of Christian and Missionary Alliance workers in Syria, his
schooling in Jerusalem and at Wheaton College, and his work with
Youth For Christ in Spain and elsewhere.

Volume: 1 Audio Tape

(MAJOR TOPICS:  Armerding, Hudson Taylor; Broadcasting station:
ELWA, Liberia; Broadcasting station: HCJB, Ecuador; Children of
missionaries; China; Christian and Missionary Alliance (CMA); Cy-
prus; Egypt; Evans, Robert Philip; Ford, Gerald Rudolph; Freed, Paul
Ernest; Fund raising; Graham, William Franklin "Billy"; India;
Indonesia; Iran; Israel; Jerusalem, Israel; Johnson, Torrey Maynard;
Language in missionary work; Language: Arabic; Language: French;
Language: German; Language: Spanish; Mass media in religion;

Missionaries--Leaves and furloughs; Missionaries--Recruitment and
training; Missions--China; Missions--Cyprus; Missions--Egypt; Missions--India; Missions--Indonesia; Missions--Iran; Missions--Morocco;
Missions--Saudi Arabia; Missions--Spain; Missions--Sri Lanka; Missions--Swaziland; Missions--Syria; Monte Carlo; Morocco; North
Carolina; Nyack Missionary Institute, NY; Presidents--United States;
Radio in missionary work; Radio in religion; Saudi Arabia; Smith,
Oswald Jeffrey; South Carolina; Spain; Sri Lanka; Swaziland; Syria;
Taylor, Kenneth Nathaniel; Trans World Radio; Truman, Harry S;
Wheaton College, IL; Youth for Christ International)

%%%%%%%%%%%%%

CN# 100
**Fuller, Charles Edward; 1887-1966**
Ephemera; 1949-1968

Newspaper clippings, sermons, radio logs, form letters to supporters, publicity materials from Fuller's *Old Fashioned Revival
Hour* radio program, several audio tapes of the program. Fuller
was one of the first evangelists to use the radio and the founder of
Fuller Seminary in California.

Vol: 1 box, 50 Audio Tapes, Phonograph Records

(MAJOR TOPICS: California; Communication; Evangelicalism;
Evangelistic work--United States; Fuller Theological Seminary, CA;
Fuller, Charles Edward Sr; Fuller, Daniel Payton; Mass media in
religion; Radio in religion; Radio Program: *Old Fashioned Revival
Hour*; Religion and music; Sermons, American)

%%%%%%%%%%%%%

CN# 88
**Gieser, Paul Kenneth (1908-1987) and M Catharine Kirk (1910-
1981)**
Papers; 1934 (1934-1940) 1978; n.d.

Oral history interview, letters to Southern Presbyterian Mission
Board and other materials mostly dealing with the Giesers' work
as medical missionaries in China before World War II.

Vol: 1 box, 3 Audio Tapes

(MAJOR TOPICS: Bell, Lemuel Nelson; Buswell, James Oliver Jr;
China; Gieser, M Catharine Kirk; Gieser, Paul Kenneth; Hockman,
Robert William; Hospitals--China; Hospitals--United States; Japan;

Korea; Medical care--China; Medical care--United States; Missionaries--Recruitment and training; Missions, Medical; Missions--China; Presbyterian Church in the United States (Southern); Presbyterian Church--Missions; Presbyterians; Sino-Japanese Conflict, 1937-1945; Stam, Elizabeth Alden Scott; Stam, John Cornelius; Walvoord, John Flipse; Wheaton College, IL; Women--Religious life; Women in missionary work; World War II)

%%%%%%%%%%%%

CN# 188
**Goforth, Jonathan (1859-1936) and Rosalind Bell-Smith (1864-1942)**
Papers; 1888-1981; n.d.

Journals, correspondence, sermon notes, book manuscripts, and other records of the Goforths, who served in the Chinese provinces of Honan and Manchuria as missionaries for the Presbyterian Church in Canada. There is a great deal of information about Jonathan's evangelistic work throughout China and Korea; the modernist-Fundamentalist split; Rosalind's career as an author; and early twentieth century Chinese society.

Vol: 3 boxes, Oversize Materials, Photographs, Slides

(MAJOR TOPICS: Boxers (Chinese political movement); Canada; Catholic Church; Catholic Church--Missions; Children of missionaries; China; Christian leadership; Church and social problems; Communism; Congresses and conferences--World Missionary Conference, 1910; Evangelistic work--Korea; Family; Feng Yu-hsiang; Finney, Charles Grandison; Fundamentalism; Goforth, Jonathan; Goforth, Rosalind; Hunger; Japan; Keswick Movement; Korea; Kuo min tang (China); Marriage; McQuilkin, Robert Crawford; Missionaries, Resignation of; Missionaries--Canada; Missions--China; Modernist-Fundamentalist controversy; Morrison, Robert; Moynan, Mary Goforth; Overseas Missionary Fellowship (China Inland Mission); Parenthood; Poverty; Prayer; Presbyterian Church in Canada; Presbyterian Church--Missions; Presbyterians; Rader, Daniel Paul; Revivals; Sermons, American; Sex role; Shanghai, China; Smith, Oswald Jeffrey; Stam, Elizabeth Alden Scott; Stam, John Cornelius; Taylor, James Hudson; United Church of Canada; Women--Religious life; Women in missionary work; Wu Pei Fu)

%%%%%%%%%%%%

CN# 36
**Gospel Recordings, Inc.; 1938-**
Records; 1939-1978; n.d.

Correspondence, tapes and manuals dealing with GR's work of
presenting the gospel via recordings in all languages and dialects
of the world.  Also includes unprocessed language tapes.

Vol: 42 boxes, 2504 Audio Tapes, Phonograph Records, Photographs

(MAJOR TOPICS: Alaska; Algeria; American Bible Society; Angola;
Argentina; Australia; Austria; Bangladesh; Belgium; Bible--Translat-
ing; Bolivia; Brazil; Burma; California; Cambodia; Cameroon; Canada;
Canary Islands; Central African Republic; Chad; Chile; China; Colom-
bia; Communication; Costa Rica; Cuba; Cyprus; Czechoslovakia;
Denmark; Ecuador; Egypt; Ethiopia; Evangelical Foreign Missions
Association; Evangelical Literature Overseas; Evangelical Missions
Information Service; Evangelistic work--Argentina; Evangelistic
work--Australia; Evangelistic work--Belgium; Evangelistic work--Brazil;
Evangelistic work--Canary Islands; Evangelistic work--France; Evan-
gelistic work--Germany; Evangelistic work--Israel; Evangelistic work---
Japan; Evangelistic work--Korea; Evangelistic work--Mexico; Evan-
gelistic work--New Zealand; Evangelistic work--Nigeria; Evangelistic
work--Paraguay; Evangelistic work--Poland; Evangelistic work--South
Africa; Evangelistic work--Soviet Union; Evangelistic work--Sudan;
Evangelistic work--Taiwan; Evangelistic work--Tibet; Evangelistic
work--United States; Evangelistic work--Uruguay; Evangelistic work---
Vietnam; Evangelistic work--Yugoslavia; Evangelistic work--Zaire;
Finland; France; Gabon; Gambia; Germany; Ghana; Gospel Record-
ings, Inc; Great Britain; Great Britain--Colonies--Kenya; Greece;
Grenada; Guatemala; Guyana; Haiti; Hawaii; Honduras; Hong Kong;
India; Indians of North America; Indians of South America; Indonesia;
Iran; Iraq; Ireland; Israel; Italy; Ivory Coast; Japan; Jordan; Kenya;
Korea; Kuwait; Language in missionary work; Language: Afrikaans;
Language: Amharic; Language: Arabic; Language: Burmese; Lan-
guage: Cantonese; Language: Chinese; Language: English; Language:
French; Language: German; Language: Japanese; Language: Korean;
Language: Mandarin; Language: Masai; Language: Portuguese; Lan-
guage: Russian; Language: Spanish; Language: Swahili; Language:
Tagal; Language: Taiwanese; Language: Turkish; Language: Viet-
namese; Laos; Lebanon; Liberia; Los Angeles, CA; Madagascar;
Malawi; Malaysia; Mali; Masai people; Kenya; Mexico; Missions--Al-
geria; Missions--Angola; Missions--Australia; Missions--Austria;
Missions--Bangladesh; Missions--Belgium; Missions--Bolivia; Mis-

sions--Brazil; Missions--Burma; Missions--Cambodia; Missions--Cameroon; Missions--Canada; Missions--Canary Islands; Missions--Central African Republic; Missions--Chad; Missions--Chile; Missions--China; Missions--Colombia; Missions--Costa Rica; Missions--Cuba; Missions--Cyprus; Missions--Denmark; Missions--Dominican Republic; Missions--Ecuador; Missions--Egypt; Missions--Ethiopia; Missions--France; Missions--Gabon; Missions--Gambia; Missions--Germany; Missions--Ghana; Missions--Great Britain; Missions--Greece; Missions--Grenada; Missions--Guinea; Missions--Guyana; Missions---Haiti; Missions--Honduras; Missions--Hong Kong; Missions--India; Missions--Indonesia; Missions--Iran; Missions--Iraq; Missions--Ireland; Missions--Israel; Missions--Italy; Missions--Ivory Coast; Missions---Japan; Missions--Jordan; Missions--Kenya; Missions--Korea; Missions--Kuwait; Missions--Laos; Missions--Lebanon; Missions--Liberia; Missions--Madagascar; Missions--Malawi; Missions--Malaya; Missions--Malaysia; Missions--Mali; Missions--Mexico; Missions--Mongolia; Missions--Mozambique; Missions--Nepal; Missions--Netherlands; Missions--New Zealand; Missions--Nicaragua; Missions--Niger; Missions--Nigeria; Missions--Norway; Missions--Pakistan; Missions--Panama; Missions--Papua New Guinea; Missions--Paraguay; Missions--Peru; Missions--Philippines; Missions--Poland; Missions--Portugal; Missions--Puerto Rico; Missions--Saudi Arabia; Missions--Senegal; Missions--Sierra Leone; Missions--Singapore; Missions--Somalia; Missions--South Africa; Missions--Soviet Union; Missions--Spain; Missions--Sri Lanka; Missions--Sudan; Missions--Sweden; Missions--Switzerland; Missions--Syria; Missions--Tahiti; Missions--Taiwan; Missions--Tanzania; Missions--Thailand; Missions--Tibet; Missions--Togo; Missions--Trinidad; Missions--Tunisia; Missions--Turkey; Missions--Uganda; Missions--United States; Missions--Upper Volta; Missions--Uruguay; Missions--Venezuela; Missions--Vietnam; Missions--Yugoslavia; Missions--Zaire; Missions--Zambia; Missions--Zimbabwe; Monaco; Mongolia; Moody Bible Institute, IL; Moravian Church--Missions; Moravians; Morocco; Mozambique; Nepal; Netherlands; New Zealand; Nicaragua; Niger; Nigeria; Norway; Pakistan; Panama; Papua New Guinea; Paraguay; Peru; Philippines; Poland; Portugal; Radio in missionary work; Radio in religion; Romania; Saudi Arabia; Senegal; Sierra Leone; Singapore; Smith, Wilbur Moorehead; South Africa; Soviet Union; Spain; Sudan; Sweden; Switzerland; Syria; Taiwan; Tanzania; Thailand; Turkey; Uganda; United States; Upper Volta; Uruguay; Venezuela; Vietnam; Wycliffe Bible Translators)

%%%%%%%%%%%%%

CN# 74
**Graham, William Franklin "Billy"; 1918-**
Ephemera; 1863; 1949-1983; n.d.

Correspondence, form letters, tapes, films, etc., gathered from
non-Billy Graham Evangelistic Association sources which relate to
Graham's family history, his work as an evangelist, and his public
image. The collection also contains audio tapes of Crusades, tapes
of television programs about Graham, as well as information on
his television work.

Vol: 2 boxes, 25 Audio Tapes, 7 Films, 1 Microfilm, Oversize
Materials, Phonograph Records, 18 Video Tapes

(MAJOR TOPICS: African Americans; Arizona; Atlanta, GA; Austra-
lia; Baptists; Barrows, Clifford B; Beavan, Gerald "Jerry"; Billy
Graham Center, IL; Billy Graham Evangelistic Association (BGEA);
Bob Jones University, SC; Brinkley, David; Bush, George Herbert
Walker; California; Canada; Caribbean; Carter, James Earl "Jimmy";
Catholic Church in United States; Charlotte, NC; Chicago, IL; China;
Christian and Missionary Alliance (CMA); Christian and Missionary
Alliance--Missions; Christianity and economics; Church and state in
the Soviet Union; Church and state in United States; Church--biblical
teaching; Civil rights movement; Coffee, Benjamin Morrow; Columbia,
S; Congresses and conferences--Explo '72; Connecticut; Costa Rica;
Counseling; Czechoslovakia; Dewey, Thomas E; District of Columbia;
Donahue, Phil; Ecumenical movement; Edman, Victor Raymond;
Egypt; Eisenhower, Dwight David; Ethiopia; Evangelicalism; Evan-
gelistic work--Australia; Evangelistic work--Canada; Evangelistic
work--Caribbean; Evangelistic work--Denmark; Evangelistic work---
Egypt; Evangelistic work--Ghana; Evangelistic work--Guatemala;
Evangelistic work--Hungary; Evangelistic work--Japan; Evangelistic
work--Korea; Evangelistic work--Liberia; Evangelistic work--Mexico;
Evangelistic work--Netherlands; Evangelistic work--New Zealand;
Evangelistic work--Soviet Union; Evangelistic work--Switzerland;
Evangelistic work--United States; Evangelistic work--Zimbabwe;
Florida; Ford, Gerald Rudolph; Ford, Leighton Frederick Sandys;
Frost, David Paradine; Georgia; Graham, William Franklin "Billy";
Great Britain; Guatemala; Haldeman, Harry Robert; Ham, Mordecai
Fowler; Hamblen, Stuart; Harper, Redd; Harvey, Paul; Homosexuality;
Howard, David Morris; Hungary; Illinois; India; Indiana; Intercultural
communications; Ireland; Isais, Juan M; Jackson, Jesse Louis; Japan;
Jews in Soviet Union; Johnson, Lyndon Baines; Jones, Robert R III
"Bob"; Judd, Walter Henry; Kennedy, John Fitzgerald; Kennedy,
Robert Francis; King, Martin Luther; Korea; Korean War; Latin

America Mission; Letourneau, Robert Gilmore; Legislators--United States; London, England; Los Angeles, CA; Mass media in religion; Mexico; Mexico City, Mexico; Missouri; Moscow, Soviet Union; Muntz, John Palmer; National Association of Evangelicals; Nehru, Jawaharlal; New York (state); New York City, NY; New York. World's Fair, 1964-1965; New Zealand; Niebuhr, Reinhold; Nixon, Richard Milhous; North Carolina; Oregon; Organizational change; Orthodox Eastern Church; Orthodox Eastern Church--Relations; Orthodox Eastern Church--Soviet Union; Pentecostals; Periodical: *Christianity Today*; Pierce, Robert Willard "Bob"; Prayer; Presidential election, 1956; Presidential election, 1960; Presidents--United States; Race relations; Radio in religion; Radio program: *Hour of Decision*; Reagan, Ronald Wilson; Religion and music; Sermons, American; Sex role; Shea, George Beverly; Simpson, Albert Benjamin; Smyth, Walter Herbert; South Africa; South Carolina; Southern Baptist Convention; Strachan, R Kenneth; Strategic Arms Limitation Treaty II (SALT II); Television in religion; Television program: *Hour of Decision*; Tennessee; Texas; Tokyo, Japan; Toronto, ON; Tozer, A W; Trinity Bible College (Florida Bible Institute), FL; Truman, Harry S; Vaus, James Arthur; Vietnamese Conflict; Washington, DC; Watergate Affair, 1972-1974; Wheaton College, IL; Wilson, Grady Baxter; World Council of Churches; World Wide Pictures; Yale University, CT; Youth--Religious life; Zamperini, Louis Silvie)

%%%%%%%%%%%

CN# 15
**Graham, William Franklin "Billy"; 1918-**
Papers; 1938-1945

Scrapbook kept by Graham containing memorabilia from evangelistic meetings he led early in his ministry. Also kept loose between the pages are handbills, newspaper clippings, programs, etc.

Vol: 1 box

(MAJOR TOPICS: Evangelistic work--United States; Graham, William Franklin "Billy"; Trinity Bible College (Florida Bible Institute), FL; Wheaton College, IL)

%%%%%%%%%%%%

CN# SC63
**Green, Willis; ?-?**
Ephemera; 1843

Letter from a missionary to Lodiana, India, to Joshua Green,
probably his brother. The letter contains descriptions of the scen-
ery and people of India as well as comments on problems in the
church in America and India.

(MAJOR TOPICS: Evangelistic work--India; Green, Willis; India;
Missions--India; Presbyterian Church--Missions; Presbyterians)

%%%%%%%%%%%%

CN# 118
**Ham, Mordecai Fowler; 1877-1961**
Ephemera; 1934-1983; n.d.

Newspaper clippings, oral history interviews with Vernon Patterson
and Grady Wilson, and microfilm of sermon note books all relating to the career of evangelist Mordecai Ham.

Vol: 1 box, 2 Folders, 3 Audio Tapes, 4 Reels of Microfilm

(MAJOR TOPICS: African Americans; Antisemitism; Charlotte, NC;
Civil rights movement; Conversion; Evangelistic work--United States;
Fundamentalism; Graham, William Franklin "Billy"; Ham, Mordecai
Fowler; Jones, Robert R Sr "Bob"; Marriage; Patterson, Vernon
William; Periodical: *Charlotte Observer, The*; Prostitution; Ramsey,
Walter J; Revivals; Sermons, American; Smith, Oswald Jeffrey; Sun-
day, William Ashley "Billy"; Wilson, Grady Baxter; Wilson, Thomas
Walter Jr)

%%%%%%%%%%%%

CN# 117
**Hamblen, Stuart; 1908-1989**
Ephemera; n.d.

A collection of recordings of songs sung by Christian country
music singer Hamblen including several he wrote.

Vol: 1 Tape, 1 Phonograph Record

(MAJOR TOPICS: Hamblen, Stuart; Religion and music)

%%%%%%%%%%%%

CN# SC40
**Hammontree, Homer; 1884-1965**
Ephemera; 1901-1965; n.d.

Correspondence, photographs, newspaper clippings, and a report
card relating to the life and ministry of evangelist Homer Hammontree and his association with Mel Trotter and Paul Beckwith.

(MAJOR TOPICS: Evangelistic work--United States; Hammontree,
Homer; Moody Bible Institute, Chicago, IL; Trotter, Melvin Ernest)

%%%%%%%%%%%%

CN# 235
**Harper, Redd; 1903-**
Ephemera; N.d.

Six tapes of country-style gospel songs; two cassettes of songs sung
by Redd Harper, one by Joe Rogers, and two eight-track stereo
tapes by Redd Harper.

Vol: 6 Audio Tapes

(MAJOR TOPICS:  Harper, Redd; Religion and music)

%%%%%%%%%%%%

CN# 137
**Hartman, Ira Everett; 1867-1951**
Papers; 1901-1958; n.d.

Primarily sermons and sermon outlines--over 250 in all--delivered
by Hartman in evangelistic services in Iowa, Nebraska and Colorado.  The sermons also contain reflections on contemporary
issues and mores. Diaries, covering 1939-47, report national and
international news, financial ledgers reflect the Great Depression.

Vol: 2 boxes

(MAJOR TOPICS: Brethren; Church and social problems; Colorado;
Eisenhower, Dwight David; Evangelical United Brethren Church;
Evangelistic work--United States; Freemasons; Hartman, Ira Everett;
Hoover, Herbert Clark; Iowa; Lincoln, Abraham; McPherson, Aimee
Semple; Nebraska; Pearson, Drew; Presidents--United States; Racism;

Roosevelt, Franklin Delano; Sermons, American; Ship: Titanic (White Star Liner); Smith, Al; Smith, Rodney "Gipsy"; Thomas, Lowell; Townsend, Francis Everett; Truman, Harry S; Wilkie, Wendell Lewis; World War II)

%%%%%%%%%%%%

CN# 377
**Hatcher, Elias Wesley; 1924-1971**
Papers; 1941-1978; n.d.

Correspondence, audio tapes, photographs, and periodicals documenting the career of Mission Aviation Fellowship pilot Hatcher in Mexico, from 1949 to 1968, and in the United States as an administrator from 1968 until his death in 1971.

Vol: 6 boxes (DC), 2 Audio Tapes, Periodicals, Photographs

(MAJOR TOPICS: Aeronautics in missionary work; Catholic Church in Mexico; Children of missionaries; Children--Religious life; Ecuador; Funeral rites and ceremonies; Hatcher, Elias Wesley; Honduras; Indians of North America; Intercultural communications; Language: Spanish; Marriage; Mellis, Charles J, Jr; Mexico; Mexico City, Mexico; Mission Aviation Fellowship (MAF); Missionaries--Leaves and furloughs; Missions--Ecuador; Missions--Honduras; Missions--Mexico; Missions--Venezuela; Saint, Nathanael "Nate"; Truxton, James Campbell; Venezuela; Wheaton College, IL; World War II; Wycliffe Bible Translators)

%%%%%%%%%%%%

CN# 39
**Hawkes, Sarah Belknap (Belle) Sherwood; 1854-1919**
Papers; 1881-1899; n.d.

Letters, reports, and photographs of an American missionary in Persia, now Iran. Subjects discussed in letters include status of women in Persia, progress of mission work, and Sherwood family affairs.

Vol: 1 box, Photographs

(MAJOR TOPICS: Courtship; Family; Feminism; Hawkes, Sarah Belknap "Belle" Sherwood; Iran; Love (Theology); Marriage; Missions--Iran; Muslims in Iran; Presbyterian Church in the United States (Southern); Presbyterians; Sex role; Women)

%%%%%%%%%%%%

CN# SC47
**Heber, Reginald; 1783-1826**
Ephemera; 1826

Manuscript of a sermon delivered by Bishop Reginald Heber of
the Anglican Church to clergy in his diocese of Calcutta, India,
sometime between 1824 and 1826. The sermon reviews the missionary situation in India.

(MAJOR TOPICS: Calcutta, India; Evangelistic work--India; Heber,
Reginald; India; Missions--India; Sri Lanka)

%%%%%%%%%%%%

CN# 232
**Hess, Esther Marguerite Nowack; 1906-**
Papers; 1931(1931-1941)1959; n.d.

Correspondence, photographs, and articles relating to Hess's
missionary work as a nurse in China with China Inland Mission
from 1931 to 1945. The documents not only trace Hess's missionary career, but also the Sino-Japanese war and her confinement to
a Japanese internment camp from 1942-1945.

Vol: 1 box, Photographs

(MAJOR TOPICS: Adolph, Paul Earnest; China; Communism--China;
Elliott, Eleanor Ruth; Evangelistic work--China; Frame, Helen Grace
Nowack; Frame, Raymond William; Hess, Esther Marguerite Nowack;
Language in missionary work; McDonald, Jessie; Medical care--China;
Missionaries--Recruitment and training; Missions, Medical; Mis-
sions--China; Overseas Missionary Fellowship (China Inland Mission);
Schoerner, Katharine Hasting Dodd; Sino-Japanese Conflict,
1937-1945; Small, Elizabeth Stair; Stam, Elizabeth Alden Scott; Wom-
en--Religious life; Women in missionary work; World War II)

%%%%%%%%%%%%

CN# 228
**Hess, Lyndon Roth; 1909-**
Interview; 1982

Taped interview with Hess in which he describes his missionary
service in Northern Rhodesia (now Zambia) between 1932 and
1975 as a teacher of missionary children, assistant to village pas-

tors and other work with the Lunda people. Topics include
cultural influences on missionary children, the national African
church, tribal tensions, Marxism, Muslim influence, medical work,
and Africa's needs and strengths.

Vol: 1 Audio Tape

(MAJOR TOPICS:  Africa Evangelical Fellowship; Baptists; Bap-
tists--Missions; Bible colleges; Brethren; Brethren Church--Missions;
Catholic Church--Missions; Catholic Church--Relations; Children of
missionaries; Christian education--Zaire; Church and state in Zambia;
Church growth; Clergy, Training of; Communism--Zambia; Hess,
Lyndon Roth; Hess, Ruth Edna De Velde; Indigenous church ad-
ministration; Intercultural communications; Jehovah's Witnesses;
Language in missionary work; Medical care--United States; Medical
care--Zambia; Methodist Church--Missions; Methodists; Missionaries,
Resignation of; Missionaries--Recruitment and training; Missions,
British; Missions, Medical; Missions--Interdenominational cooperation;
Missions--Zambia; Moody Bible Institute, IL; New York (state);
Pentecostal Church--Missions; Plymouth Brethren; Plymouth Breth-
ren--Missions; Wheaton College, IL; Zambia)

%%%%%%%%%%%%

CN# 242
**Hess, Ruth Edna DeVelde; 1909-**
Interview; 1982

Oral history interview of Hess, a missionary with the Plymouth
Brethren at Sakeji School for missionary children in Zambia. She
discusses her life as a child in Wheaton, Illinois, and schooling at
Wheaton Academy and Wheaton College, her marriage to Lyndon
Roth Hess, their calling to be teachers of missionary children, the
decision to go to Africa, their work at Sakeji School from 1932 to
1982, and the Lunda people of Zambia.

Vol: 2 reels of tape

(MAJOR TOPICS: Angola; Brethren; Brethren Church--Missions;
Children of missionaries; Christian education of adolescents; Christian
education of children; Great Britain; Hess, Lyndon Roth; Hess, Ruth
Edna De Velde; Intercultural communications; Language in missionary
work; Missionaries--Recruitment and training; Missions--Educational
work; Missions--South Africa; Missions--Zambia; Moody Bible Institute, IL; Plymouth Brethren; Plymouth Brethren--Missions; Presbyterians; Religion and music; Wheaton College, IL; Women--Reli-
gious life; Women in missionary work; Worship; Zaire; Zambia)

%%%%%%%%%%%%

CN# 200
**Hockman, Robert William (1906-1935) and Winifred
Thompson (1906- )**
Papers; 1933 (1933-1936) 1982

Letters by Robert and Winifred Hockman to his parents, 1933-35,
describing mission work in Ethiopia under the United Presbyterian
Church; scrapbook about the life and death of Robert Hockman;
taped interviews with Winifred Hockman. Extensive material on
the Italo-Ethiopian War and work of the International Red Cross.
Vol: 1 box, 2 Audio Tapes, Negatives, Photographs

(MAJOR TOPICS: Chicago, IL; China; Christian Medical Society;
Christmas; Coptic Church; Crime and criminals; Disease: Leprosy;
Egypt; Ethiopia; Haile Selassie; Hockman, Robert William; Hockman,
Winifred Thompson; Ironside, Henry Allan "Harry"; Italo-Ethiopian
War; Italy; Marriage; Medical care--China; Medical care--Ethiopia;
Missionaries--Recruitment and training; Missions, Medical; Mis-
sions--China; Missions--Egypt; Missions--Ethiopia; Moody Memorial
Church, IL; New York City, NY; Presbyterian Church--Missions;
Presbyterians; Presidents--United States; Racism; Red Cross; Roose-
velt, Franklin Delano; Seventh Day Adventists; Seventh Day Adven-
tists--Missions; Sex role; Sudan Interior Mission (SIM); Taylor, James
Hudson; Wheaton College, IL)

%%%%%%%%%%%%

CN# 405
**Holmes, Frances (1916- ) and Walter Robert (1916- )**
Papers; 1947-1960; n.d.

Collection of letters written by the Holmeses to their families in
the United States describing their work as missionaries with the
American Board of Commissioners for Foreign Missions in Sri
Lanka.  The letters concern the Holmeses' work with the Church
of South India, Jaffna College in Vaddukoddai, comments on
American and Sri Lankan political situations, Sri Lankan and
Indian culture and religion, the work of the two ABCFM hospitals
in Sri Lanka, and descriptions of their travels to and from the
field, in Europe and Southeast Asia.

Vol: 1 box

(MAJOR TOPICS:  American Board of Commissioners for Foreign Missions; Amsterdam, Netherlands; Berlin, Germany; Buddhism (theology); Buddhists in Sri Lanka; Catholic Church; Catholic Church in Sri Lanka; Catholic Church--Relations with Protestants; Children of missionaries; Christian and Missionary Alliance; Christian and Missionary Alliance--Missions; Christian education--India; Christian education--Sri Lanka; Christian education--United States; Church and state (theory); Church and state in India; Church and state in Sri Lanka; Church and state in United States; Communism; Communism--India; Communism--Sri Lanka; Congregational churches--Missions; Congregationalists; Denmark; Discrimination; Divorce; Education, Higher; Education--India; Education--Sri Lanka; Education--United States; Egypt; Faith--Cure; Family; Fundamentalism; Funeral rites and ceremonies; Gabon; Gabriel, Charles Hutchinson; Gaebelein, Arno C; Gaebelein, Frank; Gallup, George Horace III; Gambia; Germany; Great Britain; Hinduism (theology); Hindus in India; Hindus in Sri Lanka; Holmes, Walter Robert "Bob"; Hong Kong; India; Indigenous church administration; Intercultural communications; International relief; Italy; Japan; Journalism, Religious; Korean War; Language in missionary work; London, England; Marriage; Mass media in religion; Medical care--Sri Lanka; Methodist Church--Missions; Methodists; Missionaries, Resignation of; Missionaries--Leaves and furloughs; Missionaries--Salaries, pensions, etc.; Missions to Buddhists; Missions to Hindus; Missions to lepers; Missions, Medical; Missions--Educational work; Missions--Finance; Missions--India; Missions--Rural work; Missions--Sri Lanka; Missions--Vietnam; Modernist-Fundamentalist controversy; Nehru, Jawaharlal; Netherlands; Pakistan; Pentecostals; Periodical: *Christianity Today*; Racism; Radio in religion; Sex role; Soviet Union; Soviet Union--Foreign relations--United States; Sri Lanka; Switzerland; Tamils; Tokyo, Japan; Vietnam; Wheaton College, IL; Women in missionary work; Women--Religious life; Worship; Yemen)

%%%%%%%%%%%%

CN# 294
**Hour of Freedom Radio Program     1966-**
Records; 1968-1980; n.d.

Copies of broadcasts of a weekly radio program under the title HOUR OF FREEDOM featuring evangelist Howard O. Jones continuation of a program broadcast for years both in Africa and the United States.  Each program consists of a half hour of music, scripture readings, and an evangelistic sermon; includes also sermons of guest speakers, such as Ralph Bell.

Vol: 455 audio tapes

(MAJOR TOPICS:  African Americans; Bell, Ralph Shadell; Billy
Graham Evangelistic Association (BGEA); Christmas; Evangelistic
invitations; Evangelistic sermons; Evangelistic work--South Africa;
Evangelistic work--United States; Holy Spirit; Jones, Howard O; Love
(Theology); Mass media in religion; Preaching; Radio in religion;
Radio program: *Hour of Freedom*; Religion and sports; Sermons,
American; South Africa)

%%%%%%%%%%%%

CN# 94
**Hsu, John; 1944-**
Ephemera; 1979

Lecture delivered by Dr. John Hsu, a former Wheaton graduate,
in Dr. Will Norton's History of Christian Mission class, October,
1979.  Dr. Hsu spoke about his recent trip to mainland China and
his analysis of the Church's situation.  Topics discussed include the
Three Self Movement, the house church movement, and the
cultural revolution.

Vol: 1 Audio Tape

(MAJOR TOPICS: Beijing, China; Boxers (Chinese political move-
ment); Buddhism (theology); Buddhists in China; Catholic Church in
China; Catholic Church--Missions; Chou En-lai; Church and state in
China; Church growth; Communism; Confucianism; Cultural revolu-
tion--China; Hong Kong; Hsu, John; Mao Tse-tung; Missions to
Buddhists; Missions to Hindus; Muslims in China; Nee, Watchman;
Shanghai, China; Three-Self Patriotic Movement)

%%%%%%%%%%%%

CN# SC14
**Hull, James Roger; 1907-1972**
Papers; 1956-1970

Correspondence, memoranda, clippings, and a notebook relating to
Hull's activities in various Billy Graham New York Crusades
(1957, 1969, 1970) and his responsibilities as a member of the
Board of Directors of the Billy Graham Evangelistic Association.
Hull was Chairman of the 1957 Crusade, Co-chairman of the 1969
Crusade and on the Board of Directors of the 1970 Crusade.

(MAJOR TOPICS: Billy Graham Evangelistic Association (BGEA); Evangelistic work--United States; Graham, William Franklin "Billy"; Hull, James Roger; New York (state); New York City, NY)

%%%%%%%%%%%%

CN# 104
**Hunt, Bruce Finley; 1903-**
Interviews; 1980

Tapes of two oral history interviews in which Hunt discusses his boyhood in Korea, his college and seminary education at Wheaton College, Rutgers University, and Princeton Seminary, his missionary work in Korea and Manchuria, and his impressions of Korean culture.

Vol: 3 Audio Tapes

(MAJOR TOPICS: Auburn Affirmation; Blanchard, Charles Albert; Buddhism (theology); Buddhists in Korea; Catholic Church in Korea; Catholic Church--Missions; Catholic Church--Relations; Children of missionaries; China; Church and state in Korea; Church growth; Communism; Communism--Korea; Confucianism; Evangelistic work---Korea; Evans, Robert Philip; Hunt, Bruce Finley; Independent Board for Presbyterian Foreign Missions (IBPFM); Intercultural communications; Japan; Korea; Language: Korean; League of Evangelical Students; Liberation Theology; Machen, John Gresham; McIntire, Carl Curtis; Methodist Church--Missions; Methodists; Missions to Buddhists; Missions--China; Missions--Japan; Missions--Korea; Modernist-Fundamentalist controversy; Orthodox Presbyterian Church; Presbyterian Church in the United States (Southern); Presbyterian Church--Missions; Presbyterians; Princeton Seminary, NJ; Russo-Japanese War, 1905; Shinto; Totalitarianism; Wheaton College, IL)

%%%%%%%%%%%%

CN# 186
**Hursh, Marion Douglas; 1911-1982**
Papers; 1942-1982

Correspondence, small amount of manuscript material, photographs, and memorabilia concerning Hursh's work at the Sudan Interior Mission's Kano Eye Hospital, Kano, Nigeria, 1942-62.

Also, oral history interviews with Hursh about the Kano mission and life in Ethiopia.

Vol: 1 box, 2 Audio Tapes, Photographs

(MAJOR TOPICS: Bingham, Rowland Victor; Burma; Children of missionaries; Christian education--Nigeria; Disease: Leprosy; Disease: Malaria; Evangelical Churches of West Africa (ECWA); Evangelistic work--Nigeria; Family; Gospel Recordings, Inc; Graham, William Franklin "Billy"; Hursh, Marion Douglas; Illinois; India; Indigenous church administration; Islam--Relations--Christianity; Jesus people; Los Angeles, CA; Medical care--China; Medical care--Nigeria; Missionaries--Salaries, pensions, etc.; Missions, Medical; Missions--Nigeria; Moody Bible Institute, IL; Muslims in Nigeria; Nigeria; Sex role; Sudan Interior Mission (SIM); Wheaton College, IL; World War II)

%%%%%%%%%%%%%

CN# SC41
**Hwa Nan College; ?-?**
Ephemera; 1920-1931; n.d.

Correspondence, photographs, newspaper clippings about the women's Hwa Nan College in Shanghai, which was operated by the Methodist Protestant Church.

(MAJOR TOPICS: China; Education--China; Hwa Nan College, China; Medical care--China; Methodist Church--Missions; Methodists; Missions, Medical; Missions--China; Missions--Educational work; Shanghai, China)

%%%%%%%%%%%%%

CN# 138
**Hymn Writers and Composers**
Ephemera; 1878-1975; n.d.

Microfilmed contents of a scrapbook containing miscellaneous correspondence, photographs and memorabilia by and about hymn writers and composers. Included are items from Cliff Barrows, Merrill Dunlop, Lowell Mason, Homer Rodeheaver, Ira Sankey, and George Stebbins.

Vol: 1 Reel of Microfilm, Photographs

(MAJOR TOPICS: Alexander, Charles McCallon; Anglicans; Barrows, Clifford B; Bigelow and Main; Carmichael, Ralph; Church of England--Missions; Doane, William Howard; Dunlop, Merrill; Evangelistic work--United States; Excell, Edwin Othello; Gabriel, Charles Hutchinson; Hustad, Donald Paul; Moody Memorial Church, IL; Moody, Dwight Lyman; Religion and music; Rodeheaver, Homer Alvan; Sankey, Ira D; Shea, George Beverly; Smith, Edward R "Tedd"; Smith, Rodney "Gipsy"; Stebbins, George Coles; Van Alstyne, Frances Jane "Fanny" Crosby)

%%%%%%%%%%%%

CN# 352
**Interdenominational Foreign Mission Association (IFMA); 1917-**
Records; 1934-1983; n.d.

Correspondence, financial and statistical reports, form letters, minutes, promotional material, maps, photographs, etc., documenting IFMA's operation, its coordination of policy among its members and services to them. The files on IFMA's members and numerous other Christian agencies predominate. Among the topics covered are those related to the theoretical, theological or practical aspects of the missionary enterprise, such as aviation, the education of future workers, theological standards, conferences, organizational mergers, and budget planning. The documents also describe the various countries in which IFMA members operate.

Vol: 76 boxes, Oversize materials, Photographs

(MAJOR TOPICS:  Aeronautics in missionary work; Afghanistan; Africa Evangelical Fellowship; Africa Inland Mission (AIM); African Enterprise; African Americans; Ambassadors for Christ; American Missionary Fellowship; Andes Evangelical Mission; Angola; Arctic Missions, Inc; Argentina; Assemblies of God; Assemblies of God--Missions; Bahamas; Bangladesh; Baptists; Belgian Gospel Mission; Belgium; Belize; Berean Mission; Bible and Medical Missionary Fellowship; Bible colleges; Bible--Publication and distribution; Bible--Translating; Billy Graham Center, IL; Bolivia; Bolivian Indian Mission; Borneo Evangelical Mission; Brazil; Burma; CAM International; Campus Crusade for Christ; Catholic Church--Relations; Child Evangelism Fellowship; Children of missionaries; Chile; China; Chinese for Christ, Inc; Christian and Missionary Alliance (CMA); Christian and Missionary Alliance--Missions; Christian education (theory); Christian literature--Publication and distribution; Christian Medical Society; Church and state (theory); Church and state in Turkey; Church and state in United States; Church growth; Church work with children; Church work with military personnel; Church work with students;

Coggins, Wade Thomas; College students in missionary work; Colombia; Committee to Assist Ministry Education Overseas; Communism; Communism--China; Community of Latin American Evangelical Ministries; Congresses and conferences--Congress on the Church's Worldwide Mission, 1966; Congresses and conferences--Explo '72; Congresses and conferences--International Congress on World Evangelization, 1974; Congresses and conferences--Urbana Missionary Conventions; Conservative Baptist Foreign Mission Society; Corporations, Religious--Taxation; Costa Rica; Cuba; Daystar Communications; Dominican Republic; Ecuador; Ecumenical movement; Egypt; El Salvador; Elliot, Philip James; Ethiopia; Evangelical Alliance Mission, The (TEAM); Evangelical Council for Financial Accountability; Evangelical Fellowship of India; Evangelical Foreign Missions Association; Evangelical Literature Overseas; Evangelicalism; Evangelistic work (Christian theology); Evangelistic work--Soviet Union; Evangelistic work--Zaire; Far East Broadcasting Company; Free Methodist Church; Free Methodist Church--Missions; Free Will Baptist Church; Free Will Baptist Church--Missions; Frizen, Edwin Leonard Jr; Fund raising; Fundamentalism; Germany; Ghana; Gospel Missionary Union; Gospel Recordings, Inc; Graham, William Franklin "Billy"; Greater Europe Mission (GEM); Greece; Guatemala; Guyana; Haiti; Honduras; Hong Kong; Illiteracy; Independent churches; India; Indians of North America; Indians of South America; Indigenous church administration; Indonesia; Inter-Varsity Christian Fellowship; Interdenominational Foreign Mission Association (IFMA); International relief; Iran; Islam (theology); Islam--Relations--Christianity; Italy; Jamaica; Japan; Jones, Robert R Sr "Bob"; Journalism, Religious; Kane, J Herbert; Korea; Language in missionary work; Latin America Mission; Lausanne Committee for World Evangelization; Liberia; Liebenzell Mission of USA; Malawi; Malaysia; MAP International; Medical care--Liberia; Medical care--Zaire; Melvin, Billy Alfred; Methodists; Mexico; Mission Aviation Fellowship (MAF); Missionaries, Withdrawal of; Missionaries--Leaves and furloughs; Missionaries--Recruitment and training; Missionaries--Salaries, pensions, etc.; Missions Advanced Research and Communications Center (MARC); Missions to Chinese; Missions to Muslims; Missions, Medical; Missions--Agricultural work; Missions--Angola; Missions--Argentina; Missions--Bahamas; Missions--Bangladesh; Missions--Belgium; Missions--Belize; Missions--Benin; Missions--biblical teaching; Missions--Bolivia; Missions--Brazil; Missions--Burma; Missions--Caribbean; Missions--Chile; Missions--China; Missions--Colombia; Missions--Costa Rica; Missions--Cuba; Missions--Dominican Republic; Missions--Ecuador; Missions--Egypt; Missions--El Salvador; Missions--Germany; Missions--Ghana; Missions--Greece; Missions--Guatemala; Missions--Guyana; Missions--Haiti; Missions--Honduras; Missions--Hong Kong; Missions--India; Missions--Indonesia; Missions--Interdenominational cooperation; Missions--Iran; Missions--Italy; Missions--Jamaica; Missions--Japan; Missions--Korea; Missions--Liberia; Missions--Malawi; Missions--Malaysia; Missions--Mexico; Missions--Mozambique; Missions--Namibia; Missions--Nepal; Missions--Nicaragua; Missions--Nigeria; Missions--Pakistan; Missions--Panama; Missions--Paraguay; Missions--Peru; Missions--Philippines; Missions--Senegal; Missions--Sierra Leone; Missions--Singapore; Missions--South Africa; Missions--Soviet Union; Missions--Spain; Missions--Sri Lanka; Missions--Taiwan; Missions--Tanzania; Missions--Togo; Missions--United States; Missions--Upper Volta; Missions--Uruguay; Missions--Venezuela; Missions--Zaire; Missions--Zambia; Missions--Zimbabwe; Modernist-Fundamentalist controversy; Moving-pictures in church work; Mozambique; Namibia; Navigators; Nepal; New Tribes Mission; New York. World's Fair, 1964-1965; Nigeria; North Africa Mission; Nurses Christian Fellowship; Orinoco River Mission; Overseas Missionary Fellowship (China Inland Mission); Pakistan; Panama; Paraguay; Pennsylvania; Pentecostals; Periodical: *Christianity Today*; Peru; Philippines; Pocket Testament League; Prayer; Prisons--Missions and charities; Radio in missionary work; Refugees--Afghanistan; Refugees--Ethiopia; SEND Int.; Senegal; Short Terms Abroad; Sierra Leone; Singapore; Slavic Gospel Association; Smith, Oswald Jeffrey; South Africa; South America Indian Mission; South America Mission, Inc. (SAM); South China Boat Mission; Soviet Union; Spain; Sri Lanka; Student Foreign Mission Fellowship; Sudan; Sudan Interior Mission (SIM); Taiwan; Tanzania; Taylor, Clyde Willis; Townsend, William Cameron; Trans World Radio; Trinity Evangelical Divinity School, IL; Turkey; Underground Evangelism; Unevangelized Tribes Mission; United Mission to Nepal; Upper Volta; Uruguay; Venezuela; Wheaton College, IL; Wilson, J Christy Jr; Women's Union Missionary Society; Women in missionary work; Women--Religious life; World Evangelical Fellowship (WEF); World Radio Missionary Fellowship; World Relief Commission; World Vision International; Wycliffe Bible Translators; Zaire; Zambia; Zimbabwe)

%%%%%%%%%%%%

CN# 86
**International Christian Broadcasters; 1954-?**
Records; 1937-1978

A service organization intended to promote interest in Christian broadcasting, and provide help and encouragement to Christian communicators. Records include correspondence, tapes, photographs, financial reports, slides, blueprints, and memoranda relating to ICB (originally the World Conference on Mission Radio) as well as data on the World Communication Congress held in Tokyo (1970), the Muslim Conference (1974), and survey questionnaire for ICB's *World Directory of Religious Radio and Television Broadcasting.*

Vol: 35 boxes

(MAJOR TOPICS: Afghanistan; Africa Inland Mission (AIM); Alabama; Algeria; Argentina; Armerding, Carl E; Armstrong, Benjamin Leighton; Assemblies of God; Australia; Austria; Bangkok, Thailand; Bayley, Joseph Tate; Beirut, Lebanon; Belgium; Bertermann, Eugene R; Bolivia; Bowman, Robert H; Brazil; Bright, William Rohl "Bill"; Broadcasting station: ELWA, Liberia; Broadcasting station: HCJB, Ecuador; Broadcasting station: Voice of Tangier; Burma; Calcutta, India; California; Cambodia; Canada; Cerullo, Morris; Chad; Charismatic movement; Chile; China; Christian Broadcasting Network; Colombia; Colorado; Communication; Congresses and conferences--- Congress on the Church's Worldwide Mission, 1966; Congresses and conferences--Urbana Missionary Conventions; Cyprus; Czechoslovakia; Daystar Communications; Denmark; District of Columbia; Dominican Republic; Ecuador; Education--Laos; Education--Zambia; Egypt; El Salvador; Epp, Theodore H; Ethiopia; Evangelical Foreign Missions Association; Evangelical Literature Overseas; Evangelistic work--Australia; Evangelistic work--Belgium; Evangelistic work--Brazil; Evangelistic work--Canada; Evangelistic work--France; Evangelistic work--- Germany; Evangelistic work--Great Britain; Evangelistic work--Guatemala; Evangelistic work--Honduras; Evangelistic work--Japan; Evangelistic work--Mexico; Evangelistic work--New Zealand; Evangelistic work--Nigeria; Evangelistic work--Paraguay; Evangelistic work--South Africa; Evangelistic work--Soviet Union; Evangelistic work--Uruguay; Evangelistic work--Yugoslavia; Evangelistic work--Zaire; Far East Broadcasting Company; Fellowship of Christian Athletes; Fiji Islands; Finland; France; Fuller, Charles Edward Sr; Germany; Ghana; Graham, William Franklin "Billy"; Great Britain; Greece; Guatemala; Guinea; Guyana; Haiti; Hawaii; Hay, Ian M; Henry, Carl Ferdinand Howard; Hines, Jerome; Honduras; Hong Kong; Huffman, John A; Humbard, Rex; Hungary; Iceland; Illinois; India; Indonesia; Inter-Varsity Christian Fellowship; Intercultural communications; Interdenominational Foreign Mission Association (IFMA); International Christian Broadcasters; Iran; Ireland; Irwin, James Benson; Islam (theology); Islam--Relations--Christianity; Israel; Italy; Ivory Coast; Japan; Jones, Clarence Wesley; Jones, Robert R Sr "Bob"; Kamau, Timothy; Kenya; Korea; Laos; Latin America Mission; Lebanon; Liberia; London, England; Madagascar; Malaysia; Mass media in religion; Mexico; Michigan; Minnesota; Missions to Muslims; Moody Bible Institute, IL; Moody Institute of Science; Mozambique; Muslims in Algeria; Muslims in Ethiopia; Muslims in Lebanon; Muslims in Senegal; Nairobi, Kenya; National Association of Evangelicals; National Religious Broadcasters; Nepal; Netherlands; New Zealand; Nigeria;

Oklahoma; Oral Roberts University, Tulsa, OK; Organizational change; Padilla, Carlos Rene; Pakistan; Palau, Luis; Papua New Guinea; Paraguay; Philippines; Pierce, Robert Willard "Bob"; Portugal; Radio in missionary work; Radio in religion; Religion and music; Robertson, Marion Gordon "Pat"; Romania; Saudi Arabia; Savage, Robert Carlton; Schaeffer, Francis August; Senegal; Singapore; Somali; South Africa; Soviet Union; Space flight; Spain; Sri Lanka; Sudan Interior Mission (SIM); Sweden; Switzerland; Taiwan; Tanzania; Taylor, Clyde Willis; Thailand; Thiessen, Abraham Gustov; Tokyo, Japan; Trans World Radio; Tubman, William Vacanarat Shadrach; Turkey; United States; Uruguay; Van Der Puy, Abraham Cornelius; Venezuela; Vietnam; Washington, DC; Wheaton College, IL; Wisconsin; World Council of Churches; World Radio Missionary Fellowship; Yemen; Yugoslavia; Zaire; Zambia; Zimbabwe)

%%%%%%%%%%%%%

CN# 53
**International Congress on World Evangelization; 1974**
Records; 1972-1974; n.d.

Procedure books, press releases, programs, speech texts and recordings, and reports created for the Congress sponsored by the BGEA held in Lausanne, Switzerland in 1974.

Vol: 4 boxes, 45 Audio Tapes

(MAJOR TOPICS: Argentina; Australia; Bangladesh; Barrows, Clifford B; Bible--Evidences, authority, etc.; Bible--Prophecies; Billy Graham Evangelistic Association (BGEA); Bolivia; Brazil; Burma; Cambodia; Canada; Church and social problems; Church growth; Church management; Church work with youth; Church--biblical teaching; Communication; Communism; Congresses and conferences---International Congress on World Evangelization, 1974; Conversion; Dain, Arthur John; Ecuador; Ecumenical movement; Education--Laos; Egypt; Escobar, Samuel; Ethiopia; Evangelicalism; Evangelistic work---Argentina; Evangelistic work--Australia; Evangelistic work--Brazil; Evangelistic work--Canada; Evangelistic work--France; Evangelistic work--Japan; Evangelistic work--Korea; Evangelistic work--Mexico; Evangelistic work--New Zealand; Evangelistic work--South Africa; Evangelistic work--Switzerland; Evangelistic work--Taiwan; Evangelistic work--United States; Evangelistic work--Vietnam; Finland; France; Ghana; Graham, William Franklin "Billy"; Great Commission (Bible); Greece; Hawaii; Hinduism (theology); Hoke, Donald Edwin; Holy Spirit; Hong Kong; Hubbard, David Allen; India; Indonesia; Intercultural communications; Japan; Kenya; Kim, Billy (Jang Hwan); Kivengere, Festo; Korea; Language: French; Language: German;

Language: Japanese; Language: Spanish; Laos; Lausanne Covenant; Lausanne, Switzerland; Lebanon; Lindsell, Harold; Little, Paul Eagleson; Malaysia; Mass media in religion; McGavran, Donald Anderson; Mexico; Missionaries, Lay; Missions from underdeveloped areas; Missions to Hindus; Missions--Interdenominational cooperation; Missions--Theory; Mooneyham, W Stanley; New Zealand; Norway; Osei-Mensah, Gottfried B; Padilla, Carlos Rene; Pakistan; Panama; Papua New Guinea; Philippines; Portugal; Preaching; Religion and music; Schaeffer, Francis August; Shea, George Beverly; Singapore; South Africa; Spain; Sri Lanka (Ceylon); Swaziland; Switzerland; Taiwan; ten Boom, Cornelia Arnolda Johanna; Translating and interpreting; United States; Vietnam; Wati, Inchaba Bendang; Winter, Ralph D)

%%%%%%%%%%%%

CN# 285
**Johnson, Torrey Maynard; 1909-**
Interviews; 1984-1985

Three taped interviews with Johnson in which he discusses influence of Paul Rader, C. T. Dyrness, Wheaton College friends, professors, and others on his career; Wheaton College presidents Charles Blanchard and James Oliver Buswell, Jr; the founding of the National Association of Evangelicals; the founding of Youth for Christ, and his involvement in Chicago and then as International Director; and religious radio broadcasting. Also discussed are reminiscences of Robert Cook, Charles Templeton, Bob Pierce, Jack Shuler, the Palermo Brothers, Billy Graham, Herbert J. Taylor, George Wilson, Bob Jones, Carl McIntire, and others.

Vol: 5 reels of audio tape.

(MAJOR TOPICS: American Council of Christian Churches (ACCC); Baptists; Billy Graham Evangelistic Association (BGEA); Blanchard, Charles Albert; Bob Jones University, SC; Broadcasting station: HCJB, Ecuador; Broadcasting station: WMBI; Buswell, James Oliver Jr; Chaplains, Military; Chicago Gospel Tabernacle; Chicago, IL; Church and state in United States; Church work with military personnel; Cities and towns; College students--Religious life; Communication [theory]; Cook, Robert Andrew; Crawford, Percy B; Davis, Ralph T; Dunlop, Merrill; Ecumenical movement; Evangelical Free Church of America; Evangelicalism; Evangelistic invitations; Evangelistic sermons; Evangelistic work--United States; Federal Communications Commission; Graham, William Franklin "Billy"; Hearst, William Randolph; Houghton, William Henry; Illinois; Ironside, Henry Allan "Harry"; Johnson, Torrey Maynard; Jones, Robert R Sr "Bob"; Liver-

more, Thomas Leslie; Lutheran Church-Missouri Synod; Lutherans;
Machen, John Gresham; Mass media in religion; McIntire, Carl
Curtis; Minnesota; Modernist-Fundamentalist controversy; Moody
Bible Institute, IL; Moody Memorial Church, IL; National Association
of Evangelicals; National Council of Churches; National Religious
Broadcasters; Northwestern College, MN; Ockenga, Harold John;
Palermo, Louis; Palermo, Phil; Periodical: *Christian Century, The*;
Periodical: *Sword of the Lord*; Philippines; Pierce, Robert Willard
"Bob"; Preaching; Presbyterians; Rader, Daniel Paul; Radio in religion;
Radio program: *Back Home Hour*; Religion and music; Rice, John
Richard; Riley, William Bell; Shea, George Beverly; Southern Baptist
Convention; Taylor, Herbert John; Templeton, Charles B; Van Kam-
pen, Robert Cornelius; Vaus, James Arthur; Wheaton College, IL;
Wilson, George McConnell; Wisconsin; World Vision International;
Wyrtzen, John Von Casper "Jack"; Wyzenbeek, Andrew; Youth for
Christ International)

%%%%%%%%%%%%

CN# 182
**Kane, James Herbert (1910- ) and Winnifred Mary (1912-1983)**
Papers; 1934-1976; n.d.

Correspondence, speeches, articles, lecture notes, oral history
interviews relating to the Kanes' 1935-1950 careers in China as
missionaries with China Inland Mission and Herbert's subsequent
work as writer about and professor of missions.

Vol: 4 boxes, 2 Audio Tapes

(MAJOR TOPICS: American Bible Society; Anglicans; Australia;
Brethren; Brethren Church--Missions; Buddhism (theology); Buddhists
in China; Calcutta, India; Canada; Catholic Church in United States;
Catholic Church--Missions; Chamberlain, Arthur Neville; Chiang
Kai-Shek; Chicago, IL; Children of missionaries; China; Chou En-lai;
Christian education (theory); Christian education--China; Christian
education--United States; Church and social problems; Church of
Christ Uniting (COCU); Church of England; Communism; Com-
munism--China; Congresses and conferences--World Missionary
Conference, 1910; Cross-cultural studies; Cults; Ecumenical move-
ment; Edward VIII, King of England; Elizabeth II, Queen of England;
Ethnic groups; Evangelical Missions Information Service; Evangelistic
work--Korea; Faith and Order Movement; Family; Friends of Moslems
Missions; Fundamentalism; Gibb, George W; Great Britain; Hitler,
Adolph; Hockman, Robert William; Hong Kong; Houghton, Frank;
House churches; Independent churches; India; Indonesia; Intercultural
communications; International Council of Christian Churches; Interna-

tional Missionary Council; Islam (theology); Japan; Jones, Eli Stanley; Kane, James Herbert; Kane, Winnifred Mary Shepherd; Korea; Marriage; Methodists; Missionaries--Recruitment and training; Missions to Buddhists; Missions--Australia; Missions--China; Missions--Indonesia; Missions--Interdenominational cooperation; Missions--Japan; Missions--Korea; Missions--Philippines; Missions--Study and teaching; Missions--Taiwan; Modernist-Fundamentalist controversy; Moody Bible Institute, IL; Mozambique; Mussolini, Benito; National Council of Churches; Nee, Watchman; New Zealand; Overseas Missionary Fellowship (China Inland Mission); Pentecostals; People's Church, Toronto, ON; Philippines; Plymouth Brethren; Plymouth Brethren--Missions; Presbyterian Church in the United States (Southern); Presbyterians; Presidents--United States; Prisons--Missions and charities; Reformed Church in America; Roosevelt, Franklin Delano; Rural churches--China; Schoerner, Otto Frederick; Sermons, American; Sex role; Shanghai, China; Singapore; Sino-Japanese Conflict, 1937-1945; Smith, Oswald Jeffrey; Society of Friends; Society of Friends--Missions; Soviet Union; Spellman, Francis Joseph, Cardinal; Stam, Elizabeth Alden Scott; Stam, John Cornelius; Student Christian Movement; Sudan Interior Mission (SIM); Sunday, William Ashley "Billy"; T Hooft, Wa Visser; Taiwan; Trinity Evangelical Divinity School, IL; United Bible Societies; United Nations Relief and Rehabilitation Administration (UNRRA); Vatican Council II, 1962-1965; Wang Ming Tao; World Council of Churches; Women--Religious life; Women in missionary work; World Methodist Council; World War II; Wu Tze Heng)

%%%%%%%%%%%%

CN# 212
**Kathryn Kuhlman Foundation; 1957-1982**
Records; 1910-1982    n.d.

Correspondence, calendars, photographs, an oral history interview, video tapes, audio tapes, films, slides, scrapbooks, newspaper and magazine clippings, articles, memorabilia, news releases, and release forms relating to the work of the Foundation and Kathryn Kuhlman. Documents describe Kuhlman's evangelistic and healing ministry, beginning with her early life and ranging from her first years of ministry to the time of her death and the eventual winding down of the Foundation in 1982.

Vol: 3 boxes, 2118 Audio Tapes, 37 Films, Negatives, Oversize Materials,  Photographs, Slides, 1108 Video Tapes

(MAJOR TOPICS: Alabama; Argentina; Athletes--Religious life; Benin; Bible--Prophecies; California; Canada; Carson, Johnny; Charismatic movement; Chicago, IL; Christmas; Church and social problems; Colorado; Communication; Conversion; Costa Rica; Cruz, Nicky; Dispensationalism; Divorce; Douglas, Mike; El Salvador; Evangelistic sermons; Faith; Faith--Cure; Florida; Full Gospel Business Men's Fellowship; Georgia; Glossolalia; Honduras; Hong Kong; Humbard, Rex; Idaho; Illinois; India; Indiana; Indonesia; Irwin, James Benson; Jesus people; Kathryn Kuhlman Foundation; Kenya; Kuhlman, Kathryn Johanna; Los Angeles, CA; Malaysia; Mass media in religion; McDonald, James "Jimmie"; McPherson, Aimee Semple; Medical care--United States; Michigan; Minnesota; Miracles; Missions, Medical; Missouri; Moody Bible Institute, IL; Mooneyham, W Stanley; Moving-pictures in church work; Nevada; Nicaragua; Ohio; Oklahoma; Oral Roberts University, Tulsa, OK; Oregon; Paul VI (Pope); Pennsylvania; Pentecostals; Radio in religion; Rhode Island; Richardson, Don; Robertson, Marion Gordon "Pat"; Sermons, American; Sex role; Shore, Dinah; South Africa; Space flight; Sweden; Taiwan; Television in religion; Television program: *I Believe in Miracles*; Television program: *Your Faith and Mine*; ten Boom, Cornelia Arnolda Johanna; Texas; United States; Vietnam; Washington (state); Women and religion; Women authors; Women--Religious life; Women clergy)

%%%%%%%%%%%%

CN# 211
**Kerr, Maxwell A; 1912-**
Interview; 1982

Interview with Kerr in which he discusses his early life, conversion, C. O. Baptista (his work, personality, and family), technical problem-solving and innovations, his career after Baptista Films, and his assessment of the Christian film industry.

Vol: 1 Audio Tape

(MAJOR TOPICS: Anderson, Kenneth; Baptista Film Mission; Baptista, Charles Octavia; Film: *Pilgrim's Progress*; Illinois; Kerr, Maxwell A; Mass media in religion; McIntire, Carl Curtis; Michigan; Moving-pictures in church work; Moving-pictures--Moral and religious aspects; Presbyterians; Wheaton College, IL)

%%%%%%%%%%%%

CN# 247
**Knowlton, Louis E.; 1932-**
Interviews; 1983

Four taped interviews with Knowlton in which he discusses his
career in evangelistic work and  radio technology in Brazil for the
Brazilian Evangelistic Association, Inc.  Includes information on
use of radio for evangelism at Houghton College, Houghton, NY;
WMBI of Moody Bible Institute, IL; street meetings for the
Brazilian Baptist Church; radio station PRA7 of Sao Paulo, Brazil;
Christian films; church-state relations; Brazilian television; mis-
sions finance and administration.

Vol: 5 Audio Tapes

(MAJOR TOPICS: Animism; Baptists; Brazil; Broadcasting station:
WMBI; Catholic Church in Brazil; Chaplains, Military; Children of
missionaries; Church and social problems; Church and state in Brazil;
Communication; Conversion; Cults; Divorce; Evangelistic invitations;
Evangelistic work--Brazil; Finney, Charles Grandison; Graham, Wil-
liam Franklin "Billy"; Indians of South America; Knowlton, Louis E;
Liberation Theology; Mass media in religion; Missionaries--Recruit-
ment and training; Missions--Sierra Leone; Moody Bible Institute, IL;
Moving-pictures in church work; Pentecostals; Pocket Testament
League; Radio in missionary work; Radio in religion; Religion and
music; Revivals; Sex role; Television in religion; World Gospel Crusade)

%%%%%%%%%%%%

CN# SC77
**Kuhn, Isobel Miller; 1901-1957**
Papers; 1928-1929

Two personal letters and a prayer/newsletter for circulation, which
includes a personal note from Kuhn, a missionary with China
Inland Mission (CIM).  The letters include accounts of her trans--
Pacific journey to China and evangelistic opportunities there, a
description of Yangchow (new spelling, Yangzhou) in Kiangsu
Province (new spelling, Jiangsu Province), where she was in
language school, and an amusing account of a church service which
illustrates cultural differences between the Chinese and westerners.

(MAJOR TOPICS: China; Evangelistic work--China; Intercultural
communications; Kuhn, Isobel Miller; Language in missionary work;

Lisu (Tibeto-Burman tribe); Missions--China; Nowack, Ruth Louise;
Overseas Missionary Fellowship (China Inland Mission); Women
authors; Women in missionary work; Women--Religious life)

%%%%%%%%%%%%

CN# 207
**Larson, Mark Richard; 1956-**
Interview; 1982

Interview with Larson concerning his experiences as a missionary
under Sudan Interior Mission in Nigeria, 1979-1981, particularly
the agricultural mission work in the Kano area of northern Nigeria. Also in the collection is a scrapbook about the work.

Vol: 1 box, 1 Audio Tape

(MAJOR TOPICS:  Animism; Christian education--Nigeria; College
students in missionary work; Congresses and conferences--Urbana
Missionary Conventions; Education--Nigeria; Evangelical Churches of
West Africa (ECWA); Evangelistic work--Nigeria; Illiteracy; Inter-Var-
sity Christian Fellowship; Islam--Relations--Christianity; Mission-
aries--Recruitment and training; Missions from underdeveloped areas;
Missions--Agricultural work; Missions--Nigeria; Muslims in Nigeria;
Nigeria; Occult sciences; Sudan Interior Mission (SIM); Wheaton
College, IL)

%%%%%%%%%%%%

CN# 46
**Lausanne Committee on World Evangelization; 1975-**
Records; 1971-1983; n.d.

Correspondence, minutes, memoranda, reports, address manuscripts, press releases, newsletters, audio tapes, staff manuals and
other administrative materials of the Lausanne Committee, which
was set up to continue the work of the 1974 Lausanne Cong-
ress(see CN# 53) by providing liaison, encouragement, and training to Protestant evangelistic efforts around the  world. Documented events include the early planning for the 1974 International
Congress on World Evangelization(ICOWE), the creation of the
Lausanne Committee (LCWE), the 1980 Consultation on World
Evangelization (COWE) in Thailand and other events.  The
collection is subdivided by series of the following records: the
LCWE chairman (Leighton Ford); the LCWE executive secretary
(Gottfried Osei-Mensah); ICOWE director (Donald Hoke);
chairman of ICOWE and Lausanne Continuation Committee

(LCC) (A.J. Dain); director of the Simple Lifestyle Consultation
(Ronald Sider); and the COWE Wheaton office, including the
records of the director (David Howard) and program director
(Saphir Athyal).

Vol: 50 boxes, 4 Audio Tapes, Photographs

(MAJOR TOPICS: African Americans; American Bible Society;
Amsterdam, Netherlands; Anglicans; Animism; Argentina; Armerding,
Hudson Taylor; Armstrong, Benjamin Leighton; Association of Evan-
gelicals of Africa and Madagascar (AEAM); Atheism; Australia;
Bangkok, Thailand; Baptists; Belgium; Bertermann, Eugene R;
Bible--Criticism, interpretation, etc; Bible--Prophecies; Billy Graham
Center, IL; Billy Graham Evangelistic Association (BGEA); Black
Muslims; Black nationalism (United States); Bragg, Wayne G; Brazil;
Bright, William Rohl "Bill"; Buddhism (theology); Buddhists in Japan;
Burma; Cambodia; Canada; Caribbean; Catholic Church; Catholic
Church in Argentina; Catholic Church in Australia; Catholic Church in
Austria; Catholic Church in Belgium; Catholic Church in Canada;
Catholic Church in Chile; Catholic Church in France; Catholic Church
in Germany; Catholic Church in Guatemala; Catholic Church in
Ireland; Catholic Church in Italy; Catholic Church in Nigeria; Catholic
Church in Paraguay; Catholic Church in Peru; Catholic Church in
Portugal; Catholic Church in Sierra Leone; Catholic Church in Spain;
Catholic Church in United States; Catholic Church in Venezuela;
Catholic Church--Relations; Central African Republic; Chao, Samuel
H; Chile; China; Chinese in foreign countries; Christian drama; Chris-
tian education (theory); Christian leadership; Christian life; Christian
literature--Publication and distribution; Christianity and economics;
Church and social problems; Church and state in the Soviet Union;
Church development, New; Church growth--Thailand; Church of the
Nazarene; Church work with children; Church work with families;
Church work with refugees; Church work with single people; Church
work with students; Church work with women; Church--biblical teach-
ing; Cities and towns; City missions; Climenhaga, Arthur M; Coggins,
Wade Thomas; Colombia; Communication; Communication in orga-
nizations; Communism; Communism--Brazil; Communism--Colombia;
Communism--Finland; Communism--Germany; Communism--Great
Britain; Communism--India; Communism--Korea; Communism--Peru;
Communism--Soviet Union; Communism--Zambia; Congresses and
conferences--Consultation on World Evangelization, 1980; Congresses
and conferences--International Conference for Itinerant Evangelists,
1983; Congresses and conferences--International Congress on World
Evangelization, 1974; Congresses and conferences--Pan African Chris-
tian Leadership Assembly, 1976; Congresses and conferences--Urbana
Missionary Conventions; Congresses and conferences--US Congress on
Evangelism, 1969; Congresses and conferences--World Congress on

Evangelism, 1966; Congresses and conferences--World Missionary
Conference, 1910; Congresses and conferences; Conversion; Coptic
Church; Cults; Dain, Arthur John; Ecuador; Ecumenical movement;
Education, Higher; Egypt; Emery, Alan C Jr; Engstrom, Theodore
"Ted" Wilhelm; Episcopalians; Escobar, Samuel; Ethics; Ethiopia;
Evangelical Foreign Missions Association; Evangelicalism; Evangelistic
work (Christian theology); Evangelistic work--Argentina; Evangelistic
work--Australia; Evangelistic work--Austria; Evangelistic work--Bel-
gium; Evangelistic work--Brazil; Evangelistic work--Canada; Evangelis-
tic work--Central African Republic; Evangelistic work--Chile; Evan-
gelistic work--China; Evangelistic work--Colombia; Evangelistic
work--Ecuador; Evangelistic work--Egypt; Evangelistic work--Finland;
Evangelistic work--France; Evangelistic work--Germany; Evangelistic
work--Great Britain; Evangelistic work--Greece; Evangelistic work---
Guatemala; Evangelistic work--Haiti; Evangelistic work--Hong Kong;
Evangelistic work--India; Evangelistic work--Indonesia; Evangelistic
work--Ireland; Evangelistic work--Israel; Evangelistic work--Italy;
Evangelistic work--Japan; Evangelistic work--Kenya; Evangelistic
work--Korea; Evangelistic work--Mexico; Evangelistic work--Morocco;
Evangelistic work--Nepal; Evangelistic work--New Zealand; Evangelis-
tic work--Nigeria; Evangelistic work--Pakistan; Evangelistic work--Pap-
ua New Guinea; Evangelistic work--Paraguay; Evangelistic work--Peru;
Evangelistic work--Philippines; Evangelistic work--Poland; Evangelistic
work--Portugal; Evangelistic work--Sierra Leone; Evangelistic work---
Singapore; Evangelistic work--South Africa; Evangelistic work--Soviet
Union; Evangelistic work--Spain; Evangelistic work--Switzerland;
Evangelistic work--Taiwan; Evangelistic work--Thailand; Evangelistic
work--United States; Evangelistic work--Uruguay; Evangelistic work---
Venezuela; Evangelistic work--Zaire; Evangelistic work--Zambia;
Evangelistic work--Zimbabwe; Evans, Robert Philip; Family; Finland;
Finney, Charles; Ford, Leighton Frederick Sandys; France; Fund
raising; Germany; Ghana; Graham, William Franklin "Billy"; Great
Britain; Greece; Guatemala; Haiti; Haqq, Akbar Abdul; Hatori, Akira;
Hawaii; Hay, Ian M; Henry, Carl Ferdinand Howard; Hinduism
(theology); Hindus in Great Britain; Hindus in India; Hindus in Nepal;
Hispanic Americans; Hoke, Donald Edwin; Holy Spirit; Hong Kong;
House churches; Howard, David Morris; Humanism; Hunger; Illinois;
India; Indiana; Indians of Mexico; Indonesia; Intercultural communica-
tions; Interdenominational Foreign Mission Association (IFMA);
International Fellowship of Evangelical Students; International Mis-
sionary Council; Ireland; Islam (theology); Israel; Italy; Japan; Jews;
Jews in Australia; Jews in France; Jews in New Zealand; Jews in
South Africa; John Paul II (Pope); Journalism, Religious; Judaism;
Kenya; Kesler, Jay; Kivengere, Festo; Koran; Korea; Lausanne Com-
mittee for World Evangelization; Lausanne Covenant; Lausanne,
Switzerland; Lindsell, Harold; Linguistics; Little, Paul Eagleson;
London, England; MAP International; Marquardt, Horst; Mass media

in religion; Methodists; Mexico; Missionaries--Korea; Mission Aviation
Fellowship; Missions Advanced Research and Communications Center
(MARC); Missions to Buddhists; Missions to Chinese; Missions to
Hindus; Missions to Jews; Missions to Muslims; Missions--Argentina;
Missions--Australia; Missions--Austria; Missions--Belgium; Missions---
biblical teaching; Missions--Brazil; Missions--Canada; Missions--Cen-
tral African Republic; Missions--Chile; Missions--China; Missions---
Colombia; Missions--Ecuador; Missions--Egypt; Missions--Finland;
Missions--France; Missions--Germany; Missions--Great Britain; Mis-
sions--Greece; Missions--Guatemala; Missions--Haiti; Missions--Hong
Kong; Missions--India; Missions--Indonesia; Missions--Interdenomina-
tional cooperation; Missions--Ireland; Missions--Israel; Missions--Italy;
Missions--Japan; Missions--Kenya; Missions--Korea; Missions--Malawi;
Missions--Mexico; Missions--Morocco; Missions--Nepal; Missions---
New Zealand; Missions--Nigeria; Missions--Pakistan; Missions--Papua
New Guinea; Missions--Paraguay; Missions--Peru; Missions--Philip-
pines; Missions--Poland; Missions--Portugal; Missions--Sierra Leone;
Missions--Singapore; Missions--South Africa; Missions--Soviet Union;
Missions--Spain; Missions--Taiwan; Missions--Thailand; Missions---
Theory; Missions--United States; Missions--Uruguay; Missions--Venez-
uela; Missions--Zaire; Missions--Zambia; Missions--Zimbabwe; Moon-
eyham, W Stanley; Morocco; Muslims in Australia; Muslims in
Canada; Muslims in Egypt; Muslims in Indonesia; Muslims in Kenya;
Muslims in Morocco; Muslims in Philippines; Muslims in United
States; Mysticism; Nairobi, Kenya; National Council of Churches;
Nelson, Victor B; Nepal; New Jersey; New Zealand; Nigeria; Norway;
Occult sciences; Ockenga, Harold John; Organizational change;
Orthodox Eastern Church; Orthodox Eastern Church--Egypt; Or-
thodox Eastern Church--Ethiopia; Orthodox Eastern Church--Greece;
Orthodox Eastern Church--India; Orthodox Eastern Church--Rela-
tions; Orthodox Eastern Church--Soviet Union; Osei-Mensah, Gott-
fried B; Pakistan; Papua New Guinea; Pennsylvania; Periodical:
*Christianity Today*; Philadelphia, PA; Philippines; Poland; Portugal;
Poverty; Prayer; Presbyterian Church--Missions; Presbyterians; Radio
in missionary work; Radio in religion; Refugees--Cambodia; Rome,
Italy; Salvation Army; Sanny, Lorne Charles; Scripture Union; Ser-
mons, American; Sierra Leone; Singapore; Smyth, Walter Herbert;
Social change; Socialism; Sociology; Sojourners Fellowship, Washing-
ton, DC; South Africa; Soviet Union; Spain; Stott, John Robert
Walmsley; Stough, Paul Pinney; Sudan; Switzerland; Sydney, Australia;
Taylor, Clyde Willis; Television in religion; Thailand; Theology--Study
and Teaching; Tokyo, Japan; Translating and interpreting; Tribes and
tribal system; Uganda; United Bible Societies; United States; Uruguay;
Van Der Puy, Abraham Cornelius; Venezuela; Washington, DC;
Wilson, George McConnell; Wilson, Thomas Walter Jr; Winter, Ralph
D; Witchcraft; Wolgemuth, Samuel Frey; Women--Religious life;
Women in missionary work; World Council of Churches; World

Evangelical Fellowship (WEF); World Vision International; Wycliffe
Bible Translators; Youth for Christ International; Zaire; Zambia;
Zimbabwe; Zimmerman, Thomas Fletcher)

%%%%%%%%%%%%

CN# 125
**Leasor, Jane (Teresa); 1922-**
Interviews; 1982

This collection consists of two oral history interviews in which
Leasor describes among other topics, her post-graduate education
at Biblical Seminary in New York City, teaching at a secondary
school for girls and a college for women in Beirut, the Arabic
language, Islam; the place of women in Islam society, and the
relationship between various Christian churches in Lebanon.

Vol: 2 Audio Tapes

(MAJOR TOPICS: Language: Arabic; Leasor, Jane (Teresa); Islam;
Lebanon; Missionaries--Recruitment and training; Missions--Lebanon;
Women--Religious life; Women in missionary work)

%%%%%%%%%%%%

CN# 192
**Lindsell, Harold; 1913-**
Papers; 1943 (1964-1981) 1981

Correspondence, research data and writings documenting the
interests of Lindsell, an Evangelical educator, editor and writer.
The materials start from the period when he became associate
editor of *Christianity Today* magazine in 1964. The collection has
considerable information on *Christianity Today*, Wheaton College,
Gordon-Conwell Theological Seminary, and the debate over
inerrancy of Scripture.

Vol: 10 boxes, 124 Audio Tapes, Filmstrip, Oversize Materials,
Phonograph Records, Photographs, Slides

(MAJOR TOPICS: Abortion; Alabama; Ali, Muhammad; American
Board of Missions to the Jews; American Tract Society; Armerding,
Hudson Taylor; Asbury Theological Seminary, Wilmore, KY; Associa-
tion of Evangelicals of Africa and Madagascar (AEAM); Australia;
Baptists; Bell, Lemuel Nelson; Bell, Ralph Shadell; Bible--Criticism,
interpretation, etc; Billy Graham Center, IL; Billy Graham Evangelistic
Association (BGEA); Bright, William Rohl "Bill"; Bruce, Frederick

Fyvie; Buswell, James Oliver Jr; California; Cambridge University;
Camp of the Woods, MI; Campus Crusade for Christ; Capital punish-
ment; Capitalism; Carter, James Earl "Jimmy"; Catholic Church;
Catholic Church in United States; China; Christian Anti-Communism
Crusade; Christian education (theory); Christian education--United
States; Christian Holiness Association; Christian Reformed Church;
Christianity and economics; Christianity Today, Inc; Church and social
problems; Church and state in United States; Church growth; Church
League of America; Church of Christ Uniting (COCU); Charles
Wendell; Columbia Bible College, Columbia, SC; Communication;
Communism; Conference on Faith and History; Congresses and
conferences--Chicago Call Conference; Congresses and conferences---
World Congress on Evangelism, 1966; Dain, Arthur John; Dallas
Theological Seminary; Ecumenical movement; Edman, Victor Ray-
mond; Elizabeth II, Queen of England; Elliot, Elisabeth Howard;
Equal Rights Amendment; Evangelical Council for Financial Account-
ability; Evangelical Theological Society; Evangelicalism; Evangelistic
work--Australia; Evangelistic work--Guatemala; Evangelistic work---
Korea; Evangelistic work--Poland; Evangelistic work--United States;
Evolution; Faith--Cure; Feminism; Film: *Hiding Place, The*; Ford,
Gerald Rudolph; Ford, Leighton Frederick Sandys; Fuller Theological
Seminary, CA; Fuller, Charles Edward Sr; Fundamentalism; Gaebe-
lein, Frank; Gideons International; Gordon-Conwell Divinity School;
Gortner, Hugh Marjoe Ross; Graham, Ruth Bell; Graham, William
Franklin "Billy"; Guatemala; Gustafson, Roy W; Hargis, Billy James;
Harvard University, MA; Henry, Carl Ferdinand Howard; Hill, Edwin
V; Hoke, Donald Edwin; Homosexuality; Hubbard, David Allen;
Humanism; Illinois; India; Institute in Basic Youth Conflicts; Institute
of Church Growth, CA; Inter-Varsity Christian Fellowship; Interna-
tional Council on Biblical Inerrancy; Israel; Italy; Jarman, Walton
Maxey; Jehovah's Witnesses; Jerusalem, Israel; Jesus people; John
Paul II (Pope); Jones, Howard O; Judaism; Judd, Walter Henry;
Judson, Adoniram; Kantzer, Kenneth Sealer; Kennedy, John Fitz-
gerald; Kilby, Clyde Samuel; Korea; Ku Klux Klan; Kuhlman, Kathryn
Johanna; L'Engle, Madeleine; Lausanne Committee for World Evan-
gelization; Legislators--United States; Lindsell, Harold; Little, Paul
Eagleson; London, England; Los Angeles, CA; Lutheran Church-Mis-
souri Synod; Lutherans; MAP International; Marty, Martin; Mass
media in religion; Massachusetts; McGavran, Donald Anderson;
McIntire, Carl Curtis; McPherson, Aimee Semple; McQuilkin, Robert
Crawford; Miracles; Missions from underdeveloped areas; Missions---
Interdenominational cooperation; Missions--Japan; Montgomery, John
Warwick; Moral Majority; Myra, Harold; National Association of
Evangelicals; National Broadcasting Corporation; New York (state);
New York City, NY; Nixon, Richard Milhous; Nonformal education;
Ockenga, Harold John; Osei-Mensah, Gottfried B; Overseas Mission-
ary Fellowship (China Inland Mission); Oxford University; Padilla,

Carlos Rene; Paul VI (Pope); Peale, Norman Vincent; Pennsylvania;
Pentecostals; Periodical: *Christian Beacon,The*; Periodical: *Christianity
Today*; Periodical: *Eternity Magazine*; Periodical: *Southern Presbyterian
Journal*; Periodical: *United Evangelical Action*; Periodical: *Wittenburg
Door, The*; Pew, John Howard; Poland; Poverty; Presidents--United
States; Quebedeaux, Richard; Race relations; Racism; Radio Program:
*Old Fashioned Revival Hour*; Rather, Dan; Religious News Service;
Rice, John Richard; Riley, William Bell; Robertson, Marion Gordon
"Pat"; Sabbath; Schaeffer, Edith; Schaeffer, Francis August; Schlafley,
Phyllis Steward; Schlesinger, Arthur Meier Jr; Schuller, Robert Har-
old; Seume, Richard Herman; Sex role; Sexual ethics; Sino-Japanese
Conflict, 1937-1945; Smith, Wilbur Moorehead; South Africa; Southern
Baptist Convention; Speer, Robert Elliott; Sudan Interior Mission
(SIM); Sweden; Taiwan; Taylor, Clyde Willis; Taylor, Kenneth Nat-
haniel; Television in religion; Templeton, Charles B; Tennessee;
Tenney, Merrill Chapin; Thailand; Torrey, Reuben Archer Jr; Torrey,
Reuben Archer Sr; Tournier, Paul; Trinity Evangelical Divinity School,
IL; Tyndale House Publishing Co; Underground Evangelism; United
States Center for World Missions; Velikovsky, Immanuel; Vietnamese
Conflict; Wallace, George Corley; Walvoord, John Flipse; Washington,
DC; Weyerhauser, C Davis; Wheaton College, IL; Whitefield, George;
Wilson, George McConnell; Wilson, Grady Baxter; Wilson, Thomas
Walter Jr; Winter, Ralph D; World Council of Churches; World
Evangelical Fellowship (WEF); World Home Bible League; World
Vision International; World War II; Wycliffe Bible Translators; Zim-
babwe; Zimmerman, Thomas Fletcher; Zionism; Zondervan Publishing
House)

%%%%%%%%%%%%

CN# 121
**Lindsay, James Gordon; 1906-1973**
Ephemera; n.d.

Several audio tapes of the radio program *Christ for the Nations*
which include four sermon series by Pentecostal healing evangelist
Lindsay, as well as tapes of other sermons.

Vol: 54 Audio Tapes

(MAJOR TOPICS: Charismatic movement; Christ for the Nations
Ministries, Inc; Evangelistic work--United States; Faith--Cure; Judaism; Lindsay, James Gordon, Pentecostals; Sermons, American)

%%%%%%%%%%%%

CN# 315
**Little, Marie Huttenlock; 1918-**
Interviews; 1985

Two interviews with Little in which she describes her childhood in
Philadelphia; training as a nurse and further education at Philadelphia School of Bible and the University of Pennsylvania; becoming
a missionary for China Inland Mission in 1947, working in Lan-
zhou and Wu Wei, Gansu province; and her returning to the U.S.
in 1950 to become a staff worker for Inter-Varsity.

Vol: 3 Audio Tapes

(MAJOR TOPICS:  Adeney, David Howard; Adolph, Harold Paul;
Australia; Baptists; Baptists--Missions; Bible--Translating; Borden
Memorial Hospital, China; Buddhists in China; Capital punishment;
Chiang Kai-Shek; China; Christian and Missionary Alliance (CMA);
Christian education--China; Church and state in China; Com-
munism--China; Conversion; Crawford, Percy B; Education--China;
Frame, Raymond William; Glover, Robert Hall; Illiteracy; Independ-
ent churches; Inter-Varsity Christian Fellowship; Korean War; Kuhn,
Isobel Miller; Kuo min tang (China); Language in missionary work;
Language: Chinese; League of Evangelical Students; Little, Marie
Huttenlock; Little, Paul Eagleson; Mao Tse-tung; Mass media in
religion; Medical care--China; Medical care--United States; Mis-
sionaries, Withdrawal of; Missions to Buddhists; Missions, British;
Missions, Medical; Missions--China; Moody Memorial Church, IL;
Overseas Missionary Fellowship (China Inland Mission); Pennsylvania;
Radio in religion; Religion and music; Salvation Army; Schoerner,
Otto Frederick; Sex role; Shanghai, China; Sunday schools; Taylor,
James Hudson; Three-Self Patriotic Movement; Tibet; Wycliffe Bible
Translators)

%%%%%%%%%%%%

CN# SC48
**Livingstone, David; 1813-1873**
Ephemera; 1858

Letter written by Livingstone to John Kirk laying down some of
the conditions of an expedition they were planning to make to
Africa.

(MAJOR TOPICS: Livingstone, David)

%%%%%%%%%%%%

CN# 139
**Longino, Frances Rader; 1909-**
Interview; 1980

Taped oral history interview in which Longino describes her
childhood memories of evangelists Billy Sunday, Mel Trotter,
Homer Rodeheaver, and her uncle, Paul Rader; city mission work
and the Chicago Gospel Tabernacle; Pacific Garden Mission;
Winona Lake, and Cedar Lake Conference Grounds.  Also included are reminiscences of Rader's reaction to Aimee Semple
McPherson, the formation of Scripture Press, Billy Graham's early
crusades, and some of her Salvation Army activities as a musical
evangelist.

Vol: 1 Audio Tape

(MAJOR TOPICS: Biederwolf, William Edward; Chicago Gospel
Tabernacle; Chicago, IL; Cities and towns; City missions; Dunlop,
Merrill; Evangelistic work--United States; Graham, William Franklin
"Billy"; Hamblen, Stuart; Hoover, Herbert Clark; Latham, Lance;
Longino, Frances Rader; Los Angeles, CA; McPherson, Aimee Sem-
ple; Pacific Garden Mission, IL; Presidents--United States; Prohibi-
tion; Rader, Daniel Paul; Rader, Luke; Rodeheaver, Homer Alvan;
Salvation Army; Shea, George Beverly; Smith, Wilbur Moorehead;
Trotter, Melvin Ernest; Winona Lake Bible Conference, IN; Youth for
Christ International)

%%%%%%%%%%%%

CN# 2
**Lundquist, Roy; 1897-1975**
Papers; 1925-1974

Documents in collection relate mostly to a study Lundquist did on
the effect Billy Graham Crusades in thirteen cities had on crime.
Some files have information about the Moody Church of Chicago,
and to Wheaton, Illinois, politics.

Vol: 1 box

(MAJOR TOPICS: Boston, MA; California; Church and social prob-
lems; Crime and criminals; Evangelistic work--United States; Graham,
William Franklin "Billy"; Illinois; Los Angeles, CA; Lundquist, Roy;
Moody Memorial Church, IL; Texas)

%%%%%%%%%%%%

CN# 49
**Maier, Paul Luther; 19?-**
Interview; 1978

Brief interview with Maier in which he talks about the relationship
between his father Walter Arthur Maier, of the radio program *The
Lutheran Hour*, and Billy Graham. He also talks about Walter F.
Bennett and Company, an advertising firm.

Vol: 1 Audio Tape

(MAJOR TOPICS: Evangelistic work--United States; Graham, Wil-
liam Franklin "Billy"; Lutherans; Maier, Paul Luther; Maier, Walter
Arthur; Mass media in religion; Radio in religion; Radio program:
*Hour of Decision*; Radio Program: *Lutheran Hour, The*; Walter F
Bennett and Co)

%%%%%%%%%%%%

CN# 321
**Manzano, Glicerio "Jojo" Maniquis; 1952-**
Papers; 1981-1988

Three interviews with and prayer letters prepared by Manzano,
documenting his education, spiritual pilgrimage, service as office
manager with Inter-Varsity Christian Fellowship of the Philippines
and accountant for a rural hospital with International Nepal
Fellowship. Other subjects covered include: communism, Philippine Catholicism, family life, Nepali culture, the Nepali church,
and the 1987 Philippine elections.

Volume: 1 Box, 4 Audio Tapes

(MAJOR TOPICS:  Baptism; Bible colleges; Catholic Church in
Philippines; Catholic Church--Relations; Children of missionaries;
Christian education--New Zealand; Church and state in Nepal; Church
work with students; Communism--Philippines; Conversion; Education,
Higher; Education--New Zealand; Hinduism (theology); Hindus in
Nepal; Indigenous church administration; Inter-Varsity Christian
Fellowship of the Philippines; Intercultural communications; Language
in missionary work; Manzano, Glicerio "Jojo" Jr; Medical care--Nepal;
Missionaries--Philippines; Missionaries--Recruitment and training;
Missionaries--Salaries, pensions, etc.; Missions from underdeveloped
areas; Missions to Hindus; Missions, Medical; Missions--Nepal; Nepal;

Philippines; Preaching; Sunday schools; Women in missionary work; Women--Religious life)

%%%%%%%%%%%%

CN# 308
**Marks, Harvey W; 1909-**
Papers; 1954-1985

Interview of Marks in which he discusses his career in Christian film distribution, the development of Protestant Evangelical film--making, his involvement with filmmakers such as C. O. Baptista and James Frederick, film production workshops at Green Lake, Wisconsin, the church's use of films, and the effects of television on the Evangelical film industry. Also included in the collection is a copy of the notebook of the Eleventh International Workshop in Audio-Visual Education, held in 1954.

Vol: 1 Folder, 2 Audio Tapes

(MAJOR TOPICS: Anderson, Kenneth; Assemblies of God; Australia; Baptista, Charles Octavia; Baptists; California; Cathedral Films; Christian Booksellers' Association; Colorado; Communication; Disciples of Christ; Disney, Walter; Dobson, James; Evangelistic work---United States; Frederick, James K; Illinois; Lutheran Church-Missouri Synod; Lutherans; Mass media in religion; Methodists; Modernist-Fundamentalist controversy; Moody Bible Institute, IL; Moon, Irwin A; Moving-pictures in church work; Moving-pictures--Moral and religious aspects; Wisconsin)

%%%%%%%%%%%%

CN# 216
**Marquardt, Horst; 1929-**
Interview; 1982

Oral history interview in which Marquardt discusses his childhood in Germany under the Nazi government, his work for the Communist party in East Germany, his conversion to Christianity, and his career as director of Evangeliums-Rundfunk, the German branch of Trans World Radio.

Vol: 1 Audio tape

(MAJOR TOPICS: Berlin, Germany; Church and social problems; Communism; Communism--Germany; Conversion; Evangelistic work--Germany; Evangelistic work--Poland; Evangelistic work--Soviet

Union; Evangeliums Rundfunk; Fund raising; Germany; Graham,
William Franklin "Billy"; Hitler, Adolph; Hungary; International relief;
Lausanne Committee for World Evangelization; Marquardt, Horst;
Mass media in religion;  Methodists; Missions--Germany; National
Socialism; Persecution--Soviet Union; Poland; Radio in missionary
work; Radio in religion; Radio program: *Hour of Decision*;
Refugees--Germany; Soviet Union; Trans World Radio; World War
II)

%%%%%%%%%%%%

CN# 62
**Mather, Cotton; 1663-1728**
Papers; 1680-1724; n.d

Microfilm of diaries, sermons, notes, correspondence, and writings
of Mather. Originals are in the American Antiquarian Society and
the Massachusetts Historical Society. Also included in the collection is the original and a photocopy of a hand-written sermon,
1701, on Ephesians 1:3, titled "Spiritual Blessings".

Vol: 19 Microfilm, 2 folders

(MAJOR TOPICS:  Evangelistic work--North America; Evangelistic
work--United States; Frontier and pioneer life--United States; Mather,
Cotton; Occult sciences; Sermons, American; United States--Church
History--Colonial period, ca 1600-1775; United States--History--Colon-
ial period, ca 1600-1775)

%%%%%%%%%%%%

CN# 119
**McConnell, James Edwin; ?-?**
Ephemera; n.d.

One audio tape of two programs of Smilin' Ed McConnell's radio
series, probably broadcast in the 1930s or 40s.  His show consisted
mainly of popular hymns.

Vol: 1 Audio Tape

(MAJOR TOPICS: Communication; Mass media in religion; McConnell, James Edwin; Radio in religion; Religion and music)

%%%%%%%%%%%%

CN# 246
**McDonald, Jessie; 1888-1980**
Papers; 1907; 1914-1951; n.d.

Correspondence, diaries, notes, articles, photographs, and annual
reports relating to McDonald's medical work in China from
1913-1952 with China Inland Mission. The documents depict
evangelistic outreach, and the nature of health conditions in China.
The materials also describe the political and social upheavals
occurring in China during the first half of the 1900s.

Vol: 1 box, Photographs

(MAJOR TOPICS: Adolph, Paul Earnest; Beijing, China; China;
Communism--China; Education--China; Evangelistic work--China;
Feng Yu-hsiang; Hess, Esther Marguerite Nowack; Japan; Jews in
China; Korea; Kuo min tang (China); Language in missionary work;
McDonald, Jessie; Medical care--China; Missionaries, Withdrawal of;
Missionaries--Leaves and furloughs; Missions, Medical; Mis-
sions--China; Overseas Missionary Fellowship (China Inland Mission);
Pentecostals; Red Cross; Refugees--China; Sex role; Sino-Japanese
Conflict, 1937-1945; World War II)

%%%%%%%%%%%%

CN# 110
**McDowell, Donald England; 1924-**
Ephemera; 1951-1973

Collection of slides which document Protestant mission activity in
Paraguay. Scenic views, native flora, mission personnel, mission
facilities, national churchmen and pastors are some of the subjects
illustrated by the collection.

Vol: 643 Slides

(MAJOR TOPICS: Bolivia; Brazil; Evangelistic work--Paraguay;
Graham, William Franklin "Billy"; Honduras; McDowell, Donald
England; Missions--Paraguay; Paraguay; Peru; Rio de Janeiro, Brazil;
Uruguay)

%%%%%%%%%%%%

CN# 178
**McGavran, Donald Anderson; 1897-**
Papers; 1917-1976; n.d.

Audio tapes, microfilm of letters, notes, book manuscripts, minutes
of meetings and other records dealing with the career of missionary and missiologist Donald McGavran. The documents in this
collection describe his and his wife's work as missionaries in India
and the beginning and development of the Church Growth movement.

Vol: 11 Reels of Microfilm, 7 Audio Tapes

(MAJOR TOPICS: American Bible Society; Assemblies of God;
Brazil; California; Christian and Missionary Alliance (CMA); Chris-
tianity Today, Inc; Church growth; Church of Christ in the Congo;
Coggins, Wade Thomas; Disciples of Christ; Disciples of Christ--Mis-
sions; Ethiopia; Ethnic groups; Evangelical Alliance Mission, The
(TEAM); Evangelistic work--Taiwan; Evangelistic work--United
States)

%%%%%%%%%%%%

CN# 103
**McPherson, Aimee Semple; 1890-1944**
Papers; 1921-1972, n.d.

Sermon transcripts, sermon notes, films, phonograph records,
audio tapes, newspaper clippings, scrapbooks, evangelistic campaign material related to McPherson's career as evangelist, radio
speaker, and church founder.

Vol: 1 box, 21 Audio Tapes, 2 Films, 22 Reels of Microfilm, 4
Phonograph records

(MAJOR TOPICS: Angelus Temple, CA; Charismatic movement;
Communication; Creation--biblical teaching; Evangelistic work--United
States; Evolution; Faith--Cure; Fundamentalism; Healers; International
Church of the Four Square Gospel; McPherson, Aimee Semple; Pen-
tecostals; Radio in religion; Religion and science; Sermons, American;
Sex role; Women authors; Women clergy; Women--Religious life)

%%%%%%%%%%%%

CN# 363
**Mellis, Ruth Margaret; 1907-**
Interviews; 1985

Two oral history interviews about Mellis's conversion, development
as a Christian, college years at Wheaton, her work as an independent missionary, teaching in Greece and Ethiopia.

Vol: 4 Audio Tapes

(MAJOR TOPICS: Conversion; Evangelistic work--United States;
Mellis, Ruth Margaret; Missions--Ethiopia; Missions--Greece; Orphans
and orphan-asylums; Wheaton College, IL)

%%%%%%%%%%%%

CN# 136
**Mission Aviation Fellowship; 1944-**
Records; 1944-1969; n.d.

MAF was a service organized, primarily concerned with providing
transportation and logistical support to missionaries in very remote
parts of the world. This collection consists of office files, including
correspondence with MAF missionaries, with other missions
served by MAF, and the general public. Also, technical bulletins,
a radio script, publications, theses about missionary aviation, and
prayer letters.

Vol: 62 boxes, Negatives, Photographs, Oversize Material

(MAJOR TOPICS: Aeronautics in missionary work; Africa Evangeli-
cal Fellowship; Africa Inland Mission (AIM); Alaska; American Bible
Society; Anderson, Kenneth; Assemblies of God--Missions; Auca
people, Ecuador; Australia; Austria; Baptists; Baptists--Missions; Bible
Institute of Los Angeles (BIOLA), CA; Bob Jones University, SC;
Bolivia; Bowman, Robert H; Brazil; Broadcasting station: ELWA,
Liberia; Broadcasting station: HCJB, Ecuador; California; CAM
International; Catholic Church in United States; Catholic Church---
Relations; Chad; China; Christian and Missionary Alliance (CMA);
Christian and Missionary Alliance--Missions; Christian Service Bri-
gade; Church and state in Sudan; Church and state in Zaire; Church
work with students; Columbia Bible College, Columbia, SC; Com-
munism; Congresses and conferences--Congress on the Church's
Worldwide Mission, 1966; Conservative Baptist Foreign Mission
Society; Costa Rica; Cuba; Dodds, Gilbert L; Ecuador; Edman, Victor

Raymond; Elliot, Elisabeth Howard; Elliot, Philip James; Ethiopia;
Evangelical Alliance Mission, The (TEAM); Evangelical Covenant
Church--Missions; Evangelical Foreign Missions Association; Evangeli-
cal Free Church of America; Evangelical Free Church--Missions;
Evangelistic work--Nigeria; Evangelistic work--South Africa; Evangelis-
tic work--Vietnam; Far East Broadcasting Company; Fuller Theologi-
cal Seminary, CA; Gospel Recordings, Inc; Graham, William Franklin
"Billy"; Great Britain; Greater Europe Mission (GEM); Guatemala;
Hatcher, Elias Wesley; Gospel Missionary Union; Honduras; Howard,
Philip E Jr; India; Indonesia; Inter-Varsity Christian Fellowship;
Interdenominational Foreign Mission Association (IFMA); Ivory
Coast; Japan; Jones, Robert R Jr "Bob"; Kenya; Latin America Mis-
sion; Letourneau, Robert Gilmore; Letourneau, Roy; Liberia; Lindsell,
Harold; London, England; Lutheran Church--Missions; Lutheran
Church-Missouri Synod; Lutherans; Mass media in religion; McCully,
Theodore Edward, Sr; Medical care--Kenya; Methodist Church--Mis-
sions; Methodists; Mexico; Mission Aviation Fellowship (MAF); Mis-
sionaries--Recruitment and training; Missions, Medical; Missions--Aus-
tralia; Missions--Brazil; Missions--China; Missions--Costa Rica; Mis-
sions--Ecuador; Missions--Ethiopia; Missions--Honduras; Missions--In-
terdenominational cooperation; Missions--Kenya; Missions--Mexico;
Missions--Nigeria; Missions--Papua New Guinea; Missions--Philip-
pines; Missions--Soviet Union; Missions--Sudan; Missions--Tanzania;
Missions--Venezuela; Missions--Zaire; Missions--Zimbabwe; Moody
Bible Institute, IL; Moody Institute of Science; Moving-pictures in
church work; Multnomah School of the Bible; Muslims in Sudan;
National Association of Evangelicals; National Council of Churches;
Navigators; New Tribes Mission; New Zealand; Nigeria; O C Min-
istries; Overseas Missionary Fellowship (China Inland Mission);
Periodical: *Christian Century, The*; Periodical: *Christianity Today*; Peru;
Philadelphia College of the Bible, PA; Philippines; Pike, Kenneth Lee;
Radio in religion; Rockefeller, Nelson Aldrich; Russian Missionary
Society; Saint, Nathanael "Nate"; SEND International; Seventh Day
Adventists; Seventh Day Adventists--Missions; Slavic Gospel Associa-
tion; Somali (Somali Democratic Republic); South Africa; Sudan
Interior Mission (SIM); Sunday schools; Switzerland; Tanzania; Taylor,
Clyde Willis; Taylor, Kenneth Nathaniel; Thiessen, Abraham Gustov;
Townsend, William Cameron; Trans World Radio; Trotman, Dawson;
Truxton, James Campbell; Unevangelized Fields Mission; United
States--History--1919-1933; Van Der Puy, Abraham Cornelius; Vene-
zuela; Vietnam; Walter F Bennett and Co; Weyerhauser, C Davis;
Wheaton College, IL; Word of Life Fellowship; World Evangelical
Fellowship (WEF); World Home Bible League; World Vision Interna-
tional; Wycliffe Bible Translators; Youderain, Roger; Zaire; Zim-
babwe)

%%%%%%%%%%%%

CN# 140
**Mitchell, Everett; 1898-**
Interview; 1980

Oral history interview with Mitchell, who as a teenager sang invitation songs at Billy Sunday evangelistic campaigns. Mitchell discusses the evangelistic meetings in which he participated, Billy and Helen Sunday, Gipsy Smith, Chicago saloons, Homer Rodeheaver, and Mitchell's experiences with personal evangelism in Japan and Korea during the Korean War.

Vol: 1 Audio Tape

(MAJOR TOPICS: Billy Graham Center, IL; Catholic Church in United States; Catholic Church--Relations; Chicago, IL; Church and social problems; Evangelistic work--United States; Finland; Graham, William Franklin "Billy"; Japan; Korea; Korean War; McArthur, Douglas; Mitchell, Everett; Pacific Garden Mission, IL; Pius XII (Pope); Rodeheaver, Homer Alvan; Smith, Rodney "Gipsy"; Soviet Union; Sunday, Helen Amelia Thompson; Sunday, William Ashley "Billy"; Temperance; Winona Lake Bible Conference, IN)

%%%%%%%%%%%%

CN# 280
**Moe, Petra Malena "Malla"; 1863-1953**
Papers; 1893-1955; n.d.

Diaries, notebooks, correspondence, clippings, financial records, tracts, photographs, and certificates belonging to Malla Moe, missionary to South Africa, 1892-1953, under Scandinavian Alliance Mission (later The Evangelical Alliance Missions). Correspondence documents evangelistic work among South African tribes in Swaziland and Tongoland and include descriptions of the Boer War, life in African communities, and church growth.

Vol: 2 boxes, Photographs

(MAJOR TOPICS: Allenby, Edmund Henry Hunman; Boer War; Chicago, IL; Church growth; Conversion; Evangelical Alliance Mission, The (TEAM); Evangelistic work--Swaziland; Franson, Fredrik; Illinois; Illiteracy; Intercultural communications; Language in missionary work; Missionaries, Lay; Missionaries--Leaves and furloughs; Missionaries---Recruitment and training; Missions--Finance; Missions--South Africa;

Missions--Swaziland; Moe, Petra Malena "Malla"; Natal; Norway; Prayer; South Africa; Swaziland)

%%%%%%%%%%%%%

CN# SC49
**Moffat, Robert; 1795-1883**
Ephemera; 1871-1878

Collection contains a letter from Moffat, a noted missionary, to a Mr. Bergne in February, 1871, regarding the slow proceedings of Bergne's committee and Moffat's great expenses while working on his translation of the Old Testament, and an 1878 autograph with a Bible verse.

(MAJOR TOPICS: Bible--Translating; Fund raising; Moffat, Robert)

%%%%%%%%%%%%%

CN# SC36
**Moody, Dwight Lyman; 1837-1899**
Ephemera; 1891-1893; n.d.

Several letters written by evangelist Moody about his work, interest, and activities; a hand written signature card; a handbill announcing a Moody-Sankey Men's Meeting and a phonograph record of Moody reading the Beatitudes and Ira Sankey singing "God Be With You".

(MAJOR TOPICS: Evangelistic work--United States; Fund raising; Moody, Dwight Lyman; Religion and music; Sankey, Ira David)

%%%%%%%%%%%%%

CN# SC93
**Mott, John Raleigh; 1865-1955**
Ephemera; 1914

A typewritten letter to F. H. Green, from John Mott, international executive of the YMCA, commending the importance of moral and religious character as the most important qualification for teaching. Signed by Mott.

(MAJOR TOPICS: Mott, John Raleigh)

%%%%%%%%%%%%

CN# 189
**Moyan, Mary Goforth; 1903-**
Papers; 1980-1981; n.d.

Oral history interviews and color slides which deal with Moyan's memories of the personalities and work of her parents, Jonathan and Rosalind Goforth; evangelistic work in China before World War II; her own career in Christian work; and her trips in 1979 to Taiwan and in 1980 to the People's Republic of China.

Vol: 3 Audio Tapes, Slides

(MAJOR TOPICS: Agricultural societies; Boxers (Chinese political movement); Buck, Pearl Sydenstricker (Mrs Richard J Walsh); Buddhists in China; Canada; Catholic Church in China; Catholic Church---Missions; Catholic Church--Relations; Children of missionaries; China; Christian and Missionary Alliance (CMA); Church and social problems; Communication; Communism; Confucianism; Family; Feng Yu-hsiang; Finney, Charles Grandison; Fundamentalism; Goforth, Jonathan; Goforth, Rosalind; Hunger; Imperialism; Letourneau, Robert Gilmore; Marriage; McArthur, Douglas; Missions to Buddhists; Missions--China; Modernist-Fundamentalist controversy; Moynan, Mary Goforth; Muslims in China; Overseas Missionary Fellowship (China Inland Mission); Poverty; Prayer; Presbyterian Church---Missions; Presbyterians; Sex role; Smith, Oswald Jeffrey; Social change; Social classes; Stam, Elizabeth Alden Scott; Stam, John Cornelius; Taiwan)

%%%%%%%%%%%%

CN# 108
**Muntz, John Palmer; 1897-1989**
Papers; 1947-1977; n.d.

Correspondence, newspaper clippings, a book manuscript, a film script, and other items. Materials in this collection describe Muntz's early career as director of the Winona Lake Bible Conference, the early development of the Billy Graham Evangelistic Association and the criticism it received, and the careers of Billy Sunday and other evangelists.

Vol: 2 boxes, Photographs, 2 Audio Tapes

(MAJOR TOPICS: Armerding, Carl E; Australia; Beavan, Gerald "Jerry"; Billy Graham Center, IL; Billy Graham Evangelistic Association (BGEA); Bowman, Robert H; California; Ecumenical movement; Evangelistic work--Australia; Evangelistic work--New Zealand; Evangelistic work--United States; Ford, Leighton Frederick Sandys; Fundamentalism; Georgia; Graham, William Franklin "Billy"; Houghton, William Henry; Illinois; Indiana; Inter-Varsity Christian Fellowship; Jones, Robert R Jr "Bob"; Jones, Robert R Sr "Bob"; Letourneau, Robert Gilmore; Muntz, John Palmer; New York (state); New York City, NY; New Zealand; Oregon; Peale, Norman Vincent; Rice, John Richard; Riley, William Bell; Rodeheaver, Homer Alvan; Sermons, American; Smith, Wilbur Moorehead; Sunday, Helen Amelia Thompson; Sunday, William Ashley "Billy"; Voelkel, Harold; Wilson, Thomas Walter Jr; Winona Lake Bible Conference, IN; World Wide Pictures)


%%%%%%%%%%%%

CN# 176
**National Prayer Congress; 1976**
Records; 1976

Tape recordings of thirty addresses presented to the Congress, convened in Dallas, Texas. All speeches concern some aspect of prayer. Participants include Bill Bright, Charles Colson, Billy Graham, Rex Humbard, Billy Melvin, Harold Ockenga, J. Edwin Orr, Jimmy Owens, Pat Robertson, and Ben Armstrong, among others.

Vol: 16 Audio Tapes

(MAJOR TOPICS: African Americans; Armstrong, Benjamin Leighton; Barnhouse, Donald Grey Sr; Billy Graham Evangelistic Association (BGEA); Boone, Charles Eugene "Pat"; Bowman, Robert H; Bright, William Rohl "Bill"; Campus Crusade for Christ; China; Cleaver, Leroy Eldridge; Colson, Charles Wendell; Edman, Victor Raymond; Graham, Ruth Bell; Graham, William Franklin "Billy"; Great Britain; Hill, Edwin V; Hughes, Harold Everett; Kennedy, D James; Mass media in religion; Melvin, Billy Alfred; Nixon, Richard Milhous; Ockenga, Harold John; Orr, James Edwin; Prayer; Presidents--United States; Radio in religion; Robertson, Marion Gordon "Pat"; Sermons, American; Solzhenitsyn, Alexander; Soviet Union; ten Boom, Cornelia Arnolda Johanna; World War II; Zimmerman, Thomas Fletcher)

%%%%%%%%%%%%

CN# 7
**Navigators; 1943-**
Records; 1947-1974; n.d.

Correspondence, memoranda, reports, forms, and newspaper
clippings relating to the counseling and follow-up work done by
the evangelistic organization the Navigators for Billy Graham evangelistic meetings in the 1950s. For some crusades, besides manuals for counselors and advisors, staff reports, statistical reports and
clippings, there are also follow-up statistical reports on the after-
effects of the Crusade and pastors' responses to it. Also in the
collection is a notebook dating from 1953 explaining the need for a
new headquarters for the Navigators.

Vol: 5 boxes

(MAJOR TOPICS:  Billy Graham Evangelistic Association (BGEA);
California; Canada; Counseling; District of Columbia; Evangelistic
work--Canada; Evangelistic work--Great Britain; Evangelistic work---
United States; Graham, William Franklin "Billy"; Great Britain;
Haymaker, Willis Graham; Kentucky; London, England; Los Angeles,
CA; Louisiana; Michigan; Mississippi; Missouri; Navigators; New
Mexico; New York (state); New York City, NY; North Carolina; Ohio;
Organizational change; Riggs, Charles A; Sanny, Lorne Charles;
Tennessee; Texas; Toronto, ON; Trotman, Dawson; Virginia; Wash-
ington (state); Washington, DC; Youth for Christ International)

%%%%%%%%%%%%

CN# 380
**Neece James Holloway; 1941-**
Interviews; 1987

Oral history interviews in which Neece describes his conversion
and Christian education, discusses the work of a jail chaplain and
the spiritual needs of prisoners, and comments on the work of the
Good News Mission.

Vol: 4 reels of audio tape

(MAJOR TOPICS:  Alcoholics; Bible colleges; Christian educa-
tion--United States; Christian literature--Publication and distribution;
Church and social problems; Church and state in United States;
Colson, Charles Wendell; Conversion; Counseling; Crime and criminals; Divorce; Evangelistic work--North America; Evangelistic work---

The following photographs are provided courtesy of
the Billy Graham Center Library and
the Billy Graham Center Archives.

uiris de galaad pugnabat contra e-
phraim. Percusserûtq; uiri galaad e-
phraim: quia dixerat fugitiu⁹ est galaad de ephraim ⁊ habitat in medio
ephraim et manasse. Occupauerunt
galaadite uada iordanis per que e-
phraim reuersurus erat. Cunq; uenisset ad ea de ephraim numero fugiēs-
atq; dixisset obsecro ut me transire per-
mitras: dicebant ei galaadite. Nun-
quid ephrateus es? Quo dicente non
sum:interrogabât eū. Dic ergo sebbo-
leth:qđ interpretaf spica. Qui respon-
debat thebboleth:eadē littera spicam
exprimere non ualens:statimq; appre-
hensum iugulabât in ipso iordanis
transitu. Et ceciderunt in illo têpore de
ephraim quadragita duo milia. Iudicauit itaq; iepthe galaadites israhel
sex annis:⁊ mortuus est ac sepult⁹ in
ciuitate sua galaad. Post hunc iudicauit israhel abessan de bethleem:qui
habuit triginta filios et totidem filias.
Quas emittens foras marito:⁊
eiusdem numeri filijs suis accepit uxo-
res:introducens in domū suā. Qui se-
ptem annis iudicauit israhel:mortu⁹
q; est ac sepult⁹ in bethleem. Cui successi
sit ahialon zabulonites:et iudicauit
israhel decem ānis:mortuusq; est ac sepultus in zabulon. Post hūc iudicauit isrč abdon filius hellel pharatoni-
tes qui habuit quadraginta filios ⁊
triginta ex eis nepotes ascendentes su-
per septuaginta pullos asinarum:et
iudicauit israhel octo annis: mortu-
usq; est ac sepultus in pharaton terre
ephraim in monte amalech. XIII
Rursumq; filij isrč fecerūt malum
in conspectu dñi:q̃ tradidit eos
in manus philistinoꝝ quadraginta
annis. Erat aūt quidā uir de saraa

et de stirpe dan nomine manue habēs
uxorem sterilem:cui apparuit angelꝰ
dñi:et dixit ad eam. Sterilis es et abs-
q; liberis:sed concipies et paries filiū.
Caue ergo ne bibas uinū ac siceram
nec immūdum quicq; comedas:quia
concipies et paries filiū:cuj⁹ nō tāget
caput nouacula. Erit enim nazareus
dei ab infantia sua et ex matris uete-
et ipse incipiet liberare israhel de manu
philistinoꝝ. Que cū uenisset ad mari-
tū suū:dixit ei. Vir dei uenit ad me
habens uultum angelicum:terribilis
nimis. Quē cum interrogassem quis
esset ⁊ unde uenisset ⁊ quo nomine uo-
caretur noluit michi dicere: sed hoc respondit. Ecce concipies et paries filiū.
Caue ne uinū bibas nec siceram:⁊ ne
aliquo uescaris immūdo. Erit enī pu-
et nazareus ab infantia sua et ex ute-
ro matris sue:usq; ad diē mortis sue.
Orauit itaq; manue dñm et ait. Obsecro dñe ut uir dei quē misisti ueniat
iterū:et doceat nos quid nos debeam⁹
facere de puero q̃ nasciturus est. Exau-
diuitq; dñs deprecātem manue:et apparuit rursū angelꝰ dñi uxori eius se-
denti i agro. Manue aūt marit⁹ eius
non erat cū ea. Que cū uidisset angelū
festinauit et cucurrit ad uirū suū:nun-
ciauitq; ei dicēs. Ecce apparuit michi
uir quē ante uideram. Qui surrexit et
secut⁹ est uxorem suā: ueniensq; ad ui-
rum dixit ei. Tu es q̃ locut⁹ es mulieri?
Et ille respondit. Ego sū. Cui manue.
Quando inquit sermo tuus fuerit ex-
pletus: quid uis ut faciat puer aut a
quo se obseruare debebit? Dixitq; angelus dñi ad manue. Ab omnib; que
locutus sum uxori tue abstineat se: et
quicquid ex uinea nascitur non come-
dat:uinū et siceram non bibat:nullo

Folio leaf from *The Gutenberg Bible*. Mainz: J. Gutenberg and Associates, ca. 1450-55. Vol. I, folio 122, Judges xii: 3 – xiv: 15. 15⅜″ × 11¼″.

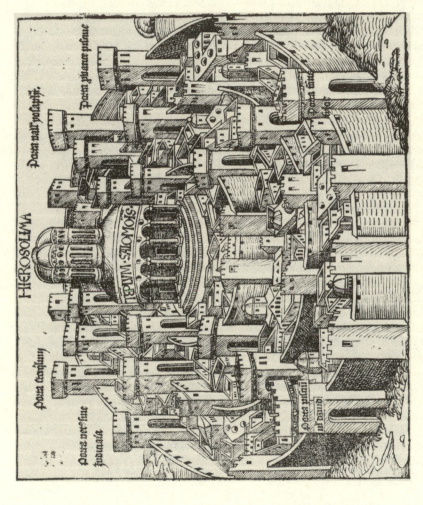

*Hierosolima* [Jerusalem]. Michael Wohlgemut. From *The Nürnburg Chronicle*. Nürnburg: Anton Koberger, 1493. Woodcut. 7½″ × 8¾″.

*Martinus Lutherus Theologus Germania Elias.* n.d. Steel engraving. 5⅜″ × 4⅛″.

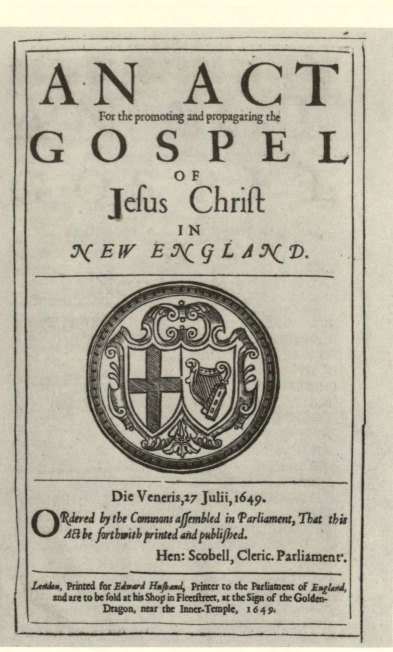

# AN ACT

For the promoting and propagating the

# GOSPEL

OF

## Jesus Christ

IN

### NEW ENGLAND.

Die Veneris, 27 Julii, 1649.

ORdered by the Commons assembled in Parliament, That this Act be forthwith printed and published.

Hen: Scobell, Cleric. Parliament'.

London, Printed for *Edward Husband*, Printer to the Parliament of *England*, and are to be sold at his Shop in Fleetstreet, at the Sign of the Golden-Dragon, near the Inner-Temple, 1649.

*An Act for the promoting and propagating the Gospel of Jesus Christ in New England. London, 1649. Pamphlet. 8⅝" × 5⅛".*

One of Cotton Mather's sermons

### Eph. I. 3. - Spiritual Blessings.

To know what Blessings are ye best and ye
chief of Blessings, is one ~~██████~~ part of or
preparation for the Blessings; yea, that
knowledge is it self one of the Blessings.

What are those Blessings, is now to be declar'd.
Hear, O Congregation; they are Spiritual
Blessings, which are of all ye most prefer-
-able Blessings.

In ye Apostolical Doxology we have here, ye
Author of those Blessings, that Bespeak our
Hallelujahs: 'Tis ye God & Father of or L. J. C.
Let us now see ye Quality of those Blessings.
There ~~██~~ is a vast variety of Blessings, wch
ye God of Heaven showers down from Heaven
upon ye children of Men. But upon His own
children, ye ~~███████~~ Blessed God multiplies
His Blessings & His Bounties, more than upon
ye rest of ye ~~██████~~ ~~███~~ Some of them
are Temporal Blessings: And ye Apostle was
undoubtedly thankful for such Blessings. God
had been favourable to him, & his Ephesians
in Temporal, & External Respects. But he
omitts ye mention of those: He mentions
only Spiritual Blessings, as being indeed the
Superlative Blessings.

Doct.

Spiritual Blessings are with every
Blessed man, the principal Bles-
-sings.

Temporal Blessings are desirable; But Spi-
-ritual Blessings are much more desirable.
Spiritual Blessings are to be valued, as the
Blessings of ye Right Hand; In Spiritual
Blessings it is, that we are fed with the
Finest of ye Wheat, & satisfied with Honey
out of ye Rock of mercy.

You may call to mind, that God has
given us an Inventory of the Blessings, wch

*Spiritual Blessings.* A sermon on Eph. 1: 3. Cotton Mather, 1701. Manuscript. 6" ×
3⅝".

*Sigillum Societatis de Promovendo Evangelio in Partibus Transmarinis: The Gift of the Society for Propagating the Gospell in Foreign Parts.* ca. 1704. Bookplate. 4¾ ″ × 3½ ″.

[John] *Wesley*. n.d. Staffordshire figure. 11″ × 5½″ × 3¼″.

*Jonathan Edwards.* R. Babson & J. Andrews. n.d. Mezzotint. 5½ ″ × 4¼ ″.

And now behold your Saviour rife,
   Who conquer'd when he fell,
And at his glorious Chariot Wheels
   Led captive Death and Hell.

Which joyful News the Angels told,
   To holy Women then,
That Chrift who lately was interr'd,
   Had now arofe again.          And

*The History of the Holy Jesus.* Boston: J. Bushell and J. Green, 1749. Illustrated children's book. 4″ × 3″ × ⅛″.

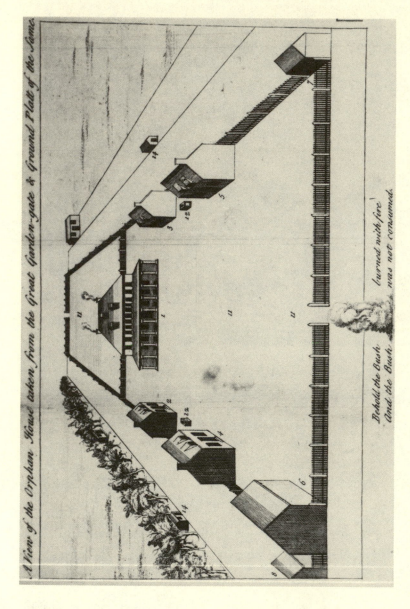

*A View of the Orphan House taken from the Great Garden-gate & Ground Platt of the Same.* From *The Orphan House Accounts.* George Whitefield, ca. 1741. 6½″ × 16½″.

A Colonial minister preaching to North-American Indians, ca. 1745. Hand-colored steel engraving. 17″ × 23¾″.

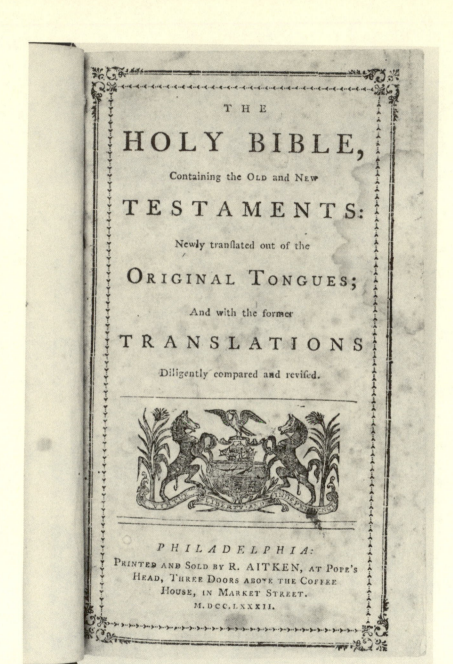

THE
# HOLY BIBLE,
Containing the OLD and NEW

# TESTAMENTS:

Newly tranflated out of the

## ORIGINAL TONGUES;

And with the former

# TRANSLATIONS

Diligently compared and revifed.

*PHILADELPHIA:*
Printed and Sold by R. AITKEN, at Pope's
Head, Three Doors above the Coffee
House, in Market Street.
M.DCC.LXXXII.

*The Holy Bible, Containing the Old and New Testaments: Newly translated out of the
Original Tongues; And with the former Translations Diligently compared and
revised. Philadelphia: R. Aitken, 1782. 6⅜" × 3⅞" × 1⅛".*

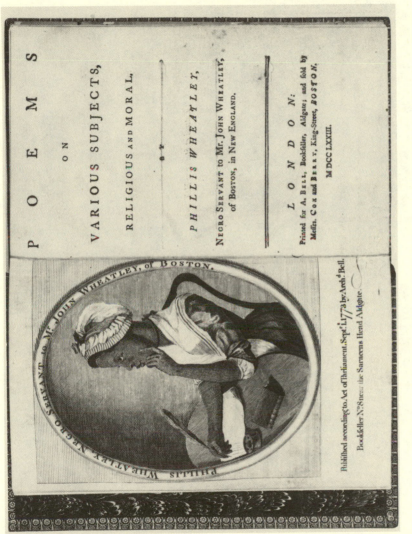

*Poems on Various Subjects, Religious and Moral.* Phillis Wheatley. London: A. Bell, 1773. 7″ × 4¾″ × ½″.

Top, *Verbum Sempiterum / Salvatori Mundi*. Third edition with amendments. John Taylor, 1701. Miniature book. 2⅛″ × 1¾″ × ¾″. Bottom, *History of the Bible*. Cooperstown: H. & E. Phinney, 1825. Miniature book. 2″ × 1⅝″ × ⅝″.

*Rev. Timothy Dwight, S.T.D., L.L.D.* B. Rogers. M. Thomas, 1817. Mezzotint. 3½″ × 2¾″.

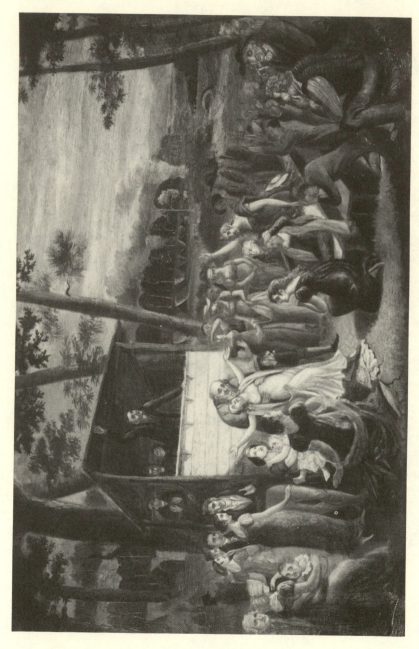

Camp meeting. Attributed to Alexander Rider. ca. 1820. Oil on pine panel. 18¾″ × 28″ × ¾″.

# CONSTITUTION

OF THE

# AMERICAN TRACT SOCIETY,

WITH

## ADDRESSES TO CHRISTIANS

RECOMMENDING THE

## DISTRIBUTION OF RELIGIOUS TRACTS,

AND

# Anecdotes

ILLUSTRATING THEIR BENEFICIAL EFFECTS.

—I handed him the *Swearer's Prayer,* and went on my journey.—
See p. 24.

---

PRINTED FOR

## THE AMERICAN TRACT SOCIETY,

BY FLAGG AND GOULD.

*Constitution of the American Tract Society, with Addresses to Christians Recommending the Distribution of Religious Tracts, and Anecdotes Illustrating Their Beneficial Effects.* Andover: Flagg & Gould, ca. 1820. Pamphlet. 6⅝″ × 4¼″ × ⅛″.

The Roads to Heaven and Hell. Attributed to Gustav Sigismund Peters. Harrisburg, ca. 1820. Hand-colored Pennsylvania German woodcut. 12" × 14¾".

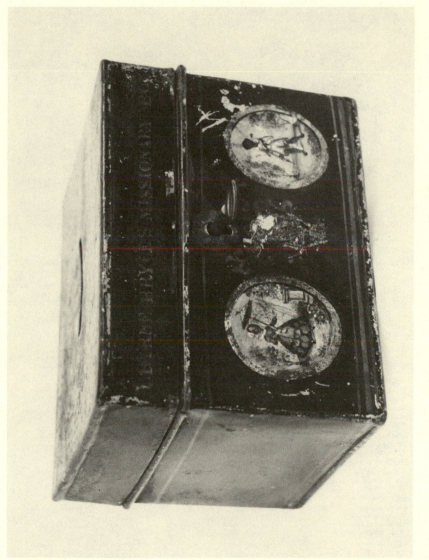

*R. Byrne Bryce's Missionary Box.* n.d. Bank. 3¾″ × 5″ × 3″.

COME all ye sons of Adam's race,
  Who're ruin'd by the fall;
Who've lost your Maker's pristine grace,
  Nor on your Saviour call:

Come listen while I tell to you
The joys of pardon'd sin;
Present the gate of Heaven in view,
And how to enter in.

But first consider on your ways—
The evils you have done;
In paths of folly all your days
And wicked ways you've run.

Your Maker's image in your breast
You've forfeited by sin,
Which yield the sweetest joy and rest
And Heavenly peace within.

Had you not sin'd, you might have now
Been fill'd with joys unknown—
The joys of those who prostrate bow
And worship round the throne.

O sad indeed that e'er you sin'd
Against your Father GOD,
Destroy'd his image from the mind,
And paths of folly trod.

O see how wretched you have been,
What happiness you've lost;
Besides the wickedness of sin,
And what it yet may cost.

Well saith the word, the Word of God,
There is no peace for thee,
The way of sinners it is hard,
And like the troubled sea

But worst of all, your days are short,
You soon must end the strife;
The running sands will quick be out
Of this frail, transient life

And then what awful scenes will rise
To your astonish'd sight!
Behold the Judge descend the skies
To bring your crimes to light!

And then your guilty, frighted soul
Must hear the sound, Depart,
Down to the gulph where torments roll
To tear each guilty Heart!

Then O, Repent, and now forsake
Your guilty, cruel sins;
And then the yoke of Jesus take,
Till free'd from sin's Remance

Repentance, 'tis a precious gace;
It melts the heart of stone,
It helps, the Saviour to embrace,
And take him for our own.

It gives to faith it's blessed power
To trust in Christ, the Lord,
And every day and every hour
To rest upon his word

But first it draws with gentler hands
It Reasons with the mind,
And makes him calmly understand
His sins must be resign'd

In this 'tis but a step remov'd
From cool reflection's thought;
Only his Heart is more reprov'd
And by the Spirit taught.

At length he yields his soul to God,
With all his sins to part;
And then the Spirit of the Lord
Moves sweetly on his Heart

Tis then he feels the blood apply'd
To wash away his guilt;
And knows that Jesus for him dy'd,
For him his blood was spilt

And now his soul dissolves in love,
And peace doth crown his days;
In Jesus' smiles he lives and moves,
And every hour is praise!

The Bible now is highly priz'd,
A pearl of price untold!
More precious are its sacred lines
Than Opher's richest gold

Tis sweeter than the honey-comb,
Or natures fond delights;
Not all the joys our senses know
So much the soul invites.

He loves the assemblys of the saints,
And all who fear the Lord;
With strong desire his spirit pants
To hear the sacred word.

Tis life and spirit from the Lord,
Tis strength and power and light,
And in the worship of his God
He finds his chief delight

But most of all his joy depends
On secret humble prayer;
When e'er to heaven his voice ascends,
Its blessings he doth share

He much delights to steal away
From every human eye—
The noise and follys of the gay,
Where none but God is nigh

And there in heavenly converse sweet
With blessings from above,
The Saviour doth his spirit meet,
And feasts his soul with love.

And thus he grace and strength obtains
To do his Master's will;
And while on earth he here remains
Doth each command fulfil

*Christian Experience. A New Heart Will I Give.* ca. 1825. Broadside. 22½ " × 7½ ".

*"In Perils Of Waters." A missionary descending the rapids in a canoe. XVI. Mainz, ca. 1835. Hand-colored lithograph. 7½" × 11¾".*

*Good Effects of Sabbath Schools.* Boston: Boston Chemical Printing Company, ca. 1838. Textile. 12″ × 11⅝″.

Missionary Abel Bingham with Indian converts. Sault Sainte Marie, Michigan. ca. 1845. Daguerreotype. 5″ × 5¾″.

*The Gospel Preached To The Heathen.* Illman & Pilbrow. Boston: Gould, Kendall & Lincoln, n.d. Hand-colored steel engraving. 7¼ ″ × 4¾ ″.

*The Plains Of Heaven.* Charles Mottram after a painting by John Martin, London: Thomas McLean, 1857. Steel engraving. 24¼" × 37¾".

*Uncle Tom's Cabin.* Abraham Lincoln & Harriet Beecher Stowe. Kansas City: Ackermann-Quigley, n.d. Poster. 26″ × 19″.

*Rest in Heaven For Thee.* Fannie Crosby, n.d. Manuscript in the hand of Fannie Crosby's secretary. 12″ × 10½″.

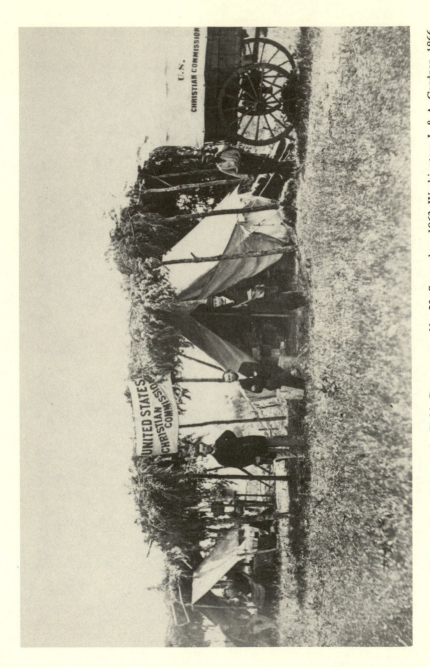

*Headquarters Christian Commission in the Field. Germantown. No. 53. September, 1863. Washington: J. & A. Gardner, 1866.*
*7" × 9".*

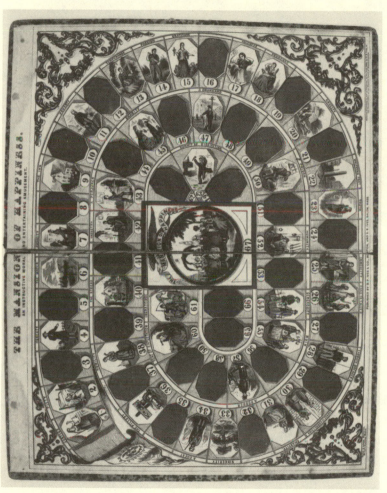

*The Mansion of Happiness. An Instructive Moral and Entertaining Amusement.* Boston: D. P. Ives & Co., 1864. First American board game. 14⅞″ × 18¼″ × ⅛″.

*If any man have not the spirit of Christ, he is none of his.*

*Go Ye Into All The World And Preach The Gospel.* n.d. Steel engraving. 8¼" × 13⅞".

*Jesus Blessing Little Children.* New York: Currier & Ives, 1867. Lithograph. 8" × 12½".

*The Tree Of Life. The Christian.* New York: N. Currier, n.d. Hand-colored lithograph. 12¼ ″ × 8¾ ″.

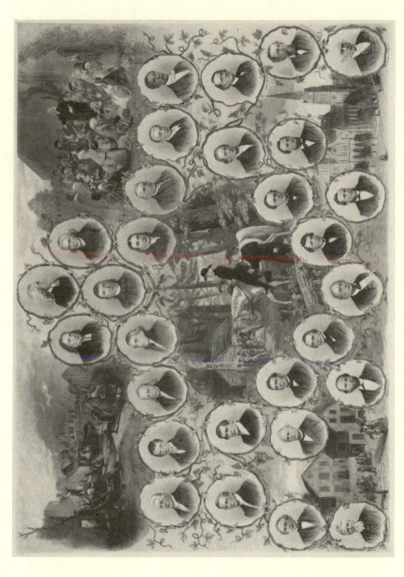

*American Methodism—1872.* J.C. Buttre after a drawing by L. Hollis. New York: The Methodist, 1872. 12¾" × 17¾".

Congregational Church, Monson, Massachusetts. ca. 1875. Stereoview. 3½″ × 7″.

*Temperance Crusade Almanac—1875.* New York: R.H. McDonald & Co.,
1874. Pamphlet. 6½ ″ × 3¾ ″ × ⅛ ″.

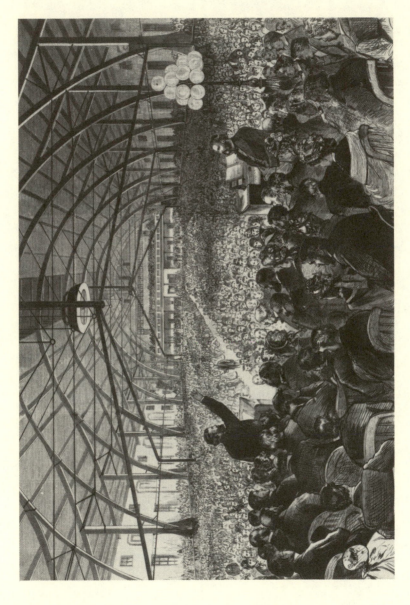

*The Revivalists In Brooklyn—Opening Service Of Messrs. Moody and Sankey In The Rink. Harper's Weekly, November 6, 1875. Wood engraving. 13½″ × 20⅝″.*

*Are You Saved?* R. A. Torrey & Charles M. Alexander. Newark, N.J.: The Whitehead & Hoag Co., 1896. Celluloid button. $5/8'' \times 1'' \times 1/8''$.

*Mr. C. Taylor, Evangelist, and his Son Charlie.* n.d. Photographic postcard. 3⅜″ × 5¼″.

*What Will You Do With Jesus: Life Is Short, Death Is Sure, Sin's The Cause, Christ's The Cure.* Turn-of-the-century tract token. 1″ × 1″ × ⅛″.

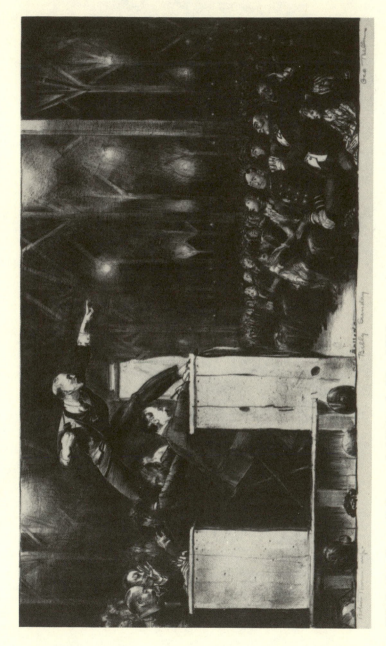

*Billy Sunday*. George Bellows, n.d. Lithograph. 9" × 16¼".

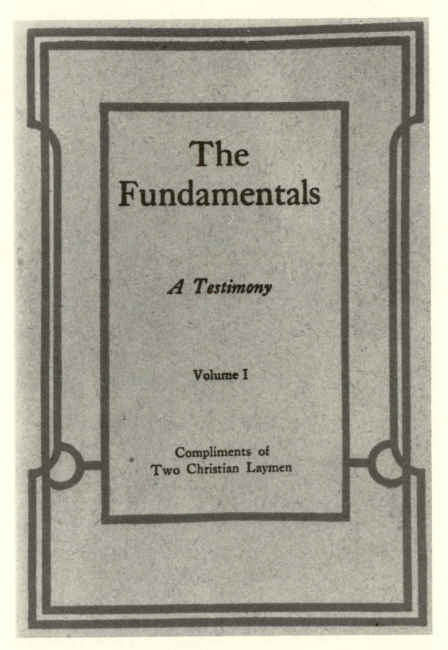

# The Fundamentals

*A Testimony*

Volume I

Compliments of
Two Christian Laymen

*The Fundamentals: A Testimony to the Truth. Vol. I.* Chicago: Testimony Publishing
Company, n.d. Book. 7½ ″ × 5¼ ″ × ⅜ ″.

*A Man May Be Down But He's Never Out.* Frederick Duncan. Salvation Army, 1919. Poster. 39½″ × 29¾″.

*Nothing to do but lay hold!* E.J. Pace, n.d. Lantern slide. 3¼″ × 4″ × ⅛″.

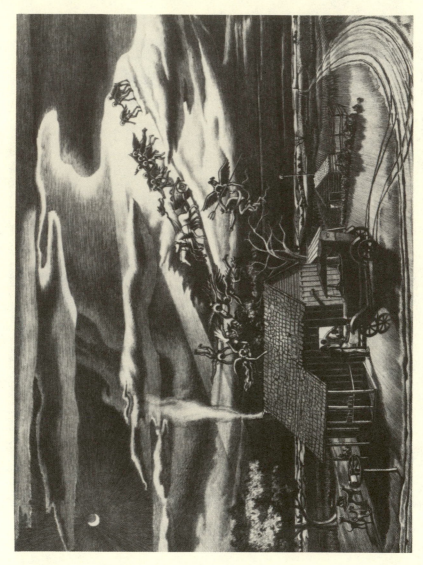

*Swing Low Sweet Chariot.* John McCrady, n.d. Lithograph. 10⅞″ × 14¾″.

# 8 Great Days Of REVIVAL

## with Students of Wheaton College

**BILLY GRAHAM**

Choruses!

Instrumental Numbers!

Dynamic Preaching!

Solos!

**Billy Graham,** A Young Southern Evangelist With A Burning Message You Will Never Forget!

**Al Smith,** Nationally-known Composer, Song Leader, Radio Artist!

**Lloyd Fesmire,** Pianist, Trombonist, Formerly With Percy Crawford's Famous Brass Quartet!

## APRIL 13 = 20

### The Church With The Sign "JESUS SAVES"

**MOLINE, MICH.**

Tune in Mel Trotter's Morning Mission Broadcast, Tuesday - Thursday, 7 - 7:30 A.M.

Great YOUTH RALLY, Sunday, April 20, at 3 P. M.

*8 Great Days of Revival with Students of Wheaton College.* Billy Graham. ca. 1945. Handbill. 9″ × 6″.

Even a child is known
by his doings...
Prov. 20:11a

RALLY
DAY

*Don't Forget!*
*See you at Sunday school on Sunday*

*Rally Day.* S.P. Co., n.d. Postcard. 5½ " × 3½ ".

*Get Right With God.* Brother Harrison Mayes, n.d. Painted aluminum roadside sign. 72″ × 48″ × 1″.

*The Revival.* Roy K. Pace, 1985. Wood carving. 11½" × 12½" × 16".

*Gift of vision from God.* Howard Finster, n.d. Mixed media. 4″ × 6½″.

*Homage to Grünewald.* Jeff Thompson, 1981. Assemblage. 17½" × 12¼" × 7¼".

*Searching: I Take The Blind To See The Show*. Michael Mallard, 1985. Acrylic collage. 47½ ″ × 54 ″ × 1½ ″.

*Historical Dislocations: The Expulsion.* Chris Anderson, 1987. Oil on paper. 44½ ″ × 32½ ″.

*Going Home.* George Lorio, 1985. Hand-painted wooden assemblage. 12½″ × 7″ × 15″.

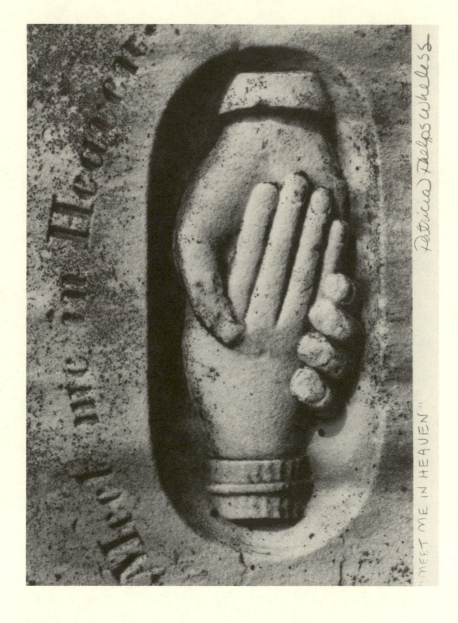

*Meet Me In Heaven.* Patricia Phelps Wheless, 1985. Photograph. 16″ × 20″.

Certificate of membership as an auxiliary of the Woman's Union Missionary Society. n.d. 12⅝″ × 16½″. (BGC Archives.) CN 379, Records of Woman's Union Missionary Society.

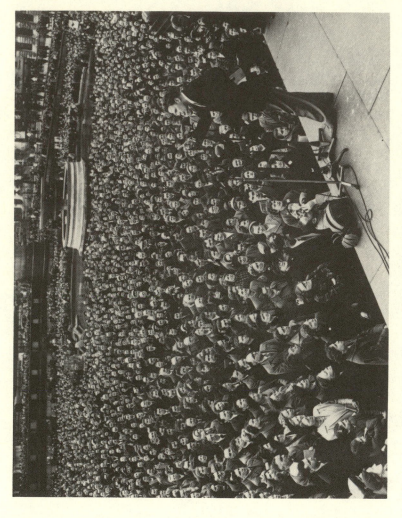

Billy Graham preaching to a crowd in Trafalgar Square during his 1954 London Crusade. Black and white photograph. (BGC Archives.) CN 17, Records of the Billy Graham Evangelistic Association, Vice President of Crusade Organization and Team Activities.

# OUTFIT LIST

—◆—

The following list is but suggestive, so good judgment must be exercised by the Candidate in making selections.

Portable Typewriter. Folding Arm Chair. Drapery for Curtains and Covers. Clock. Lamp and Lantern. Bed. Springs and Mattress. Woolen Blankets. Sheets. Pillows and Pillow Cases. Granite chamber set with covered pail. Towels, large and small. Dishes, Knives, Forks, Spoons and accessories. Table Linen. Sundry kitchen utensils. Sundry supplies for general use, including a *few* tools. Stationery, assorted. Medicines and supplies ordinarily used in the home, to which add a Clinical Thermometer. Sundry sewing materials. Sundry toilet articles. Clothing of summer weight. Some woolen underwear, light weight. Shoes, easy fitting, low heels for walking. Hose, to include some of woolen material.

Many articles of clothing and food supplies may be purchased to advantage in Kenya. Some provisions and extra clothing should be taken to Congo. Take wearing apparel in use, personal belongings and Bible study library.

———

Before purchasing bed or typewriter, write Business Manager about special prices and refer to him for all information regarding packing and shipping goods. Sewing machine, if required, should be purchased in Africa.

———

### AFRICA INLAND MISSION
373 CARLTON AVENUE, BROOKLYN, N. Y.

Handbill produced by Africa Inland Mission, listing items considered necessary for missionaries going to Africa. ca. 1930s. 5½ ″ × 8¼ ″. (BGC Archives.) CN 81, Records of Africa Inland Mission.

Africa Inland Mission worker, Mr. Fraser, and young African boy. Black and white lantern slide taken by AIM missionary Laura Collins. ca. early 1900s. (BGC Archives.) CN 422, Photographs of Laura Collins.

Handbill publicizing Paul Rader's message in 1919 at the Moody Tabernacle in Chicago. Rader was a well-known evangelist during the 1910s, 1920s, and 1930s, and was senior pastor of Moody Tabernacle from 1915 to 1921. 3½″ × 5½″. (BGC Archives.) CN 330, Records of Moody Memorial Church.

United States; Faith; Fund raising; Gangs; Good News Mission; Homosexuality; M-2 program, CA; Multnomah School of the Bible, WA; Neece, James Holloway; Preaching; Prison Fellowship; Prisoners--United States; Prisons--Missions and charities; Race relations; Redemption; Sex role; Sin; Voluntarism; Wheaton College, IL; Worship)

%%%%%%%%%%%%

CN# 185
**Nichols, Albert Sylvanus (1896-  ) and Muriel Murray (1899-1980)**
Papers; 1904(1923-1925)1952

Correspondence, photographs, negatives and miscellaneous documents concerning family events and career decisions. Bulk of letters were sent to family during a two year period while the Nichols were serving as missionaries to Sierra Leone, where Albert was director of Industrial Education at Albert Academy.

Vol: 2 boxes, Negatives, Photographs

MAJOR TOPICS: Brethren; Brethren--Missions; Intercultural communications; Missionaries--Recruitment and training; Missions--Educational work; Missions--Sierra Leone; Nichols, Albert Sylvanus; Nichols, Muriel Murray; Sex role; Sierra Leone; United Brethren in Christ; United Brethren in Christ--Missions)

%%%%%%%%%%%%

CN# 222
**O C Ministries; 1951-**
Records; 1950-1983

Correspondence, reports, minutes, manuscripts, handbooks, directories, photographs, etc., relating to the mission's work since its origin in 1950 and official founding in 1951. Documents describe the founding and expansion of the mission, the activities of its various divisions, its work around the world of assisting national churches and other missions in evangelism and discipleship.

Vol: 6 boxes, Photographs

(MAJOR TOPICS:  Argentina; Athletes--Religious life; Australia; Brazil; Chiang Kai-Shek; Children of missionaries; Chile; China; Christian education--Philippines; Christian leadership; Church development, New; Church growth; Church work with military personnel; College students in missionary work; Colombia; Communication;

Communism; Communism--China; Congresses and conferences--Congress on the Church's Worldwide Mission, 1966; Congresses and conferences--International Congress on World Evangelization, 1974; Congresses and conferences--Urbana Missionary Conventions; Dominican Republic; Ecumenical movement; Evangelistic work--Asia; Evangelistic work--Australia; Evangelistic work--Caribbean; Evangelistic work--Dominican Republic; Evangelistic work--France; Evangelistic work-- Greece; Evangelistic work--Taiwan; Evangelistic work--Vietnam; France; Germany; Graham, William Franklin "Billy"; Great Commission (Bible); Greece; Guatemala; Hillis, Charles Richard "Dick"; Hong Kong; Independent churches; India; Indigenous church administration; Indonesia; Korea; Kuo min tang (China); Luis Palau Evangelistic Team; Mass media in missionary work; Mass media in religion; Mexico; Missionaries, Resignation of; Missionaries--Recruitment and training; Missions--Argentina; Missions--Australia; Missions--Brazil; Missions--Chile; Missions--Colombia; Missions--Dominican Republic; Missions--Europe; Missions--France; Missions--Germany; Missions--Greece; Missions--Guatemala; Missions--Hong Kong; Missions--India; Missions--Indonesia; Missions--Japan; Missions---Korea; Missions--Mexico; Missions--Philippines; Missions--Singapore; Missions--Sri Lanka; Missions--Taiwan; Missions--Uruguay; Missions--Venezuela; Missions--Vietnam; Navigators; O C Ministries; Overseas Missionary Fellowship (China Inland Mission); Palau, Luis; Pentecostals; Philippines; Religion and sports; Schaeffer, Bud Stanley; Singapore; Sports Ambassadors; Sri Lanka; Taiwan; Television in religion; Uruguay; Venezuela; Winona Lake Bible Conference, IN; World Vision International; Youth for Christ International)

%%%%%%%%%%%%

CN# 43
**Old Fashioned Faith, The**
Ephemera

A tape mostly of gospel music, including selections by Homer Rodeheaver, Gipsy Smith, and the Princeton Theological Seminary Chorus. The lecture "Acres of Diamonds" by Russell Conwell is also included.

Vol: 1 Audio Tape

(MAJOR TOPICS: Conwell, Russell Herman; Evangelistic work---United States; Religion and music; Rodeheaver, Homer Alvan; Smith, Rodney "Gipsy"; Sunday, William Ashley "Billy")

%%%%%%%%%%%%

CN# 42
**Old Time Gospel Music of the 30s and 40s**
Ephemera

A tape of gospel music, including songs by Homer Rodeheaver, F. Carlton Booth, and George Beverly Shea.

1 Audio Tapes

(MAJOR TOPICS:  Evangelistic work--United States; Religion and music; Rodeheaver, Homer Alvan; Shea, George Beverly)

%%%%%%%%%%%%

CN# 219
**Ogren, Bertil A; 1914-**
Interviews; 1982

Oral history interviews with Ogren in which he describes his recruitment as a lay missionary in the Belgian Congo from 1948-1956; his work there beginning and running the LECO Press, which served the needs of members of the Congo Protestant Council and relations between Africans and Western missionaries.

Vol: 2 Audio Tapes

(MAJOR TOPICS:  Agricultural societies; Baptists; Baptists--Missions; Bible--Publication and distribution; Catholic Church---Missions; Children; Children of missionaries; Church and state in Zaire; Church of Christ in the Congo; Congo Protestant Council; Conversion; Education--Zaire; Evangelical Covenant Church; Evangelical Covenant Church--Missions; Illinois; Intercultural communications; Mass media in missionary work; Medical care--Zaire; Missionaries, Lay; Missionaries--Recruitment and training; Missions--Zaire; Occult sciences; Ogren, Bertil A; Race relations; Racism; Sex role; Social change; Zaire)

%%%%%%%%%%%%

CN# 56
**OMS International, Inc; 1901-**
Records; 1963-1978; n.d.

OMS (formerly the Oriental Missionary Society) is a mission agency of the Wesleyan tradition involved in evangelism, church planting, education and broadcasting. The collection contains news releases, prayer letters, reports, field studies all relating to OMS' administration and ministries.

Vol: 1 box

(MAJOR TOPICS: Brazil; China; Christian literature--Publication and distribution; Climenhaga, Arthur M; Ecuador; Evangelical Foreign Missions Association; Evangelistic work--Taiwan; Greece; Haiti; Hong Kong; India; Indonesia; Japan; Korea; Mass media in religion; Mass media in missionary work; Missions, Medical; Missions--Educational work; Nigeria; OMS International, Inc; Radio in missionary work; Spain; Taiwan)

%%%%%%%%%%%%

CN# 355
**Orr, James Edwin; 1912-1987**
Papers; 1936;1951-1953;1979; n.d.

Letters between Orr and correspondents in Latin America about evangelistic activities, mainly on that continent, although there is description of meetings Orr held in New Zealand, Australia, India and South Africa. Most of the letters deal with meetings held by Orr in Brazil in 1951 and 1952.

Vol: 1 box

(MAJOR TOPICS:  Airmail From God, Inc; Angola; Argentina; Australia; Baptist Mid-Missions; Baptists; Baptists--Missions; Bolivia; Brazil; Chaplains, Military; Chile; Church work with students; Evangelism in Depth; Evangelistic work--Argentina; Evangelistic work---Australia; Evangelistic work--Brazil; Evangelistic work--Guatemala; Evangelistic work--India; Evangelistic work--New Zealand; Evangelistic work--Paraguay; Evangelistic work--South Africa; Evangelistic work---Uruguay; Faith--Cure; Fellowship Foundation; Fundamentalism; Graham, William Franklin "Billy"; Guatemala; Haiti; International Church of the Four Square Gospel; Latin America Mission; McIntire, Carl Curtis; Methodist Church--Missions; Methodists; Missions--Angola; Missions--Bolivia; Missions--Brazil; Missions--Mozambique; Modernist-Fundamentalist controversy; Mozambique; New Zealand; Nicaragua; OMS International, Inc; Orr, James Edwin; Palau, Luis; Paraguay; Pike, Kenneth Lee; Presbyterian Church--Missions; Presbyterians; South Africa; Strachan, R Kenneth; ten Boom, Cornelia Arnolda Johanna; Trotman, Dawson; World Gospel Crusade; Wycliffe Bible Translators; Youth for Christ International)

%%%%%%%%%%%%

CN# 215
**Overseas Missionary Fellowship (China Inland Mission) US
Home Council; 1901-**
Records; 1853-1957; n.d.

Correspondence, minutes, directories, newsletters, brochures,
photographs, and other records documenting the mission's origins
in North America; the activities of its workers in China up to 1951;
its influence on the Christian church in China; the political, military, and social events in the Far East in the first half of the 20th
century; the mission's withdrawal from China in 1951; and its reorganization as Overseas Missionary Fellowship (previously China
Inland Mission).

Vol: 7 boxes, Oversize Materials, Photographs

(MAJOR TOPICS: Adolph, Harold Paul; Baptism; Belief and doubt;
Bible--Publication and distribution; Borden Memorial Hospital, China;
Borden, William Whiting; Boxers (Chinese political movement);
Broomhall, Alfred James; Catholic Church--Missions; Chefoo Schools;
Chiang Kai-Shek; Children of missionaries; China; Christian leader-
ship; Christian martyrs; Church and state in China; Church growth;
Church work with military personnel; Church work with women;
Clergy; Communication; Communism; Communism--China; Con-
gresses and conferences--World Missionary Conference, 1910; Conver-
sion; Courtship; Crime and criminals; Death; Disease: Leprosy; Ecu-
menical movement; Education--China; Education--Laos; Elliott,
Eleanor Ruth; Espionage; Ethnocentrism; Evangelical Alliance Mis-
sion, The (TEAM); Evangelistic work--Taiwan; Evangelistic work---
Tibet; Family; Feng Yu-hsiang; Floods; Ford, H. T.; Frame, Helen
Grace Nowack; Freed, Paul Ernest; Friedenshort Deaconess Mission;
Frost, Henry Weston; Funeral rites and ceremonies; Glossolalia;
Glover, Robert Hall; Goforth, Jonathan; Great Britain; Hitler, Adolph;
Hospitals--China; Houghton, Frank; Howard, Philip E Jr; Hunter,
George W; Illiteracy; Indigenous church administration; Indonesia;
Intercultural communications; Japan; Kane, J Herbert; Kuhn, Isobel
Miller; Kuhn, John Becker; Kuo min tang (China); Language in
missionary work; Language: Mongolian; Linguistics; Lisu people,
Tibet; Malaysia; Marriage; Mass media in missionary work; Mass
media in religion; Medical care--China; Missionaries, Resignation of;
Missionaries--Australia; Missionaries--Canada; Missionaries--Great
Britain; Missionaries--Recruitment and training; Missions in literature;
Missions, British; Missions, Medical; Missions--Australia; Mis-
sions--Canada; Missions--China; Missions--Educational work; Mis

sions--Hong Kong; Missions--Indonesia; Missions--Interdenominational cooperation; Missions--Japan; Missions--Laos; Missions--Malaysia; Missions--Mongolia; Missions--New Zealand; Missions--Philippines; Missions--Singapore; Missions--Thailand; Missions--Theory; Missions--Tibet; Missions--United States; New Zealand; Organizational change; Orphans and orphan-asylums; Overseas Missionary Fellowship (China Inland Mission); Pennsylvania; Pentecostals; Philadelphia, PA; Philippines; Poverty; Prayer; Prisons--Missions and charities; Revivals; Rural churches--China; Schoerner, Katharine Hasting Dodd; Schoerner, Otto Frederick; Sex role; Sexual ethics; Shanghai, China; Singapore; Sino-Japanese Conflict, 1937-1945; Slavery; Social change; Soviet Union; Stam, Elizabeth Alden Scott; Stam, John Cornelius; Taiwan; Taylor, Frederick Howard; Taylor, James Hudson; Three-Self Patriotic Movement; Tibet; Torrey, Reuben Archer Sr; Women authors; Women--Religious life; Women in missionary work; World Council of Churches; World War I; World War II)

%%%%%%%%%%%%

CN# SC64
**Palestine Missionary Society; ?-?**
Ephemera; 1821

Letter from S. W. Colburn to Mrs. Mary Gerish. The letter describes the purpose of the Society, which was to set up mission stations in Asia Minor and Palestine and especially to attempt the conversion of Jews to Christianity. The letter also asks for financial and prayer support.

(MAJOR TOPICS: Evangelistic work--Israel; Missions--Israel; Palestine Missionary Society)

%%%%%%%%%%%%

CN# 172
**Pan African Christian Leadership Assembly (PACLA); 1976**
Records; 1975-1978; n.d.

Correspondence, reports, news releases, minutes of meetings, and other materials which describe the origins, planning, purpose, and results of the PACLA meeting of Evangelical Protestants held in Nairobi, Kenya in December 1976.

Vol: 2 boxes, Oversize Materials, Photographs

MAJOR TOPICS: Algeria; All Africa Conference of Churches (AACC); Angola; Billy Graham Evangelistic Association (BGEA);

Botswana; Cameroon; Cassidy, Michael A; Church and state in Kenya; Church and state in Zaire; Congresses and conferences--International Congress on World Evangelization, 1974; Congresses and conferences--Pan African Christian Leadership Assembly, 1976; Dain, Arthur John; Ecumenical movement; Education--Kenya; Egypt; Egypt General Mission; Ethiopia; Evangelistic work--South Africa; Evangelistic work--Tanzania; Evangelistic work--Uganda; Evangelistic work--Zaire; Gabon; Ghana; Graham, William Franklin "Billy"; Ivory Coast; Kenya; Kivengere, Festo; Lindsell, Harold; Madagascar; Missions--Interdenominational cooperation; Missions--Zaire; Morocco; Mozambique; Nairobi, Kenya; Namibia; Nigeria; Osei-Mensah, Gottfried B; Senegal; Sierra Leone; Smyth, Walter Herbert; South Africa; Tanzania; Tunisia; Uganda; Upper Volta; Zaire; Zambia; Zimbabwe

%%%%%%%%%%%%

CN# 5
**Patterson, Vernon William; 1892-**
Papers; 1921-1985; n.d.

Correspondence, clippings book, forms, newsletters relating to Patterson's extremely active participation in evangelistic activities in the Charlotte, North Carolina, area and particularly to his involvement in the work of Billy Sunday and the early career of Billy Graham.

Vol: 2 boxes

(MAJOR TOPICS: Billy Graham Evangelistic Association (BGEA); Christian Businessman's Committee; Evangelicalism; Evangelistic work--United States; Fundamentalism; Graham, William Franklin "Billy"; Ham, Mordecai Fowler; North Carolina; Patterson, Vernon William; Sunday, William Ashley "Billy"; Youth for Christ International)

%%%%%%%%%%%%

CN# 367
**Perkins, John M; 1930-**
Papers; 1983-1987

Interview with Perkins, founder and President Emeritus of Voice of Calvary Ministries (VOCM). Subjects covered include: Perkins' childhood in rural Mississippi, his conversion, the formation of VOCM, Perkins' philosophy of holistic ministry (integrating evangelism, social action and community development) and leadership development; racial and social conditions and attitudes in

Mississippi among Christians and the general public; Perkins's arrest, imprisonment and recovery; and the extension of his ministry to Pasadena. Also in the collection are videotapes of presentations by him on the relationship between Christianity and social justice.

Vol: 3 Reels of Audio Tape, 5 Videotapes

(MAJOR TOPICS: African Americans; Christian education--United States; Church and social problems; Church and state in United States; Church work with youth; Cities and towns; City missions; Conversion; Education--United States; Evangelicalism; Evangelistic work (Christian theology); Evangelistic work--United States; Family; Fund raising; Mendenhall Ministries, The (TMM); Mississippi; Perkins, John M; Perkins, Vera Mae; Race relations; Racism; Social change; Voice of Calvary Ministries; Women--Religious life)

%%%%%%%%%%%%

CN# 227
**Pinney, John Book; 1806-1882**
Ephemera; 1836 (1836-1880) 1975

Biographical data from Fannie Spooner, Pinney's daughter; a 1975 thesis about Pinney and two reels of microfilm containing reports by Pinney, 1836 and 1868-80, and letters, 1878-79, to New York Colonization Society about the status of an American colony in Liberia and its educational facilities for freed blacks. Includes discussion of how slavery affected Liberia, the educational needs of American blacks, and the early history of missionary efforts in West Africa by the Presbyterian Church and the American Colonization Society.

Vol: 1 box, 2 Reels of Microfilm

(MAJOR TOPICS: African Americans; American Colonization Society; Education--Liberia; Liberia; Missions--Liberia; Muslims in Liberia; Pinney, John Book; Presbyterian Church--Missions; Presbyterians; Slavery)

%%%%%%%%%%%%

CN# 264
**Pioneer Ministries; 1939-**
Records; 1939-1983; n.d.

Correspondence, reports, photographs, slides, tapes, curriculum
materials, manuals, etc., relating to the work of the PM (formerly
Pioneer Girls) in North American churches. Documents describe
PM's origins, philosophy of ministry, work with sister movements
in other countries, and the framework of the organization's program, which includes local church committees, volunteer help,
camping, study materials for young people and supervisory staff,
and the training of leaders.

Vol: 8 boxes, Artifacts, 17 Audio Tapes, 5 Films, Filmstrips,
Periodicals, Slides

(MAJOR TOPICS: Boys--Societies and clubs; Canada; Chicago, IL;
Children's clubs; Children--Conversion to Christianity; Children--Reli-
gious life; Christian education (theory); Christian education, Outdoor;
Christian education of adolescents; Christian education of children;
Christian education--United States; Christian literature--Publication
and distribution; Christian Service Brigade; Church work with children;
Church work with students; Church work with youth; Edman, Victor
Raymond; Evangelistic work--Canada; Evangelistic work--United
States; Girls--Societies and clubs; Patterson, Virginia; Pioneer Ministries; Taylor, Herbert John; Thiessen, Lois; Vacation schools, Chris-
tian; Wheaton College, IL; Youth--Religious life; Youth--Societies and
clubs)

%%%%%%%%%%%%

CN# 341
**Plymire, Victor Guy; 1881-1956**
Papers; 1908-1957; n.d.

Letters, articles, photographs, maps, diary and other material
relating to the career of Assemblies of God missionary Plymire.
The collection contains information not only on his evangelistic
work among various strata of Tibetan society but also about
Tibetan culture and society, the Buddhist religion, and Plymire's
evangelistic/exploration expedition of 1927-28 which crossed from
northeastern to southwestern Tibet;

Vol: 3 boxes, Oversize Material, Photographs, 2 Video Tapes

(MAJOR TOPICS:  Assemblies of God; Assemblies of God--Missions;
Baptism; Beijing, China; Belief and doubt; Buddhism (theology);
Buddhists in Tibet; Children of missionaries; China; Chou En-lai;
Christian literature-- Publication and distribution; Church and state in
China; Communism; Communism--China; Conversion; Dalai Lama;
Evangelistic work--China; Evangelistic work--Tibet; Footbinding;
Indigenous church administration; Kuo min tang (China); Lamaism;
Marriage; Medical care--Tibet; Missionaries, Withdrawal of; Mis-
sionaries--Leaves and furloughs; Missionaries--Recruitment and
training; Missions to Buddhists; Missions, Medical; Missions--China;
Missions--Tibet; Overseas Missionary Fellowship (China Inland Mis-
sion); Pentecostalism--China; Pentecostalism--Tibet; Pentecostals;
Plymire, Victor Guy; Prayer; Prisoners--China; Prisoners--Tibet;
Religion and music; Three-Self Patriotic Movement; Tibet; World War
I; World War II; Worship; Wright, James Elwin)

%%%%%%%%%%%%

CN# 274
**Prison Fellowship Ministries; 1976-**
Records; 1975-1982; n.d.

Correspondence, memoranda, reports, newspaper clippings and
other documents describing the founding and development of
PFM.  Among the subjects covered in the files are: the part played
in the organization by Charles Colson, the realities of prison
ministry, the conditions of prisons in the United States, relations
between organizations involved in prison ministries, the testimonies of inmates, and the relationship between PFM and its con-
stituents.

Vol: 21 boxes, photographs

(MAJOR TOPICS:  African Americans; Albuquerque, NM; Atlanta,
GA; Belief and doubt; Billy Graham Evangelistic Association
(BGEA); Canada; Capital punishment; Charlotte, NC; Chicago, IL;
Christian education of adults; Christian education--United States;
Christian literature--Publication and distribution; Christianity Today,
Inc; Church and social problems; Church and state in United States;
Church work with women; Colson, Charles Wendell; Columbia, SC;
Conversion; Counseling; Discrimination; Education--United States;
Evangelicalism; Evangelistic work--Canada; Evangelistic work--United
States; Faith; Falwell, Jerry; Fund raising; Hispanic Americans;
Hughes, Harold Everett; Illinois; Journalism, Religious; Los Angeles,
CA; Loux, Gordon; Mass media in religion; Michigan; Montana;
Moving-pictures in church work; New Mexico; New York City, NY;
Nixon, Richard Milhous; Periodical: *Christianity Today*; Periodical:

*Wittenburg Door, The*; Perkins, John M; Philadelphia, PA; Prayer; Prayer groups; Prison Fellowship; Prisoners--United States; Prisons---Missions and charities; PTL Network; Racism; Schaeffer, Francis August; Sex role; Social change; Tennessee; Texas; Voluntarism; Washington (state); Washington, DC; Watergate Affair, 1972-1974; West Virginia; Weyerhauser, C Davis; Women--Religious life; Worship)

%%%%%%%%%%%%

CN# 356
**Prison Ministry Videos**
Records; 1985-1986; n.d.

The material in this collection consists of edited video programs produced by the staff of the Institute of Prison Ministries of the Billy Graham Center. Most of the tapes are interviews with chaplains, judges and others involved in local, state or federal prison systems.

Vol: 11 Video Tapes

(MAJOR TOPICS: Billy Graham Center, IL; Burger, Warren Earl; Church and state in United States; Crime and criminals; Evangelistic work--United States; Hatfield, Mark Odom; Legislators--United States; Meese, Edwin III; Prisoners--United States; Prisons--Missions and charities; Supreme Court)

%%%%%%%%%%%%

CN# 203
**Rader, Luke; 18?-19?**
Ephemera; n.d.

One audio tape containing brief radio broadcast messages of Rader, "America's Pioneer Radio Evangelist"; includes hymns, poems, songs, and scripture readings by Rader accompanied by organ, piano and orchestra.

Vol: 1 Audio Tape

(MAJOR TOPICS: Evangelistic work--United States; Fundamentalism; Mass media in religion; Rader, Luke; Radio in religion)

%%%%%%%%%%%%

CN# 38
**Rader, Daniel Paul; 1879-1938**
Ephemera; 1916-1938; 1971; n.d.

Newsletters, sermon manuscripts, scrapbooks, programs, pamphlets, video tape copy of a 1928 film, etc. documenting the career of evangelist Rader. The material deals mostly with his pioneer radio work and the church he founded, the Chicago Gospel Tabernacle. Additional material includes sermons of preachers who spoke at the Tabernacle and reports about mission activity around the world supported by the Tabernacle.

Vol: 1 box, 2 Audio Tapes, 5 Reels of Microfilm, Negatives, Oversize   Materials, Photographs, Slides, 1 Video Tape

(MAJOR TOPICS: Apostasy; Belief and doubt; Bible colleges; Bible--Evidences, authority, etc.; Bible--Inspiration; Bible--Prophecies; Biederwolf, William Edward; Blanchard, Charles Albert; Broadcasting station: HCJB, Ecuador; Bryan, William Jennings; Canada; Chicago Gospel Tabernacle; Chicago, IL; Children; China; China--History--- 1912-1937; Christian and Missionary Alliance (CMA); Christian and Missionary Alliance--Missions; Christian education, Outdoor; Christian education--United States; Christian leadership; Christmas; Church and social problems; Church work with youth; City missions; Communication; Conversion; Crowds; Cults; Death; Devil; Deyneka, Peter Sr; Dunlop, Merrill; Easter; Evangelistic invitations; Evangelistic sermons; Evangelistic work--Canada; Evangelistic work--Great Britain; Evangelistic work--Japan; Evangelistic work--Korea; Evangelistic work--Poland; Evangelistic work--Soviet Union; Evangelistic work--United States; Faith; Faith--Cure; Family; Fascism; Feng Yu-hsiang; Forgiveness; Freedom (Theology); Fuller, Charles Edward Sr; Fund raising; Fundamentalism; Funeral rites and ceremonies; Great Britain; Greece; Heaven; Holy Spirit; Independent churches; Ireland; Japan; Johnson, Albert Mussey; Johnson, Bessilyn Morris; Jones, Clarence Wesley; Judaism; Latham, Lance; Los Angeles, CA; Love (Theology); Mass media in religion; Michigan; Minneapolis, MN; Miracles; Missionaries--Recruitment and training; Missions to Jews; Missions--biblical teaching; Missions--China; Missions--India; Missions--Japan; Missions--Korea; Missions--Soviet Union; Modernist-Fundamentalist controversy; Moody Memorial Church, IL; Mussolini, Benito; Obedience; Persecution--Soviet Union; Prayer; Prophecy (Christianity); Rader, Daniel Paul; Rader, Luke; Radio audiences; Radio broadcasting; Radio in missionary work; Radio in religion; Religion and music; Religion and science; Repentance; Riley, William Bell; Rodeheaver, Homer Alvan; Salvation; Salvation Army; Sanctification; Sermons,

American; Simpson, Albert Benjamin; Sin; Smith, Oswald Jeffrey; Soviet Union; Toronto, ON; Wheaton College, IL; Women--Religious life; Worship)

%%%%%%%%%%%%

CN# 378
**Railroad Evangelistic Association; 1941-**
Records; 1941-1985

Tax exemption correspondence, constitutions, tracts, membership application of the REA, an organization created by railroad workers for fellowship and evangelism. There are only a very few items in this collection. They describe the structure of the organization and a little bit about its purpose. Tracts give the testimonies of some of the members.

Vol: 1 Box, Photograph

(MAJOR TOPICS:  Corporations, Religious--Taxation; Evangelistic work--United States; Railroad Evangelistic Association)

%%%%%%%%%%%%

CN# 238
**Redpath, Alan; 1907-**
Ephemera; 1958-1961

Tapes of sermons preached by Redpath at the Moody Memorial Church in Chicago. The topics include "The Spirit-filled Life" and "Assurance of Salvation".

Vol: 2 Audio Tapes

(MAJOR TOPICS:  Holy Spirit; Moody Memorial Church, IL; Redpath, Alan; Sermons, American)

%%%%%%%%%%%%

CN# 124
**Renich, Helen Torrey; 1916-**
Papers; 1920-1982; n.d.

Tapes of interviews with Renich in which she talks about her grandfather, Reuben Archer Torrey Sr, and describes her experiences growing up in China as a child of missionaries and going through culture shock when she came to the United States to attend Wheaton College. Also in the collection are photographs of her family life in China and Chinese nationals, ca. 1920-30s.

Vol: 2 Audio Tapes, Photographs

(MAJOR TOPICS: Adolescence; Australia; Belief and doubt; Boxers (Chinese political movement); Buswell, James Oliver Jr; Chiang Kai-Shek; Children of missionaries; China; Edman, Victor Raymond; Education, Higher; Evangelistic work--Australia; Evangelistic work---Canada; Evangelistic work--United States; Family; Footbinding; Fundamentalism; Graham, Ruth Bell; Graham, William Franklin "Billy"; Illinois; Intercultural communications; Japan; Medical care---China; Missions, Medical; Missions--China; Missions--Educational work; Moody Bible Institute, IL; Presbyterian Church--Missions; Presbyterians; Renich, Helen Torrey; Sex role; Sino-Japanese Conflict, 1937-1945; Torrey, Reuben Archer Jr; Torrey, Reuben Archer Sr; Wheaton College, IL; World War II)

%%%%%%%%%%%%

CN# 95
**Riley, William Bell; 1861-1947**
Ephemera; 1903-1945; n.d.

Materials, including home movies, and microfilm of notebooks and scrapbooks, relating to Riley's career as a minister and as a major leader of Protestant Fundamentalists in the United States.

Vol: 2 Films, 10 Reels of Microfilm

(MAJOR TOPICS: Balfour Declaration; Baptists; Bible--Criticism, interpretation, etc; Bryan, William Jennings; Catholic Church in United States; Catholic Church--Relations; Chapman, John Wilbur; Christian Science; Church and social problems; Communism; Creation--biblical teaching; Darrow, Clarence Seward; Evangelistic work--United States; Evolution; Fundamentalism; Hitler, Adolph; McPherson, Aimee Semple; Millennialism; Modernist-Fundamentalist controversy; Mormons and Mormonism; Northern Baptist Convention; Northwestern College, MN; Palestine; Prohibition; Religion and science; Riley, William Bell; Sermons, American; Smith, Rodney "Gipsy"; Soviet Union; Spurgeon, Charles Haddon; Sunday, William Ashley "Billy"; Temperance; Torrey, Reuben Archer Sr; World Christian Fundamentals Association; World War II)

%%%%%%%%%%%%

CN# 101
**Roberts, Robert William; 1875-1964**
Papers; 1907-1916; n.d.

Correspondence, account books, photographs, and other records mostly concerned with Roberts' tasks as a worker for the American Sunday School Union from 1907-1913.

Vol: 1 box, Photographs

(MAJOR TOPICS: American Sunday School Union; Evangelistic work--United States; Illinois; Roberts, Robert William; Sunday schools; Wisconsin)

%%%%%%%%%%%%

CN# 229
**Robie, L C; 1892-?**
Ephemera; 1979; n.d.

Two tapes of an interview with Robie in which he discusses his experiences during his 42 year career as an evangelist in California, New York and Pennsylvania, beginning ca. 1920.

Vol: 2 Audio Tapes

(MAJOR TOPICS:  Assemblies of God; Church and social problems; Church work with youth; Conversion; Crime and criminals; Evangelistic work--United States; Faith--Cure; Finney, Charles Grandison; Methodists; Michigan; New York (state); Pentecostals; Prayer; Prohibition; Revivals; Robie, L C; Youth--Religious life)

%%%%%%%%%%%%

CN# 130
**Rodeheaver, Homer Alvan; 1880-1955**
Ephemera; 1916-1941; n.d.

Several items in this collection relate to Rodeheaver's music publishing company, Homer A. Rodeheaver Company.  Other materials include newspaper clippings, copies of *Rodeheaver's Musical News*; tapes of Rodeheaver singing solo and in duets with Virginia Asher, and letters sent to friends.

Vol: 1 box, 2 Audio Tapes

(MAJOR TOPICS: Evangelistic work--United States; Religion and music; Rodeheaver, Homer Alvan; Sunday, William Ashley "Billy"; Van Alstyne, Frances Jane "Fanny" Crosby)

%%%%%%%%%%%%

CN# 60
**Ruch, Andrew (?-1966) and Martha (?- )**
Papers; 1921-1936

Letters written by the Ruchs to family and other correspondents about their experiences in Kenya as missionaries of Africa Inland Mission.

Vol: 1 box

(MAJOR TOPICS: Africa Inland Mission (AIM); Egypt; Evangelistic work--Kenya; Kenya; Kikuyu people, Kenya; Language: Swahili; Livingstone, David; Missions, Medical; Missions--Educational work; Missions--Kenya; Moody Bible Institute, IL; Nairobi, Kenya; Medical care--Kenya; Presidents--United States; Roosevelt, Theodore; Ruch, Andrew; Ruch, Martha; Women--Religious life; Women in missionary work)

%%%%%%%%%%%%

CN# 52
**Salzman, Esther; 1906-**
Interview; 1978

Oral history interview taped with Salzman, a Wheaton alumna and missionary to China in the 1940s and the Philippines from 1950-1972.

Vol: 1 Audio Tape

(MAJOR TOPICS: Beijing, China; Catholic Church in China; Catholic Church--Missions; Catholic Church--Relations; China; Church and state in China; Communism--China; Edman, Victor Raymond; Foot-binding; Missions, Medical; Missions--China; Missions--Educational work; Missions--Philippines; Philippines; Prohibition; Salzman, Esther; Sex role; Shanghai, China; Wheaton College, IL; Women--Religious life; Women in missionary work; World War II)

%%%%%%%%%%%%

CN# SC57
**Sankey, Ira David; 1840-1908**
Ephemera; 1887-1899; n.d.

Collection of materials relating to Ira Sankey, singer and song-writer, and close associate of Dwight L. Moody. Items include a letter to Edward Bok about evangelist Henry Ward Beecher, some handwritten autobiographical materials, and autographs.

(MAJOR TOPICS: Beecher, Henry Ward; Evangelistic work--United States; Religion and music; Sankey, Ira David)

%%%%%%%%%%%%

CN# 250
**Savage, Robert Carlton; 1914-**
Interview; 1983

Interview in which Savage discusses his work as a missionary evangelist in Columbia (1942-1944), and his work in Ecuador for missionary radio station HCJB and Youth for Christ (1944-1969).

Vol: 1 Audio Tape

(MAJOR TOPICS: Broadcasting station: HCJB, Ecuador; Catholic Church in Colombia; Catholic Church in Ecuador; Catholic Church--- Relations; Christian and Missionary Alliance (CMA); Christian and Missionary Alliance--Missions; Christian education--Colombia; Christian martyrs; Church and state in Colombia; Church and state in Ecuador; Church development, New; Church growth; Church growth--Colombia; Church work with youth; Colombia; Discrimination; Ecuador; Evangelical Alliance Mission, The (TEAM); Evangelistic work--Colombia; Evangelistic work--Ecuador; Film: *Mr Texas*; Gospel Missionary Union; Graham, Ruth Bell (Mrs); Graham, William Franklin "Billy"; Indians of South America; Indigenous church administration; Intercultural communications; International Christian Broadcasters; Jesuits; John XXIII (Pope); Johnson, Torrey Maynard; Jones, Clarence Wesley; Language in missionary work; Language: Spanish; Larson, Reuben Emmanuel; Mass media in missionary work; Mass media in religion; Missionaries--Recruitment and training; Missions--Colombia; Missions--Ecuador; Missions--Rural work; Missions--South America; Moody Films; Moving-pictures in church work; Race relations; Racism; Radio audiences; Radio in missionary work; Radio in religion; Radio stations; Rural churches--Colombia; Savage, Robert Carlton; Seventh Day Adventists; Seventh Day Adventists---

Missions; Sunday schools; Television in religion; Vatican Council II, 1962-1965; World Radio Missionary Fellowship; World War II; World Wide Pictures; Youth for Christ International

%%%%%%%%%%%%%

CN# 256
**Sawyer, Helen Irvin (1923- ) and Malcolm Maurice (1919- )**
Interviews; 1983

Four interviews in which the Sawyers discuss their childhood; schooling; activities in China and Laos for the Christian and Missionary Alliance from 1948-1975 including church planting, training of pastors, and medical assistance to Khamu and Hmong peoples and running a Bible school; and their work with Hmong refugees in the Chicago area.

Vol: 4 Audio Tapes

(MAJOR TOPICS:  Animism; Bible colleges; Bible--Translating; Buddhists in China; Buddhists in Laos; Catholic Church; Catholic Church--Relations; Children of missionaries; China; Christian and Missionary Alliance (CMA); Christian and Missionary Alliance--Missions; Christian literature--Publication and distribution; Church and social problems; Church and state in China; Church and state in Laos; Church and state in Vietnam; Church work with refugees; Clergy, Training of; Communism--China; Communism--Laos; Communism--Vietnam; Conversion; Education--Laos; Education--Vietnam; Ekvall, Robert Brainerd; Evangelistic work--Vietnam; Gospel Recordings, Inc; Hmong people, Laos; Hong Kong; Illinois; Illiteracy; Intercultural communications; Khamu people, Laos; Language in missionary work; Language: Chinese; Language: French; Medical care--Laos; Medical care--Vietnam; Missionaries--Leaves and furloughs; Missionaries--Recruitment and training; Missions to Buddhists; Missions, Medical; Missions--China; Missions--Interdenominational cooperation; Missions--Laos; Missions--Tibet; Prayer; Refugees--Laos; Religion and music; Sawyer, Helen Irvin; Sawyer, Malcolm Maurice; Sex role; Shanghai, China; Thailand; Tibet; Vietnam; Women--Religious life; Women in missionary work)

%%%%%%%%%%%%

CN# 132
**Schaeffer, Bud; 1927-**
Ephemera; 1955-1979

Prayer letters written by the Schaeffers about their mission work with Sports Ambassadors, a branch of the evangelistic organization Overseas Crusades. Materials relate their experiences in the Philippines, Australia, and the United States with sending various athletes to foreign nations to share their faith.

Vol: 1 box

(MAJOR TOPICS: Athletes--Religious life; Australia; California; Evangelistic work--Australia; Evangelistic work--Taiwan; Ford, Leighton Frederick Sandys; Graham, William Franklin "Billy"; Hillis, Charles Richard "Dick"; Illinois; Los Angeles, CA; Missions--Philippines; O C Ministries; Palau, Luis; Philippines; Schaeffer, Bud Stanley; Sports; Sports Ambassadors; Taiwan; Thailand; Wilson, Grady Baxter)

%%%%%%%%%%%%

CN# 220
**Schaeffer, Francis August; 1912-1984**
Ephemera; 1963

One tape of an informal discussion with questions following an address by evangelist and author Schaeffer at Wheaton College in 1963.

Vol: 1 Audio Tape

(MAJOR TOPICS: L'Abri Fellowship, Switzerland; Schaeffer, Francis August; Sermons, American; Wheaton College, IL)

%%%%%%%%%%%%

CN# 83
**Scheel, Richard Edgar; 1923-1989**
Papers; 1950-1970

Audio tapes, slides, letters, photographs of Scheel, a medical doctor, all relating to the work of the Sudan Interior Mission in Ethiopia.

Vol: 1 box, 3 Audio Tapes, Slides

(MAJOR TOPICS: Africa Inland Mission (AIM); American Revolution Bicentennial, 1776-1976; Broadcasting station: ELWA, Liberia; Christian Blind Mission; Church and social problems; Coptic Church; Cuba; Edman, Victor Raymond; Evangelical Alliance Mission, The (TEAM); Evangelistic work--Ethiopia; Haile Selassie; Hockman, Robert William; Hospitals--Nigeria; Illinois; Islam--Relations--Christianity; Italo-Ethiopian War; Kenya; Knighton, J Raymond "Ray"; Medical care--Ethiopia; Mission Aviation Fellowship (MAF); Missions, Medical; Missions--Educational work; Missions--Ethiopia; Moody Memorial Church, IL; Muslims in Ethiopia; Rift Valley Academy, Kenya; Scheel, Richard Edgar; Social change; Somali (Somali Democratic Republic); Soviet Union; Sudan; Sudan Interior Mission (SIM); Wheaton College, IL;

%%%%%%%%%%%%%

CN# 51
**Schoerner, Katharine Hasting Dodd; 1908-**
Interview; 1978

Oral history interview taped with Schoerner, a Wheaton alumna and missionary to China from 1931-1951. Also in the collection are five letters written during her stay in China describing her life there.

Vol: 1 Audio Tape, 1 Folder

(MAJOR TOPICS: Buddhists in China; Children of missionaries; China; Communism; Communism--China; Confucianism; Intercultural communications; Japan; Kuo min tang (China); Missions to Buddhists; Missions--China; Missions--Educational work; Overseas Missionary Fellowship (China Inland Mission); Schoerner, Katharine Hasting Dodd; Schoerner, Otto Frederick; Shanghai, China; Stam, Elizabeth Alden Scott; Taoism; Wheaton College, IL; Women--Religious life; Women in missionary work; World War II)

%%%%%%%%%%%

CN# 55
**Schoerner, Otto Frederick; 1906-**
Interviews; 1978-1979

Oral history interviews taped with Schoerner, a Wheaton alumnus and missionary to China from 1931-51. Narrative covers his life in Sinkiang, Honan, and Kangsu provinces. Also in the collection is a photograph of the staff of the Borden Memorial Hospital in China.

Vol: 2 Audio Tapes, 1 Photograph

(MAJOR TOPICS: Borden Memorial Hospital, China; Buddhists in China; Chiang Kai-Shek; China; Church and state in China; Cities and towns; Communism; Communism--China; Confucianism; Evangelistic work--China; Hunter, George W; Japan; Korean War; Kuo min tang (China); Missions to Buddhists; Missions, Medical; Missions--China; Mongolia; Moody Bible Institute, IL; Muslims in China; Overseas Missionary Fellowship (China Inland Mission); Schoerner, Katharine Hasting Dodd; Schoerner, Otto Frederick; Shanghai, China; Soviet Union; Stam, Elizabeth Alden Scott; Wheaton College, IL; World War II)

%%%%%%%%%%%

CN# 270
**Schulenburg, Ray Harvey; 1909-**
Interview; 1984

Oral history interview with Schulenburg in which he discusses his conversion and involvement in Christian work, his memories of Paul Rader and the Chicago Gospel Tabernacle, the early days of Youth for Christ, evangelistic preaching, and city missions.

Vol: 1 Audio Tape

(MAJOR TOPICS: African Americans; Chicago Gospel Tabernacle; Chicago, IL; Children--Conversion to Christianity; Children--Religious life; Christian and Missionary Alliance (CMA); Christian education--United States; Church work with children; Church work with youth; Cities and towns; Criswell, Wallie Amos; Evangelistic invitations; Evangelistic sermons; Evangelistic work--United States; Illinois; Ironside, Henry Allan "Harry"; Johnson, Albert Mussey; Johnson, Torrey Maynard; Jones, Clarence Wesley; Jones, Howard; Kentucky; Latham, Lance; Missionaries--Recruitment and training; Missions--Finance; Moody Memorial Church, Chicago, IL; Pentecostals; Philpot, Ford; Rader, Daniel Paul; Religion and music; Schulenburg, Ray Harvey; Smith, Oswald Jeffrey; World Wide Christian Couriers; Youth for Christ International)

%%%%%%%%%%%%

CN# 181
**Schultz, Earl Wesley, Jr; 1924-**
Papers; 1947-1969

Office files of Schultz during his tenure as Director of the Hampstead, Maryland, Youth for Christ organization. Includes correspondence with YFC leaders, and topical files covering Hampstead YFC, YFC Eastern (U.S.) Region, YFC/USA, and YFC International.

Vol: 6 boxes, Photographs, Phonograph Records

(MAJOR TOPICS: American Council of Christian Churches (ACCC); Appelman, Hyman Jedidiah; Bihl, Carl J "Kelly"; Billy Graham Evangelistic Association (BGEA); Bob Jones University, SC; Church work with youth; Cook, Robert Andrew; Cults; Ecuador; Eisenhower, Dwight David; Engstrom, Theodore "Ted" Wilhelm; Evangelistic work--Japan; Evangelistic work--United States; Federal Bureau of Investigation; Gideons International; Graham, William Franklin "Billy"; Hong Kong; India; Indiana; International Council of Christian Churches; International Society of Christian Endeavor; Japan; Johnson, Torrey Maynard; Kesler, Jay Lewis; Maryland; McIntire, Carl Curtis; National Council of Churches; New Jersey; Pennsylvania; Presidents--United States; Schultz, Earl Wesley Jr; Venezuela; Wilson, Thomas Walter Jr; Winona Lake Bible Conference, IN; Wolgemuth, Samuel Frey; World Council of Churches; World Vision International; Young Life; Youth for Christ International)

%%%%%%%%%%%%

CN# 32
**Seminar on the Authority of Scripture; 1966**
Records; 1966

Copies of the papers read at the meeting held in Wenham, MA. Also a list of participants, a schedule of events, and copies of the text of the communique and resolutions adopted by the meeting.

Vol: 1 box

(MAJOR TOPICS: Bible--Criticism, interpretation, etc; Bible--Inspiration; Congresses and conferences--Seminar on the Authority of the Bible, 1966; Sermons, American; Theology; Walvoord, John Flipse)

%%%%%%%%%%%%

CN# 316
**Seymour, Deborah J.; 1960-**
Interviews; 1985-1986

Two interviews with Seymour who grew up as a child of missionaries in Papua New Guinea and worked as an English teacher in Honduras with World Gospel Mission and Churches of Christ in Christian Union from 1983 to 1985. Topics discussed include her parents' missionary work, her childhood among tribal people, Latin American culture and her own life and work in Honduras.

Vol: 3 Audio Tapes

(MAJOR TOPICS: Animism; Cargo movement; Catholic Church in Honduras; Catholic Church--Relations; Children of missionaries; Children--Conversion to Christianity; Children--Religious life; Christian education of adolescents; Christian education--Honduras; Christian life; Church and social problems; Church work with students; College students in missionary work; Conversion; Counseling; Education, Higher--Honduras; Education--Honduras; Education--Philosophy; Evangelicalism; Evangelistic work--Honduras; Honduras; Indigenous church administration; Intercultural communications; Language in missionary work; Missionaries--Recruitment and training; Missions--Educational work; Missions--Honduras; Missions--Paupa New Guinea; Papua New Guinea; Polygamy; Sex role; Seymour, Deborah J; Social change; Women clergy; Women in missionary work; Women---Religious life; World Gospel Mission; Worship; Youth--Religious life)

%%%%%%%%%%%%

CN# 201
**Shedd, Russell Philip; 1929-**
Interviews; 1982

Five hours of taped interviews, concerning Shedd's upbringing by missionary parents in Bolivia; education at Wheaton College, Faith Seminary, PA, and the University of Edinburgh; evangelism opportunities in Scotland, 1953-55; and work with the Conservative

Baptist Foreign Mission Society in Portugal, 1959-62, and Bolivia, 1962-82.

Vol: 3 Audio Tapes

(MAJOR TOPICS:  Argentina; Baptists; Baptists--Missions; Billy Graham Evangelistic Association (BGEA); Bolivia; Bolivian Indian Mission; Brazil; Catholic Church; Catholic Church in Bolivia; Catholic Church in Portugal; Children of missionaries; Conservative Baptist Foreign Mission Society; Evangelistic work--Argentina; Evangelistic work--Brazil; Evangelistic work--Paraguay; Film: *Mr Texas*; Graham, William Franklin "Billy"; Great Britain; Inter-Varsity Christian Fellowship; Liberation Theology; Lutherans; McIntire, Carl Curtis; Missions--Bolivia; Missions--Brazil; Missions--Europe; Missions--Great Britain; Missions--Portugal; Pentecostals; Portugal; Sex role; Shedd, Russell Philip; Uruguay; Wheaton College, IL)

%%%%%%%%%%%%

CN# 269
**Shoemaker, Samuel Moore; 1893-1963**
Papers; 1907-1963

Appointment books, audio tapes, magazines, articles, newspaper clippings, a pamphlet, phonograph records, photographs, and programs covering the years of Shoemaker's career as an Episcopalian preacher, author, radio preacher, and spiritual advisor-counselor. Includes taped sermons from the radio program *Faith at Work*.

Vol: 3 boxes, 31 Audio Tapes, Phonograph Records, Photographs

(MAJOR TOPICS:  Alcoholics Anonymous; Conversion; Episcopalians; Evangelistic work--United States; Faith; Free will and determinism; Freedom (Theology); Graham, William Franklin "Billy"; Mass media in religion; Mental health; New York (state); New York City, NY;  Pennsylvania; Prayer; Radio in religion; Radio program: *Faith at Work*; Sermons, American; Shoemaker, Samuel)

%%%%%%%%%%%%

CN# 179
**Short Terms Abroad; 1965-1976**
Records; 1965-1976

Correspondence, personnel files, bulletins, newspapers, posters, publications, legal documents, photographs, mailing lists, minutes of meetings, and other items pertaining to the operation of the organization. Short Terms Abroad brought together individuals with particular skills (such as teaching or construction) and an interest in serving as missionaries for a limited time with missions having temporary needs for those skills.

Vol: 18 boxes, Photographs, Oversize Materials

(MAJOR TOPICS: Baptists; Baptists--Missions; Charismatic movement; Frizen, Edwin Leonard Jr; Missionaries, Lay; Missionaries--Recruitment and training; Missions--Educational work; Missions--United States; Organizational change; Pentecostal Church--Missions; Presbyterian Church--Missions; Presbyterians; Radio in missionary work; Short Terms Abroad; Taylor, Clyde Willis; Taylor, Kenneth Nathaniel; United States; Voluntarism)

%%%%%%%%%%%%%

CN# 224
**Shufelt, John Stratton; 1910-**
Papers; 1930-1979; n.d.

Reports, newspaper clippings, handbills, photographs, and other ephemera relating to Shufelt's evangelistic activities as a song leader for Youth for Christ, Jack Shuler, John R. Rice, Harry Ironside and others. This collection also contains information on the Wheaton Revival of 1950.

Vol: 1 box

(MAJOR TOPICS:  Amsterdam, Netherlands; Appelman, Hyman Jedidiah; Belgium; Buswell, James Oliver Jr; California; Canada; Christ for America; Church and social problems; Church work with youth; Cities and towns; City missions; Denmark; Evangelistic work---Belgium; Evangelistic work--Canada; Evangelistic work--Germany; Evangelistic work--Great Britain; Evangelistic work--Netherlands; Evangelistic work--United States; France; Germany; Graham, William Franklin "Billy"; Great Britain; Illinois; Ironside, Henry Allan "Harry"; Johnson, Torrey Maynard; Los Angeles, CA; Netherlands; Norway; Pennsylvania; Periodical: *Sword of the Lord*; Revivals; Rice, John Richard; Shufelt, John Stratton; Sweden; Templeton, Charles B; Voice of Christian Youth; Washington  (state); Wheaton College, IL; Wheaton Revival, 1950; Whitefield, George; Winona Lake Bible Conference, IN; Youth for Christ International; Youth--Religious life)

%%%%%%%%%%%%%

CN# SC73
**Shuler, Jack; 1918-**
Ephemera; 1951

Brochures, posters, and newspaper clippings used in "Key to Life"
evangelistic campaign of evangelist Jack Shuler in Grand Rapids,
Michigan, September 9-October 15, 1951, sponsored by the Christian Businessmen's Committee of Grand Rapids.

(MAJOR TOPICS: Evangelistic work--United States; Shuler, Jack)

%%%%%%%%%%%%%

CN# 237
**Slavic Gospel Association; 1934-**
Records; 1922 (1974-1981) 1983; n.d.

Correspondence, minutes, prayer letters, audio tapes, films and
other  materials of the SGA, a mission concerned primarily with
work among Slavic peoples, although it also had for a time missionaries to Indians in Alaska.  Records deal with the early career
of Peter Deyneka Sr.; work of individual missionaries; long range
planning for the mission; radio ministry; literature publication and
distribution; and evangelism in Europe, North America and South
America.  There is  also a great deal of information about the
church in eastern Europe.  Most of the documents in the collection are post-1974.

Vol: 32 boxes, 108 Audio Tapes, 72 Films, Oversize materials,
Phonograph Records, Photographs, Slides, 1 Video Tape

(MAJOR TOPICS: Alaska; Albania; Aleut people, USA; Alliluyeva,
Svetlana; Appelman, Hyman Jedidiah; Argentina; Australia; Austria;
Baptism; Barrows, Clifford B; Belief and doubt; Bible colleges;
Bible--Prophecies; Bible--Publication and distribution; Bob Jones
University, SC; Bowman, Robert H; Brazil; Broadcasting station:
HCJB, Ecuador; Bulgaria; Campus Crusade for Christ; Canada;
Catholic Church--Relations; Charismatic movement; Chicago, IL;
Child Evangelism Fellowship; Children; Children's clubs; Children---
Conversion to Christianity; Children--Religious life; China; Christian
education, Outdoor; Christian education--Argentina; Christian educa-
tion--Canada; Christian education--Tanzania; Christian educa-
tion--United States; Christian education--Zaire; Christian leadership;
Christian literature--Publication and distribution; Church and state in
Poland; Church and state in the Soviet Union; Church work with

children; Church work with refugees; Church work with youth; Communism; Conversion; Cook, Robert Andrew; Czechoslovakia; Deyneka, Peter Jr; Deyneka, Peter Sr; Dodds, Gilbert L; Education--Argentina; Education--Canada; Education--Poland; Eisenhower, Dwight David; Eskimos; Evangelism to Communist Lands; Evangelistic work--Argentina; Evangelistic work--Australia; Evangelistic work--Brazil; Evangelistic work--Canary Islands; Evangelistic work--France; Evangelistic work--Germany; Evangelistic work--Great Britain; Evangelistic work--Israel; Evangelistic work--Paraguay; Evangelistic work--Poland; Evangelistic work--Soviet Union; Evangelistic work--United States; Evangelistic work--Uruguay; Evangelistic work--Yugoslavia; Far East Broadcasting Company; Forgiveness; France; Fund raising; Germany; Grace; Great Britain; Heaven; House churches; Hungary; International relief; Israel; Italy; Jesus to the Communist World; Johnson, Torrey Maynard; Language: Russian; Language: Spanish; Lausanne Committee for World Evangelization; Livingstone, David; Love (Theology); Marriage; Missionaries, Lay; Missionaries--Recruitment and training; Missions--Argentina; Missions--Educational work; Missions--Korea; Missions--Poland; Missions--Soviet Union; Moscow, Soviet Union; New Zealand; Nixon, Richard Milhous; Nonformal education; Ockenga, Harold John; Open Doors with Brother Andrew; Organizational change; Orthodox Eastern Church; Orthodox Eastern Church--Relations; Pacific Garden Mission, IL; Paraguay; Persecution--Poland; Persecution--Soviet Union; Poland; Prayer groups; Preaching; Presidents--United States; Prisoners--Soviet Union; Radio audiences; Radio in religion; Radio program: *Hour of Decision*; Radio program: *Unshackled*; Redemption; Refugees--Austria; Refugees--Germany; Refugees--Italy; Regeneration (Theology); Religion and music; Repentance; Resurrection; Romania; Rome, Italy; Rosell, Mervin E "Merv"; Rural churches--Brazil; Salvation; Samaritan's Purse; Sanctification; SEND International; Sermons, American; Shanghai, China; Sin; Slavic Gospel Association; Smith, Oswald Jeffrey; Solzhenitsyn, Alexander; Soviet Union; Sunday schools; Sweden; Sydney, Australia; Trans World Radio; Underground Evangelism; Uruguay; Vacation schools, Christian; van der Bijl, Andrew; Vins, Georgi; Virgin birth; Wheaton College, IL; Women--Religious life; World Radio Missionary Fellowship; Worship; Wurmbrand, Richard; Wyrtzen, John Von Casper "Jack"; Youth for Christ International; Youth--Religious life; Yugoslavia)

%%%%%%%%%%%%%

CN# 164
**Small, Elizabeth Stair; 1904-**
Interview; 1980

Oral history interview with Small in which she describes her
missionary experiences in China from 1931 to 1948. Topics discussed include education at Moody Bible Institute, Chinese customs, evangelism methods, contacts with Chinese communists, the
church in China, and the place of women in Chinese society.

Vol: 1 Audio Tape

(MAJOR TOPICS: Chiang Kai-Shek; China; Communism; Hmong
people, China; Kuo min tang (China); Missions--China; Missions--Ed-
ucational work; Moody Bible Institute, IL; Overseas Missionary
Fellowship (China Inland Mission); Shanghai, China; Small, Elizabeth
Stair; Stam, Elizabeth Alden Scott; Totalitarianism; Wisconsin; World
War II)

%%%%%%%%%%%%%

CN# SC50
**Small, Samuel White; 1851-1931**
Ephemera; 1910

Second page of letter signed by evangelist Small on his stationery
and side portrait photograph of Small. Photograph is in photo file.

(MAJOR TOPICS: Evangelistic work--United States; Small, Samuel
White)

%%%%%%%%%%%%%

CN# 173
**Smith, Judson; 1837-1906**
Papers; 1878-1913; n.d.

Correspondence, reports, a will, newspaper clippings, and miscel-
leanous receipts concerning Smith's personal affairs, a trip to the
British Isles and Paris (1882), and deputation visits to Turkey
(1888), China, and Japan (1898) as Corresponding and Foreign
Secretary to the American Board of Commissioners for Foreign
Missions, 1884-1906.

Vol: 2 boxes

(MAJOR TOPICS: American Board of Commissioners for Foreign Missions; Anglicans; China; Church of England--Missions; Congresses and conferences--World Missionary Conference, 1888; Congregational churches--Missions; Congregationalists; France; Great Britain; Hong Kong; Japan; London, England; Medical care--Turkey; Methodist Church--Missions; Methodists; Missions, Medical; Missions--China; Missions--Hong Kong; Missions--Japan; Missions--Turkey; Moody, Dwight Lyman; Oberlin College, OH; Overseas Missionary Fellowship (China Inland Mission); Paris, France; Presbyterian Church--Missions; Presbyterians; Shanghai, China; Smith, Judson; Spurgeon, Charles Haddon; Turkey)

%%%%%%%%%%%%%

CN# 322
**Smith, Oswald Jeffrey; 1889-1986**
Papers; 1890-1986; n.d.

Correspondence, audio tapes, hymn and poem manuscripts, lantern slides, phonograph records, negatives, photographs, tracts, posters, audio tapes, clippings, scrapbooks, etc. related to Smith's career as an evangelist, pastor, author and editor, hymn writer and poet, colporteur, and promoter of missions involvement. Documents span Smith's education, colporteur work in Kentucky and Canada, and his pastoring the Dale Presbyterian Church, Toronto Alliance Tabernacle, and Gospel Tabernacle of Los Angeles, the Cosmopolitan Tabernacle (in Toronto), Toronto Gospel Tabernacle, and Toronto's People's Church.

Vol: 12 boxes, 75 Reels and 11 Cassettes of Audio Tape, Negatives, Phonograph Records, Photographs, Slides (Lantern)

(MAJOR TOPICS: Ackley, B D; African Americans; Alexander, Charles McCallon; Baptism; Bible--Prophecies; Bible colleges; Billy Graham Evangelistic Association; Booth, William Bramwell; Canada; Catholic Church; Catholic Church--Relations with Protestants; Chapman, John Wilbur; China; Christian and Missionary Alliance; Christian drama; Christian education (theory); Christian education--Indonesia; Christian literature--Publication and distribution; Church--biblical teaching; Cities and towns; Communism; Conversion; Deyneka, Peter Sr; Dunlop, Merrill; Ethiopia; Evangelicalism; Evangelistic invitations; Evangelistic sermons; Evangelistic work (theory); Evangelistic work---Canada; Evangelistic work--Iceland; Evangelistic work--Poland; Evangelistic work--United States; Faith; Family; Film: *Mr Texas*; Frost, Henry Weston; Fund raising; Fundamentalism; Gospel musicians; Graham, William Franklin "Billy"; Greece; Haile Selassie; Hamblen,

Stuart; Hammontree, Homer; Harper, Redd; Holy Spirit; Iceland;
Independent churches; Indigenous church administration; Indonesia;
Ironside, Henry Allan "Harry"; Jehovah's Witnesses; Jerusalem, Israel;
Journalism, Religious; Kentucky; Marshall, Peter; Mass media in
religion; McDonald, James "Jimmie"; Millennialism; Missionaries--Re-
cruitment and training; Missions, Medical; Missions--China; Mis-
sions--Indonesia; Missions--Rural work; Missions--Study and teaching;
Modernist-Fundamentalist controversy; Moody, Dwight Lyman; Nyack
Missionary Institute, NY; Palermo, Louis; Palermo, Phil; People's
Church (Toronto, ON); Poland; Prayer; Preaching; Presbyterians;
Rader, Daniel Paul; Radio in religion; Radio program: *Back Home
Hour*; Religion and music; Riley, William Bell; Rodeheaver, Homer
Alvan; Sankey, Ira D; Sermons, American; Shea, George Beverly;
Simpson, Albert Benjamin; Smith, Oswald Jeffrey; Smith, Rodney
"Gipsy"; Spurgeon, Charles Haddon; Sunday, William Ashley "Billy";
Toronto, ON; Torrey, Reuben Archer Sr; Trotter, Melvin Ernest;
World Literature Crusade; World Wide Christian Couriers; World
War II)

%%%%%%%%%%%%

CN# 109
**Smith, Rodney "Gipsy"; 1860-1947**
Ephemera; 1909-1935

Newspaper clippings, phonograph records and audio tapes relating
to the career of evangelist Gipsy Smith. A postcard photograph of
Smith and his wife is also included in the collection, as well as a
photograph of Smith with three unidentified people.

Vol: 1 box, 1 Audio Tape, Phonograph Records, Photographs

(MAJOR TOPICS: Evangelistic work--United States; Haymaker,
Willis Graham; Religion and music; Smith, Rodney "Gipsy")

%%%%%%%%%%%%

CN# 204
**South America Mission, Inc; 1914-**
Records; 1905 (1921-1955)1981; n.d.

Correspondence, legal documents, minutes of meetings, publications, reports, and linguistic materials related to the history and
activities of the mission, formerly Inland South America Missionary Union, incorporated 1921. The documents describe SAM's
work with Indian tribes in the interior of Bolivia, Brazil, Colombia,
Paraguay, and Peru. Subjects covered include tribal customs,

evangelistic methods, literature distribution, church planting, theological education, translation of the Bible into Indian languages, and aviation.

Vol: 3 boxes, 10 Reels of Microfilm, Oversize Material

(MAJOR TOPICS: Bible--Translating; Brazil; Evangelistic work--Brazil; Evangelistic work--Paraguay; Gospel Recordings, Inc; Indians of South America; Indigenous church administration; Intercultural communications; Language in missionary work; Language: Spanish; Missions--Argentina; Missions--Bolivia; Missions--Brazil; Missions--Chile; Missions--Paraguay; Missions--Peru; Missions--Study and teaching; Norwood, G Hunter; Paraguay; Ridderhof, Joy Fanny; South America Mission, Inc. (SAM) )

%%%%%%%%%%%%

CN# 90
**Spotts, George Franklin; 1944-**
Interview; 1979

An interview with Spotts discussing his experiences as a Teen Team member and later permanent Youth for Christ staff member in France. Subjects included club projects, response of the French nationals to evangelism, and analysis of overseas YFC work.

Vol: 1 Audio Tape

(MAJOR TOPICS: Adolescence; Catholic Church in France; Evangelistic work--France; France; Spotts, George Franklin; Youth for Christ International)

%%%%%%%%%%%%

CN# SC110
**Stam, Helen Priscilla; 1934-**
Ephemera; 1934-1939

A few newspaper clippings about the childhood of Stam, describing the murder in China by Communist soldiers of her missionary parents, John and Elizabeth Stam, when she was a baby; her rescue in China by local Christians; and the hopes of her grandparents that she would become a missionary.

(MAJOR TOPICS: Children of missionaries; China; Christian martyrs; Communism--China; Missions--China; Stam, Elizabeth Alden Scott; Stam, Helen Priscilla; Stam, John Cornelius)

%%%%%%%%%%%%

CN# 281
**Stauffacher, Florence Minch (1881-1959) and John W (1878-1944)**
Papers; 1902-1973

Correspondence, diaries, manuscripts, notes, clippings, photographs, etc., relating to the Stauffachers' work as missionaries with Africa Inland Mission. The materials document their careers from the earliest stages, describing their responsibilities and everyday life, primarily in Kenya and the Belgian Congo, but also in Uganda and Tanzania, their developing relationship by correspondence prior to Mrs. Stauffacher's arrival in Kenya and their subsequent marriage, as well as including a general history of AIM.

Vol: 3 boxes, Photographs

(MAJOR TOPICS: Africa Inland Mission (AIM); Church and state in Kenya; Church and state in Zaire; Congresses and conferences--Urbana Missionary Conventions; Courtship; Education--Kenya; Evangelistic work--Tanzania; Evangelistic work--Zaire; Hurlburt, Charles E; Illinois; Kenya; Masai people, Kenya; Medical care--Kenya; Missionaries--Leaves and furloughs; Missionaries--Recruitment and training; Missions--Kenya; Missions--Tanzania; Missions--Uganda; Missions---Zaire; Scott, Peter Cameron; Stauffacher, Florence P. Minch; Stauffacher, John; Student Volunteer Movement; Tanzania; Tucker, Alfred Robert; Uganda; Zaire)

%%%%%%%%%%%%

CN# 109
**Stough, Henry Wellington; 1870-1939**
Ephemera; 1911-1939; n.d.

Miscellaneous materials from Stough's career as an evangelist, including sermon notes, autobiographical manuscript, photographs, a microfilmed scrapbook of Stough's 1915 campaigns in Altoona and Lancaster, PA, a xeroxed copy of a scrapbook of newspaper clippings, pamphlets from the Evansville, IN, 1916, campaign and a photograph of Stough with William Jennings Bryan.

Vol: 1 box, 1 Reel of Microfilm, Photographs

(MAJOR TOPICS: Alexander, Charles McCallon; Bryan, William Jennings; Chapman, John Wilbur; Church and social problems; Cities and towns; City missions; Faith--Cure; Fundamentalism; Independent churches; Indiana; Interdenominational Association of Evangelists; Jones, Samuel Porter; McPherson, Aimee Semple; Mills, B Fay; Moody, Dwight Lyman; Prohibition; Sermons, American; Stough, Henry Wellington; Sunday, William Ashley "Billy"; Whitefield, George; Winona Lake Bible Conference, IN)

%%%%%%%%%%%

CN# 89
**Stough, Paul Pinney; 1901-**
Interviews; 1979-1980

Series of interviews with Stough, a missionary of Africa Inland Mission who served in the Belgian Congo and Kenya. Collection includes information on the work of evangelist Henry W. Stough, history of Wheaton College, and the spread of Christianity in Africa.

Vol: 3 Audio Tapes

(MAJOR TOPICS: Africa Inland Church; Africa Inland Mission (AIM); American Colonization Society; Becker, Carl K Jr; Belgium; Blanchard, Jonathan; Catholic Church in Zaire; Catholic Church--Missions; Catholic Church--Relations; Christian literature--Publication and distribution; Church and social problems; Church and state in Kenya; Church and state in Zaire; Congo Protestant Council; Davis, Ralph T; Evangelical Literature Overseas; Evangelistic work--United States; Evangelistic work--Zaire; Gospel Recordings, Inc; Graham, William Franklin "Billy"; Hurlburt, Charles E; Independent churches; Intercultural communications; International Missionary Council; Kenya; Kivengere, Festo; Mau Mau movement; Medical care--Kenya; Medical care--United States; Missions, Medical; Missions--Educational work; Missions--Kenya; Missions--Zaire; Pennsylvania; Pinney, John Book; Prisoners--Kenya; Prohibition; Scott Theological College, Machakos, Kenya; Stough, Henry Wellington; Stough, Paul Pinney; Sunday, William Ashley "Billy"; World Council of Churches; Zaire)

%%%%%%%%%%%

CN# 61
**Sunday, William Ashley (1862-1935) and Helen Amelia (1868-1957)**
Papers; 1882 (1888-1957) 1974; n.d.

Several hundred photographs and 29 reels of microfilm containing correspondence, sermons, reports, revival ephemera, scrapbooks dealing mainly with the career of evangelist Billy Sunday from its beginning to his death and about the work of his wife Helen, who besides acting as his chief advisor and manager was a Fundamentalist leader in her own right, especially after his death. The collection also contains information about the Prohibition movement in America and life on the home front during World War 1.

Vol: 29 reels of microfilm; photographs

(MAJOR TOPICS: Ackley, B D; Adolescence; Alexander, Charles McCallon; Asher, Virginia Healey (Mrs William); Barrows, Clifford B; Biederwolf, William Edward; Billy Graham Evangelistic Association (BGEA); Bob Jones University, SC; Bok, Edward; Boston, MA; Bryan, William Jennings; California; Chapman, John Wilbur; Chicago, IL; Christian leadership; Church and social problems; Church and state in United States; Church--biblical teaching; Cities and towns; City missions; Clark, Harry D; Colorado; Cook, Robert Andrew; Coolidge, Calvin; Curley, James; Daniels, Joseph; DeMille, Cecil B; Deyneka, Peter Sr; District of Columbia; Evangelistic work--United States; Fundamentalism; Gaebelein, Arno C; Georgia; Hammontree, Homer; Haymaker, Willis Graham; Hillis, Charles Richard "Dick"; Hoover, Herbert Clark; Houghton, William Henry; Huffman, John A; Illinois; Independent churches; Interdenominational Evangelist League; Iowa; Ironside, Henry Allan "Harry"; Johnson, Torrey Maynard; Jones, Robert R Jr "Bob"; Jones, Robert R Sr "Bob"; Kentucky; Lansing, Robert; Legislators--United States; Letourneau, Robert Gilmore; Lorimer, George H; Louisiana; Mack, Connie; Maryland; Mass media in religion; Matthews, Robert; Mayo, Charles; Mayo, William J; McAdoo, William Gibbs; McLoughlin, William; Messer, Wilbur; Michigan; Minnesota; Mississippi; Missouri; Mott, John Raleigh; Moving-pictures in church work; Moving-pictures--Moral and religious aspects; Nationalism; New Jersey; New York City, NY: New York (state); Norris, John Franklyn; Ohio; Oklahoma; Pacific Garden Mission, IL; Parenthood; Pegler, Westbrook; Pennsylvania; Prayer; Presidents--United States; Prohibition; Radio program: *Hour of Decision*; Radio program: *Unshackled*; Religion and sports; Rhode Island; Rice, John Richard; Roberson, Lee; Rockefeller, John Davison Jr; Rodeheaver, Homer Alvan; Roosevelt, Franklin Delano; Roosevelt, Theodore; Rosell, Mervin E "Merv"; Saulnier, Harold; Sermons, American; Seventh Day Adventists; Sex role; Smith, Oswald Jeffrey; Smith, Wilbur Moorehead; Smyth, Walter Herbert; Sports; Sunday, Helen Amelia Thompson; Sunday, William Ashley "Billy"; Tennessee; Texas; Torrey, Reuben Archer Sr; Trotter, Melvin Ernest; Virginia; Virginia Asher Business Women Councils; Walker, Robert; Walter F Bennett and Co; Wanamaker, John; Washington (state); Washington, DC; West Virginia; Williams, Milan B; Wilson, George McConnell; Wilson, Thomas Walter Jr; Winona Lake Bible Conference, IN; Women--Religious life; World War I; Wyrtzen, John Von Casper

"Jack"; Young Men's Christian Association (YMCA); Youth for Christ International)

%%%%%%%%%%%%

CN# 29
**Sunday, William Ashley "Billy"; 1862-1935**
Ephemera; 1914-1971; n.d.

Miscellaneous materials collected from various sources about the career of evangelist Sunday, including newspaper clippings, bulletins, counselor training materials, promotional pieces, correspondence, audio tapes, photographs, postcards, scrapbooks, a film relating to Sunday's ministry as an evangelist and Homer Rodeheaver's publishing activities.

Vol: 3 boxes, 2 Audio Tapes, 1 Film, 1 Reel of Microfilm, Phonograph Records, Photographs

(MAJOR TOPICS: Asher, Virginia Healey (Mrs William); Boston, MA; Church and state in United States; Counseling; Evangelistic work--United States; Fundamentalism; Harding, Warren Gamaliel; Ingersoll, Robert G "Bob"; Massachusetts; New York City, NY; Ohio; Presidents--United States; Rodeheaver, Homer Alvan; Sermons, American; Smith, Rodney "Gipsy"; Sunday, Helen Amelia Thompson; Sunday, William Ashley "Billy")

%%%%%%%%%%%%

CN# 266
**Sundquist, Ruth; 1920-**
Interviews; 1984

Two interviews with Sundquist in which she describes her work first in Kentucky home missions as a Christian education worker with the Evangelical Free Church, and then her missionary career in China and Hong Kong between 1947-1982 as an administrator for a Sunday School and orphanage. Topics discussed include her call to be a missionary, language school in China, Chinese attitudes toward the Kuo min tang and Communist parties, Americans in China, and the social needs of Hong Kong.

Vol: 2 Audio Tapes

(MAJOR TOPICS: African Americans; Children--Conversion to Christianity; China; Christian education of children; Christian education--China; Christian education--Hong Kong; Christian educa-

tion--United States; Church and social problems; Church work with
children; Church work with refugees; Communism--China; Evangelical
Free Church of America; Evangelical Free Church--Missions; Illinois;
Kentucky; Kuo min tang (China); Language in missionary work;
Missionaries--Recruitment and training; Missions to Chinese; Mis-
sions--China; Missions--Hong Kong; Missions--United States; Moody
Bible Institute, IL; Orphans and orphan-asylums; Religion and under-
developed areas; Salvation; Salvation Army; Sunday schools; Women---
Religious life; Women in missionary work)

%%%%%%%%%%%%

CN# 79
**Survey of Inquiries at the 1962 Greater Chicago Crusade**
Records; 1963-1963

A questionnaire prepared by Aubrey Leon Morris containing 100
correspondents' responses to questions relating to the Billy Graham Chicago Crusade of 1962.

Vol: 1 box

(MAJOR TOPICS: Belief and doubt; Billy Graham Evangelistic
Association (BGEA); Chicago, IL; Conversion; Evangelicalism; Evangelistic invitations; Evangelistic sermons; Faith)

%%%%%%%%%%%%

CN# 129
**Talmage, Thomas Dewitt; 1832-1902**
Ephemera; 1870 (1891-1894) 1897

Letter to a Dr. McKenzie inviting him to the dedication of Talmage's new tabernacle in Brooklyn; letter from Talmage refuting
the charge that he had visited an actor to increase his speaking
abilities; and news articles by Talmage clipped from the *Ladies
Home Journal*.

Vol: 1 box

(MAJOR TOPICS: Evangelistic work--United States; Talmage, Thomas Dewitt)

%%%%%%%%%%%%

CN# 20
**Taylor, Herbert John; 1893-1978**
Papers; 1916-1976; n.d.

Correspondence, photographs, reports, publications, posters,
minutes of meetings, and other documentation of long involvement
of Taylor (a Chicago businessman) in the leadership of such
organizations as Child Evangelism, Youth for Christ, Young Life,
National Association of Evangelicals, Fuller Seminary, Christian
Workers Foundation, and Inter-Varsity as well as his role in the
planning and development of Billy Graham's Chicago crusades and
of Key '73. Other records deal with his business career, his deep
involvement in Rotary, (of which he was International President),
his wartime service on the Price Adjustment Board, and his
interest in Chicago civic affairs.

Vol: 81 boxes, 5 Films, Photographs

(MAJOR TOPICS: African Enterprise; Africa Inland Mission (AIM);
Alexander, John W; American Bible Society; American Tract Society;
Arkansas; Armerding, Hudson Taylor; Australia; Barnhouse, Donald
Grey Sr; Barrows, Clifford B; Bayley, Joseph Tate; Bible Memory
Association (BMA); Bihl, Carl J "Kelly"; Billy Graham Evangelistic
Association (BGEA); Boice, James Montgomery; Bolten, John;
Boys--Societies and clubs; Bright, William Rohl "Bill"; Buswell, James
Oliver Jr; Butt, Howard E Jr; CAM International; Campus Crusade
for Christ; Chicago Evangelistic Institute; Chicago, IL; Child Evan-
gelism Fellowship; Children's clubs; Children--Conversion to Chris-
tianity; Children--Religious life; Christian Service Brigade; Christian
Worker's Foundation; Christianity Today, Inc; Church and state in
United States; Church work with single people; Church work with
students; City missions; Congresses and conferences--Explo '72;
Congresses and conferences--Urbana Missionary Conventions; Con-
gresses and conferences--World Congress on Evangelism, 1966; Cook,
Robert Andrew; Counseling; Dallas Theological Seminary; De Haan,
Richard; Deyneka, Peter Sr; Edman, Victor Raymond; Engstrom,
Theodore "Ted" Wilhelm; Evangelical Alliance Mission, The (TEAM);
Evangelical Foreign Missions Association; Evangelicalism; Evangelistic
work--Australia; Evangelistic work--Japan; Evangelistic work--New
Zealand; Evangelistic work--United States; Evans, Robert Philips;
Fellowship of Christian Athletes; Fuller Theological Seminary, CA;
Fuller, Charles Edward Sr; Fundamentalism; Girls--Societies and
clubs; Gospel Films, Inc; Gothard, William; Graham, William Franklin
"Billy"; Greater Europe Mission (GEM); Hansen, Kenneth Norman;
Hawaii; Henry, Carl Ferdinand Howard; Hillis, Charles Richard

"Dick"; Hoke, Donald Edwin; Hubbard, David Allen; Hummel, Charles E; Illinois; Institute in Basic Youth Conflicts; Inter-Varsity Christian Fellowship; Interdenominational Foreign Mission Association (IFMA); Johnson, Torrey Maynard; Jones, Robert R Sr "Bob"; Key '73; L'Abri Fellowship; Latin America Mission; Lindsell, Harold; Methodists; Missions--Interdenominational cooperation; Moody Bible Institute, IL; Moody Institute of Science; Moody Memorial Church, IL; Moving-pictures in church work; Moving-pictures--Moral and religious aspects; National Association of Evangelicals; National Black Evangelistic Association; National Religious Broadcasters; Navigators; Nelson, Victor B; New England Fellowship (NEF); New York (state); New York City, NY; New Zealand; North Carolina; O C Ministries; Ockenga, Harold John; Organizational change; Pacific Garden Mission, IL; Periodical: *Christianity Today*; Periodical: *Decision*; Philadelphia, PA; Philippines; Pierce, Robert Willard "Bob"; Pioneer Ministries; Prayer groups; Presidents--United States; Radio in religion; Radio Program: *Old Fashioned Revival Hour*; Rayburn, James C Jr; Rice, John Richard; Riggs, Charles A; Rodeheaver, Homer Alvan; Salvation Army; Sanny, Lorne Charles; Saulnier, Harry G; Servicemaster; Shea, George Beverly; Short Terms Abroad; Skinner, Thomas; Slavic Gospel Association; Smyth, Walter Herbert; Stone, W Clement; Student Foreign Mission Fellowship; Sudan Interior Mission (SIM); Sunday schools; Sweeting, George; Taylor, Clyde Willis; Taylor, Herbert John; Taylor, Kenneth Nathaniel; Television in religion; Trotman, Dawson; Trotter, Melvin Ernest; Unevangelized Fields Mission; Urban Outreach; Vacation schools, Christian; Voice of Calvary Ministries; Weyerhauser, C Davis; Wheaton College, IL; Wiersbe, Warren W; Wilson, George McConnell; Wilson, Thomas Walter Jr; Wolgemuth, Samuel Frey; Woods, C Stacey; Word of Life Fellowship; World Evangelical Fellowship (WEF); World Relief Commission; World Vision International; World War I; World War II; World Wide Pictures; Wright, James Elwin; Wycliffe Bible Translators; Young Life; Young Men's Christian Association, United States; Youth for Christ International; Youth--Religious life; Youth--Societies and clubs)

%%%%%%%%%%%%

CN# SC92
**Taylor, James Hudson; 1832-1905**
Ephemera; 1896-1898

Two letters to Mr. Sloan, one written aboard the "Oceania" (June 2, 1896) and the other en route to Wan-hsien, China (Dec. 26, 1898), discussing C.I.M. affairs, including a legacy and contributions, conferences, and concerns for friends and co-workers.

(MAJOR TOPICS: Fund raising; Overseas Missionary Fellowship
(China Inland Mission); Taylor, James Hudson)

%%%%%%%%%%%%

CN# 78
**ten Boom, Cornelia Arnolda Johanna; 1892-1983**
Papers; 1902-1983; n.d.

Letters, photographs, audio tapes, diary, notebooks, and other
material relating to the life of the Dutch Christian worker Corrie
ten Boom. Material includes information on: her father Casper,
her imprisonment in a concentration camp during World War II,
her work among refugees after the war, her travels as an evangelist, the work of her two foundations, and the production of the
film *The Hiding Place*.

Vol: 3 boxes, 9 Audio Tapes, Photographs

(MAJOR TOPICS: Amsterdam, Netherlands; Argentina; Australia;
Barrows, Clifford B; Belief and doubt; Billy Graham Evangelistic
Association (BGEA); Book: *Hiding Place, The*; Charismatic movement; Children; Children's clubs; Christian education of adolescents;
Christian education of children; Christian education--Netherlands;
Christian giving; Christian leadership; Christian life; Christian litera-
ture--Publication and distribution; Christian martyrs; Church and
social problems; Communication; Corrie ten Boom Stichting (Founda-
tion); Evangelistic work--Argentina; Evangelistic work--Australia;
Evangelistic work--South Africa; Evangelistic work--Taiwan; Evangelis-
tic work--United States; Film: *Hiding Place, The*; Forgiveness; Fund
raising; Germany; Girls--Societies and clubs; Graham, William Frank-
lin "Billy"; Jews in Netherlands; Language: Dutch; Language: German;
Language: Spanish; Mass media in religion; Missions to Jews;
Moving-pictures in church work; New Zealand; Pentecostals; Prayer;
Preaching; Prisons--Missions and charities; Reconciliation; Refugees---
Germany; Refugees--Netherlands; Resurrection; Sermons, American;
South Africa; Taiwan; ten Boom, Betsie; ten Boom, Casper; ten
Boom, Cornelia Arnolda Johanna; van der Bijl, Andrew; Women
authors; Women--Religious life; World War II; World Wide Pictures;
Youth--Societies and clubs)

%%%%%%%%%%%%%

CN# 44
**Tenney, Helen Margaret Jaderquist; 1904-1978**
Papers; 1910-1980; n.d.

Correspondence, scrapbook, drafts, articles, research notes, and
other documents relating to Tenney's active participation on a
number of Evangelical ministries but particularly to her work with
the Women's Union Missionary Society (WUMS). The bulk of
the collection consists of the manuscript of her history of the
WUMS.

Vol: 6 boxes, Photographs

(MAJOR TOPICS: American Baptist Foreign Mission Society; Bap-
tists; Baptists--Missions; China; Doremus, Sarah D; Evangelicalism;
Evangelistic work--United States; India; Interdenominational Foreign
Mission Association (IFMA); Japan; Medical care--China; Medical
care--India; Missions, Medical; Missions--China; Missions--Educational
work; Missions--India; Missions--Interdenominational cooperation;
Missions--Japan; National Association of Evangelicals; Pakistan;
Philippines; Tenney, Helen Jaderquist; Woman's American Baptist
Foreign Mission Society; Women's Union Missionary Society; World
War II)

%%%%%%%%%%%%%

CN# 260
**Thiessen, Jeannette Louise Martig; 1928-**
Interviews; 1983

Three taped interviews with Mrs. Thiessen in which she discusses
her family life in Illinois, favorite professors and her education at
Wheaton College, nurses' training, and years in India, 1952-1974,
working with her husband under the sponsorship of the Mennonite
Church, Mission to Leprosy, and American Leprosy Missions.
Topics include Indian caste system, politics, economics, literacy,
hospital work with lepers, the Indian church, education of American children in India and culture shock on furloughs.

Vol: 3 Audio Tapes

(MAJOR TOPICS: American Leprosy Missions, Inc; Bible colleges;
Camp meetings; Children of missionaries; Christian education, Outdoor; Christian education--India; Christian leadership; Church and
social problems; Church and state in India; Church work with refu-

gees; Clergy, Training of; College students in missionary work; Congresses and conferences--Urbana Missionary Conventions; Conversion; Counseling; Disease: Leprosy; Edman, Victor Raymond; Education---India; Elliot, Philip James; Evangelistic work--India; Gandhi, Mahatma; Holy Spirit; Howard, David Morris; Illinois; India; Indigenous church administration; Intercultural communications; Judson, Adoniram; Language in missionary work; Letourneau, Robert Gilmore; McGavran, Donald Anderson; MAP International; Medical care---India; Medical care--Nigeria; Medical care--United States; Mennonite Church--Missions; Missionaries, Resignation of; Missionaries--Leaves and furloughs; Missionaries--Recruitment and training; Missions to lepers; Missions, Medical; Missions--India; Nehru, Jawaharlal; Nursing; Olford, Stephen Frederick; Prayer; Redpath, Alan; Refugees---India; Taylor, James Hudson; Thiessen, Jeannette Louise Martig; Wheaton College, IL; Winona Lake Bible Conference, IN; Women---Religious life; Women in missionary work; Worship)

%%%%%%%%%%%%

CN# 84
**Thiessen, Vera Edna; 1919-**
Papers; 1946-1975; n.d.

Correspondence describing Thiessen's experiences and work as a medical missionary of the Africa Inland Mission (AIM) in the Belgian Congo.

Vol: 1 box

(MAJOR TOPICS: Africa Inland Mission (AIM); Baptists; Baptists--Missions; Belgian Gospel Mission; Brethren; Brethren Church---Missions; British Missionary Society; Christian and Missionary Alliance (CMA); Church and state in Zaire; Communism--Zaire; Congo Protestant Council; Conservative Baptist Foreign Mission Society; Evangelistic work--Tanzania; Evangelistic work--Uganda; Evangelistic work--Zaire; Gration, John A; Heart of Africa Mission (HAM); Jehovah's Witnesses; Kenya; Langford, Sidney; Litchman, Bernard Leonard "Jack"; Mau Mau movement; Medical care--Zaire; Methodists; Missions, Medical; Missions--China; Missions--Educational work; Missions--Zaire; Plymouth Brethren; Plymouth Brethren--Missions; Pocket Testament League; Rimmer, Harry; Rosell, Mervin E "Merv"; Seume, Richard Herman; Stam, Peter; Studd, Charles Thomas; Tanzania; Thiessen, Vera; Uganda; Wheaton College, IL; Zaire)

%%%%%%%%%%%%

CN# 107
**Torrey, Reuben Archer Sr; 1856-1928**
Papers; 1892-1936; n.d.

Correspondence, sermon notes, Sunday School lessons, newspaper clippings, brochures, memorial booklet, and photographs from Torrey's career as evangelist, teacher, author, and family man.

Vol: 3 boxes, Negatives, Photographs, 1 Folder, Oversize Materials

(MAJOR TOPICS: Alexander, Charles McCallon; Beijing, China; Bible Institute of Los Angeles (BIOLA), CA; China; Evangelistic work--New Zealand; Evangelistic work--United States; Family; Fundamentalism; Moody Bible Institute, IL; New Zealand; Overseas Missionary Fellowship (China Inland Mission); Riley, William Bell; Sermons, American; Sunday schools; Torrey, Reuben Archer Sr)

%%%%%%%%%%%%

CN# SC 97
**Torrey, Reuben Archer, Jr; 1887-1980**
Papers; 1942-1966; n.d.

Correspondence and excerpts from correspondence, pamphlets, reports, articles, and narrative accounts relating to the work of Torrey, the only son of evangelist R. A. Torrey, Sr. Torrey's career included work as a missionary, liaison officer for Chiang Kai-Shek to the American forces in China, and director of the Korean Amputee Rehabilitation Project. Documents in the collection include descriptions of Torrey's internment by the Japanese in China, the great physical and spiritual needs of the people in South Korea following the war there, and the development of the rehabilitation program under Torrey's administration.

(MAJOR TOPICS: Chiang Kai-Shek; China; Ecumenical movement; Evangelistic work--China; Korea; Korean War; Missions, Medical; Missions--China; Missions--Cooperative movement; Missions--Korea; Presbyterian Church--Missions; Presbyterians; Refugees--Korea; Torrey, Reuben Archer Jr; Torrey, Reuben Archer Sr)

%%%%%%%%%%%%

CN# 331
**Torrey, Reuben Archer, III; 1918-**
Interview; 1986

An oral history interview in which Torrey discusses his childhood in China as the son of Presbyterian missionaries; his experiences at boarding schools in China and Korea; his grandfather, Dr. R. A. Torrey; his work as an Episcopal parish priest in the U. S.; teaching at an Episcopal seminary in Korea; and his founding of a retreat center in Korea, Jesus Abbey.

Vol: 2 Audio Tapes, 1 Video Tape

(MAJOR TOPICS: Children of missionaries; Episcopalians; Missions--China; Missions--Korea; Prayer; Presbyterians; Presbyterian church--Missions; Torrey, Reuben Archer III; Torrey, Reuben Archer Jr; Torrey, Reuben Archer Sr)

%%%%%%%%%%%%

CN# 183
**Tournier, Paul; 1898-**
Ephemera; 1961

Two taped segments translated from the French, in which psychiatrist Paul Tournier discusses medicine as personal dialogue as well as scientific knowledge and the importance of including the spiritual as part of the dialogue. Also includes biographical details which illustrate this aspect of medicine.

Vol: 2 Audio Tapes

(MAJOR TOPICS: Counseling; Psychiatry and religion; Switzerland; Wheaton College, IL)

%%%%%%%%%%%%

CN# 190
**Travers, Alan; 19?-**
Interviews; 1981

Interviews with Travers about his work with Trans World Radio, from 1959 to 1981, and the use of radio in missionary work. Travers discusses the history of TWR, technical and administrative details and policy of the organization, the locations of its stations throughout the world, how the staff function in the stations and relate to the countries in which they serve, how the German branch of TWR (Evangeliums Rundfunk) was started and how it functions within the structure of TWR.

Volume: 4 Reels of Audio Tape

(MAJOR TOPICS: Africa Evangelical Fellowship; Angola; Animism; Apartheid; Arabs; Argentina; Armenians; Armstrong, Benjamin Leighton; Australia; Berlin, Germany; Brazil; Canada; Charismatic movement; Children of missionaries; China; Christianity and politics; Clergy, Training of; Communism; Czechoslovakia; Egypt; Evangeliums Rundfunk; Family; Far East Broadcasting Company; Federal Communications Commission; France; Freed, Paul Ernest; Fund raising; Fundamentalism; Germany; Hong Kong; House churches; India; Indigenous church administration; Intercultural communications; Islam--Relations--Christianity; Italy; Japan; Kenya; Language in missionary work; Language: Arabic; Language: Chinese; Language: French; Language: German; Liberia; Marquardt, Horst; Mass media in religion; Methodists; Missionaries--Recruitment and training; Missions to Muslims; Missions--Angola; Missions--Brazil; Missions--China; Missions--France; Missions--India; Missions--Indonesia; Missions--Iran; Missions--Liberia; Missions--Morocco; Missions--Mozambique; Missions--Palestine; Missions--Portugal; Missions--Saudi Arabia; Missions--Spain; Missions--Sri Lanka; Missions--Study and teaching; Missions--Syria; Monaco; Monte Carlo; Morocco; Mozambique; Muslims in Egypt; Nairobi, Kenya; National Religious Broadcasters; National Socialism; Netherlands; New Jersey; North Carolina; Panama; Presidents--United States; Portugal; Radio in missionary work; Radio in religion; Saudi Arabia; South Africa; Soviet Union; Spain; Sri Lanka (Ceylon); Sudan Interior Mission (SIM); Syria; Tokyo, Japan; Trans World Radio; Travers, Alan; Truman, Harry S; Wheaton College, IL; World Radio Missionary Fellowship; World War II; Worship)

%%%%%%%%%%%%

CN# 47
**Trotter, Melvin Ernest; 1870-1940**
Papers; 1899-1972; n.d.

Correspondence, annual reports, newspaper clippings, sermon notes, photographs, audio tape, memorabilia related to the life and work of evangelist and rescue mission worker Mel Trotter.

Vol: 8 boxes, 1 Audio Tape, 3 Reels of Microfilm, Negatives, Photographs

(MAJOR TOPICS: Ackley, B D; Alexander, Charles McCallon; Brotherhood of Rescue Mission Superintendents; Cities and towns; City missions; Evangelistic work--United States; Fundamentalism; Hammontree, Homer; Ironside, Henry Allan "Harry"; Jones, Robert R Sr "Bob"; Mel Trotter Rescue Mission, Grand Rapids, MI; Monroe, Harry; Morgan, G Campbell; Northfield Bible Conference, MA; Pacific Garden Mission, IL; Prohibition; Rader, Daniel Paul; Radio program: *Unshackled*; Rodeheaver, Homer Alvan; Sermons, American; Sunday, William Ashley "Billy"; Torrey, Reuben Archer Sr; Trotter, Melvin Ernest; Vandenberg, Arthur H )

%%%%%%%%%%%%%

CN# 111
**Troutman, Charles Henry Jr; 1914-**
Papers; 1924-1979; n.d.

Correspondence, minutes, reports, manuals, and other records concerning Troutman's career in Christian work among university students, with Inter-Varsity in the United States and Australia (in both countries he served as chief executive officer) and then with Latin America Mission.

Vol: 21 boxes, Photographs, Slides, Phonograph Records

(MAJOR TOPICS: Afghanistan; Alabama; Alexander, John W; American Bible Society; Anglicans; Argentina; Arizona; Arkansas; Armerding, Hudson Taylor; Australia; Australian Conference of the World Council of Churches; Australian Council of Churches; Barnhouse, Donald Grey Jr; Bayley, Joseph Tate; Beavan, Gerald "Jerry"; Bible--Criticism, interpretation, etc; Billy Graham Evangelistic Association (BGEA); Bolivia; Bolten, John; Brazil; Bright, William Rohl "Bill"; Burma; California; Campus Crusade for Christ; Canada; Catholic Church; Chicago, IL; Chile; China; Christian leadership; Christian literature--Publication and distribution; Christian Medical Society; Christian Nurses' Fellowship; Christianity Today, Inc; Church and social problems; Church of England; Church work with military personnel; Church work with students; Civil rights movement; College students in missionary work; College students--Religious life; Colombia; Colorado; Communication; Communism; Congresses and conferences--International Congress on World Evangelization, 1974; Congresses and conferences--Urbana Missionary Conventions; Connecticut; Costa Rica; Cuba; Dain, Arthur John; Delaware; District of Columbia; Ecuador; Ecumenical movement; Ethiopia; Evangelical Literature Overseas; Evangelicalism; Evangelistic work--Argentina; Evangelistic work--Australia; Evangelistic work--Brazil; Evangelistic work--Canada; Evangelistic work--Ecuador; Evangelistic work--Germany; Evangelistic work--Great Britain; Evangelistic work--Guatemala; Evangelistic work--Japan; Evangelistic work--Korea; Evangelistic work--Mexico; Evangelistic work--New Zealand; Evangelistic work---Poland; Evangelistic work--Portugal; Evangelistic work--Taiwan; Evangelistic work--United States; Evangelistic work--Vietnam; Fellowship Foundation; Florida; Ford, Leighton Frederick Sandys; Gaebelein, Frank; Georgia; Germany; Glossolalia; Goldwater, Barry Morris; Graham, William Franklin "Billy"; Great Britain; Guatemala; Haines, Margaret; Harvard University, MA; Haymaker, Willis Graham; Hillis, Charles Richard "Dick"; Hong Kong; Houghton, William Henry; Howard, David Morris; Hustad, Donald Paul; Idaho; Illinois; India; Indiana; Indonesia; Inter-Varsity Christian Fellowship; Intercultural communications; International Council of Christian Churches; International Students, Inc; InterVarsity Christian Fellowship--Great Britain; Iowa; Japan; Kansas; Kentucky; Keswick Movement; Korea; Kraakevik, James Henry; Langford, Sidney; Latin America Mission; Liberation Theology; Little, Paul Eagleson; London, England; Los Angeles, CA; Louisiana; Machen, John Gresham; Maine; Malaysia; Maryland; Massachusetts; Medical care--United States; Mexico; Michigan; Minnesota; Missions, Medical; Missions--Argentina; Missions--Australia; Missions--Bolivia; Missions--Brazil; Missions--Burma; Missions--Canada; Missions--Chile; Missions--China; Missions--Colombia; Missions--Costa Rica; Missions--Cuba; Missions--Ecuador; Missions--Educational work; Missions--Ethiopia; Missions--Great Britain; Missions--Guatemala; Missions--Hong Kong; Missions--Indonesia; Missions--Interdenominational cooperation; Missions--Japan; Missions--Korea; Missions--Malaysia; Missions--Mexico; Missions--Nicaragua; Missions--Panama; Missions--Peru; Missions--Philippines; Missions--Portugal; Missions--Taiwan; Missions--United States; Missions--Vietnam; Missouri; Montana; National Association of Evangelicals; National Council of Churches; National Negro Evangelical Association; Navajo Indians; Navigators; Nebraska; New Hampshire; New Jersey; New Mexico; New York (state); New York City, NY; New Zealand; Nicaragua; Niebuhr, Reinhold; Nonformal education; North Dakota; Nurses Christian Fellowship; Oberlin College, OH; Ockenga, Harold John; Officers' Christian Union; Ohio; Oklahoma; Oregon; Orr, James Edwin; Panama; Pennsylvania; Pentecostals; Periodical: *Christianity Today*; Periodical: *Eternity Magazine*; Periodical: *His*; Peru; Philippines; Portugal; Rhode Island; Riggs, Charles A; Schaeffer, Francis August; Schoerner, Katharine Hasting Dodd; Schoerner, Otto Frederick; Scripture Union; Singapore; South Carolina; South Dakota; Strachan, R Kenneth; Student Foreign Mission Fellowship; Switzerland; Sydney, Australia; Taiwan; Taylor, Clyde Willis; Taylor, Herbert John; Taylor, Kenneth Nathaniel; Tennessee; Tenney, Merrill Chapin; Texas; Troutman, Charles H Jr; United States; Utah; Vermont; Vietnam; Washington (state); West Virginia;

Winter, Ralph D; Woods, C Stacey; World Christian Fellowship; World Council of Churches; World War II; Wycliffe Bible Translators; Wyoming; Wyrtzen, John Von Casper "Jack"; Yale University, CN; Young Life; Youth for Christ International; Youth--Religious life)

%%%%%%%%%%%%

CN# 135
**Tucker, Alfred Robert; 1849-1914**
Papers; 1890-1927; n.d.

Correspondence, maps, clippings, pamphlets, photographs, sketches relating to Tucker, Anglican Bishop of Uganda. Materials deal with church affairs in Uganda and Kenya, and a biography of Tucker planned by Mary Carus-Wilson.

Vol: 2 boxes, Photographs

(MAJOR TOPICS: Anglicans; Catholic Church in Uganda; Catholic Church--Missions; Catholic Church--Relations; Church and social problems; Church and state in Uganda; Church Missionary Society, England; Church of England; Church of England--Missions; Education--Kenya; Evangelistic work--Uganda; Kenya; Medical care--Uganda; Missions, Medical; Missions--Uganda; Tucker, Alfred Robert; Uganda; Zanzibar)

%%%%%%%%%%%%

CN# 313
**Van Kampen, Robert Cornelius; 1910-1989**
Papers; 1944 (1959-1982) 1982

Correspondence, minutes, reports, manuscripts, photographs, audio tapes, clippings, etc., related to Van Kampen's responsibilities on the Board of Directors of the Billy Graham Evangelistic Association as well the boards of BGEA subsidiaries or affiliated institutions (Billy Graham Benevolent Fund, Billy Graham Evangelistic Film Ministry, Inc., Billy Graham Evangelistic Trust, Billy Graham Foundation, Grason Company, World Evangelism and Christian Education Fund, World Wide Pictures, World Wide Publications), and Wheaton College's Board of Trustees. The documents focus on administrative and planning activities.

Vol: 3 boxes, 6 Audio Tapes, Photographs

(MAJOR TOPICS: Abortion; Auca people, Ecuador; Australia; Barrows, Clifford B; Bell, Lemuel Nelson; Bible colleges; Billy Gra-

ham Center, IL; Billy Graham Evangelistic Association (BGEA);
Boston, MA; Campus Crusade for Christ; Chicago, IL; Christian
education (theory); Christian education--United States; Church and
social problems; Church and state in United States; Congresses and
conferences--International Congress on World Evangelization, 1974;
Congresses and conferences--World Congress on Evangelism, 1966;
Corporations, Religious--Taxation; Cults; Edman, Victor Raymond;
Education, Higher; Evangelicalism; Evangelistic invitations; Evangelis-
tic sermons; Evangelistic work--Australia; Evangelistic work--Liberia;
Evangelistic work--United States; Evangelistic work--Venezuela;
Falwell, Jerry; Feminism; Ferm, Lois Roughan; Ford, Leighton Frede-
rick Sandys; Graham, William Franklin "Billy"; Haile Selassie; Hall,
Myrtle; Hawaii; Hoke, Donald Edwin; Hustad, Donald Paul; Italy;
Jones, Robert R Sr "Bob"; Liberia; London, England; Mass media in
religion; McDonald, James "Jimmie"; Mooneyham, W Stanley;
Moving-pictures in church work; Muslims in Nigeria; National As-
sociation of Evangelicals; New York. World's Fair, 1964-1965; Nixon,
Richard Milhous; Periodical: *Sword of the Lord*; Presidents--United
States; Race relations; Radio in religion; Refugees--Vietnam; Religion
and music; Rice, John Richard; Saint, Rachel; Sex role; Shea, George
Beverly; Smith, Edward R "Tedd"; Smith, Wilbur Moorehead; Smyth,
Walter Herbert; South Africa; Soviet Union; Sydney, Australia; Taylor,
Clyde Willis; Television in religion; Texas; Van Kampen, Robert
Cornelius; Venezuela; Vietnamese Conflict; Watergate Affair,
1972-1974; Wheaton College, IL; White, John Wesley; Woods, C
Stacey; World Wide Pictures; Young Life; Youth for Christ Inter-
national)

%%%%%%%%%%%%

CN# 105
**Votaw, Paul Dean; 1917-**
Interview; 1980

Oral history interview in which Votaw describes his boyhood;
education at Wheaton College, Dallas Seminary, and Princeton
Seminary; and missionary activities in Syria and Lebanon.

Vol: 2 Audio Tapes

(MAJOR TOPICS: Armerding, Hudson Taylor; Bayley, Joseph Tate;
Buswell, James Oliver Jr; Catholic Church in Syria; Catholic Church---
Relations; Chicago, IL; Ecumenical movement; Edman, Victor Ray-
mond; Egypt; Evangelistic work--Israel; Henry, Carl Ferdinand How-
ard; Illinois; Israel; Jerusalem, Israel; Language: Arabic; Lebanon;
MacKay, John Alexander; Missions--Educational work; Mis-

sions--Lebanon; Missions--Syria; Muslims in Syria; Presbyterian
Church--Missions; Presbyterians; Syria; Taylor, Kenneth Nathaniel;
Votaw, Paul Dean; Wheaton College, IL; Zionism)

%%%%%%%%%%%%

CN# 358
**Wagner, Charles Peter; 1930-**
Papers; 1965-1987

Correspondence, memoranda, minutes, reports, promotional
materials, news releases, clippings, article and address manuscripts,
photographs and negatives. The materials document Wagner's
activities as a member of the Lausanne Committee for World
Evangelization, its Executive Committee and as chairperson of its
Strategy Working Group as well as his activities as a missionary
and educator.

Volume: 9 boxes, Oversize Materials, Photographs, Negatives

(MAJOR TOPICS: Bible--Inspiration; Bolivia; Chile; Christian
education--United States; Church and social problems; Church work
with emigrants; Church work with refugees; Congresses and confer-
ences--International Congress on World Evangelization, 1974; Dayton,
Edward Risedorph; Ecumenical movement; Ethiopia; Evangelicalism;
Evangelistic work (Christian theology); Evangelistic work--United
States; Ford, Leighton Frederick Sandys; Fuller Theological Seminary,
CA; Henry, Carl Ferdinand Howard; Hispanic Americans; Hubbard,
David Allen; Judaism; Lausanne Committee for World Evangelization;
Liberation Theology; McGavran, Donald Anderson; Missionaries---
Korea; Missions Advanced Research and Communications Center
(MARC); Missions to Jews; Missions--Chile; Missions--Inter-
denominational cooperation; Missions--Korea; Ockenga, Harold John;
Osei-Mensah, Gottfried B; Padilla, Carlos Rene; Pentecostals; Peru;
Refugees--Cambodia; Stott, John Robert Walmsley; Taylor, Clyde
Willis; United States Center for World Missions; Wagner, Charles
Peter; Winter, Ralph D; Zimmerman, Thomas Fletcher)

%%%%%%%%%%%%

CN# 167
**Walkwitz, Naomi Hildebrand; 1934-**
Interview; 1980

An interview with Walkwitz in which she describes her childhood
experiences, education and marriage to Roger Walkwitz, their careers as missionaries to the tribal peoples of the Philippines under

Far East Gospel Crusade between 1958-1980. Includes discussion of Philippine customs, tribal practices of Christian groups, training of singing gospel teams, education in the Christian and national schools, relationship with Roman Catholics, and Philippine governmental policies.

Vol: 1 Audio Tape

(MAJOR TOPICS: Animism; Catholic Church in Philippines; Catholic Church--Relations; Children of missionaries; Chinese Communists; Christian education--Philippines; Evangelistic work--Philippines; Family; Intercultural communications; Linguistics; Mass media in missionary work; Missions--Educational work; Missions--Philippines; Mozambique; Philippines; SEND International; Tenney, Merrill Chapin; Walkwitz, Naomi Hildebrand; Walkwitz, Roger; Women---Religious life; Women in missionary work)

%%%%%%%%%%%%%

CN# 166
**Walkwitz, Roger; 1929-**
Interview; 1980

Taped interview with Walkwitz in which he describes his early life in Wheaton, Illinois, attendance at Wheaton College, and experiences of 23 years in the Philippines (1958-1980) as a missionary with Far Eastern Gospel Crusade. Among the activities described are translation, church planting in the tribal areas, education, and evangelism.

Vol: 1 Audio Tape

(MAJOR TOPICS: Catholic Church in Philippines; Catholic Church---Relations; Christian education--Philippines; Communism; Dodds, Gilbert L; Evangelistic work--Philippines; Graham, William Franklin "Billy"; Korean War; Missions--Educational work; Missions--Philippines; Philippines; SEND International; Walkwitz, Roger; Wheaton College, IL)

%%%%%%%%%%%%%

CN# 75
**Warner, Mrs. Elizabeth Howard; 1912-**
Interviews; 1978

Tapes of two interviews with Mrs. Warner, a Wheaton alumna and missionary to China from 1936 to 1941. Subjects discussed include childhood experiences in China while her father taught school in Canton, college life at Wheaton, and her ministry at the Door of Hope Mission in Canton and Hong Kong.

Vol: 1 Audio Tape

(MAJOR TOPICS: Boston, MA; Buddhists in China; Buswell, James Oliver Jr; Children of missionaries; China; Church and state in China; Communism; Confucianism; Education--China; Gieser, Paul Kenneth; Gordon-Conwell Divinity School; Hong Kong; House churches; Medical care--China; Missions to Buddhists; Missions, Medical; Missions---China; Missions--Educational work; Sex role; Sino-Japanese Conflict, 1937-1945; Soviet Union; Tenney, Merrill Chapin; Wheaton College, IL; Women--Religious life; Women in missionary work; World War II)

%%%%%%%%%%%%%

CN# 193
**Washington Street Mission; 1910-**
Records; 1914-1982; n.d.

Sermon notes for almost every book of the Bible; brochures; programs; pamphlets and tracts used by Robert J. Brown and Robert O. Miller, successive superintendents of the mission between the years 1911-1940; financial reports; minutes; by-laws; estate settlement records; clippings; fund-raising brochures; statistical reports of the Mission's activities.

Vol: 7 boxes, Oversize Materials, Photographs

(MAJOR TOPICS: Armstrong, Herbert W; Bahaism; Brethren; Catholic Church; Charismatic movement; Christian Science; Church and social problems; Cities and towns; City missions; Communism; Cults; Evangelistic work--United States; Faith--Cure; Jehovah's Witnesses; Letourneau, Robert Gilmore; Miller, Robert O; Missions--United States; Mormons and Mormonism; Pentecostals; Plymouth Brethren; Poverty; Roberts, Granville Oral; Seventh Day Adventists; Sunday, Helen Amelia Thompson; Sunday, William Ashley "Billy"; Washington Street Mission, Springfield, IL; World Wide Church of God)

%%%%%%%%%%%%%

CN# 373
**Weary, Dolphus; 1946-**
Interview; 1987

Interview describing Weary's childhood, education and religious training in rural Mississippi, conversion, leadership in Voice of Calvary Ministries and Mendenhall Ministries, impressions of John Perkins, and racial conditions in Mississippi.

Vol: 2 Audio Tapes

(MAJOR TOPICS:  African Americans; Athletes--Religious life; Children of missionaries; Christian education--United States; Church and social problems; Church work with students; Church work with youth; Conversion; Education--United States; Evangelicalism; Evangelistic work (Christian theology); Evangelistic work--United States; Fletcher, Artis Edward; Mass media in missionary work; Mendenhall Ministries, The (TMM); Missionaries--Recruitment and training; Mississippi; Perkins, John M; Perkins, Vera Mae; Race relations; Racism; Radio in religion; Religion and sports; Vacation schools, Christian; Voice of Calvary Ministries; Weary, Dolphus; Women--Religious life)

%%%%%%%%%%%%%

CN# 31
**Wesley, John; 1703-1791**
Ephemera; 1782; 1889-1902;1938; n.d.

One autographed letter, signed by Wesley to "Sammy", written while he was in London during October, 1782.  Several newspaper clippings and a scrapbook of clippings relating to the 100th anniversary of Wesley's death.

Vol: 1 box

(MAJOR TOPICS: Clergy; Methodists; Theology; Wesley, Charles; Wesley, John)
%%%%%%%%%%%%%

CN# SC 101
**Whitefield, George; 1714-1770**
Ephemera; 1766

Letter from Whitefield to Rev. Mr. Reader, December 10, 1766, thanking him for copies of one of Reader's sermons.

(MAJOR TOPICS: Evangelistic work--United States; Whitefield, George)

%%%%%%%%%%%%

CN# 109
**Whosoever Heareth, Inc.; 1942-**
Records; 1943-1975; n.d.

Correspondence, legal documents, financial records, notebooks, clippings, pamphlets, brochures, and sermon tapes related to the career of lawyer-evangelist Clift Brannon and two of the organizations he set up, Whosoever Heareth, Inc. and the Clift Brannon Evangelistic Association. Includes a copy of the data on the Soul Winner's New Testament, an edited version of the New Testament, with notes to be used for individual and group evangelism.

Vol: 1 box, 9 Audio Tapes, Books, Oversize Materials, Pamphlets

(MAJOR TOPICS: Baptists; Bible--Publication and distribution; Brannon, Clifton; Clift Brannon Evangelistic Association; Communication; Evangelistic work--United States; Mass media in religion; Radio in religion; Southern Baptist Convention; Whosoever Heareth, Inc; Winona Lake Bible Conference, IN)

%%%%%%%%%%%%

CN# SC 66
**Wilson, Mary Jane; ?-1836**
Ephemera; 1836

Letter written by Wilson, a missionary of the American Board of Commissioners of Foreign Missions, from South Africa to her uncle in Virginia. The letter describes her new baby; the attempt of missionaries Daniel Lindley and Henry Venable to establish a mission station at Moesega in the territory and under the protection of the Matabele ruler Moselekatse; local marriage customs, the severe drought in Grigua town, and impressions of Robert Moffat and others.

(MAJOR TOPICS: American Board of Commissioners for Foreign Missions; Evangelistic work--South Africa; Lindley, Daniel; Missions--South Africa; South Africa; Venable, Henry Isaac; Wilson, Alexander Erwin; Wilson, Mary Jane)

%%%%%%%%%%%%%

CN# 93
**Winsor, Earl Austin; 1897-19?**
Interviews; 1979-1980; n.d.

Tapes of three interviews with Winsor in which he discusses his
years at Wheaton as student (1919-1920) and teacher (1920-1925
and 1939-1949) and his experiences in Africa under Africa Inland
Mission, serving in what is now Zaire. Most of the interviews deal
with Wheaton personalities; mission experiences, especially those
relating to his education work; and his reflections on African
government, churches, tribal customs, and health practices.

Vol: 3 Audio Tapes

(MAJOR TOPICS: Africa Inland Mission (AIM); Belgium; Blanchard,
Charles Albert; Buswell, James Oliver Jr; Church and state in Kenya;
Church and state in Zaire; Education--Kenya; Evangelistic
work--Zaire; Hurlburt, Charles E; Intercultural communications;
Kenya; Massachusetts; Missions--Finance; Missions--Zaire; Rethy
Academy, Zaire; Simba Rebellion; Straw, Perry; Winsor, Earl A)

%%%%%%%%%%%%%

CN# 306
**Winston, George Murray; 1926-**
Papers; 1952-1987

Two oral history interviews with and prayer letters of George
Winston, missionary with Belgian Gospel Mission and Greater
Europe Mission in Belgium from 1952, which describe his work as
a church planter and mission and Bible institute administrator.
The documents also describe Winston's early life as a child of
missionaries, his education at Wheaton College, and Belgian
culture.

Vol: 1 box, 4 Audio Tapes

(MAJOR TOPICS: Belgian Gospel Mission; Belgium; Bible colleges;
Catholic Church in Belgium; Catholic Church--Relations; Children of
missionaries; Christian education (theory); Christian education--Bel-
gium; Church and state in Belgium; Cities and towns; Conversion;
Education--Belgium; Elliot, Elisabeth Howard; Elliot, Philip James;
Evangelicalism; Evangelistic work--Belgium; Greater Europe Mission
(GEM); Howard, David Morris; Howard, Philip E Jr; Independent
churches; Intercultural communications; Interdenominational coopera-

tion; International relief; Missionaries' wives; Missionaries--Recruitment and training; Missions--Belgium; Sex role; Theological Education by Extension (TEE); Wheaton College, IL; Winston, George Murray; Women in missionary work; Women--Religious life; World War II)

%%%%%%%%%%%%

CN# 343
**Wolgemuth, Samuel Frey; 1914-**
Papers; 1962-1981

Administrative correspondence, reports, minutes, memoranda, newsletters, publications, promotional material, photographs, and slides, documenting Wolgemuth's term (1965-1973) as president of Youth for Christ. The correspondence with YFC staff, and representatives of other Christian organizations, predominates.

Vol: 15 boxes, Photographs, Slides

(MAJOR TOPICS: Alexander, John W; Armerding, Hudson Taylor; Australia; Beavan, Gerald "Jerry"; Bible--Translating; Billy Graham Evangelistic Association (BGEA); Brethren; Brethren--Missions; Brethren in Christ Church; Brethren in Christ Church--Missions; Bright, William Rohl "Bill"; California; Campus Crusade for Christ; Christian education--Taiwan; Church and state in United States; Church work with children; Church work with youth; Colorado; Congresses and conferences--US Congress on Evangelism, 1969; Cook, Robert Andrew; Daley, Richard J; Dausey, Gary; Dayton, Edward Risedorph; Engstrom, Theodore "Ted" Wilhelm; Evangelistic work (Christian theology); Evangelistic work--Australia; Evangelistic work---Brazil; Evangelistic work--Canada; Evangelistic work--France; Evangelistic work--India; Evangelistic work--Japan; Evangelistic work---Philippines; Evangelistic work--United States; France; Fund raising; Graham, William Franklin "Billy"; Great Britain; Hillis, Charles Richard "Dick"; Hubbard, David Allen; India; Indiana; Inter-Varsity Christian Fellowship; Israel; Japan; Kesler, Jay Lewis; Key '73; Latin America Mission; Maryland; Melvin, Billy Alfred; Michigan; Minnesota; Missions Advanced Research and Communications Center (MARC); Missouri; Mooneyham, W Stanley; Myra, Harold; National Association of Evangelicals; Navigators; New Mexico; New York (state); Nixon, Richard Milhous; Ohio; Oregon; Palermo, Louis; Palermo, Phil; Pennsylvania; Philippines; Pierce, Robert Willard "Bob"; Presidents--United States; Prisons--Missions and charities; Religion and music; Sanny, Lorne Charles; Schultz, Earl Wesley Jr; Skinner, Thomas; South Carolina; Taiwan; Taylor, Clyde Willis; Taylor, Herbert John; Troutman, Charles H Jr; United States; Virginia; Washington (state); Washington, DC; Wheaton College, IL; Wilson, George McConnell; Wilson, Thomas Walter Jr; Wolgemuth, Samuel Frey; Women--Religious life; World Relief Commission; World Vision International; Young Life; Youth for Christ International;)

%%%%%%%%%%%%

CN# 379
**Women's Union Missionary Society; 1860-1974**
Records; 1860-1983; n.d.

Records of the WUMS, known after 1972 as United Fellowship For Christian Service. Founded in 1860 by Sarah Platt Doremus, it was intended as a vehicle for sending single women as missionaries to Asia. The materials in the collection consist of correspondence, reports, personnel files, legal documents, financial files, scrapbooks, and photographs, documenting the Society's medical and educational work in Burma, China, India, Pakistan, and Japan.

Vol. 50 boxes, Oversize material, Photographs

(MAJOR TOPICS: Baptists; Baptists--Missions; Buddhists in Japan; Burma; Calcutta, India; China; Christian literature--Publication and distribution; Communism-- China; Corporations, Religious--Taxation; Doremus, Sarah Platt; Education-- China; Education--India; Education--Japan; Education--Pakistan; Evangelistic work--India; Great Britain; India; Japan; Language in missionary work; Marriage; Medical care--China; Medical care--India; Medical care--Pakistan; Missionaries, Resignation of; Missionaries, Withdrawal of; Missionaries--Leaves and furloughs; Missionaries--Salaries, pensions, etc.; Missions to Buddhists; Missions to Chinese; Missions to Hindus; Missions to Muslims; Missions, Medical; Missions--Burma; Missions--China; Missions--Finance; Missions--India; Missions--Japan; Missions--Nepal; Missions--Pakistan; Muslims in India; Nepal; New York (state); New York City, NY; Nursing; Orphans and orphan-asylums; Pakistan; Refugees--Tibet; Shanghai, China; Sunday-school; Tibet; Vacation schools, Christian; Women's Union Missionary Society; Women's missionary societies; Women--Religious life; World War II)

%%%%%%%%%%%%

CN# 210
**World Bible Study Fellowship; 1948-1982**
Records; 1935-1982; n.d.

Correspondence, newsletters, minutes of meetings, correspondence course, photographs, and other materials related to the work of the WBSF, which included publishing and distribution of Bible studies for use around the world in prisons, hospitals, and leper colonies, and for use of missionaries and national Christian workers.

Vol: 3 boxes, Photographs

(MAJOR TOPICS: Arizona; Baptism; Belief and doubt; California; Cameroon; Christian education--Cuba; Christian education--Haiti; Christian education--Japan; Christian education--Nigeria; Christian education--Philippines; Christian literature--Publication and distribution; Christmas; Church and social problems; Colombia; Colorado; Conversion; Cuba; Education--Angola; Education--Nigeria; Evangelistic work--Caribbean; Evangelistic work--Haiti; Evangelistic work--Japan; Evangelistic work--Nigeria; Evangelistic work--Philippines; Evangelistic work--Spain; Evangelistic work--United States; Feiner, Berea St John; Florida; Georgia; Ghana; Haiti; Idaho; Illinois; India; Japan; Kansas; Language: French; Language: Portuguese; Language: Spanish; Louisiana; Marriage; Mass media in religion; Methodists; Minnesota; Missions, Medical; Missions--Angola; Missions--Vietnam; New York (state); Nigeria; Ohio; Pennsylvania; Pentecostals; Philippines; Portugal; Prisoners--United States; Prisons--Missions and charities; Radio in religion; Salvation; Spain; Tennessee; Vietnam; Virginia; Washington (state); World Bible Study Fellowship; Youth--Religious life)

%%%%%%%%%%%%

CN# 14
**World Congress on Evangelism; 1966**
Records; 1966

Biographical sketches, participants' lists, form letters, programs, audio tapes of speeches, and study papers of the Congress held in Berlin. Besides the English materials, there are study papers in French and German and programs, correspondence and speech transcripts in German, French, and Spanish.

Vol: 2 boxes, 13 Audio Tapes

(MAJOR TOPICS: Auca people, Ecuador; Berlin, Germany; Bible---
Inspiration; Church growth; Church work with youth; Church--biblical
teaching; Communication; Congresses and conferences--World Con-
gress on Evangelism, 1966; Conversion; Crowds; Ecuador; Elliot,
Philip James; Ethiopia; Evangelicalism; Evangelistic invitations; Evan-
gelistic work--Germany; Evangelistic work--United States; Faith;
Fundamentalism; Germany; Graham, William Franklin "Billy"; Great
Commission (Bible); Halverson, Richard C; Haqq, Akbar Abdul;
Henry, Carl Ferdinand Howard; Hoffmann, Oswald Carl Julius; Holy
Spirit; Hudson, Arthur William Goodwin; Language: English;
Language: German; Language: Spanish; Missions--Ecuador; Mis-
sions--Interdenominational cooperation; Obedience; Ockenga, Harold
John; Pache, Rene; Persecution; Saint, Nathanael "Nate"; Stott, John
Robert Walmsley; Theology, Practical; Wycliffe Bible Translators

%%%%%%%%%%%%%

CN# SC65
**Wright, Joseph K; 18?-?**
Ephemera; 1856

Letter by Presbyterian missionary Wright to his brother William in
which he describes his activities in China and the Taiping rebellion.

(MAJOR TOPICS: China; Evangelistic work--China; Missions--China;
Shanghai, China; Taiping Rebellion)

%%%%%%%%%%%%%

CN# 85
**Wrighton, William Hazer; 1884-1962**
Papers; 1903-1963; n.d.

Sermons and clippings, articles, manuscripts, notebooks, personal
records, correspondence and miscellaneous items relating to the
career of Wrighton as teacher and minister.

Vol: 4 boxes

(MAJOR TOPICS: Bible--Criticism, interpretation etc.; Congresses
and conferences--Finney Sesquicentennial; Coolidge, Calvin; Culbertson, William; Evangelical Alliance Mission, The (TEAM); Evangelistic
work--United States; Finney, Charles Grandison; Fuller Theological
Seminary, CA; Gessewein, Armin Richard; Graham, William Franklin
"Billy"; Howard, Philip E Jr; Lindsell, Harold; Moody Bible Institute,
IL; New England Fellowship (NEF); Orr, James Edwin; Periodical:

*Christianity Today*; Periodical: *Sunday School Tines, The*;
Presidents--United States; Sermons, American; Wheaton College, IL;
Wrighton, William Hazer)

%%%%%%%%%%%%

CN# 40
**Wyzenbeek, Andrew; 1888-1985**
Interview; 1978

Tape of interview with Chicago manufacturer and inventor Wyzenbeek who was very active as a layman in evangelistic work.
Among other topics, he discusses his acquaintance with Billy
Sunday, Paul Rader, Peter Deyneka; the beginnings of the Chicago
Gospel Tabernacle; and the beginning of Paul Rader's radio
ministry. The collection also contains a folder with a short handwritten autobiography.

Vol: 1 box, 1 Audio Tape

(MAJOR TOPICS: Chicago Gospel Tabernacle; Deyneka, Peter Sr;
Edman, Victor Raymond; Evangelistic work--United States; Gideons
International; Graham, William Franklin "Billy"; Johnson, Torrey
Maynard; Michigan; Moody Memorial Church, IL; Rader, Daniel
Paul; Radio in religion; Slavic Gospel Association; Sunday, William
Ashley "Billy"; Trotter, Melvin Ernest; Wheaton College, IL; Wyzen-
beek, Andrew; Youth for Christ, International)

%%%%%%%%%%%%

CN 397
**York, Consuella Batchelor; 1923-**
Papers; 1953-1989; n.d.

Clippings, photographs, handbooks, cards, sermons, oral history
interviews and other records mainly with concerned York's ministry as a chaplain at the Cook County Jail, but also describing her
childhood growing up on the south side of Chicago, conversion,
religious education, criticism she has received as a woman preacher, and her work as a pastor.

Vol: 1 box, 5 Reels of Audio Tapes, Photographs, 1 Video Tape

(MAJOR TOPICS: African Americans; Belief and doubt; Capital
punishment; Chicago, IL; Church and social problems; Clergy, Training of; Conversion; Crime and criminals; Drug abuse; Faith; Gangs;
Muslims in United States; Preaching; Prisons--Missions and charities;

Sermons, American; Women clergy; Women--Religious life; York, Consuella Batchelor)

%%%%%%%%%%%%

CN# 48
**Youth for Christ, International; 1944-**
Records; 1944-1981; n.d.

Correspondence, minutes of meetings, clippings, newsletters, manuals, press releases, audio and video tapes, photographs, phonograph records, posters, yearbooks, and more about the founding, development and activities of YFCI, an organization involved in evangelism and nurture among high school age people. Also included are copies of YFC's television special and its radio program *Reality*.

Vol: 23 boxes, 24 Audio Tapes, Oversize Material, Phonograph Records, Photographs, 13 Video Tapes

(MAJOR TOPICS: Adams, Lane G; Adolescence; Alabama; Alaska; Amsterdam, Netherlands; Ankerberg, Floyd; Argentina; Arizona; Arkansas; Atheism; Australia; Austria; Barrows, Clifford B; Belgium; Bible--Memorizing; Bihl, Carl J "Kelly"; Bolivia; Boone, Deborah Ann "Debbie"; Brazil; Bryant, Anita; California; Canada; Carlson, Frank; Carmichael, Ralph; Cash, Johnny; Catholic Church in France; Chicago, IL; Chile; China; Christian Service Brigade; Church work with students; Church work with youth; Cities and towns; City missions; Colombia; Colorado; Colson, Charles Wendell; Communism; Connecticut; Conversion; Cook, Robert Andrew; Cosby, Bill; Counseling; Cuba; Culbertson, William; Cyprus; Czechoslovakia; Dallas Theological Seminary; Delaware; Deyneka, Peter Sr; District of Columbia; Dodds, Gilbert L; Dulles, John Foster; Ecuador; Edman, Victor Raymond; Engstrom, Theodore "Ted" Wilhelm; Ethiopia; Evangelicalism; Evangelistic work--Argentina; Evangelistic work--Australia; Evangelistic work--Austria; Evangelistic work--Belgium; Evangelistic work--Brazil; Evangelistic work--Caribbean; Evangelistic work--Chile; Evangelistic work--Cuba; Evangelistic work--Ecuador; Evangelistic work--Finland; Evangelistic work--Germany; Evangelistic work--Ghana; Evangelistic work--Great Britain; Evangelistic work---Greece; Evangelistic work--Guatemala; Evangelistic work--Haiti; Evangelistic work--Hong Kong; Evangelistic work--Hungary; Evangelistic work--Indonesia; Evangelistic work--Ireland; Evangelistic work--Israel; Evangelistic work--Italy; Evangelistic work--Japan; Evangelistic work--Korea; Evangelistic work--Lebanon; Evangelistic work--Mexico; Evangelistic work--Netherlands; Evangelistic work--New Zealand; Evangelistic work--Nigeria; Evangelistic work--Peru; Evan-

gelistic work--Poland; Evangelistic work--Portugal; Evangelistic work---
Singapore; Evangelistic work--South Africa; Evangelistic work--Swe-
den; Evangelistic work--Switzerland; Evangelistic work--Taiwan;
Evangelistic work--United States; Evangelistic work--Venezuela;
Evangelistic work--Vietnam; Evangelistic work--Yugoslavia; Family;
Finland; Florida; Ford, Leighton Frederick Sandys; France; Gangs;
Georgia; Germany; Ghana; Graham, Ruth Bell; Graham, William
Franklin "Billy"; Great Britain; Greece; Guatemala; Guyana; Hal-
verson, Richard C; Hamblen, Stuart; Harper, Redd; Harvey, Paul;
Hatfield, Mark Odom; Hawaii; Hillis, Charles Richard "Dick"; Hong
Kong; Humbard, Rex; Hungary; Idaho; Illinois; India; Indiana; In-
donesia; Iowa; Ireland; Israel; Italy; Japan; Johnson, Torrey Maynard;
Jordan; Kansas; Kentucky; Kesler, Jay Lewis; Korea; Landry, Thomas
Wade; Legislators--United States; Letourneau, Robert Gilmore;
Liberia; London, England; Los Angeles, CA; Maine; Manning, Ernest
G; Maryland; Mass media in religion; Massachusetts; Mexico; Michi-
gan; Minnesota; Missions--Finland; Missions--Great Britain; Mississip-
pi; Missouri; Montana; Muntz, John Palmer; Nebraska; Netherlands;
Nevada; New Hampshire; New Jersey; New Mexico; New York (state);
New York City, NY; New Zealand; Nigeria; Nixon, Richard Milhous;
Nonformal education; North Carolina; North Dakota; Norway; Ocken-
ga, Harold John; Ohio; Oklahoma; Organizational change; Pacific
Garden Mission, IL; Papua New Guinea; Pennsylvania; Philippines;
Pierce, Robert Willard "Bob"; Pollock, John Charles; Presi-
dents--United States; Radio in religion; Rhode Island; Riley, William
Bell; Roberts, Granville Oral; Rodeheaver, Homer Alvan; Rosell,
Mervin E "Merv"; Savage, Robert Carlton; Schaeffer, Francis August;
Schuller, Robert Harold; Schultz, Earl Wesley Jr; Sermons, American;
Shea, George Beverly; Shufelt, John Stratton; Singapore; Skinner,
Thomas; Smith, Oswald Jeffrey; Smith, Wilbur Moorehead; Smyth,
Walter Herbert; South Africa; South Carolina; South Dakota; Soviet
Union; Spain; Story-telling; Sunday, Helen Amelia Thompson; Swe-
den; Switzerland; Taiwan; Taylor, Herbert John; Taylor, Kenneth
Nathaniel; Templeton, Charles B; Tennessee; Texas; Toronto, ON;
Troutman, Charles H Jr; Tubman, William Vacanarat Shadrach;
Uruguay; Utah; Vaus, James Arthur; Venezuela; Vermont; Vietnam;
Virginia; Walker, Robert; Washington (state); Washington, DC;
Waters, Ethel; West Virginia; Wilson, George McConnell; Wilson,
Grady Baxter; Wilson, Thomas Walter Jr; Winona Lake Bible Con-
ference, IN; Wirt, Sherwood Eliot; Wisconsin; Wolgemuth, Samuel
Frey; World War II; Wyoming; Wyrtzen, John Von Casper "Jack";
Youth for Christ International; Youth--Religious life; Youth--Societies
and clubs; Yugoslavia)

# Appendix I: Select List of Archives and Manuscript Repositories in the United States with Documents Relevant to the Evangelical Movement

Listed below are repositories which have the records of Evangelical institutions and/or leaders or which have documents relevant to the study of American Evangelicalism.

%%%%%

**ALABAMA**

Woman's Missionary Union, Auxiliary to the Southern Baptist
 Convention
P.O. Box 830010
Birmingham, AL   35283-0010
(205) 991-8100

Archives include organization records and publications relating to Southern Baptist evangelistic efforts in both the United States and the rest of the world from 1880 to the present.

%%%%%

**ARKANSAS**

John Brown University
Library
Siloam Springs, AR   72761
(501) 524-3131

Sermon notes, correspondence, audio tapes and other materials of
John Brown, Sr. (1879-1957), founder of the university and itinerant
evangelist.

%%%%%

**CALIFORNIA**

Biola University
Archives
Rose Memorial Library
13800 Biola Avenue
La Mirada, CA   90639
(213) 944-0351, ext. 3255

Records of the institution.  Also the papers of Lyman Stewart (1840-
1923), a founder of Union Oil Company and one of the sponsors of
the publication of *The Fundamentals*.

Center for Mennonite Brethren Studies
4824 E. Butler
Fresno, CA   93727-5097
(209) 453-2225

Records of the denomination and materials about individual Mennonites.

Death Valley National Monument
Scotty's Castle
National Park Service
Death Valley, California    92328
(619) 786-2331 or 786-2392

Personal and business papers of Bessilyn Morris Johnson [nee Pen-
niman] (1872-1943) and Albert Mussey Johnson (1872-1948).  Johnson
was a Chicago businessman.  He and his wife supported various Fundamentalist and Evangelical causes, notably evangelist Paul Rader.
Researchers should inquire through the Superintendent to use
Archives.

Every Home for Christ
20232 Sonburst Street
Chatsworth, CA 91311
(818) 341-7870

Records of the organization.

Fuller Theological Seminary
Du Plessis Center
Box K
Pasadena, CA    91182
(818) 584-5308

Papers of Pentecostal leader David Du Plessis (1905-1987); records of
Pentecostal history and papers of individual Pentecostals; materials on
the ecumenical movement, including the files of the west coast depository for the National Council of Churches.  Also at Fuller, in the
library, are the records of the institution, papers of seminary founder
and evangelist Charles E. Fuller (1887-1968), recordings of broadcasts
of *The Old Fashioned Revival Hour* radio program.

Loma Linda University
Department of Archives and Special Collections
Heritage Room
Loma Linda, CA    92350
(714) 824-4942

Records of the university and collections dealing with the history of
the Seventh Day Adventist church.

National Archives--Pacific Southwest Region
24000 Avilia Road
Laguna Niguel, CA    92677
(714) 643-92677

The vice-presidential papers of Richard M. Nixon (1913- ) including correspondence with evangelist Billy Graham (1918- ).


World Vision
Archives
919 West Huntington Drive
Monrovia, CA    91016
(818) 357-7979

Two separate archives are maintained, one for the records of the United States branch of WV and one for the international headquarters.  WV is an interdenominational agency of Evangelical tradition engaged primarily in child care, community development, emergency relief, evangelism leadership development, and public health.  Materials document the founding of WV by Bob Pierce (1914-1978), its growth and development, film and television ministry, and radio broadcasts.


%%%%%

**COLORADO**


Christian and Missionary Alliance
Archives
P.O. Box 3500
Colorado Springs, CO 80935-3500
(719) 599-5999, ext. 370

Records of the denomination.

The Navigators
Record Management Center
P.O. Box 6000
Colorado Springs, CO 80934
(719) 598-1212, ex. 369

Records of the Navigators' (founded in 1933) worldwide activities of
lay evangelism, discipling and training.  Also the papers of founder
Dawson Trotman (1906-1956), documenting his development of the
concepts on which the work of the Navigators is based.


%%%%%

**CONNECTICUT**


Yale University Divinity School
Library
409 Prospect Street, New Haven, CT    06510
(203) 432-5301

Library contains the records of many individuals and organizations
relevant to Fundamentalist studies, such as Dwight L. Moody
(1837-1899), John R. Mott (1865-1955), William W. Borden
(1887-1913), Liston Pope (1909-1974), George Sherwood Eddy
(1871-?), Kenneth Scott Latourette (1884-1968), the World Student
Christian Movement, World Council of Churches, the National Campus Ministry Association, the student division of the YMCA, the committee which produced the Revised Standard Version of the Bible, the
American Home Missionary Society, and the Student Volunteer Movement.


Yale University
Library
Manuscripts and Archives
Box 1603A Yale Station
New Haven, CT 06520-7429
(203) 432-1744

The correspondence of Idahoan Republican politician J. E. Babb
(1864-1934) includes discussion of the Modernist-Fundamentalist controversy and the theory of evolution; papers of James Lockwood
Wright which cover the years 1828 to 1858 and include information on

revivals in the New Haven, CT area and his evangelistic work among black residents of the town.


%%%%%

## DISTRICT OF COLUMBIA


General Conference of Seventh Day Adventists
Office of Archives and Statistics
6840 Eastern Avenue Washington, DC   20012
(202) 722-6372

Documents, records, correspondence, publications, photographs, re-cordings, films, etc. that have historical and cultural value to the SDA Church, particularly material produced or collected by the General Conference as an institution.


Library of Congress
Library of Congress Annex
Manuscript Division
2nd Street and Independence Avenue, S.E.
Washington, DC   20540
(202) 426-5383

Includes various relevant collections, such as the papers of William Jennings Bryan (1860-1925), George Whitefield (1714-1770), Dwight L. Moody (1837-1899), Billy Sunday (1862-1935), Clarence Darrow (1857-1938), Peter Marshall (1902-1949), G. Bromley Oxnam (1891-1963), John Haynes Holmes (1879-1964), Reinhold Niebuhr (1892-1971), founder of the Free Methodist Church Benjamin Titus Roberts (1823-1893), and records of Moral Rearmament, Inc. The papers of gospel singer Ethel Waters (1900-1977) are in the music division of LC.

%%%%%

**FLORIDA**

The Sherry DuPree Archives
P.O. Box 163
Gainesville, FL 32602-0613
(904) 395-5407, 392-0895, 392-0896

A private collection of material related to black Holiness and Pentecostal history from the 1880s to the present. Included in the collection
are Work Projects Administration reports on black churches; books;
denominational magazines; dissertations; and voluminous files of
clippings about black churches, storefront churches, Pentecostals, and
gospel music.

%%%%%

**GEORGIA**

Atlanta Historical Society
3101 Andrews Drive, N.W.
Atlanta, GA   30355
(404) 261-1837

Papers of evangelists Samuel Porter Jones (1847-1906) and Samuel W.
Small (1851-1931); a scrapbook about Billy Sunday's evangelistic
meetings.

University of Georgia Libraries
Hargrett Rare Book and Manuscript Library
Athens, GA   30602
(404) 542-7123

Papers of evangelist Samuel Porter Jones (1847-1906).

%%%%%

**ILLINOIS**

Aurora University
Library
The Jenks Memorial Collection
Aurora, IL   60507
(708) 844-5445

Records of Advent Christian General Conference churches, leaders, missionaries, organizations. Includes the papers of William Miller (1782-1849) and an extensive collection of Millerite and early Adventist periodicals and other publications.

Bethany/Northern Baptist Theological Seminary
Library
Butterfield and Meyers Roads
Oak Brook, IL   60521
(708) 620-2214

Records of the Bethany and Northern Baptist seminaries, the Brethren and Baptists who teach and study there, and the Norwegian Theological Seminary archives.

Brethren Historical Library and Archives
1451 Dundess Avenue
Elgin, IL   60120
(708) 742-5100

Records of the Church of the Brethren, including information on individual Brethren active in peace movement, international relief and service, foreign missions, race relations, social welfare, refugee resettlement, and other church programs.

Chicago Historical Society
Clark Street at North Avenue
Chicago, IL   60614
(312) 642-4600

Records of the Church Federation of Greater Chicago, records of the Chicago Sunday Evening Club, and materials about lecturer and agnostic Robert Ingersoll (1833-1899) in the David Davis papers.

Evangelical Covenant Church of America
Archives and Historical Library
North Park College and Theological Seminary
5125 Spaulding Avenue
Chicago, IL 60625
(312) 583-2700, ext. 5267

Records of the Evangelical Covenant Church as well as North Park
College and Theological Seminary. Also the private papers of some
pastors and missionaries of the denomination.


Evangelical Lutheran Church in America
Archives
8765 Higgins Road
Chicago, IL   60631-4198
(312) 380-2818 or 1-800-NET-ELCA

Records of the ECLA and its predecessors, the American Lutheran
Church, the Association of Evangelical Churches, and the Lutheran
Church in America. Also the records of the Lutheran Council in the
USA, its predecessor the National Lutheran Council and 34 related
organizations of Lutherans, such as Lutheran World Relief and Lu-
theran Educational Conference of North America; Christ Seminary-
Seminex; Evangelical Lutherans in Motion; and personal papers of
Lutheran church leaders.


Moody Bible Institute Library
820 North LaSalle Street
Chicago, IL   60610
(312) 329-4140

Papers of Dwight L. Moody (1837-1899), R. A. Torrey Sr. (1856-1928),
James M. Gray (1851-1935) and the records of the Institute.


Southern Illinois University at Carbondale
Morris Library
Special Collections
Carbondale, IL   62901
(618) 453-2543

Records of The Christian Century magazine, a leading publication of
liberal Protestant Christianity. Also papers of lecturer and agnostic
Robert Ingersoll (1833-1899).

Trinity Evangelical Divinity School
Archives
2065 Half Day Road
Deerfield, IL   60015
(312) 945-8800

Papers of Evangelical historian and theologian Wilbur Moorehead
Smith (1894-1976) and records of the Evangelical Free Church of
America.

University of Chicago Library
Department of Special Collections
1100 E. 57th Street
Chicago, IL   60637
(312) 702-8705

Includes records of the American Institute of Sacred Literature (1880-
1943); the Baptist Minister's Conference of Chicago (1889-1910);
Divinity School, Office of the Dean (1890-1942), including papers of
Shailer Mathews and correspondence concerning the Modernist-
Fundamentalist controversy); the Northwestern Baptist Education
Society (1871-1925); the Clarence Darrow papers (including press
releases from the Scopes trial); and papers of Divinity School faculty
members, including Thomas W. Goodspeed (1842-1927), William R.
Harper (1856-1906), and Ira M. Price (1856-1939) as well as some
documents about the activities of Baptists.

Wheaton College
Buswell Memorial Library
Special Collections
Wheaton, IL  60187
(708) 260-5705

Records of the institution plus papers of presidents Jonathan Blanchard (1811-1892), Charles Albert Blanchard (1848-1925), James
Oliver Buswell, Jr. (1895-1980), Victor Raymond Edman (1900-1967),
and Hudson Taylor Armerding (1918- ).  The materials for the last
two men are mainly administrative files, with little personal correspondence.  Also in the college special collections department are: the
records of the National Christian Association, the American Scientific
Affiliation, and the Christian Sociological Society; a hymnal collection
of 2200 volumes; the manuscripts for Kenneth Taylor's *Living Bible*
and *Taylor's Bible Story Book*; the papers of pastor Louis Evans Sr.
(1897- ) who founded the Fellowship of Christian Athletes; and the
papers of hymn writer Edith Margaret Clarkson (1915- ).

Woman's Christian Temperance Union National Headquarters
Frances E. Willard Memorial Library
1730 Chicago Avenue
Evanston, IL   60201
(312) 864-1396

Records of the WCTU and papers of Francis Willard (1839-1898);
other documents related to the temperance movement, women's history and social reform in the late 19th century.


%%%%%

**INDIANA**


Anderson University
Church of God School of Theology
Byrd Memorial Library
Archives
Anderson, IN   46012-3462
(317) 641-4274 or 641-4526

Records of institutions of the Church of God denomination, including
colleges and the Warner Press (formerly Gospel Trumpet Press) and
papers of private individuals.


Archives of the Mennonite Church
1700 South Main
Goshen, IN   46526
(219) 535-7477

Records of the denomination and material about individual Mennonites.


Bethel College
Bowen Library
United Missionary Historical Collection
Mishawaka, IN   46545
(219) 259-8511

Records of the Missionary Church; records of Bethel College; private
papers including the papers of radio evangelist Quinton J. Everest
(1907- ).  Photographs of camp meetings.

Christian Theological Seminary
Manuscript Collection
1000 West 42nd Street
Indianapolis, IN   46208
(317) 924-1331

Records of the Christian Church (Disciples of Christ).  Papers of missionaries, educators and church leaders, including Frederick Doyle Kershner (1875-1954), editor of *The Christian Evangelist*.


Free Methodist World Headquarters
Marston Memorial Historical Center
901 College Avenue
Winona Lake, IN 46590
(219) 267-7656

Records of the denomination and its predecessors.  Also a few miscellaneous items from Methodists, such as letters of John Wesley (1703-1791).


DePauw University
Roy O. West Library
Archives of Depauw University and Indiana United Methodism
Greencastle, IN   46135
(317) 653-4501

Records of Methodist organizations in Indiana and papers of individual Methodists.


Fort Wayne Bible College
S. A. Lehman Memorial Library
Archives
919 West Rudisill Blvd.
Fort Wayne, IN   46807
(219) 456-2111, ext. 252

Records of the College, an affiliate of the Missionary Church.

Grace College and Theological Seminary
Morgan Library
200 Seminary Drive
Winona Lake, IN   46590
(219) 372-5177

Papers of evangelist Billy Sunday (1862-1935), records of the Winona
Lake Christian Assembly (an important Fundamentalist conference
center), and the records of the Grace Brethren churches.


Huntington College
Richard Lyn Library
United Brethren Archives
2303 College Avenue
Huntington, IN   46750
(219) 356-6000, ext. 1064

Records of Huntington College and of the denomination, Church of
the United Brethren in Christ.


Indiana Historical Society Library
315 West Ohio Street
Indianapolis, IN   46202
(317) 232-1879

Records of many individual Indiana congregations; records of the
Indiana Council of Churches; photographs of Billy Sunday (1862-1965)
and other evangelists (Inbody Collection).


World Gospel Mission
Box WGM
Marion, IN 46952
(317) 664-7331

Records of World Gospel Mission, a mission of the Wesleyan tradition
involved in church planting, Christian education, evangelism and medicine.

%%%%%

## IOWA

Northwestern College
Ramaker Library
Dutch Heritage Collection
101 Seventh Street, S.W.
Orange City, IA 51041
(712) 737-4821

Manuscripts relating to the college and to the Reformed Church in America, particularly in the midwestern and western parts of the United States.

%%%%%

## KANSAS

Dwight D. Eisenhower Library
Abilene, KS   67410
(913) 263-4751

Includes correspondence between Eisenhower (1890-1969) and evangelist Billy Graham (1918- ).

Mennonite Library and Archives
North Newton, KS   67117
(316) 283-2500, ext. 305

Records of the General Conference Mennonite denomination, Bethel College (including materials on the modernist-Fundamentalist controversy of the 1920s), personal papers of Mennonites, and records of Mennonite para-church groups.  The collection also has many oral history interviews and other materials about pacifism and conscientious objectors.

%%%%%%

**KENTUCKY**


Asbury Theological Seminary
B. L. Fisher Library
Wilmore, KY    40390
(606) 858-3581

Relevant holdings include the official records of Asbury Theological
Seminary, the papers of founder Henry Clay Morrison (1857-1942),
past presidents Julian Claudius McPheeters (1889- ?) and Frank Bate-
man Stanger (1914- ) and former faculty or board members such as
John Haywood Paul (1877- ?), Frank Paul Morris, John Wesley Bee-
son (1866- ?), and Paul Stromberg Rees (1900- ). Also of interest are
the papers of William Webster White, founder of Biblical Seminary in
New York; biblical scholar Howard Kuist; devotional writer Hannah
Whitall Smith (1832-1911); evangelists Harmon A. Baldwin (1869-
1936), Charles William Butler (1873-1960), Ford Philpot (1917-), and
Christian Wismer Ruth (1865-1941); mission organizations such as
OMS International, Missionary World Service and Evangelism, Pen-
tecost Bands of India; the Japan Mission of the American Board of
Commissioners for Foreign Missions; and of missionaries such as Eli
Stanley Jones (1884-1973) of India, Earl Arnett Seamands (1891- ?) of
India, Ernest F. Ward (1850-1937) of India, and Alexander J. Reid of
Zaire. The records of the Christian Holiness Association (formerly
National Camp Meeting Association and National Holiness Associa-
tion) are a rich source of material on campmeetings, study conferen-
ces, local holiness associations, and the development of numerous
cooperative efforts within the Holiness movement.


Kentucky Christian College
Lusby Memorial Library
College and Landsdown
Grayson, KY 41143
(606) 474-6613

Records of the college and faculty, as well as the papers of evangelist
R. B. Neal and the Gospel Dollar League.

Southern Baptist Theological Seminary
Billy Graham Room
2825 Lexington Road
Louisville, KY   40206
(800) 626-5525

Films, newspaper clippings, forms, and other materials from evangelistic meetings held by Billy Graham (1918- ).  Also copies of many of
the programs of Graham's *Hour of Decision* radio program from the
1950s through the 1970s.


Transylvania University
Library
300 N. Broadway
Lexington, KY 40508
(606) 233-8242

A few documents about the Campbellites, including notes of lectures
given by Alexander Campbell (1788-1866) and a statement on the
establishment of the Lancaster Christian Church in Lancaster, Kentucky.


University of Kentucky
Libraries
Special Collections and Archives
111 King Library North
Lexington, KY   40506-0039
(606) 257-8611

Sermon notes and scrapbook of evangelist Mordecai Ham (1877-1961).


%%%%%%

**MASSACHUSETTS**

Gordon College
Archives
255 Grapevine Road
Wenham, MA 01984
(508) 927-2300, ext. 4140

Records of the college and papers of Adoniram Judson Gordon (1836-
1895).

Gordon-Conwell Seminary
Burton L. Goddard Library
130 Essex Street
S. Hamilton, MA 01982-2361
(508) 468-7111, ext. 585

Records of the seminary, papers of the first president Frederic Leonard Chapell (1836-1900), some scrapbooks and other materials of Harold John Ockenga (1905-1985).

Harvard University Archives
Pusey Library
Cambridge, MA    02138
(617) 495-2461

Scrapbooks of Social Gospel theologian Francis G. Peabody
(1847-1936).

Northfield Mount Hermon School
Northfield, MA    01360
(413) 498-5311

The school archives includes photocopies of Dwight L. Moody's correspondence, genealogies, photographs of Moody and his family, and
records of his evangelistic campaigns.  There is also a great deal of
material from the Northfield Summer Conference (begun in 1886) and
some early records of the Student Volunteer Movement.  Moody's
birthplace is also located on campus and contains much memorabilia.
The attached museum includes originals and copies of Moody correspondence, newspaper clippings, information about the 1937 Moody
Centenary, scrapbooks, photographs and photocopies of sermon notes.

%%%%%

## MICHIGAN

Andrews University
James White Library
Adventist Heritage Center
Berrien Springs, MI   49104
(616) 471-3274

Extensive collection of Millerite and early Seventh Day Adventist
material, including biographies, sermons, and evangelistic aids pertaining to SDA evangelists from the church's beginnings to the present.

Calvin College and Seminary Archives
Grand Rapids, MI 49506
(616) 957-6313

Records of the college and seminary, minutes of denominational
boards and Christian Reformed congregations, files of Christian
Reformed Missions, and periodicals such as *Missionary Monthly* and
*The Banner*.

Hope College
The Joint Archives of Holland
Holland, MI 49423
(616) 394-7798

Records of Hope College, Western Theological Seminary, and the
Holland Historical Trust as well as denominational and congregational
files of the Reformed Church in America and the personal papers of
ministers.

University of Michigan
Bentley Historical Library
Michigan Historical Collections
1150 Beal Avenue
Ann Arbor, MI   48109
(313) 764-3482

Contains copies of printed sermons, books, pamphlets and articles by
Fundamentalist leader Carl McIntire (1906- ), papers of hymn writer
George Bennard (1873-1958), miscellaneous material by and about

Dwight L. Moody (1837-1899), records of the Prohibition Party
(including material on the Christian Amendment Movement), records
of anti-abortion groups, and papers of Howard Hyde Russell
(1855-1946), founder of the Anti-Saloon League.


%%%%%

**MINNESOTA**


Bethel College and Theological Seminary
Carl H. Lundquist Library
3949 Bethel Drive
St. Paul, MN 55112
(612) 638-6184

Records of the Baptist General Conference (formerly the Swedish
Baptist General Conference), including its world and home mission
boards, Bethel College and Seminary, benevolent institutions, individual churches and the denominational leadership. Historically strong
emphasis on evangelism and missions by Baptists.


Luther Theological Seminary
Archives of American Lutheran Church
St. Paul, MN   55108
(612) 641-3205

Records of the denomination and its antecedents as well as some
material from individual Lutherans.


Northwestern College
McAlister Library
3003 N. Snelling Road
Roseville, MN   55113
(612) 631-5241

Papers of the college and its founder, William Bell Riley (1861-1947),
including books, manuscripts and scrapbooks.

University of Minnesota
10 Walter Library
Archives
117 Pleasant Street SE
Minneapolis, MN   55455
(612) 624-0562

Records of the Office of the President and papers of Howard Haycroft
contain information on debate over evolution between William Bell
Riley (1861-1947) and the university faculty.  Records regarding
student religious activities are located in the unprocessed records of
the Coordinator of Religious Activities and the personal papers of
Robert Ross.


University of Minnesota
101 Walter Library
Social Welfare History Archives
Minneapolis, MN   55455
(612) 624-6394

Includes the archives of the YMCA of the USA (1250 linear feet;
20,000 photographs; 10,000 volumes).


%%%%%

**MISSOURI**


Assemblies of God
Archives
1445 Boonville Avenue
Springfield, MO   65802
(417) 862-2781, ext. 4400

Records of the denomination and private papers of Pentecostals such
as evangelist Charles Sydney Price (1880? -1947).  Many recorded sermons and radio programs, by preachers such as Jack Coe (1918-1956)
and Charles Morse Ward (1909- ).  Tapes of the Pentecostal Fellowship of North America annual meetings and other records of the
organization.  Films of various events, including the 1949 AG General
Council.  Video interviews with missionaries and church leaders.
Records of the Pentecostal World Conference.

Church of the Nazarene International Headquarters
Archives
6401 The Paseo
Kansas City, MO   64131
(816) 333-7000, ext. 437

Records of the denomination and papers of individuals.


Concordia Historical Institute
801 DeMun Avenue
St. Louis, MO   63105
(314) 721-5934, ext. 297 or 351.

Records of the Lutheran Church-Missouri Synod plus other collections
of individual Lutherans, such as the papers of radio preacher Walter
Maier (1893-1950).  Copies of LC-MS radio, television and film productions.


Presbyterian Church in America Historical Archives
12330 Conway Road
St. Louis, Missouri  63141
(314) 469-9077

Records of the Presbyterian Church in America and its agencies; con-
servative organizations within the PCUS (pre-PCA); the Reformed
Presbyterian Church, Evangelical Synod and its agencies; the Bible
Presbyterian Church; the Evangelical Presbyterian Church; Reformed
Presbyterian Church, General Synod; World Presbyterian Missions;
Covenant Theological Seminary; and *The Presbyterian Journal*.  The
papers of Max Belz, James Oliver Buswell, Jr. (1895-1980); Gordon
Haddon Clark (1902- ); R. Laird Harris (1911- ); James and Pauline
McAlpine; William Andrew McIlwaine (1893- ?); Harry H. Meiners;
John Barton Payne (1922- ); Robert G. Rayborn; John Edward Rich-
ards (1911- ); G. Gregg Singer; Morton Howison Smith (1923- ); Peter
Stam, Jr. (1892- ?); George Aiken Taylor (1920- ); and Francis Schaef-
fer (1912-1984).  Other materials about Presbyterians.

United Pentecostal Church International
Historical Center
8855 Dunn Road
Hazelwood, MO    63042-2299
(314) 837-7300

Materials from the early beginnings of the Pentecostal movement in
the twentieth century as well as records of the United Pentecostal
Church International and papers of individual Pentecostals.

William Jewell College
William E. Partee Center for Baptist Historical Studies
Liberty, MO    64068
(816) 781-7700, ext. 5490 or 5341

The Partee Center is the official depository for the Missouri Baptist
Convention, which dates back to 1834.  It includes material from various types of Baptists, including Southern Baptists, Primitive Baptists
and American Baptists.

%%%%%

**NEW JERSEY**

Archives and History Center of the United Methodist Church
36 Madison Avenue
Madison, NJ    07940
(201) 822-2787, or 822-2826

Records of the UMC and its antecedents plus papers of individual
Methodists.

New Brunswick Theological Seminary
Gardner A. Sage Library
21 Seminary Place
New Brunswick, NJ    08901
(201) 247-5243

Seminary archives, including sermons, lecture notes and administrative
records, 1784 to the present.

New Brunswick Theological Seminary
Gardner A. Sage Library
Reformed Church in America Archives
21 Seminary Place
New Brunswick, NJ    08901
(201) 246-1779

Records of the Reformed Church in America, including local church records, missionary correspondence, and denominational minutes of missionary societies.

%%%%%%

**NEW YORK**

American Baptist Historical Society
1106 South Goodman Street
Rochester, NY   14620
(716) 473-1740

Papers of J. C. Massee (1871-1958), John Roach Stratton (1875-1929), and Walter Rauschenbusch (1861-1918), among other Baptists.

American Bible Society
Library
1865 Broadway
New York, NY    10023
(212) 581-7400, ext. 495

Archives of the ABS, including information about Scripture distribution, translation and production in the United States and abroad (with special emphasis on Latin America, South America, the Far East and the Near East) from 1816 through the present.  In addition, the ABS maintains the archives of various auxiliary societies formerly affiliated with the ABS, the American Bible Revision Committee, and the archives of the United Bible Societies.

Foundation for Christian Living
66 East Main Street
Pawling, NY    12564
(914) 855-5000

Papers of minister, author, radio speaker Norman Vincent Peale
(1898- ), 878 sermons on audio tape, 212 on video tape.


Hamilton College
Burke Library
Clinton, NY    13323
(315) 859-7135

Papers of preacher, educator and theologian Oren Root, Jr.
(1838-1907) including material on biblical inerrancy and the debate
over evolution.


The King's College
Briarcliff Manor, NY 10510
(914) 944-5605 or 5543

The media library of the college has many original films and video
copies of broadcasts of the early television evangelism program of
Percy Crawford (1902-1960), called *Youth on the March*. The Archives
has the records of the college as well as papers of the Crawford
family.


National Board of the Young Women's Christian Association
Archives
726 Broadway
New York, NY    10003
(212) 614-2700

Files of the YWCA and private papers of some staff members.


Salvation Army
Archives and Research Center
145 West 15th Street
New York, NY    10011
(212) 337-7428

Official records of the Salvation Army in the United States, reflecting
both its religious and social service activities.  Includes the personal

papers of Salvationists, including founder General William Booth (1829-1912) and his daughter Evangeline Booth (1965-1950).

Syracuse University
George Arents Research Library
Special Collections
Syracuse, NY   13210
(315) 423-3335, 423-2697

Includes papers of evangelist Dwight L. Moody (1837-1899), minister Norman Vincent Peale (1898- ) and theologian Carl F. H. Henry (1913- ), the first editor of *Christianity Today*.

%%%%%%

**NORTH CAROLINA**

Atlanta Christian College
Carolina Discipliana Library
Lee Street
Wilson, NC   27893
(919) 237-3161, ext. 262

Materials about Disciples of Christ history, especially in North Carolina.  Also much material on related religious groups.

Archives of the Moravian Church in America, Southern Province
4 E. Bank Street
Winston-Salem, NC  27101
(919) 722-1742

Records of the Moravian Church's southern province in America and material about individual Moravians.

Mount Olive College
Moye Library
Free Will Baptist Historical Collection
Mount Olive, NC   28365
(919) 658-2502, ext. 126

Materials relating to the Free Will Baptist churches, especially in
North Carolina.  Documents relating to the activities of individual
Baptists.


Presbyterian Study Center (Montreat)
Box 849
Montreat, NC   28757
(704) 669-7061

Records of the Presbyterian Church, U.S. (Southern) and antecedents;
papers of prominent church leaders.  Also records of the Associate
Reformed Presbyterian Church and the Cumberland Presbyterian
Church.  Papers of prominent Presbyterians.


Wake Forest University
Room 207, Z. Smith Reynolds Library
North Carolina Baptist Historical Collection
Post Office Box 7777, Reynolda Station
Winston-Salem, NC   27109
(919) 761-5472

Printed materials including annuals, minutes, newspapers and other
publications and records of Baptist churches, organizations and individuals, including some materials relating to Primitive, Black, Free
Will Baptists and Conservative Baptists in North Carolina.

%%%%%

**OHIO**

Bluffton College
Mennonite Historical Library
Bluffton, OH 45817
(419) 358-8015, ext. 271

Materials on Mennonites and Anabaptists in the eastern United States,
Canada, Switzerland, France, and Germany as well as the archives of
the college, the Central District Conference of the General Conference Mennonite Church, and the Africa Inter-Mennonite Mission.

Malone College
Everett L. Cattell Library
515 25th St. NW
Canton, OH  44709-3897
(216) 489-7393

Archives of the Evangelical Friends Church-Eastern Region, including
the record books of the Ohio Yearly Meeting of the Friends (1760-
1965) as well as the papers of missionaries to China and India.

Oberlin College
Archives
320 Mudd Learning Center
Oberlin, OH 44074
(216) 775-8285, ext. 247

Papers of evangelist Charles Finney (1792-1875); records of the college
and various faculty, some of whom were involved in missions and
evangelistic activities.

Ohio Historical Society
1985 Velma Avenue
Columbus, OH   43211
(614) 466-1500

Papers of Washington Gladden (1836-1918), scrapbook of clippings
about Billy Sunday (1862-1935), manuscript of autobiography of Methodist circuit rider Peter Cartwright (1785-1872), some records of Free

Will Baptist churches; and the papers of many influential Baptists, Methodists, and Presbyterians, such as pastors.

Wilberforce University
Rembert E. Stokes Learning Resources Center
Archives and Special Collections
Wilberforce, OH 45384-1003
(513) 376-2911, ext. 628

Records of the African Methodist Episcopal Church and the papers of some of its bishops and other Methodists.

%%%%%

**OKLAHOMA**

Oral Roberts University
Archives
7777 South Lewis
Tulsa, OK   74171
(918) 495-6750

Records of ORU, the Oral Roberts Evangelistic Association, and private papers.

Pentecostal Holiness Church
Archives
P.O. Box 12609
Oklahoma City, OK   73157
(405) 787-7110

Records of the denomination including the World Missions department and some materials from individual Pentecostals.

%%%%%

## OREGON

Luis Palau Evangelistic Association
Archives
P. O. Box 1173
Portland, OR 97207-1173
(503) 643-0777

Records of the organization, a global evangelistic ministry also
involved in counseling, publishing, and broadcasting.

Northwest Christian College
Learning Resources Center
828 E. 11th Avenue
Eugene, OR 97401
(503) 343-1641

Materials about Disciples of Christ churches, leaders and organizations
in the Pacific Northwest.

%%%%%

## PENNSYLVANIA

American Baptist Archives Record Center
P.O. Box 851
Valley Forge, PA 19482-0851
(215) 768-2373 or 2378

Official non-current records of the past and present national organizations of American Baptists and the Baptist World Alliance as well as
some material of the Free Will Baptist movement.

Geneva College
MacCartney Collection
Beaver Falls, PA 15010
(412) 847-6692

Papers of Presbyterian pastor, preacher, and author Clarence E. Mac-
Cartney (1879-1957).

Haverford College
Library
Quaker Collection
Haverford, PA    19041-1392
(215) 896-1161

Records of the Society of Friends.


Lancaster Mennonite Historical Society
Archives
2215 Mill Stream Road
Lancaster, PA    17602-1499
(717) 393-9745

Records of the Lancaster and Atlantic Coast conferences of the Mennonite Church, Eastern Mennonite Board of Missions and Charities,
papers of individual Mennonites and local church-related educational
institutions, 1710 to the present.


Mennonite Historians of Eastern Pennsylvania
24 Main Street
Souderton, PA    18964
(215) 723-1700

Papers of several significant Mennonites, including Bishop John E.
Lapp (1906-1988) and J. G. Clemens (1874-1965) among other collections.


Messiah College
Archives of the Brethren in Christ Church and Messiah College
Grantham, PA    17027
(717) 766-2511

Records of the Brethren in Christ Church, including the *Evangelical
Visitor* (official paper of the denomination) and the minutes of the
General Conference from 1871 to the present.  Also in the Archives
are the private papers of Brethren in Christ leaders such as Arthur
Climenhaga (1916- ), who served as executive secretary of the National
Association of Evangelicals; Henry Ginder; Charles Byers; and C. N.
Hostetter, Jr.

The Moravian Archives
41 West Locust Street
Bethlehem, PA    18018
(215) 866-3255

Records of the Moravian Church's northern province in America and
material about individual Moravians.


New Castle Free Public Library
207 E. North Street
New Castle, PA 16101
(412) 658-6659

A few letters and sermons of Dwight L. Moody (1837-1899) and Ira
Sankey (1840-1908).


Pittsburgh Theological Seminary
Clifford E. Barbour Library
616 North Highland Avenue
Pittsburgh, PA    15206
(412) 362-5610

Records of the seminary and faculty, as well as some documents relating to antecedent denominations of the United Presbyterian Church
and other material about Presbyterians.


Office of History, Presbyterian Church (USA)
425 Lombard Street
Philadelphia, PA    19147
(215) 627-1852

Records of several Presbyterian denominations as well as other collections such as the papers of evangelist J. Wilbur Chapman (1859-1918),
author and theologian J. Gresham Machen (1881-1937), and Stuart
Merriam; records of the National Council of Churches (formerly the
Federal Council of Churches); files on the 1930s trial of the Presbyterian Church of the USA vs Carl McIntire; records of the Presbyterian Evangelistic Summer Committee of Philadelphia (1899-1969) and
the Labor Temple, Presbytery of New York.  Papers of prominent
Presbyterians.

WEC International
Box 1707
Fort Washington, PA 19034-8707
(215) 646-2322

Formerly the Worldwide Evangelization Crusade. Records of the
organization, an interdenominational mission agency involved in
church planting, theological education, evangelism, Bible translation,
medicine, literacy, literature, radio, and rural development.


Westminster Theological Seminary
Archives
Chestnut Hill, P. O. Box 27009
Philadelphia, PA 19118
(215) 887-5511

Papers of theologian, educator and conservative Protestant leader J.
Gresham Machen (1881-1937). Also the papers of theologian Cornelius Van Til and biblical scholars Ned B. Stonehouse (1902-1962)
and Edward J. Young (1907-1968).


Young People's Church of the Air, Inc.
P.O. Box 86
Flourtown, PA 19031
(215) 628-3500

Records and memorabilia of radio and television evangelist Percy
Crawford (1902-1960), his wife Ruth Crawford Porter (1916-1986), and
their programs *Youth on the March, Young People's Church of the Air,*
and *Pinebrook Praises*. Also information on the youth camps they ran:
Pinebrook, Shadowbrook and Mountainbrook. Also the older files of
Crawford Broadcasting Co., a conservative, Evangelical radio station.

%%%%%%

## SOUTH CAROLINA

Bob Jones University
J. S. Mack Library
Greenville, SC   29614
(803) 242-5100

Records of the institution, papers of the Jones family, papers of W. O.
H. Garman (1899- ) and G. Archer Weniger (1915- ).

Columbia Bible College and Graduate School of Bible and Missions
Learning Resources Center
7435 Monticello Road, P.O. Box 3122
Columbia, SC   29230
(803) 754-4100, ext. 372

Records of the institution as well as private papers of College presidents Robert C. McQuilkin (1886-1952), J. Alan Fleece (1909- ), and
J. Robertson McQuilkin (1927- ).

South Carolina Baptist Historical Society
Special Collections Department
University Library
Furman University
Greenville, SC   29613
(803) 294-2194

Records of Baptists and their organizations in South Carolina.

University of South Carolina
South Caroliniana Library
Manuscripts Division
Columbia, SC   29208
(803) 777-5183

Much material on religious activities of South Carolinians, including
missionaries to Africa and China, and of African Methodist Episcopals, Presbyterians, Baptists, Catholics, Christians, Lutherans,
Methodists, Protestant Episcopals, Quakers, and Unitarians. Files of
the Christian Action Council, which include information on Billy
Graham and his 1950 crusade in Columbia, SC. Papers (1928-1974) of

religious journalist Louis Welborn Cassels (1922-1974) include materials on science and religion, the ecumenical movement, parochial-public school conflicts and religious views on various current social issues. Papers (1928-1967) of Cornelia Dabney Tucker (1881- ?) including material on her efforts to expose communism in the National Council of Churches.


%%%%%%

## SOUTH DAKOTA


North American Baptist Seminary
North American Baptist Archives
1321 W. 22nd Street
Sioux Falls, SD    57105
(605) 335-9071

Records of the denomination and seminary, as well as materials about individual Baptists.


%%%%%%

## TENNESSEE


Cleveland State Community College
Library
Box 1205
Cleveland, TN 37311
(615) 472-7141

Some documents about the history of the Church of God.


Disciples of Christ Historical Society
1101 Nineteenth Avenue, South
Nashville, TN    37212
(615) 327-1444

Records of the Christian Church (Disciples of Christ), the Churches of Christ and the Independent Christian Churches and Churches of Christ.

East Tennessee State University
Archives of Appalachia
Box 22450A
Johnson City, TN 37614-0002
(615) 929-5339

Records of the Appalachian Preaching Mission, an interdenominational yearly evangelistic campaign which was held from 1954 to 1980.
Archives includes 320 audio tapes of sermons.  Also at the Archives
are audio and video tapes of interviews with members of snake
handling churches in Tennessee and North Carolina.


Emmanual School of Religion
Library
1 Walker Drive
Johnson City, TN 37601
(615) 926-1186

Documents of the churches of the Campbell/Stone movement, such as
the Christian Churches and Churches of Christ, the Christian Church
(Disciples of Christ), and Churches of Christ.


Free Will Baptist Bible College
Free Will Baptist Historical Collection
3606 West End Avenue
Nashville, TN   37205
(615) 383-1340

Records of the denomination and individual Baptists.


Southern Baptist Historical Library and Archives
901 Commerce Street, Suite 400
Nashville, TN   37203-3620
(615) 244-0344

Records of denominational agencies and private papers of individual
Baptists and organizations including J. Franklyn Norris (1877-1952)
and Amzi Clarence Dixon (1854-1925).

Vanderbilt University
Jean and Alexander Heard Library
Vanderbilt Television News Archive
Nashville, TN    37240-0007
(615) 322-2927

Tapes of the national networks nightly news programs recorded every
night since 1968, as well as some special news programs recorded
since 1968.  Some of these programs include stories on Protestant
Fundamentalists and Evangelicals in the news such as Jerry Falwell
(1933- ), Jim Bakker (1940- ), Tammy Bakker (1942-), Jimmy Lee
Swaggart (1935- ), Oral Roberts (1918-), Billy Graham (1918- ), as
well as stories about television evangelism, church and state, and other
subjects.


%%%%%

**TEXAS**


Abilene Christian University
Margaret and Herman Brown Library
Center for Restoration Studies
ACU Station, Box 8177
Abilene, TX 79699
(915) 674-2344

Documents of the Campbell/Stone movement.


CAM International
8625 La Prada Drive
Dallas, TX 75228
(214) 327-8206

Records of the mission (formerly the Central American Mission) as
well as much material from Dr. C. I. Scofield (1843-1921).

Dallas Theological Seminary
Archives
3909 Swiss Avenue
Dallas, TX 75204
(214) 824-3094

Archives has the records of the seminary and the International Council
on Biblical Inerrancy, as well as the papers of Lewis Sperry Chafer
(1871-1952), W. H. Griffith Thomas (1861-1924), William K. Harrison
and Mrs. Graeme M. MacDonald.


Episcopal Church, USA
Archives
606 Rathervue Place
Austin, TX   78705
(512) 472-6816

Official repository for the national records of the Episcopal Church.
The Archives also has the papers of prominent Episcopalians such as
minister and broadcaster Samuel Shoemaker (1893-1963).


Letourneau College
The Mary Estes Library
Longview, TX   75607
(214) 753-0231

Records of businessman and Fundamentalist leader Robert G. Letourneau (1888-1969), including notes and audio cassettes for speeches he
gave between 1937 and 1967.


Scofield Memorial Church
7730 Abrams Road
Dallas, TX 75231
(214) 349-6043

Records of the church as well as papers of Dr. C. I. Scofield (1843-
1921).

Southwestern Assemblies of God College
Nelson Memorial Library
1200 Sycamore
Waxahachie, TX 75165
(214) 937-4010, ext. 59

Oral history interviews and other documents relating to the history of
the Assemblies in the south central and southwestern United States.

Southwestern Baptist Theological Seminary
A. Webb Roberts Library
P.O. Box 22000-2E
Fort Worth, TX   76122
(817) 923-1921, ext. 3330

Materials relating to Baptist churches in Texas and papers of Texas
Baptists such as George Truett (1867-1944), Benajah Henry Carroll
(1843-1914), Lee Rutland Scarborough (1870-1945), and Hyman
Appelman (1902-1983). Also copies of many of the programs of
Graham's *Hour of Decision* radio program from the 1950s through the
1970s.

%%%%%

**VIRGINIA**

CBN University
Library
Special Collections
1000 Centerville Turnpike
Virginia Beach, VA   23464-9882
(804) 523-7473

Publications of the Christian Broadcasting Network, records of CBN
University, film and papers of early Evangelical filmmaker C. O. Baptista (1895-1965), and papers relating to founder Pat Robertson
(1930-).

Eastern Mennonite College
Menno Simons Historical Library
Harrisonburg, VA 22801
(703) 433-2771, Ext. 153

Official records and private papers relating to the Virginia Mennonite
Conference and its subsidiary organizations, and the records of Eastern Mennonite College and Seminary as well as individual Mennonites.


Liberty University
Archives
Box 20000
Lynchburg, VA
(804) 582-2000

Records of the institution plus miscellaneous clippings and other
material on Jerry Falwell (1933- ) and the Moral Majority movement.


University of Virginia Library
Special Collections Department
Manuscripts Division
Charlottesville, VA   22903
(804) 924-3025

Letters of Bob Jones (1883-1968) to Collins Denny (1854-1943) in the
Collins Denny Collection (#2672) comprising the papers of the prominent Southern Methodist bishop, teacher, author, and lawyer.


%%%%%

**WEST VIRGINIA**


Bethany College
T. W. Phillips Library
Alexander Campbell Archives
Bethany, WV 26032
(304) 829-7321

Papers of Bethany College founder Alexander Campbell (1788-1866),
his father Thomas Campbell (1763-1854), and their associates and
family.  The Campbells were early leaders in the Restoration movement, from which the Disciples of Christ, the Church of Christ and the
Christian Church developed.

%%%%%

**WISCONSIN**

Seventh Day Baptist Center
3120 Kennedy Road
Janesville, WI 53545
(608) 752-5055

Records of the denomination and material about individual Baptists.

# Appendix II: Select List of Libraries and Research Centers in the United States with Collections Relevant to the Evangelical Movement

The majority of libraries listed below are those found in leading Evangelical institutions of higher education which have substantial collections supporting the study of topics within the American Evangelical movement, with emphasis on church history, evangelism, missions, and conservative theology. Added to these are several large research libraries known for their outstanding historical collections on missionary activities. Also included are some research centers affiliated with Evangelical agencies which gather and disseminate information to the Evangelical community.

%%%%%

**CALIFORNIA**

Azusa Pacific University
Marshburn Memorial Library
929 E. Alosta
Azusa, CA  91702-7000
(818) 969-3434, ext. 3272

This interdenominational liberal arts university serves as the official college of the Free Methodist Church, Church of God (Anderson, Indiana), and five other denominations.

**Subject strengths**: Holiness movement, Missionaries--United States, United States--Church history.

**Special collections**: John Hess Memorial Holiness Collection, Clifford M. Drury Collection on the Missionary in the American West.

Biola University
Rose Memorial Library
13800 Biola Ave.
La Mirada, CA 90639-0001
(213) 944-0351, ext. 3255

Founded in 1908 as the Bible Institute of Los Angeles by those who
promoted the publication of *The Fundamentals*, the university includes
the Rosemead School of Psychology, the School of Intercultural Studies, and Talbot Theological Seminary. The library holds a complete
file of *The King's Business*.

**Subject strengths**: Bible--Criticism, interpretation, etc., Counseling,
Evangelicalism, Missions, Pastoral theology, Theology.

**Special collections**: (See Appendix I--Biola University.)


Fuller Theological Seminary
McAlister Library
135 North Oakland Ave.
Pasadena, CA 91182
(818) 584-5218

Founded by Charles E. Fuller and Harold John Ockenga, the seminary
is an interdenominational institution with schools of psychology, theol-
ogy, and world mission. Charter members of the faculty were
Everett F. Harrison, Carl F. H. Henry, Harold Lindsell, and Wilbur
M. Smith. Edward John Carnell served as first resident president.
Library holdings include the personal collections of Professors Everett
Harrison, Robert Bower, George Eldon Ladd, and Dr. Wilbur Smith.

**Subject strengths**: Bible--Criticism, interpretation, etc., Church growth,
Counseling, Feminism, Missions, Pentecostalism, Philosophy, Religion,
Theology.

**Special collections**: (See Appendix I--Fuller Theological Seminary.)

Missions Advanced Research and
Communication Center (MARC)
919 West Huntington Drive
Monrovia, CA 91016
(818) 357-7979

MARC is a ministry of World Vision International. "It attempts to
assess the status of world evangelization continually and to explore
possible better futures for efforts to share the Good News with all the
world." It publishes the *MARC Newsletter*. In support of this information gathering, MARC uses the Information Resource Center Library
at World Vision.

**Subject strengths**: Missions, Medical.

**Special collections**: (See Appendix I--World Vision.)


Point Loma Nazarene College
Ryan Library
3900 Lomaland Drive
San Diego, CA 92106-2899
(619) 221-2312

Founded in Los Angeles in 1902, this liberal arts college was one of
the first to serve the Church of the Nazarene.

**Subject strengths**: Church of the Nazarene, Holiness movement, United States--Church history.

**Special collections**: 19th and 20th Century Christian Holiness
Movement Collection.


Westmont College
Roger John Voskuyl Library
955 La Paz Road
Santa Barbara, CA 93108-1099
(805) 565-6000, ext. 522

Founded in 1940 by Ruth W. Kerr of Kerr Manufacturing Company,
this interdenominational liberal arts college considers itself to be an
"enthusiastically Evangelical Christian college."

**Subject strengths**: Christianity and culture, Evangelicalism, Religion,
Theology, United States--Church history.

**Special collections**: The Christ and Culture Collection focuses on the interaction of Christian faith and culture.


%%%%%

**COLORADO**


Denver Conservative Baptist Seminary
Carey S. Thomas Library
Location: 3401 S. University Blvd.
          Englewood, CO 80110
Mailing address: P.O. Box 10,000
          Denver, CO  80210
(303) 781-8691

Founded in 1950, the seminary serves the needs of the Conservative Baptist denomination.  Library holdings include the personal collection of Vernon Grounds.

**Subject strengths**: Baptists, Bible--Criticism, interpretation, etc., Christian education, Conservative Baptist Association of America, Missions, Philosophy, Pastoral theology, Preaching, Theology.

**Special collections**: Baptistica Collection.


%%%%%

**CONNECTICUT**


Hartford Seminary Library
77 Sherman Street
Hartford, CT  06105
(203) 232-4451

Founded in 1834, the Hartford Seminary is interdenominational.  The Kennedy School of Missions was affiliated with the seminary.  Although a large portion of the original Hartford collection was sold to Emory University for the Pitts Theology Library, two major special collections of interest to scholars of missions remain.  The Hartford Seminary Foundation publishes *The Muslim World*, formerly titled *The Moslem World*.

**Subject strengths:** Missions, Missions to Muslims.

**Special collections:** Duncan Black Macdonald Collection on Islam and the A. C. Thompson Collection of nineteenth-century missiological materials.


Yale University Divinity School
Library
409 Prospect Street
New Haven, CT  06511
(203) 432-5290


The Divinity Library was established as a separate collection in 1932. The missions collection is one of the finest in the United States and now supports the research needs of the nearby Overseas Ministries Study Center, publisher of *The International Bulletin of Missionary Research* (490 Prospect Street, New Haven, CT  06511, Telephone: 203-624-6672).

**Subject strengths:** Bible--Criticism, interpretation, etc., Church history, Church work with students, Evangelistic work, Missions, Missions--China, Theology, United States--Church history.

**Special collections:** China Missions, Day Historical Library of Foreign Missions, Missions Pamphlet Collection.  For a more complete description of the Archives and Manuscripts Collection, **see** Appendix I--Yale University Divinity School.


%%%%%

**DISTRICT OF COLUMBIA**


Howard University
School of Divinity Library
1400 Shepherd St. NE
Washington, D.C.  20017
(202) 636-8914


Howard University traces its roots to 1866 when plans were laid for the founding of the Howard Normal and Theological Institute for the Education of Teachers and Preachers.  Today the school emphasizes the preparation of professional religious leaders, an international cross-cultural inquiry into human values, and graduate study primarily in the cultural and religious heritage of African Americans.

**Subject strengths**: African Americans, Bible--Criticism, interpretation, etc., Church and social problems, Church history, Pastoral theology, Theology, United States--Church history.

**Special collections**: Black Religious Studies Collection.

%%%%%

**FLORIDA**

Miami Christian College Library
2300 NW 135th St.
Miami, FL 33167
(305) 953-1130

Founded in 1949 as the interdenominational Miami Bible Institute, the school is now affiliated with Trinity Evangelical Divinity School (Deerfield, IL). The library collection incorporates the Winona Lake School of Theology collection, including the personal library of William Biederwolf.

**Subject strengths**: Bible--Criticism, interpretation, etc., Pastoral theology, Religion, Theology.

%%%%%

**GEORGIA**

MAP International Library
Box 50
2200 Glynco Parkway
Brunswick, GA 31520
(912) 265-6010

MAP is an interdenominational agency which cooperates with other agencies to provide medical supplies, health training, and other development resources. The library collects materials on all aspects of health and development, especially primary health care.

**Subject strengths**: Missions, Medical.


%%%%%

**ILLINOIS**


Bethany/Northern Baptist Theological Seminary
Library
Butterfield & Meyers Roads
Oak Brook, IL  60521
(708) 620-2214

The Seminary Library serves two institutions.  Founded in 1905,
Bethany serves the Church of the Brethren.  Northern Baptist Seminary is affiliated with the American Baptist Convention, having been
founded in 1913 by conservatives opposing the theological education of
the University of Chicago Divinity School.

**Subject strengths**: American Baptists, American Tract Society, Baptists, Bible--Criticism, interpretation, etc., Church of the Brethren,
Evangelicalism, Holiness movement, Missions, Peace, Pietism, Religion, United States--Church history.

**Special collections**: Abraham H. Cassel Collection contains a nearly
complete collection of the American Tract Society publications;
Donald Dayton Collection of nineteenth century Evangelicalism.  (See
**also**: Appendix I--Bethany/Northern Baptist Theological Seminary.)


Moody Bible Institute Library
820 N. LaSalle Dr.
Chicago, IL  60610
(312) 329-4138

The Institute was founded in 1886 as an interdenominational Bible
school by Dwight L. Moody.  Past presidents included R. A. Torrey,
James M. Gray, Will H. Houghton, William Culbertson, and George
Sweeting.  The library holds a complete file of *Moody Monthly* and its
predecessors: *The Institute Tie*, *The Christian Worker's Magazine*, and
*The Moody Bible Institute Monthly*.

**Subject strengths**: Bible--Criticism, interpretation, etc., Christian education, Church music, Evangelicalism, Evangelistic work, Fundamen-

talism, Missions, Pastoral theology, Theology; Culbertson, William; Gray, James Martin; Houghton, William Henry; Moody, Dwight Lyman; Sweeting, George; Torrey, Reuben Archer, Sr.

**Special collections**: Moodyana Collection, Rare Book Collection includes early Bibles and rare theology works. For a more complete description, **see** Appendix I--Moody Bible Institute.

North Park Theological Seminary
Mellander Library
5125 N. Spaulding Ave.
Chicago, IL  60625
(312) 583-2700

Founded in 1891, North Park is affiliated with the Evangelical Covenant Church, a denomination rooted in the pietistic renewal of the Swedish Lutheran Church and influenced by the American Evangelical revival movement.

**Subject strengths**: Bible--Criticism, interpretation, etc., Evangelical Covenant Church, Evangelicalism, Pastoral theology, Pietism, Theology.

**Special collections**: (**See** Appendix I--Evangelical Covenant Church of America.)

Slavic Gospel Association
Box 1122
Wheaton, IL  60189
(708) 690-8900

This interdenominational Evangelical mission agency engages in radio broadcasting, literature production, Bible distribution, theological education by extension, and evangelistic work. A specialized library collection supports an Institute of Soviet and East European Studies.

**Subject strengths**: Missions--Europe, Eastern, Missions--Soviet Union.

Trinity Evangelical Divinity School
Rolfing Memorial Library
2065 Half Day Road
Deerfield, IL  60015
(708) 945-8800, ext. 317

Sponsored by the Evangelical Free Church of America, in 1963 the
seminary made special efforts to expand curriculum and add outstanding scholars from many denominations, who were "noted for their
defense of orthodox Christianity and committed to earnest piety and
the Evangelical faith."   The library supports doctoral programs in
ministry, missiology, and education, and holdings include the personal
collections of Carl F. H. Henry and Wilbur M. Smith.

**Subject strengths**: Bible--Criticism, interpretation, etc., Christian education, Church history, Counseling, Evangelical Free Church of America, Evangelicalism, Fundamentalism, Missions, Pastoral theology, Philosophy, Religion, Theology.

**Special collections**: (**See** Appendix I--Trinity Evangelical Divinity
School.)

Wheaton College
Buswell Memorial Library
Franklin & Irving
Wheaton, IL  60187-5593
(708) 260-5908

Founded in 1860, Wheaton College is an interdenominational Christian liberal arts college supporting M.A. programs in Christian education, communications, counseling, missions, and theology.  Past presidents included Jonathan Blanchard, Charles Blanchard, J. Oliver Buswell, V. Raymond Edman, and Hudson T. Armerding.

**Subject strengths**: Bible--Criticism, interpretation, etc., Christian education, Church history, Communication, Counseling, Hymnology, Keswick Movement, Mormons and Mormonism, Religion, Theology.

**Special collections**: Stephen Barabas Keswick Collection, Mormonism
Collection, Hymnal Collection, Faculty and Alumni Collection;
*Sojourners* Collection.  (**See also** Appendix I--Wheaton College.)

%%%%%

**INDIANA**

Grace Theological Seminary
Morgan Library
200 Seminary Dr.
Winona Lake, IN  46590
(219) 372-5177

The Fellowship of Grace Brethren Churches founded the seminary in
1937 as a result of deep concerns "about the inroads of modern unbelief in the general field of higher education, and particularly in the
institution which they had been supporting."  Library holdings include
the personal collection of Alva J. McClain, first president of Grace
Schools.

**Subject strengths**: Bible--Criticism, interpretation, etc., Christian education, Grace Brethren, Missions.  (**See also** Appendix I--Grace
College and Theological Seminary.)

%%%%%

**IOWA**

Emmaus Bible College Library
2570 Asbury Road
Dubuque, IA  52001-3096
(319) 588-8000, ext. 240

Affiliated with the open Plymouth Brethren, Emmaus Bible School
originated in Toronto with evening school classes begun in September,
1941.  From 1954 until its 1984 relocation to Dubuque, Emmaus was
located in Oak Park, Illinois.  Correspondence courses are available in
125 languages.

**Subject strengths**: Bible--Criticism, interpretation, etc., Plymouth
Brethren.

%%%%%

**KENTUCKY**

Asbury Theological Seminary
B.L. Fisher Library
N. Lexington Ave. SPO 152
Wilmore, KY  40390
(606) 858-3581, ext. 229

Interdenominational within the Wesleyan-Arminian tradition, the seminary was established in 1923 by Henry Clay Morrison, President of Asbury College.  The missions and evangelism collection serves the E. Stanley Jones School of World Mission and Evangelism.

**Subject strengths**: Bible--Criticism, interpretation, etc., Faith--cure, Holiness movement, Evangelistic work, Methodists, Missions, Pastoral theology, Theology.

**Special collections**: Alfred E. Price Healing Collection.  (**See also** Appendix I--Asbury Theological Seminary.)

Southern Baptist Theological Seminary
James P. Boyce Centennial Library
2825 Lexington Rd.
Louisville, KY  40280
(502) 897-4807

This Southern Baptist seminary supports doctoral programs in Christian education, church music, and theology.  For many years, Lewis Drummond was the Billy Graham professor of evangelism at Southern.

**Subject strengths**: Baptists, Bible--Criticism, interpretation, etc., Christian education, Church history, Church music, Evangelistic work, Hymnology, Missions, Philosophy, Religion, Southern Baptist Convention, Theology.

**Special collections**: Baptist Historical Collection, Everett Helm Music Collection, William F. Albright Archaeology Collection, Converse Hymnology Collection, R. Pierce Beaver Missions Collection, Ingersoll Music Collection.  (**See also** Appendix I--Southern Baptist Theological Seminary, Billy Graham Room.)

%%%%%

## MASSACHUSETTS

Gordon-Conwell Theological Seminary
Burton L. Goddard Library
130 Essex Street
South Hamilton, MA  01982
(508) 468-7111, ext. 585

Gordon-Conwell is the major Evangelical seminary in New England.
A merger in 1969 joined the Conwell School of Theology and the
Gordon Divinity School with Harold John Ockenga as first president.

**Subject strengths:** Bible--Criticism, interpretation, etc., Christian education, Church history, Counseling, Evangelicalism, Evangelistic work,
Missions, Pastoral theology, Preaching, Theology.

**Special collections:** Mercer Collection of Assyro-Babylonian Materials,
Roger Babson Collection of Rare Bibles.  (**See also:** Appendix I--
Gordon-Conwell Seminary.)

%%%%%

## MICHIGAN

Calvin College and Seminary Library
3207 Burton St. SE
Grand Rapids, MI  49546-4301
(616) 957-6297

Serving the Christian Reformed Church, the college and seminary
were established in 1876.

**Subject strengths:** Calvinism, Christian Reformed Church, Pastoral
theology, Philosophy, Reformed Church in America, Religion, Theology.

**Special collections:** H. H. Meeter Calvinism Research Collection, The
Colonial Origins Collection consists of resources on the Christian
Reformed Church, its leaders, its Dutch origins, and closely related

institutions.  (**See also**: Appendix I--Calvin College and Seminary Archives.)


%%%%%

**MINNESOTA**


Bethel College and Theological Seminary
Carl H. Lundquist Library
3949 Bethel Dr.
St. Paul, MN  55112
(612) 638-6184

Affiliated with the Baptist General Conference of America, the college and seminary were founded in 1871.  Prior to its 1914 move to St. Paul, the early years of Bethel Theological Seminary were spent as the Swedish Department of the Divinity School of the University of Chicago and its predecessor, Baptist Union Theological Seminary.

**Subject strengths**: Baptist General Conference, Baptists, Bible--Criticism, interpretation, etc., Church history, Evangelicalism, Pietism, Practical theology, Puritans, Theology.

**Special collections**: Skarstedt Collection of Pietistic Literature, Carl Nelson Collection of Devotional Books, Klingberg Puritan Collection. (**See also**: Appendix I--Bethel Theological Seminary.)


Northwestern College
McAlister Library
3003 North Snelling Ave.
Roseville, MN  55113
(612) 631-5241

This interdenominational school was founded in 1902 by William Bell Riley as a Bible and Missionary Training School in the First Baptist Church of Minneapolis. Billy Graham served as second president. The library holds complete files of: *School and Church*, *Christian Fundamentals in School and Church*, and *The Christian Fundamentalist*.

**Subject strengths**: Bible--Criticism, interpretation, etc., Christian education, Fundamentalism.  (**See also** Appendix I--Northwestern College.)

%%%%%

## MISSISSIPPI

Reformed Theological Seminary Library
5422 Clinton Blvd.
Jackson, MS  39209-3099
(601) 922-4988, ext. 252

Founded in 1964 out of a "need for a seminary committed to the inerrancy of Scripture and historic Reformed theology as set forth by the
Westminster Confession of Faith with its compelling demands for
evangelism and Christian nurture," the seminary serves various Presbyterian and Reformed denominations.

**Subject strengths**: Bible--Criticism, interpretation, etc., Calvinism,
Christian education, Counseling, Evangelistic work, Pastoral theology,
Presbyterians, Religion, Theology.

**Special collections**: George A. Blackburn Memorial Collection
(Southern Presbyterian history and theology).

%%%%%

## MISSOURI

Assemblies of God Theological Seminary
Cordas C. Burnett Library
1445 Boonville Ave.
Springfield, MO  65802
(417) 862-3344, ext. 5505

Begun in 1973, the seminary serves the ministry needs of the
Assemblies of God.

**Subject strengths**: Assemblies of God, Bible--Criticism, interpretation,
etc., Communication, Counseling, Holy Spirit, Missions, Pentecostalism, Philosophy, Theology.  (**See also** Appendix I--Assemblies of God.)

Covenant Theological Seminary
J. Oliver Buswell, Jr. Library
12330 Conway Road
St. Louis, MO  63141
(314) 434-4044

Founded in 1956 as an agency of the Evangelical Presbyterian Church, the seminary now serves the ministry needs of the Presbyterian Church of America.

**Subject strengths**: Bible--Criticism, interpretation, etc., Calvinism, Church history, Practical theology, Presbyterian Church in America, Puritans, Theology.

**Special collections**: Blackburn Library Collection (Southern Presbyterians), Tait Puritan and Rare Book Collection. (**See also** Appendix I-- Presbyterian Church in America Historical Archives.)


Nazarene Theological Seminary
William Broadhurst Library
1700 E. Meyer Blvd.
Kansas City, MO  64131
(816) 333-6254, ext. 41

Established in 1944, the seminary is sponsored by the Church of the Nazarene.

**Subject strengths**: Bible--Criticism, interpretation, etc., Christian education, Church history, Church of the Nazarene, Holiness movement, Methodists, Missions, Philosophy, Theology.

**Special collections**: History of the Church of the Nazarene Collection, James P. McGraw Memorial Wesleyana-Methodistica Collection. (**See also** Appendix I--Church of the Nazarene International Headquarters.)

%%%%%

**NEW JERSEY**

Drew University Library
36 Madison Avenue
Madison, NJ  07940
(201) 408-3471

The university began in 1866 as Drew Theological Seminary, "the only seminary founded directly by the General Conference of the Methodist Church and the first in American Methodism to operate entirely on the graduate professional level." Now the university is affiliated with the United Methodist Church and offers a Ph.D. program in Methodist Studies.

**Subject strengths**: Bible--Criticism, interpretation, etc., Church history, Church music, Hymnology, Methodists, Missions, Religion, Theology, United States--Church history.

**Special collections**: Luke Tyerman Collection of Methodist Pamphlets, Tipple and Maser Collections of Wesleyana, David Creamer Hymnology Collection, Walter Koehler Collection in Reformation History; a vast collection of Methodistica. (**See also** Appendix I-- Archives and History Center of the United Methodist Church.)

Princeton Theological Seminary
Robert E. Speer Library
Mercer Street & Library Pl., P.O. Box 111
Princeton, NJ  08542-0111
(609) 497-7940

Founded in 1812, the seminary is affiliated with the Presbyterian Church (USA).  During the modernist-Fundamentalist controversy, Princeton stood for Presbyterian orthodoxy.  Even though several faculty left to start Westminster Theological Seminary, the president participates in the Fellowship of Evangelical Seminary Presidents. Library holdings include portions of the personal collection of Benjamin B. Warfield.

**Subject strengths**: Baptism, Baptists, Bible--Criticism, interpretation, etc., Calvinism, Church history, Church music, Hymnology, Missions, Presbyterians, Puritans, Religion, Theology, United States--Church history.

**Special collections**: Louis F. Benson Collection of Hymnology, Grosart Library of Puritan and Nonconformist Theology, Agnew Baptist Collection deals with the controversy over the proper form of baptism, Sprague Early American Theological Pamphlets.


%%%%%

**NEW YORK**


Houghton College
Willard J. Houghton Library
Houghton, NY  14744
(716) 567-9240


Founded in 1883, the college is affiliated with the Wesleyan Church.

**Subject strengths**: Bible and science, Christian education, Missions, Religion and science, Theology, The Wesleyan Church.

**Special collections**: John Wesley Collection, Science and Christian Faith Collection.


Nyack College and Alliance Theological Seminary Library
Nyack, NY 10960-3698
(914) 358-1710, ext. 750


Founded by A. B. Simpson, the early emphasis of these Christian and Missionary Alliance schools was on programs promoting evangelistic work and missions.

**Subject strengths**: Bible--Criticism, interpretation, etc., Christian and Missionary Alliance, Church music, Missions, Pastoral theology, Religion, Theology.  For the major denominational collection, **see** Appendix I--Christian and Missionary Alliance.

Union Theological Seminary
Burke Library
3061 Broadway
New York, NY 10027
(212) 280-1504

Founded in 1836, the seminary strongly supported higher criticism of
the Bible and academic freedom in the modernist-Fundamentalist controversy of the late-nineteenth century. Its library holds one of the
finest historical collections on world missions, the Missionary Research
Library.

**Special collections**: Following the Edinburgh World Missionary Council in 1910 and with the guidance of John R. Mott, the Foreign Missions Conference of North America founded the Missionary Research
Library in 1914. The collection of over 100,000 books, periodicals,
reports, and archives was relocated to the seminary in 1929. The
seminary continues to collect missions materials broadly, with special
emphasis on the Protestant mission boards now known as the Division
of Overseas Ministries of the National Council of Churches of Christ
in the U.S.A.

%%%%%

**NORTH CAROLINA**

SIM International Resource Center
Box 7900
14830 Choate Circle
Charlotte, NC 28241-8819
(704) 588-1503

This interdenominational Evangelical mission agency engages primarily
in church planting, community development, broadcasting, theological
education, medicine, and support of national churches. Formerly
known as Sudan Interior Mission, SIM International now serves areas
outside Africa, including Latin America and Asia. The resource center collects books, periodicals, and vertical file materials on countries
and types of service.

**Subject strengths**: Missions--Africa, Missions--Asia, Missions--Latin
America.

%%%%%%

**OKLAHOMA**

Oral Roberts University
John Messick Learning Resources Center
7777 S. Lewis Ave.
Tulsa, OK  74171-0007
(918) 495-6723

Opening in 1965, the university serves a broad interdenominational
constituency within the Charismatic and Pentecostal traditions.

**Subject strengths**: Bible--Criticism, interpretation, etc., Charismatic
movement, Christianity and culture, Faith--Cure, Holy Spirit, Pastoral
theology, Pentecostalism, Theology.

**Special collections**: Holy Spirit Research Center. (**See also**
Appendix I--Oral Roberts University.)


%%%%%%

**OREGON**


George Fox College
Murdock Learning Resource Center
Newberg, OR  97132-2698
(503) 538-8383, ext. 303

George Fox is affiliated with the Northwest Yearly Meeting of Friends
which has been influenced by the Wesleyan holiness and Evangelical
movements.

**Subject strengths**: Missions, Peace, Society of Friends.

**Special collections**: Quaker Collection, Peace Collection.

Western Conservative Baptist Seminary
Cline-Tunnell Library
5511 SE Hawthorne Blvd.
Portland, OR  97215
(503) 233-8561, ext. 323

Affiliated with the Conservative Baptists, the seminary serves the wider
Evangelical community.  Programs include the doctor of ministry and
doctor of psychology.

**Subject strengths**: Baptists, Bible--Criticism, interpretation, etc.,
Church music, Counseling, Missions, Pastoral theology, Religion,
Theology.

**Special collections**: Oregon Baptist History Collection.


Western Evangelical Seminary
George Hallauer Memorial Library
4200 SE Jennings Avenue
Portland, OR  97267-9095
(503) 654-5182

Beginning in 1947, the seminary serves the needs of the Pacific Northwest for an Evangelical school of theology in the Arminian-Wesleyan
tradition.  Denominational affiliations include the Brethren in Christ
Church, The Evangelical Church, the Evangelical Methodist Church,
the Free Methodist Church, the Northwest Yearly Meeting of Friends
Church, the Missionary Church, and The Wesleyan Church.

**Subject strengths**: Bible--Criticism, interpretation, etc., Christian education, Church history, Church music, Counseling, Holiness movement,
Methodists, Missions, Pastoral theology, Theology.

**Special collections**: Free Methodist Church Historical Collection, Curriculum Library, E. J. Petticord Music Collection.

%%%%%%

**PENNSYLVANIA**

Philadelphia College of Bible Library
200 Manor Ave.
Langhorne, PA  19047
(215) 752-5800, ext. 230

The college developed from the merger of two Bible schools, National
Bible Institute and Philadelphia School of the Bible, co-founded by C.
I. Scofield and William L. Pettingill.

**Subject strengths**: Bible--Criticism, interpretation, etc., Christian education, Church music, Evangelicalism, Evangelistic work, Hymnology,
Missions, Theology.

**Special collections**: Hymnals Collection, C. I. Scofield Library of Biblical Studies, Jamieson Missionary Research Collection.


Westminster Theological Seminary
Montgomery Library
Location: Willow Grove Ave. & Church Rd.
 Glenside, PA
Mailing address: Chestnut Hill,
 P.O. Box 27009
 Philadelphia, PA  19118
(215) 572-3821

Westminster is an interdenominational seminary within the Reformed
tradition, formed by Robert Dick Wilson, J. Gresham Machen, Oswald
T. Allis, and Cornelius Van Til after the reorganization of Princeton
Theological Seminary in 1929.  The library supports Ph.D. programs in
Historical and Theological Studies and Hermeneutics and Biblical
Interpretation, and holdings include portions of the personal collec-
tions of Wilson, Machen, Allis, Caspar Wistar Hodge, Geerhardus
Vos, Edward J. Young, and Ned B. Stonehouse.

**Subject strengths**: Bible--Criticism, interpretation, etc., Calvinism,
Church history, City missions, Counseling, Evangelicalism, Pastoral
theology, Presbyterians, Theology.

**Special collections**: The Rare Book Room houses a strong collection
of early Reformed theology and an extensive collection of Latin,

Greek, and English Bibles. (**See also** Appendix I--Westminster Theological Seminary.)


%%%%%

**SOUTH CAROLINA**


Bob Jones University
J.S. Mack Library
Greenville, SC  29614
(803) 242-5100, ext. 6010

Founded in 1927 by Methodist Bob Jones, Sr., today the university serves an interdenominational, Fundamentalist constituency.

**Subject strengths**: Bible--Criticism, interpretation, etc., Christian education, Church music, Fundamentalism, Theology.

**Special collections**: Bob Jones University Press Publications, Fundamentalism File. (**See also** Appendix I--Bob Jones University.)


Columbia Bible College and Graduate School of Bible and Missions
Learning Resources Center
7435 Monticello Road, P.O. Box 3122
Columbia, SC  29230
(803) 754-4100, ext. 277

Founded in 1923 by Robert C. McQuilkin, the school promoted the Keswick Movement.  The library supports M. Div. and M.A. programs.

**Subject strengths**: Bible--Criticism, interpretation, etc., Christian Education, Church growth, Evangelicalism, Evangelistic work, Missions, Pastoral theology, Theology.

**Special collections**: Visual Aids for Religious Education and Christian Service Collection, Missionary Curios Collection. (**See also** Appendix I--Columbia Bible College and Seminary.)

%%%%%

**TENNESSEE**

Lee College and the Church of God School of Theology
William G. Squires Library
260 11th Street NE, P.O. Box 3448
Cleveland, TN  37320-3448
(615) 478-7428

Affiliated with the Church of God (Cleveland, Tenn.), the school
stands in the traditions of the Holiness movement and Pentecostalism.

**Subject strengths**: Holiness movement, Pentecostalism.

**Special collections**: Pentecostal Research Library Collection.

Sunday School Board
Southern Baptist Convention
E.C. Dargan Research Library
127 Ninth Ave., N.
Nashville, TN  37234
(615) 251-2124

The Sunday School Board serves the educational needs of Southern
Baptists.

**Subject strengths**: Baptists, Christian education, Southern Baptist
Convention, Sunday schools, Theology.

**Special collections**: Southern Baptist History Community Archives and
Collection. (**See also** Appendix I--Southern Baptist Historical Library
and Archives.)

Tennessee Temple University
Cierpke Memorial Library
1815 Union
Chattanooga, TN  37404
(615) 493-4250

Founded in 1946 by Highland Park Baptist Church, an independent
Baptist church under the leadership of Lee Roberson, the school is
"evangelistic, missionary and premillenial."   Library collections support

an M.S. in Education, with a major in Christian School Administration and Supervision.

**Subject strengths**: Baptists, Christian education, Evangelistic work, Fundamentalism, Missions.

**Special collections**: Religious Education Collection, Educational Curriculum Collection.


%%%%%

**TEXAS**


Dallas Theological Seminary
Turpin Library
3909 Swiss Ave.
Dallas, TX  75204-6411
(214) 841-3750

Founded in 1924 as Evangelical Theological College with Lewis Sperry Chafer as first president, the seminary is well known for its strong Th.M. and Th.D. programs and its publication, *Bibliotheca Sacra*. John F. Walvoord served as second president.

**Subject strengths**: Bible--Criticism, interpretation, etc., Bible--Prophecies, Christian education, Church history, Evangelicalism, Missions, Practical theology, Theology.

**Special collections**: (**See also**: Appendix I--Archives, Dallas Theological Seminary.)


Southwestern Baptist Theological Seminary
Roberts Library
2001 W. Seminary Drive, P.O. Box 22,000-2E
Fort Worth, TX  76122
(817) 923-1921, ext. 2770

The seminary is an outgrowth of the theological department of Baylor University and governed by the Southern Baptist Convention.  Presidents included B. H. Carroll and L. R. Scarborough.  The library supports doctoral programs in theology, religious education, and church music.

**Subject strengths**: Baptists, Bible--Criticism, interpretation, etc., Christian education, Church history, Church music, Communication, Counseling, Evangelistic work, Hymnology, Missions, Pastoral theology, Preaching, Theology.

**Special collections**: (See Appendix I--Southwestern Baptist Theological Seminary.)


%%%%%

**VIRGINIA**


Foreign Mission Board
Southern Baptist Convention
Jenkins Research Library
3806 Monument Ave.
P.O. Box 6767
Richmond, VA  23230
(804) 353-0151, ext. 435

The Foreign Mission Board is one of the largest Protestant sending agencies in the United States and engages in church planting, relief work, radio and television broadcasting, health and development work. David Barrett, editor of the *World Christian Encyclopedia*, now works with the board to update statistics on Christianity worldwide for the AD 2000 project. The board publishes *The Commission*.

**Subject strengths**: Missions, Global Statistics, World Affairs.


Liberty University Library
Lynchburg, VA  24506
(804) 582-2220

Thomas Road Baptist Church, pastored by the Rev. Jerry Falwell, governs this independent Baptist university founded in 1971.

**Subject strengths**: Baptists, Christian education, Fundamentalism.

**Special collections**: Church League of America Collection. (**See also** Appendix I--Liberty University.)

## FINDING OTHER COLLECTIONS:

### A. Reference Sources for Denominations, Their Educational Institutions, and Interdenominational Agencies

Melton, J. Gordon. *The Encyclopedia of American Religions*. 2d. ed.
   Detroit, Mich.: Gale Research, 1987.

Describes most American Protestant denominations and classifies
them according to broad categories of tradition. For each denomination, lists periodicals and approved educational facilities. Excellent
indexes facilitate usefulness.

*National Evangelical Directory*. Carol Stream, Ill.: National Association
   of Evangelicals. Annual.

Lists address and telephone information for a wide range of Evangelical agencies. Included are all member denominations and churches of
the National Association of Evangelicals, the member missionary
societies of the Evangelical Foreign Missions Association and Interdenominational Foreign Missions Association, and publishers in the
Evangelical Press Association. The section "Education/Christian Education" lists most Evangelical seminaries and graduate schools, Christian liberal arts colleges, and Bible colleges.

*Yearbook of American & Canadian Churches*. Prepared and edited in
   the Communication Unit of the National Council of the Churches
   of Christ in the U.S.A. Nashville: Abingdon Press. Annual.

In addition to brief descriptions and directory information for many
denominations, the yearbook lists theological seminaries, Bible colleges, church-related colleges and universities, religious periodicals,
and service agencies. In the "Statistical and Historical Section" will be
found a brief directory of main depositories of church history materials
and sources in North America.

### B. Guides to Special Collections

*American Library Directory*. New York: R. R. Bowker Co. Annual.

Provides current directory information for most libraries in the United
States and Canada.

Ash, Lee. *Subject Collections*. New York: R. R. Bowker. Most
    recent edition.

Arranges and describes special collections under specific subject headings. Most useful for searching specific topics such as names of
denominations, persons, etc. Coverage is quite uneven for broad subjects such as "Fundamentalism" or "Holiness and Pentecostal Movement."

*Directory of Special Libraries and Information Centers*. Detroit, Mich.:
    Gale Research. Most recent edition.

Describes special libraries and some special collections in the United
States and Canada; arranged by institutional or library name.

Howell, J. B., ed. *Special Collections in Libraries of the Southeast*.
    Jackson, Miss.: published for the Southeastern Library Association
    by Howick House, 1978.

Example of regional and state guides to special collections; arranged
by state and city.

*Special Collections in College and University Libraries*. Compiled by
    MODOC Press, Inc. New York: Macmillan Publishing, 1989.

Provides statistics on collection size and describes special collections;
arranged by state and institutional name.

*Subject Directory of Special Libraries and Information Centers, v.4:
    Social Sciences and Humanities Libraries*. Detroit, Mich.: Gale
    Research. Most recent edition.

The section on "Religion/Theology Libraries" provides a broad overview of special libraries and special collections. Entries arranged
alphabetically by institutional or library name.

# Index

The index refers primarily to the Archives section. However, references are made to other sections where appropriate. In most cases, subject headings are those of the Library of Congress. Some entries are arranged under form headings in order to group them together. Magazines and other periodical titles are preceded by the term "Periodical"; names of radio and television stations by "Broadcasting station"; movies by the term "Film"; radio programs by "Radio program"; television programs by "Television program"; languages by the term "Language"; names of meetings, such as congresses, conferences, workshops, and seminars, by "Congresses and conferences." Many topics are subdivided geographically by country. Thus, there are entries for Christian education--Angola, Christian education--Belgium, etc. References are to page numbers.

**About the Compilers**

ROBERT D. SHUSTER is Director of Archives at the Billy Graham Center at Wheaton College. He is the author of *The Papers of William and Helen Sunday: A Guide to the Microfilm Edition* and several articles on religious archives.

JAMES STAMBAUGH is Director of the Billy Graham Center Museum.

FERNE WEIMER is Director of the Billy Graham Center Library. She specializes in the development and growth of church and theological libraries outside of the United States.